YO-AAZ-326

Physical Anthropology *05/06*

Fourteenth Edition

EDITOR

Elvio Angeloni

Pasadena City College

Elvio Angeloni received his B.A. from UCLA in 1963, his M.A. in anthropology from UCLA in 1965, and his M.A. in communication arts from Loyola Marymount University in 1976. He has produced several films, including *Little Warrior,* winner of the Cinemedia VI Best Bicentennial Theme, and *Broken Bottles,* shown on PBS. He also served as an academic adviser on the instructional television series, *Faces of Culture.*

McGraw-Hill/Dushkin

2460 Kerper Blvd., Dubuque, IA 52001

Visit us on the Internet
http://www.dushkin.com

Credits

1. **The Evolutionary Perspectives**
   Unit photo—© Getty Images/Nick Koudis
2. **Primates**
   Unit photo—© Digital Vision/Punchstock
3. **Sex and Society**
   Unit photo—© Getty Images/Ryan McVay
4. **The Fossil Evidence**
   Unit photo—© 2004 by PhotoDisc, Inc.
5. **Late Hominid Evolution**
   Unit photo—© Getty Images/Steve Cole
6. **Human Diversity**
   Unit photo—© CORBIS/Royalty-Free
7. **Living With the Past**
   Unit photo—© Getty Images/Stevel Cole

Copyright

Cataloging in Publication Data
Main entry under title: Annual Editions: Physical Anthropology. 2004/2005.
1. Physical Anthropology—Periodicals. I. Angeloni, Elvio, *comp.* II. Title: Physical Anthropology.
ISBN 0–07–307908–1   658'.05   ISSN 1074–1844

Fourteenth Edition

Cover image © Adalberto Rios Szalay/Sexto Sol/Getty Images and Photos.com
Printed in the United States of America   1234567890QPDQPD987654   Printed on Recycled Paper

Editors/Advisory Board

Members of the Advisory Board are instrumental in the final selection of articles for each edition of ANNUAL EDITIONS. Their review of articles for content, level, currentness, and appropriateness provides critical direction to the editor and staff. We think that you will find their careful consideration well reflected in this volume.

Preface

In publishing ANNUAL EDITIONS we recognize the enormous role played by the magazines, newspapers, and journals of the public press in providing current, first-rate educational information in a broad spectrum of interest areas. Many of these articles are appropriate for students, researchers, and professionals seeking accurate, current material to help bridge the gap between principles and theories and the real world. These articles, however, become more useful for study when those of lasting value are carefully collected, organized, and reproduced in a low-cost format, which provides easy and permanent access when the material is needed. That is the role played by ANNUAL EDITIONS.

This fourteenth edition of *Annual Editions: Physical Anthropology* contains a variety of articles relating to human evolution. The writings were selected for their timeliness, relevance to issues not easily treated in the standard physical anthropology textbook, and clarity of presentation.

Whereas textbooks tend to reflect the consensus within the field, *Annual Editions: Physical Anthropology 05/06* provides a forum for the controversial. We do this in order to convey to the student the sense that the study of human development is an evolving entity in which each discovery encourages further research and each added piece of the puzzle raises new questions about the total picture.

Our final criterion for selecting articles is readability. All too often, the excitement of a new discovery or a fresh idea is deadened by the weight of a ponderous presentation. We seek to avoid that by incorporating essays written with enthusiasm and with the desire to communicate some very special ideas to the general public.

Included in this volume are a number of features that are designed to be useful for students, researchers, and professionals in the field of anthropology. While the articles are arranged along the lines of broadly unifying subject areas, the *topic guide* can be used to establish specific reading assignments tailored to the needs of a particular course of study. Other useful features include the *table of contents* abstracts, which summarize each article and present key concepts in bold italics.

In addition, each unit is preceded by an *overview* that provides a background for informed reading of the articles, emphasizes critical issues, and presents *key points* to consider in the form of questions. Also included are *World Wide Web* sites that are coordinated to follow the volume's units.

In contrast to the usual textbook that by its nature cannot be easily revised; this book will be continually updated to reflect the dynamic, changing character of its subject. Those involved in producing *Annual Editions: Physical Anthropology 05/06* wish to make the next one as useful and effective as possible. Your criticism and advice are welcomed. Please complete and return the postage-paid *article rating form* on the last page of the book and let us know your opinions. Any anthology can be improved, and this one will continue to be.

Elvio Angeloni

Elvio Angeloni
Editor

Contents

UNIT 1
The Evolutionary Perspectives

The concepts in bold italics are developed in the article. For further expansion, please refer to the Topic Guide.

UNIT 2
Primates

The concepts in bold italics are developed in the article. For further expansion, please refer to the Topic Guide.

UNIT 3
Sex and Society

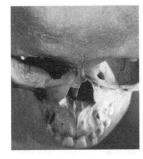

UNIT 4
The Fossil Evidence

The concepts in bold italics are developed in the article. For further expansion, please refer to the Topic Guide.

UNIT 5
Late Hominid Evolution

The concepts in bold italics are developed in the article. For further expansion, please refer to the Topic Guide.

UNIT 6
Human Diversity

UNIT 7
Living With the Past

The concepts in bold italics are developed in the article. For further expansion, please refer to the Topic Guide.

The concepts in bold italics are developed in the article. For further expansion, please refer to the Topic Guide.

Topic Guide

This topic guide suggests how the selections in this book relate to the subjects covered in your course. You may want to use the topics listed on these pages to search the Web more easily.

On the following pages a number of Web sites have been gathered specifically for this book. They are arranged to reflect the units of this *Annual Edition*. You can link to these sites by going to the DUSHKIN ONLINE support site at *http://www.dushkin.com/online/*.

ALL THE ARTICLES THAT RELATE TO EACH TOPIC ARE LISTED BELOW THE BOLD-FACED TERM.

Aggression
10. What Are Friends For?
14. Dim Forest, Bright Chimps
15. Rethinking Primate Aggression
16. Disturbing Behaviors of the Orangutan
21. Apes of Wrath
28. Hard Times Among the Neanderthals

Anatomy
4. Profile of an Anthropologist: No Bone Unturned
20. What's Love Got to Do With It?
22. Hunting the First Hominid
23. Food for Thought: Dietary Change Was a Driving Force in Human Evolution
26. *Erectus* Rising
27. The Scavenging of "Peking Man"
28. Hard Times Among the Neanderthals
29. Rethinking Neanderthals
30. The Gift of Gab
31. We are All Africans
32. The Lost Man
35. Does Race Exist? A Proponent's Perspective
36. Does Race Exist? An Antagonist's Perspective

Archaeology
4. Profile of an Anthropologist: No Bone Unturned
26. *Erectus* Rising
29. Rethinking Neanderthals
32. The Lost Man

Bipedalism
20. What's Love Got to Do With It?
22. Hunting the First Hominid
23. Food for Thought: Dietary Change Was a Driving Force in Human Evolution
24. Scavenger Hunt

Blood groups
34. Black, White, Other
35. Does Race Exist? A Proponent's Perspective
36. Does Race Exist? An Antagonist's Perspective

Burials
29. Rethinking Neanderthals

Catastrophism
1. The Growth of Evolutionary Science

Chain of being
1. The Growth of Evolutionary Science

Communication
30. The Gift of Gab

Culture
13. Got Culture?
29. Rethinking Neanderthals

Darwin, Charles
1. The Growth of Evolutionary Science
3. 15 Answers to Creationist Nonsense
41. Dr. Darwin

Disease
5. Go Ahead, Kiss Your Cousin
6. Curse and Blessing of the Ghetto
7. The Saltshaker's Curse
40. The Viral Superhighway
41. Dr. Darwin

DNA (deoxyribonucleic acid)
6. Curse and Blessing of the Ghetto
31. We are All Africans
34. Black, White, Other

Dominance hierarchy
10. What Are Friends For?
16. Disturbing Behaviors of the Orangutan
20. What's Love Got to Do With It?
21. Apes of Wrath

Ethnicity
32. The Lost Man
35. Does Race Exist? A Proponent's Perspective
36. Does Race Exist? An Antagonist's Perspective

Evolution
1. The Growth of Evolutionary Science
2. Darwin's Influence on Modern Thought
3. 15 Answers to Creationist Nonsense
33. Skin Deep
35. Does Race Exist? A Proponent's Perspective
36. Does Race Exist? An Antagonist's Perspective
37. The Bare Truth

Evolutionary perspective
1. The Growth of Evolutionary Science
2. Darwin's Influence on Modern Thought
3. 15 Answers to Creationist Nonsense
22. Hunting the First Hominid
25. Chasing Dubois's Ghost
33. Skin Deep
35. Does Race Exist? A Proponent's Perspective
36. Does Race Exist? An Antagonist's Perspective
37. The Bare Truth
41. Dr. Darwin

Family systems
5. Go Ahead, Kiss Your Cousin
19. A Woman's Curse?

Forensic anthropology
4. Profile of an Anthropologist: No Bone Unturned
35. Does Race Exist? A Proponent's Perspective
41. Dr. Darwin

World Wide Web Sites

The following World Wide Web sites have been carefully researched and selected to support the articles found in this reader. The easiest way to access these selected sites is to go to our DUSHKIN ONLINE support site at *http://www.dushkin.com/online/*.

AE: Physical Anthropology 05/06

The following sites were available at the time of publication. Visit our Web site—we update DUSHKIN ONLINE regularly to reflect any changes.

General Sources

American Anthropological Association (AAA)
http://www.aaanet.org/

Maintained by the AAA, this site provides links to AAA's publications (including tables of contents of recent issues, style guides, and others) and to other anthropology sites.

Anthromorphemics
http://www.anth.ucsb.edu/glossary/index2.html

A glossary of anthropological terms is available at this Web site.

Anthropology in the News
http://www.tamu.edu/anthropology/news.html

Texas A&M provides data on news articles that relate to anthropology, including biopsychology and sociocultural anthropology news.

Anthropology on the Web
http://www.as.ua.edu/ant/lib/web1.htm

This Web site provides addresses and tips on acquiring links to regional studies, maps, anthropology tutorials, and other data.

Anthropology 1101 Human Origins Website
http://www.geocities.com/Athens/Acropolis/5579/TA.html

Exploring this site, which is provided by the University of Minnesota, will lead to a wealth of information about our ancient ancestors and other topics of interest to physical anthropologists.

Anthropology Resources on the Internet
http://www.socsciresearch.com/r7.html

Links to Internet resources of anthropological relevance, including Web servers in different fields, are available here. *The Education Index* rated it "one of the best education-related sites on the Web."

Anthropology Resources Page
http://www.usd.edu/anth/

Many topics can be accessed from this University of South Dakota site. South Dakota archaeology, American Indian issues, and paleopathology resources are just a few examples.

Library of Congress
http://www.loc.gov

Examine this extensive Web site to learn about resource tools, library services/resources, exhibitions, and databases in many different subfields of anthropology.

The New York Times
http://www.nytimes.com

Browsing through the archives of the *New York Times* will provide a wide array of articles and information related to the different subfields of anthropology.

Physical Anthropology Resources
http://www.killgrove.org/osteo.html

This Web site provides numerous links to other resources from the Web covering all aspects of physical anthropology.

UNIT 1: The Evolutionary Perspectives

Charles Darwin on Human Origins
http://www.literature.org/Works/Charles-Darwin/

This Web site contains the text of Charles Darwin's classic writing, *Origin of Species,* which presents his scientific theory of natural selection.

Enter Evolution: Theory and History
http://www.ucmp.berkeley.edu/history/evolution.html

Find information related to Charles Darwin and other important scientists at this Web site. It addresses preludes to evolution, natural selection, and more. Topics cover systematics, dinosaur discoveries, and vertebrate flight.

Fossil Hominids FAQ
http://www.talkorigins.org/faqs/homs/

Some links to materials related to hominid species and hominid fossils are provided on this site. The purpose of the site is to refute creationist claims that there is no evidence for human evolution.

Harvard Dept. of MCB—Biology Links
http://mcb.harvard.edu/BioLinks.html

This site features sources on evolution and links to anthropology departments and laboratories, taxonomy, paleontology, natural history, journals, books, museums, meetings, and many other related areas.

UNIT 2: Primates

African Primates at Home
http://www.indiana.edu/~primate/primates.html

Don't miss this unusual and compelling site describing African primates on their home turf. "See" and "Hear" features provide samples of vocalizations and beautiful photographs of various types of primates.

Electronic Zoo/NetVet-Primate Page
http://netvet.wustl.edu/primates.htm

This site touches on every kind of primate from A to Z and related information. The long list includes Darwinian theories and the *Descent of Man,* the Ebola virus, fossil hominids, the nonhuman Primate Genetics Lab, the Simian Retrovirus Laboratory, and zoonotic diseases, with many links in between.

Laboratory Primate Newsletter
http://www.brown.edu/Research/Primate/other.html

This series of Web sites on primates includes links to a large number of primate sites.

UNIT 3: Sex and Society

American Anthropologist
http://www.aaanet.org/aa/index.htm

Check out this site, the home page of *American Anthropologist,* for general information about anthropology as well as articles relating to such topics as biological research.

www.dushkin.com/online/

American Scientist
http://www.amsci.org/amsci.html

Investigating this site will help students of physical anthropology to explore issues related to sex and society.

Bonobo Sex and Society
http://songweaver.com/info/bonobos.html

Accessed through Carnegie Mellon University, this site includes a *Scientific American* article discussing a primate's behavior that challenges traditional assumptions about male supremacy in human evolution.

UNIT 4: The Fossil Evidence

The African Emergence and Early Asian Dispersals of the Genus *Homo*
http://www.uiowa.edu/~bioanth/homo.html

Read this classic article to learn about what the Rift Valley in East Africa has to tell us about early hominid species. An excellent bibliography is included.

Anthropology, Archaeology, and American Indian Sites on the Internet
http://dizzy.library.arizona.edu/library/teams/sst/anthro/

This Web page points out a number of Internet sites of interest to different kinds of anthropologists, including physical and biological anthropologists. Visit this page for links to electronic journals and more.

Long Foreground: Human Prehistory
http://www.wsu.edu/gened/learn-modules/top_longfor/lfopen-index.html

This Washington State University site presents a learning module covering three major topics in human evolution: Overview, Hominid Species Timeline, and Human Physical Characteristics. It also provides a helpful glossary of terms and links to other Web sites.

UNIT 5: Late Hominid Evolution

Human Prehistory
http://users.hol.gr/~dilos/prehis.htm

The evolution of the human species, beginning with the *Australopithecus* and continuing with *Homo habilis, Homo erectus,* and *Homo sapiens,* is examined on this site. Also included are data on the people who lived in the Palaeolithic and Neolithic Age and are the immediate ancestors of modern man.

UNIT 6: Human Diversity

Hominid Evolution Survey
http://www.geocities.com/SoHo/Atrium/1381/index.html

This survey of the Hominid family categorizes known hominids by genus and species. Beginning with the oldest known species, data include locations and environments, physical characteristics, technology, social behaviors, charts, and citations.

Human Genome Project Information
http://www.ornl.gov/TechResources/Human_Genome/home.html

Obtain answers about the U.S. Human Genome Project from this site, which details progress, goals, support groups, ethical, legal, and social issues, and genetics information.

OMIM Home Page-Online Mendelian Inheritance in Man
http://www3.ncbi.nlm.nih.gov/omim/

This database from the National Center for Biotechnology Information is a catalog of human genes and genetic disorders. It contains text, pictures, and reference information of great interest to students of physical anthropology.

The Human Diversity Resource Page
http://community-1.webtv.net/SoundBehavior/DIVERSITYFORSOUND/

This page will provide useful resource links for understanding the power of human differences. Differences can challenge assumptions and lead to appreciation. The basic premise of appreciation is understanding. Being open to a level of personal understanding allows for differences to be noticed.

UNIT 7: Living With the Past

Ancestral Passions
http://www.canoe.ca/JamBooksReviewsA/ancestral_morell.html

This review of Virginia Morell's book, *Ancestral Passions,* a biography of the famously dysfunctional Leakey family, will likely spur you to the bookstore in order to learn more about the history of paleontology and the thrill and trials of the hunt for human origins. It is this evolutionary detective story that is the book's true drama. Jump over to *http://url.co.nz/african_trip/tanzania.html* to read an individual's account of a recent trip "In the Cradle of Humankind."

Forensic Science Reference Page
http://www.lab.fws.gov

Look over this site from the U.S. Fish and Wildlife Forensics Lab to explore topics related to forensic anthropology.

Zeno's Forensic Page
http://forensic.to/forensic.html

A complete list of resources on forensics is presented on this Web site. It includes general information sources, DNA/serology sources and databases, forensic medicine anthropology sites, and related areas.

We highly recommend that you review our Web site for expanded information and our other product lines. We are continually updating and adding links to our Web site in order to offer you the most usable and useful information that will support and expand the value of your Annual Editions. You can reach us at: *http://www.dushkin.com/annualeditions/.*

UNIT 1
The Evolutionary Perspectives

Unit Selections

Key Points to Consider

- In nature, how is it that design can occur without a designer, orderliness without purpose?

- What is "natural selection?" How does Gregor Mendel's work relate to Charles Darwin's theory?

- In what ways has Charles Darwin influenced modern thought?

- What is "forensic anthropology?" How can it be applied in modern society?

- Why is Tay-Sachs disease so common among Eastern European Jews?

- What is the "saltshaker's curse" and why are some people more affected by it than others?

- Should cousin marriage be legal?

- How should we assess the importance of nature versus nurture?

- Is alcholism a disease? Explain your opinion.

 **Links: www.dushkin.com/online/**
These sites are annotated in the World Wide Web pages.

Charles Darwin on Human Origins
  http://www.literature.org/Works/Charles-Darwin/
Enter Evolution: Theory and History
  http://www.ucmp.berkeley.edu/history/evolution.html
Fossil Hominids FAQ
  http://www.talkorigins.org/faqs/homs/
Harvard Dept. of MCB—Biology Links
  http://mcb.harvard.edu/BioLinks.html

As we reflect upon where science has taken us over the past 300 years, it should come as no surprise that we have been swept along a path of insight into the human condition (See "Go Ahead, Kiss Your Cousin" and "Of Mice, Men and Genes") as well as heightened controversy as to how to handle this potentially dangerous and/or unwanted knowledge of ourselves.

Certainly, Gregor Mendel, in the late nineteenth century, could not have anticipated that his study of pea plants would ultimately lead to the better understanding of over 3,000 genetically caused diseases, such as sickle-cell anemia, Huntington's chorea, and Tay-Sachs. Nor could he have foreseen the present-day controversies over such matters as cloning and genetic engineering.

The significance of Mendel's work, of course, was his discovery that hereditary traits are conveyed by particular units that we now call "genes," a then-revolutionary notion that has been followed by a better understanding of how and why such units change. It is knowledge of the process of "mutation," or alteration of the chemical structure of the gene, that is now providing us with the potential to control the genetic fate of individuals. This does not mean, however, that we should not continue to look at the role the environment plays in the origins of what might be better termed "genetically influenced conditions," such as alcoholism. (See "What You Can Learn From Drunk Monkeys.")

The other side of the evolutionary coin, as discussed in "The Growth of Evolutionary Science" and "Darwin's Influence on Modern Thought," is natural selection, a concept provided by Charles Darwin and Alfred Wallace. Natural selection refers to the "weeding out" of unfavorable mutations and the perpetuation of favorable ones.

As our understanding of evolutionary processes continues to be refined, unfortunately, it also continues to be badly understood by the public in general. Thus, we have the need for "15 Answers to Creationist Nonsense."

It seems that as we gain a better understanding of both of these processes, mutation and natural selection, and grasp their relevance to human beings, we draw nearer to that time when we may even control the evolutionary direction of our species. Knowledge itself, of course, is neutral—its potential for good or ill—being determined by those who happen to be in a position to use it. Consider the possibility of eliminating some of the harmful hereditary traits discussed in "Curse and Blessing of the Ghetto" and "The Saltshaker's Curse," both by Jared Diamond. While it is true that many deleterious genes do get weeded out of the population by means of natural selection, there are other harmful ones, Diamond points out, that may actually have a good side to them and will therefore be perpetuated. It may be, for example, that some men are dying from a genetically caused overabundance of iron in their blood systems in a trade-off that allows some women to absorb sufficient amounts of the element to guarantee their own survival. The question of whether we should eliminate such a gene would seem to depend on which sex we decide should reap the benefit.

Anthropological applications to everyday life seem to have no boundaries. For example, Patrick Huyghe, in "Profile of an Anthropologist: No Bone Unturned," describes "forensic anthropology," a whole new field involving the use of physical similarities and differences between people in order to identify human remains.

The issue of just what is a beneficial application of scientific knowledge, however, is a matter for debate. Who will have the final word as to how these technological breakthroughs will be employed in the future? Even with the best of intentions, how can we be certain of the long-range consequences of our actions in such a complicated field? Note, for example, the sweeping effects of ecological change upon the viruses of the world, seem to be paving the way for new waves of human epidemics.

Generally speaking, there is an element of purpose and design in our machinations. Yet, even with this clearly in mind, the whole process seems to be escalating out of human control. It seems that the entire world has become an experimental laboratory in which we know not what we do until we have already done it.

As we read the essays in this unit and contemplate the significance of genetic diseases for human evolution, we can hope that a better understanding of congenital diseases will lead to a reduction of human suffering. At the same time, we must remain aware that someone, at some time, may actually use the same knowledge to increase rather than reduce the misery that exists in the world.

The Growth of Evolutionary Science

Douglas J. Futuyma

Today, the theory of evolution is an accepted fact for everyone but a fundamentalist minority, whose objections are based not on reasoning but on doctrinaire adherence to religious principles.

—James D. Watson, 1965*

In 1615, Galileo was summoned before the Inquisition in Rome. The guardians of the faith had found that his "proposition that the sun is the center [of the solar system] and does not revolve about the earth is foolish, absurd, false in theology, and heretical, because expressly contrary to Holy Scripture." In the next century, John Wesley declared that "before the sin of Adam there were no agitations within the bowels of the earth, no violent convulsions, no concussions of the earth, no earthquakes, but all was unmoved as the pillars of heaven." Until the seventeenth century, fossils were interpreted as "stones of a peculiar sort, hidden by the Author of Nature for his own pleasure." Later they were seen as remnants of the Biblical deluge. In the middle of the eighteenth century, the great French naturalist Buffon speculated on the possibility of cosmic and organic evolution and was forced by the clergy to recant: "I abandon everything in my book respecting the formation of the earth, and generally all of which may be contrary to the narrative of Moses." For had not St. Augustine written, "Nothing is to be accepted save on the authority of Scripture, since greater is that authority than all the powers of the human mind"?

When Darwin published *The Origin of Species*, it was predictably met by a chorus of theological protest. Darwin's theory, said Bishop Wilberforce, "contradicts the revealed relations of creation to its Creator." "If the Darwinian theory is true," wrote another clergyman, "Genesis is a lie, the whole framework of the book of life falls to pieces, and the revelation of God to man, as we Christians know it, is a delusion and a snare." When *The Descent of Man* appeared, Pope Pius IX was moved to write that Darwinism is "a system which is so repugnant at once to history, to the tradition of all peoples, to exact science, to observed facts, and even to Reason herself, [that it] would seem to need no refutation, did not alienation from God and the leaning toward materialism, due to depravity, eagerly seek a support in all this tissue of fables."[1] Twentieth-century creationism continues this battle of medieval theology against science.

One of the most pervasive concepts in medieval and post-medieval thought was the "great chain of being," or *scala naturae*.[2] Minerals, plants, and animals, according to his concept, formed a gradation, from the lowliest and most material to the most complex and spiritual, ending in man, who links the animal series to the world of intelligence and spirit. This "scale of nature" was the manifestation of God's infinite benevolence. In his goodness, he had conferred existence on all beings of which he could conceive, and so created a complete chain of being, in which there were no gaps. All his creatures must have been created at once, and none could ever cease to exist, for then the perfection of his divine plan would have been violated. Alexander Pope expressed the concept best:

> Vast chain of being! which from God
>   began,
> Natures aethereal, human, angel, man,
> Beast, bird, fish, insect, what no eye
>   can see,
> No glass can reach; from Infinite to
>   thee,
> From thee to nothing.—On superior
>   pow'rs
> Were we to press, inferior might on
>   ours;
> Or in the full creation leave a void,
> Where, one step broken, the great
>   scale's destroy'd;
> From Nature's chain whatever link
>   you strike,
> Tenth, or ten thousandth, breaks the
>   chain alike.

Coexisting with this notion that all of which God could conceive existed so as to complete his creation was the idea that all things existed for man. As the philosopher Francis Bacon put it, "Man, if we look to final causes, may be regarded as the centre of the world... for the whole world works together in the service of man… all things seem to be going about man's business and not their own."

"Final causes" was another fundamental concept of medieval and post-medieval thought. Aristotle had distinguished final causes from efficient causes, and the Western world saw no reason to doubt the reality of both. The "efficient cause" of an event is the mechanism responsible for its occurrence: the cause of a ball's movement on a pool table, for example, is the impact of the cue or another ball. The "final cause," however, is the goal, or purpose for its occurrence: the pool ball moves because I wish it to go into the corner pocket. In post-medieval thought there was a final cause—a purpose—for everything; but purpose implies intention, or foreknowledge, by an intellect. Thus the existence of the world, and of all the creatures in it, had a purpose; and that purpose was God's design. This was self-evident, since it was possible to look about the world and see the palpable evidence of God's design everywhere. The heavenly bodies moved in harmonious orbits, evincing the intelligence and harmony of the divine mind; the adaptations of animals and plants to their habitats likewise reflected the devine intelligence, which had fitted all creatures perfectly for their roles in the harmonious economy of nature.

Before the rise of science, then, the causes of events were sought not in natural mechanisms but in the purposes they were meant to serve, and order in nature was evidence of divine intelligence. Since St. Ambrose had declared that "Moses opened his mouth and poured forth what God had said to him," the Bible was seen as the literal word of God, and according to St. Thomas Aquinas, "Nothing was made by God, after the six days of creation, absolutely new." Taking Genesis literally, Archbishop Ussher was able to calculate that the earth was created in 4004 B.C. The earth and the heavens were immutable, changeless. As John Ray put it in 1701 in *The Wisdom of God Manifested in the Works of the Creation*, all living and nonliving things were "created by God at first, and by Him conserved to this Day in the same State and Condition in which they were first made."[3]

The evolutionary challenge to this view began in astronomy. Tycho Brahe found that the heavens were not immutable when a new star appeared in the constellation Cassiopeia in 1572. Copernicus displaced the earth from the center of the universe, and Galileo found that the perfect heavenly bodies weren't so perfect: the sun had spots that changed from time to time, and the moon had craters that strongly implied alterations of its surface. Galileo, and after him Buffon, Kant, and many others, concluded that change was natural to all things.

A flood of mechanistic thinking ensued. Descartes, Kant, and Buffon concluded that the causes of natural phenomena should be sought in natural laws. By 1755, Kant was arguing that the laws of matter in motion discovered by Newton and other physicists were sufficient to explain natural order. Gravitation, for example, could aggregate chaotically dispersed matter into stars and planets. These would join with one another until the only ones left were those that cycled in orbits far enough from each other to resist gravitational collapse. Thus order might arise from natural processes rather than from the direct intervention of a supernatural mind. The "argument from design"—the claim that natural order is evidence of a designer—had been directly challenged. So had the universal belief in final causes. If the arrangement of the planets could arise merely by the laws of Newtonian physics, if the planets could be born, as Buffon suggested, by a collision between a comet and the sun, then they did not exist for any purpose. They merely came into being through impersonal physical forces.

From the mutability of the heavens, it was a short step to the mutability of the earth, for which the evidence was far more direct. Earthquakes and volcanoes showed how unstable terra firma really is. Sedimentary rocks showed that materials eroded from mountains could be compacted over the ages. Fossils of marine shells on mountain-tops proved that the land must once have been under the sea. As early as 1718, the Abbé Moro and the French academician Bernard de Fontenelle had concluded that the Biblical deluge could not explain the fossil-

ized oyster beds and tropical plants that were found in France. And what of the great, unbroken chain of being if the rocks were full of extinct species?

To explain the facts of geology, some authors—the "catastrophists"—supposed that the earth had gone through a series of great floods and other catastrophes that successively extinguished different groups of animals. Only this, they felt, could account for the discovery that higher and lower geological strata had different fossils. Buffon, however, held that to explain nature we should look to the natural causes we see operating around us: the gradual action of erosion and the slow buildup of land during volcanic eruptions. Buffon thus proposed what came to be the foundation of geology, and indeed of all science, the principle of uniformitarianism, which holds that the same causes that operate now have always operated. By 1795, the Scottish geologist James Hutton had suggested that "in examining things present we have data from which to reason with regard to what has been." His conclusion was that since "rest exists not anywhere," and the forces that change the face of the earth move with ponderous slowness, the mountains and canyons of the world must have come into existence over countless aeons.

If the entire nonliving world was in constant turmoil, could it not be that living things themselves changed? Buffon came close to saying so. He realized that the earth had seen the extinction of countless species, and supposed that those that perished had been the weaker ones. He recognized that domestication and the forces of the environment could modify the variability of many species. And he even mused, in 1766, that species might have developed from common ancestors:

If it were admitted that the ass is of the family of the horse, and different from the horse only because it has varied from the original form, one could equally well say that the ape is of the family of man, that he is a degenerate man, that man and ape have a common origin; that, in fact, all the families among plants as well as animals have come from a single stock, and that all animals are descended from a single animal, from which have sprung in the course of time, as a result of process or of degeneration, all the other races of animals. For if it were once shown that we are justified in establishing these families; if it were granted among animals and plants there has been (I do not say several species) but even a single one, which has been produced in the course of direct descent from another species... then there would no longer be any limit to the power of nature, and we should not be wrong in supposing that, with sufficient time, she has been able from a single being to derive all the other organized beings.[4]

This, however, was too heretical a thought; and in any case, Buffon thought the weight of evidence was against common descent. No new species had been observed to arise within recorded history, Buffon wrote; the sterility of hybrids between species appeared an impossible barrier to such a conclusion; and if species had emerged gradually, there should have been innumerable intermediate variations between the horse and ass, or any other species. So Buffon concluded: "But this [idea of a common ancestor] is by no means a proper representation of nature. We are assured by the authority of revelation that all animals have participated equally in the grace of direct Creation and that the first pair of every species issued fully formed from the hands of the Creator."

Buffon's friend and protégé, Jean Baptiste de Monet, the Chevalier de Lamarck, was the first scientist to take the big step. It is not clear what led Lamarck to his uncompromising belief in evolution; perhaps it was his studies of fossil molluscs, which he came to believe were the ancestors of similar species living today. Whatever the explanation, from 1800 on he developed the notion that fossils were not evidence of extinct species but of ones that had gradually been transformed into living species. To be sure, he wrote, "an enormous time and wide variation in successive conditions must doubtless have been required to enable nature to bring

the organization of animals to that degree of complexity and development in which we see it at its perfection"; but "time has no limits and can be drawn upon to any extent."

Lamarck believed that various lineages of animals and plants arose by a continual process of spontaneous generation from inanimate matter, and were transformed from very simple to more complex forms by an innate natural tendency toward complexity caused by "powers conferred by the supreme author of all things." Various specialized adaptations of species are consequences of the fact that animals must always change in response to the needs imposed on them by a continually changing environment. When the needs of a species change, so does its behavior. The animal then uses certain organs more frequently than before, and these organs, in turn, become more highly developed by such use, or else "by virtue of the operations of their own inner senses." The classic example of Lamarckism is the giraffe: by straining upward for foliage, it was thought, the animal had acquired a longer neck, which was then inherited by its off-spring.

In the nineteenth century it was widely believed that "acquired" characteristics—alterations brought about by use or disuse, or by the direct influence of the environment—could be inherited. Thus it was perfectly reasonable for Lamarck to base his theory of evolutionary change partly on this idea. Indeed, Darwin also allowed for this possibility, and the inheritance of acquired characteristics was not finally proved impossible until the 1890s.

Lamarck's ideas had a wide influence; but in the end did not convince many scientists of the reality of evolution. In France, Georges Cuvier, the foremost paleontologist and anatomist of his time, was an influential opponent of evolution. He rejected Lamarck's notion of the spontaneous generation of life, found it inconceivable that changes in behavior could produce the exquisite adaptations that almost every species shows, and emphasized that in both the fossil record and among living animals there were numerous "gaps" rather than intermediate forms between species. In England, the

philosophy of "natural theology" held sway in science, and the best-known naturalists continued to believe firmly that the features of animals and plants were evidence of God's design. These devout Christians included the foremost geologist of the day, Charles Lyell, whose *Principles of Geology* established uniformitarianism once and for all as a guiding principle. But Lyell was such a thorough uniformitarian that he believed in a steady-state world, a world that was always in balance between forces such as erosion and mountain building, and so was forever the same. There was no room for evolution, with its concept of steady change, in Lyell's world view, though he nonetheless had an enormous impact on evolutionary thought, through his influence on Charles Darwin.

Darwin (1809–1882) himself, unquestionably one of the greatest scientists of all time, came only slowly to an evolutionary position. The son of a successful physician, he showed little interest in the life of the mind in his early years. After unsuccessfully studying medicine at Edinburgh, he was sent to Cambridge to prepare for the ministry, but he had only a half-hearted interest in his studies and spent most of his time hunting, collecting beetles, and becoming an accomplished amateur naturalist. Though he received his B.A. in 1831, his future was quite uncertain until, in December of that year, he was enlisted as a naturalist aboard *H.M.S. Beagle*, with his father's very reluctant agreement. For five years (from December 27, 1831, to October 2, 1836) the *Beagle* carried him about the world, chiefly along the coast of South America, which it was the *Beagle's* mission to survey. For five years Darwin collected geological and biological specimens, made geological observations, absorbed Lyell's *Principles of Geology*, took voluminous notes, and speculated about everything from geology to anthropology. He sent such massive collections of specimens back to England that by the time he returned he had already gained a substantial reputation as a naturalist.

Shortly after his return, Darwin married and settled into an estate at Down where he remained, hardly traveling even to London, for the rest of his life.

Despite continual ill health, he pursued an extraordinary range of biological studies: classifying barnacles, breeding pigeons, experimenting with plant growth, and much more. He wrote no fewer than sixteen books and many papers, read voraciously, corresponded extensively with everyone, from pigeon breeders to the most eminent scientists, whose ideas or information might bear on his theories, and kept detailed notes on an amazing variety of subjects. Few people have written authoritatively on so many different topics: his books include not only *The Voyage of the Beagle, The Origin of Species*, and *The Descent of Man, but also The Structure and Distribution of Coral Reefs* (containing a novel theory of the formation of coral atolls which is still regarded as correct), *A Monograph on the Sub-class Cirripedia* (the definitive study of barnacle classification), *The Various Contrivances by Which Orchids are Fertilised by Insects, The Variation of Animals and Plants Under Domestication* (an exhaustive summary of information on variation, so crucial to his evolutionary theory), *The Effects of Cross and Self Fertilisation in the Vegetable Kingdom* (an analysis of sexual reproduction and the sterility of hybrids between species), *The Expression of the Emotions in Man and Animals* (on the evolution of human behavior from animal behavior), and *The Formation of Vegetable Mould Through the Action of Worms*. There is every reason to believe that almost all these books bear, in one way or another, on the principles and ideas that were inherent in Darwin's theory of evolution. The worm book, for example, is devoted to showing how great the impact of a seemingly trivial process like worm burrowing may be on ecology and geology if it persists for a long time. The idea of such cumulative slight effects is, of course, inherent in Darwin's view of evolution: successive slight modifications of a species, if continued long enough, can transform it radically.

When Darwin embarked on his voyage, he was a devout Christian who did not doubt the literal truth of the Bible, and did not believe in evolution any more than did Lyell and the other English scientists he had met or whose books he had read. By the time he returned to England in 1836 he had made numerous observations that would later convince him of evolution. It seems likely, however, that the idea itself did not occur to him until the spring of 1837, when the ornithologist John Gould, who was working on some of Darwin's collections, pointed out to him that each of the Galápagos Islands, off the coast of Ecuador, had a different kind of mockingbird. It was quite unclear whether they were different varieties of the same species, or different species. From this, Darwin quickly realized that species are not the discrete, clear-cut entities everyone seemed to imagine. The possibility of transformation entered his mind, and it applied to more than the mockingbirds: "When comparing… the birds from the separate islands of the Galápagos archipelago, both with one another and with those from the American mainland, I was much struck how entirely vague and arbitrary is the distinction between species and varieties."

In July 1837 he began his first notebook on the "Transmutation of Species." He later said that the Galápagos species and the similarity between South American fossils and living species were at the origin of all his views.

> During the voyage of the *Beagle* I had been deeply impressed by discovering in the Pampean formation great fossil animals covered with armour like that on the existing armadillos; secondly, by the manner in which closely allied animals replace one another in proceeding southward over the continent; and thirdly, by the South American character of most of the productions of the Galápagos archipelago, and more especially by the manner in which they differ slightly on each island of the group; none of these islands appearing to be very ancient in a geological sense. It was evident that such facts as these, as well as many others, could be explained on the supposition that species gradually become modified; and the subject has haunted me.

The first great step in Darwin's thought was the realization that evolution had occurred. The second was his brilliant insight into the possible cause of evolutionary change. Lamarck's theory of "felt needs" had not been convincing. A better one was required. It came on September 18, 1838, when after grappling with the problem for fifteen months, "I happened to read for amusement Malthus on Population, and being well prepared to appreciate the struggle for existence which everywhere goes on from long-continued observation of the habits of animals and plants, it at once struck me that under these circumstances favorable variations would tend to be preserved, and unfavorable ones to be destroyed. The result of this would be the formation of new species. Here, then, I had at last got a theory by which to work."

Malthus, an economist, had developed the pessimistic thesis that the exponential growth of human populations must inevitably lead to famine, unless it were checked by war, disease, or "moral restraint." This emphasis on exponential population growth was apparently the catalyst for Darwin, who then realized that since most natural populations of animals and plants remain fairly stable in numbers, many more individuals are born than survive. Because individuals vary in their characteristics, the struggle to survive must favor some variant individuals over others. These survivors would then pass on their characteristics to future generations. Repetition of this process generation after generation would gradually transform the species.

Darwin clearly knew that he could not afford to publish a rash speculation on so important a subject without developing the best possible case. The world of science was not hospitable to speculation, and besides, Darwin was dealing with a highly volatile issue. Not only was he affirming that evolution had occurred, he was proposing a purely material explanation for it, one that demolished the argument from design in a single thrust. Instead of publishing his theory, he patiently amassed a mountain of evidence, and finally, in 1844, collected his thoughts in an essay on natural selection. But he still didn't publish. Not until 1856, almost twenty years after he became an evolutionist, did he begin what he planned to be a massive work on the subject, tentatively titled *Natural Selection*.

Then, in June 1858, the unthinkable happened. Alfred Russel Wallace (1823–

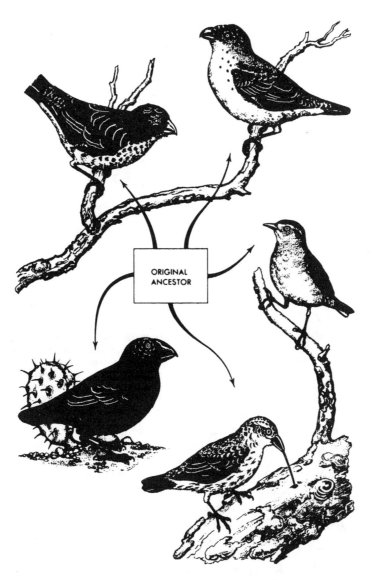

Figure 1. *Some species of Galápagos finches. Several of the most different species are represented here; intermediate species also exist. Clockwise from lower left are a male ground-finch (the plumage of the female resembles that of the tree-finches); the vegetarian tree-finch; the insectivorous tree-finch; the warbler-finch; and the woodpecker-finch, which uses a cactus spine to extricate insects from crevices. The slight differences among these species, and among species in other groups of Galápagos animals such as giant tortoises, were one of the observations that led Darwin to formulate his hypothesis of evolution.* **(From D. Lack, Darwin's Finches [Oxford: Oxford University Press, 1944].)**

1913), a young naturalist who had traveled in the Amazon Basin and in the Malay Archipelago, had also become interested in evolution. Like Darwin, he was struck by the fact that "the most closely allied species are found in the same locality or in closely adjoining localities and… therefore the natural sequence of the species by affinity is also geographical." In the throes of a malarial fever in Malaya, Wallace conceived of the same idea of natural selection as Darwin had, and sent Darwin a manuscript "On the Tendency of Varieties to Depart Indefinitely from the Original Type."

Darwin's friends Charles Lyell and Joseph Hooker, a botanist, rushed in to help Darwin establish the priority of his ideas, and on July 1, 1858, they presented to the Linnean Society of London both Wallace's paper and extracts from Darwin's 1844 essay. Darwin abandoned his big book on natural selection and condensed the argument into a 490-page "abstract" that was published on November 24, 1859, under the title *The Origin of Species by Means of Natural Selection; or, the Preservation of Favored Races in the Struggle for Life*. Because it was an abstract, he had to leave out many of the de-

tailed observations and references to the literature that he had amassed, but these were later provided in his other books, many of which are voluminous expansions on the contents of *The Origin of Species*.

The first five chapters of the *Origin* lay out the theory that Darwin had conceived. He shows that both domesticated and wild species are variable, that much of that variation is hereditary, and that breeders, by conscious selection of desirable varieties, can develop breeds of pigeons, dogs, and other forms that are more different from each other than species or even families of wild animals and

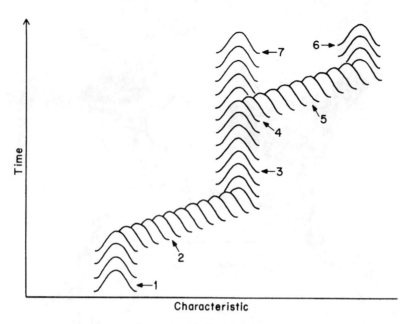

Figure 2. *Processes of evolutionary change. A characteristic that is variable (1) often shows a bell-shaped distribution--individuals vary on either side of the average. Evolutionary change (2) consists of a shift in successive generations, after which the characteristic may reach a new equilibrium (3). When the species splits into two different species (4), one of the species may undergo further evolutionary change (5) and reach a new equilibrium (6). The other may remain unchanged (7) or not. Each population usually remains variable throughout this process, but the average is shifted, ordinarily by natural selection.*

plants are from each other. The differences between related species then are no more than an exaggerated form of the kinds of variations one can find in a single species; indeed, it is often extremely difficult to tell if natural populations are distinct species or merely well-marked varieties.

Darwin then shows that in nature there is competition, predation, and a struggle for life.

Owing to this struggle, variations, however slight and from whatever cause proceeding, if they be in any degree profitable to the individuals of a species, in their infinitely complex relations to other organic beings and to their physical conditions of life, will tend to the preservation of such individuals, and will generally be inherited by the offspring. The offspring, also, will thus have a better chance of surviving, for, of the many individuals of any species which are periodically born, but a small number can survive. I have called this principle, by which each slight variation, if useful, is preserved, by the term natural selection, in or-

der to mark its relation to man's power of selection.

Darwin goes on to give examples of how even slight variations promote survival, and argues that when populations are exposed to different conditions, different variations will be favored, so that the descendants of a species become diversified in structure, and each ancestral species can give rise to several new ones. Although "it is probable that each form remains for long periods unaltered," successive evolutionary modifications will ultimately alter the different species so greatly that they will be classified as different genera, families, or orders.

Competition between species will impel them to become more different, for "the more diversified the descendants from any one species become in structure, constitution and habits, by so much will they be better enabled to seize on many and widely diversified places in the polity of nature, and so be enabled to increase in numbers." Thus different adaptations arise, and "the ultimate result is that each creature tends to become more and more improved in relation to its conditions. This improvement inevitably leads to the greater advancement of the

organization of the greater number of living beings throughout the world." But lowly organisms continue to persist, for "natural selection, or the survival of the fittest, does not necessarily include progressive development—it only takes advantage of such variations as arise and are beneficial to each creature under its complex relations of life." Probably no organism has reached a peak of perfection, and many lowly forms of life continue to exist, for "in some cases variations or individual differences of a favorable nature may never have arisen for natural selection to act on or accumulate. In no case, probably, has time sufficed for the utmost possible amount of development. In some few cases there has been what we must call retrogression of organization. But the main cause lies in the fact that under very simple conditions of life a high organization would be of no service.…"

In the rest of *The Origin of Species*, Darwin considers all the objections that might be raised against his theory; discusses the evolution of a great array of phenomena—hybrid sterility, the slave-making instinct of ants, the similarity of vertebrate embryos; and presents an enormous body of evidence for evolution. He draws his evidence from comparative anatomy, embryology, behavior, geographic variation, the geographic distribution of species, the study of rudimentary organs, atavistic variations ("throwbacks"), and the geological record to show how all of biology provides testimony that species have descended with modification from common ancestors.

Darwin's triumph was in synthesizing ideas and information in ways that no one had quite imagined before. From Lyell and the geologists he learned uniformitarianism: the cause of past events must be found in natural forces that operate today; and these, in the vastness of time, can accomplish great change. From Malthus and the nineteenth-century economists he learned of competition and the struggle for existence. From his work on barnacles, his travels, and his knowledge of domesticated varieties he learned that species do not have immutable essences but are variable in all their properties and blend into one another gradually. From his familiarity with the works of Whewell, Herschel, and other philosophers of science he developed a powerful method of pursuing science, the "hypothetico-deductive" method, which consists of formulating a hypothesis or speculation, deducing the logical predictions that must follow from the hypothesis, and then testing the hypothesis by seeing whether or not the predictions are verified. This was by no means the prevalent philosophy of science in Darwin's time.[5]

Darwin brought biology out of the Middle Ages. For divine design and unknowable supernatural forces he substituted natural material causes that could be studied by the methods of science. Instead of catastrophes unknown to physical science he invoked forces that could be studied in anyone's laboratory or garden. He replaced a young, static world by one in which there had been constant change for countless aeons. He established that life had a history, and this proved the essential view that differentiated evolutionary thought from all that had gone before.

For the British naturalist John Ray, writing in 1701, organisms had no history—they were the same at that moment, and lived in the same places, doing the same things, as when they were first created. For Darwin, organisms spoke of historical change. If there has indeed been such a history, then fossils in the oldest rocks must differ from those in younger rocks: trilobites, dinosaurs, and mammoths will not be mixed together but will appear in some temporal sequence. If species come from common ancestors, they will have the same characteristics, modified for different functions: the same bones used by bats for flying will be used by horses for running. If species come from ancestors that lived in different environments, they will carry the evidence of their history with them in the form of similar patterns of embryonic development and in vestigial, rudimentary organs that no longer serve any function. If species have a history, their geographical distribution will reflect it: oceanic islands won't have elephants because they wouldn't have been able to get there.

Once the earth and its living inhabitants are seen as the products of historical change, the theological philosophy embodied in the great chain of being ceases to make sense; the plenitude, or fullness, of the world becomes not an eternal manifestation of God's bountiful creativity but an illusion. For most of earth's history, most of the present species have not existed; and many of those that did exist do so no longer. But the scientific challenge to medieval philosophy goes even deeper. If evolution has occurred, and if it has proceeded from the natural causes that Darwin envisioned, then the adaptations of organisms to their environment, the intricate construction of the bird's wing and the orchid's flower, are evidence not of divine design but of the struggle for existence. Moreover, and this may be the deepest implication of all, Darwin brought to biology, as his predecessors had brought to astronomy and geology, the sufficiency of efficient causes. No longer was there any reason to look for final causes or goals. To the questions "What purpose does this species serve? Why did God make tapeworms?" the answer is "To no purpose." Tapeworms were not put here to serve a purpose, nor were planets, nor plants, nor people. They came into existence not by design but by the action of impersonal natural laws.

By providing materialistic, mechanistic explanations, instead of miraculous ones, for the characteristics of plants and animals, Darwin brought biology out of the realm of theology and into the realm of science. For miraculous spiritual forces fall outside the province of science; all of science is the study of material causation.

Of course, *The Origin of Species* didn't convince everyone immediately. Evolution and its material cause, natural selection, evoked strong protests from ecclesiastical circles, and even from scientists.[6] The eminent geologist Adam Sedgwick, for example, wrote in 1860 that species must come into existence by creation,

> a power I cannot imitate or comprehend; but in which I can believe, by a legitimate conclusion of sound reason drawn from the laws and harmonies of Nature. For I can see in all around me a design and purpose, and a mutual adaptation of parts which I *can* comprehend, and which prove that there is exterior to, and above, the mere phenomena of Nature a great prescient and designing cause.... The pretended physical philosophy of modern days strips man of all his moral attributes, or holds them of no account in the estimate of his origin and place in the created world. A cold atheistical materialism is the tendency of the so-called material philosophy of the present day.

Among the more scientific objections were those posed by the French paleontologist François Pictet, and they were echoed by many others. Since Darwin supposes that species change gradually over the course of thousands of generations, then, asked Pictet, "Why don't we find these gradations in the fossil record... and why, instead of collecting thousands of identical individuals, do we not find more intermediary forms?... How is it that the most ancient fossil beds are rich in a variety of diverse forms of life, instead of the few early types Darwin's theory leads us to expect? How is it that no species has been seen to evolve during human history, and that the 4000 years which separates us from the mummies of Egypt have been insufficient to modify the crocodile and the ibis?" Pictet protested that, although slight variations might in time alter a species slightly, "all known facts demonstrate... that the prolonged influence of modifying causes has an action which is constantly restrained within sufficiently confined limits."

The anatomist Richard Owen likewise denied "that... variability is progressive and unlimited, so as, in the course of generations, to change the species, the genus, the order, or the class." The paleontologist Louis Agassiz insisted that organisms fall into discrete groups, based on uniquely different created plans, between which no intermediates could exist. He chose the birds as a group that showed the sharpest of boundaries. Only a few years later, in 1868, the fossil *Archaeopteryx*, an exquisite intermediate between birds and reptiles, demolished Agassiz's argument, and he had no more to say on the unique character of the birds.

Within twelve years of *The Origin of Species*, the evidence for evolution had been so thoroughly accepted that philosopher and mathematician Chauncey Wright could point out that among the students of science, "orthodoxy has been won over to the doctrine of evolution." However, Wright continued, "While the general doctrine of evolution has thus been successfully redeemed from theological condemnation, this is not yet true of the subordinate hypothesis of Natural Selection."

Natural selection turned out to be an extraordinarily difficult concept for people to grasp. St. George Mivart, a Catholic scholar and scientist, was not unusual in equating natural selection with chance. "The theory of Natural Selection may (though it need not) be taken in such a way as to lead man to regard the present organic world as formed, so to speak, *accidentally*, beautiful and wonderful as is the confessedly haphazard result." Many like him simply refused to understand that natural selection is the antithesis of chance and consequently could not see how selection might cause

adaptation or any kind of progressive evolutionary change. Even in the 1940s there were those, especially among paleontologists, who felt that the progressive evolution of groups like the horses, as revealed by the fossil record, must have had some unknown cause other than natural selection. Paradoxically, then, Darwin had convinced the scientific world of evolution where his predecessors had failed; but he had not convinced all biologists of his truly original theory, the theory of natural selection.

Natural selection fell into particular disrepute in the early part of the twentieth century because of the rise of genetics—which, as it happened, eventually became the foundation of the modern theory of evolution. Darwin's supposition that variation was unlimited, and so in time could give rise to strikingly different organisms, was not entirely convincing because he had no good idea of where variation came from. In 1865, the Austrian monk Gregor Mendel discovered, from his crosses of pea plants, that discretely different characteristics such as wrinkled versus smooth seeds were inherited from generation to generation without being altered, as if they were caused by particles that passed from parent to offspring. Mendel's work was ignored for thirty-five years, until, in 1900, three biologists discovered his paper and realized that it held the key to the mystery of heredity. One of the three, Hugo de Vries, set about to explore the problem as Mendel had, and in the course of his studies of evening primroses observed strikingly different variations arise, *de novo*. The new forms were so different that de Vries believed they represented new species, which had arisen in a single step by alteration or, as he called it, mutation, of the hereditary material.

In the next few decades, geneticists working with a great variety of organisms observed many other drastic changes arise by mutation: fruit flies (Drosophila), for example, with white instead of red eyes or curled instead of straight wings. These laboratory geneticists, especially Thomas Hunt Morgan, an outstanding geneticist at Columbia University, asserted that evolution must proceed by major mutational steps, and

that mutation, not natural selection, was the cause of evolution. In their eyes, Darwin's theory was dead on two counts: evolution was not gradual, and it was not caused by natural selection. Meanwhile, naturalists, taxonomists, and breeders of domesticated plants and animals continued to believe in Darwinism, because they saw that populations and species differed quantitatively and gradually rather than in big jumps, that most variation was continuous (like height in humans) rather than discrete, and that domesticated species could be altered by artificial selection from continuous variation.

The bitter conflict between the Mendelian geneticists and the Darwinians was resolved in the 1930s in a "New Synthesis" that brought the opposing views into a "neo-Darwinian" theory of evolution.[7] Slight variations in height, wing length, and other characteristics proved, under careful genetic analysis, to be inherited as particles, in the same way as the discrete variations studied by the Mendelians. Thus a large animal simply has inherited more particles, or genes, for large size than a smaller member of the species has. The Mendelians were simply studying particularly well marked variations, while the naturalists were studying more subtle ones. Variations could be very slight, or fairly pronounced, or very substantial, but all were inherited in the same manner. All these variations, it was shown, arose by a process of mutation of the genes.

Three mathematical theoreticians, Ronald Fisher and J. B. S. Haldane in England and Sewall Wright in the United States, proved that a newly mutated gene would not automatically form a new species. Nor would it automatically replace the preexisting form of the gene, and so transform the species. Replacement of one gene by a mutant form of the gene, they said, could happen in two ways. The mutation could enable its possessors to survive or reproduce more effectively than the old form; if so, it would increase by natural selection, just as Darwin had said. The new characteristic that evolved in this way would ordinarily be considered an improved adaptation.

Sewall Wright pointed out, however, that not all genetic changes in species need be adaptive. A new mutation might be no better or worse than the preexisting gene—it might simply be "neutral." In small populations such a mutation could replace the previous gene purely by chance—a process he called random genetic drift. The idea, put crudely, is this. Suppose there is a small population of land snails in a cow pasture, and that 5 percent of them are brown and the rest are yellow. Purely by chance, a greater percentage of yellow snails than of brown ones get crushed by cows' hooves in one generation. The snails breed, and there will now be a slightly greater percentage of yellow snails in the next generation than there had been. But in the next generation, the yellow ones may suffer more trampling, purely by chance. The proportion of yellow offspring will then be lower again. These random events cause fluctuations in the percentage of the two types. Wright proved mathematically that eventually, if no other factors intervene, these fluctuations will bring the population either to 100 percent yellow or 100 percent brown, purely by chance. The population will have evolved, then, but not by natural selection; and there is no improvement of adaptation.

During the period of the New Synthesis, though, genetic drift was emphasized less than natural selection, for which abundant evidence was discovered. Sergei Chetverikov in Russia, and later Theodosius Dobzhansky working in the United States, showed that wild populations of fruit flies contained an immense amount of genetic variation, including the same kinds of mutations that the geneticists had found arising in their laboratories. Dobzhansky and other workers went on to show that these variations affected survival and reproduction: that natural selection was a reality. They showed, moreover, that the genetic differences among related species were indeed compounded of the same kinds of slight genetic variations that they found within species. Thus the taxonomists and the geneticists converged onto a neo-Darwinian theory of evolution: evolution is due not to mutation *or* natural selection, but to both. Random mutations provide abundant genetic variation; natural selection, the antithesis of randomness,

sorts out the useful from the deleterious, and transforms the species.

In the following two decades, the paleontologist George Gaylord Simpson showed that this theory was completely adequate to explain the fossil record, and the ornithologists Bernhard Rensch and Ernst Mayr, the botanist G. Ledyard Stebbins, and many other taxonomists showed that the similarities and differences among living species could be fully explained by neo-Darwinism. They also clarified the meaning of "species." Organisms belong to different species if they do not interbreed when the opportunity presents itself, thus remaining genetically distinct. An ancestral species splits into two descendant species when different populations of the ancestor, living in different geographic regions, become so genetically different from each other that they will not or cannot interbreed when they have the chance to do so. As a result, evolution can happen without the formation of new species: a single species can be genetically transformed without splitting into several descendants. Conversely, new species can be formed without much genetic change. If one population becomes different from the rest of its species in, for example, its mating behavior, it will not interbreed with the other populations. Thus it has become a new species, even though it may be identical to its "sister species" in every respect except its behavior. Such a new species is free to follow a new path of genetic change, since it does not become homogenized with its sister species by interbreeding. With time, therefore, it can diverge and develop different adaptations.

The conflict between the geneticists and the Darwinians that was resolved in the New Synthesis was the last major conflict in evolutionary science. Since that time, an enormous amount of research has confirmed most of the major conclusions of neo-Darwinism. We now know that populations contain very extensive genetic variation that continually arises by mutation of pre-existing genes. We also know what genes are and how they become mutated. Many instances of the reality of natural selection in wild populations have been documented, and there is extensive evidence that many

species form by the divergence of different populations of an ancestral species.

The major questions in evolutionary biology now tend to be of the form, "All right, factors x and y both operate in evolution, but how important is x compared to y?" For example, studies of biochemical genetic variation have raised the possibility that nonadaptive, random change (genetic drift) may be the major reason for many biochemical differences among species. How important, then, is genetic drift compared to natural selection? Another major question has to do with rates of evolution: Do species usually diverge very slowly, as Darwin thought, or does evolution consist mostly of rapid spurts, interspersed with long periods of constancy? Still another question is raised by mutations, which range all the way from gross changes of the kind Morgan studied to very slight alterations. Does evolution consist entirely of the substitution of mutations that have very slight effects, or are major mutations sometimes important too? Partisans on each side of all these questions argue vigorously for their interpretation of the evidence, but they don't doubt that the major factors of evolution are known. They simply emphasize one factor or another. Minor battles of precisely this kind go on continually in every field of science; without them there would be very little advancement in our knowledge.

Within a decade or two of *The Origin of Species*, the belief that living organisms had evolved over the ages was firmly entrenched in biology. As of 1982, the historical existence of evolution is viewed as fact by almost all biologists. To explain how the fact of evolution has been brought about, a theory of evolutionary mechanisms—mutation, natural selection, genetic drift, and isolation—has been developed.[8] But exactly what is the evidence for the fact of evolution?

NOTES

1. Andrew Dickson White, *A History of the Warfare of Science with Theology in Christendom* vol. I (London: Macmillan, 1896; reprint ed., New York: Dover, 1960).

2. A. O. Lovejoy, *The Great Chain of Being* (Cambridge, Mass.: Harvard University Press, 1936).

3. Much of this history is provided by J. C. Greene, *The Death of Adam: Evolution and its Impact on Western Thought* (Ames: Iowa State University Press, 1959).

4. A detailed history of this and other developments in evolutionary biology is given by Ernst Mayr, *The Growth of Biological Thought: Diversity, Evolution, Inheritance* (Cambridge, Mass.: Harvard University Press, 1982).

5. See D. L. Hull, *Darwin and His Critics* (Cambridge, Mass.: Harvard University Press, 1973).

6. Ibid.

7. E. Mayr and W. B. Provine, *The Evolutionary Synthesis* (Cambridge, Mass.: Harvard University Press, 1980).

8. Our modern understanding of the mechanisms of evolution is described in many books. Elementary textbooks include G. L. Stebbins, *Processes of Organic Evolution*, (Englewood Cliffs, N.J.: Prentice-Hall, 1971), and J. Maynard Smith, *The Theory of Evolution* (New York: Penguin Books, 1975). More advanced textbooks include Th. Dobzhansky, F. J. Ayala, G. L. Stebbins, and J. W. Valentine, *Evolution* (San Francisco: Freeman, 1977), and D. J. Futuyma, *Evolutionary Biology* (Sunderland, Mass.: Sinauer, 1979). Unreferenced facts and theories described in the text are familiar enough to most evolutionary biologists that they will be found in most or all of the references cited above.

James D. Watson, a molecularbiologist, shared the Nobel Prize for his work in discovering the structure of DNA.

Darwin's Influence on Modern Thought

Great minds shape the thinking of successive historical periods. Luther and Calvin inspired the Reformation; Locke, Leibniz, Voltaire and Rousseau, the Enlightenment. Modern thought is most dependent on the influence of Charles Darwin

by Ernst Mayr

Clearly, our conception of the world and our place in it is, at the beginning of the 21st century, drastically different from the zeitgeist at the beginning of the 19th century. But no consensus exists as to the source of this revolutionary change. Karl Marx is often mentioned; Sigmund Freud has been in and out of favor; Albert Einstein's biographer Abraham Pais made the exuberant claim that Einstein's theories "have profoundly changed the way modern men and women think about the phenomena of inanimate nature." No sooner had Pais said this, though, than he recognized the exaggeration. "It would actually be better to say 'modern scientists' than 'modern men and women,'" he wrote, because one needs schooling in the physicist's style of thought and mathematical techniques to appreciate Einstein's contributions in their fullness. Indeed, this limitation is true for all the extraordinary theories of modern physics, which have had little impact on the way the average person apprehends the world.

The situation differs dramatically with regard to concepts in biology. Many biological ideas proposed during the past 150 years stood in stark conflict with what everybody assumed to be true. The acceptance of these ideas required an ideological revolution. And no biologist has been responsible for more—and for more drastic—modifications of the aver-age person's worldview than Charles Darwin.

Darwin's accomplishments were so many and so diverse that it is useful to distinguish three fields to which he made major contributions: evolutionary biology; the philosophy of science; and the modern zeitgeist. Although I will be focusing on this last domain, for the sake of completeness I will put forth a short overview of his contributions—particularly as they inform his later ideas—to the first two areas.

A SECULAR VIEW OF LIFE

Darwin founded a new branch of life science, evolutionary biology. Four of his contributions to evolutionary biology are especially important, as they held considerable sway beyond that discipline. The first is the non-constancy of species, or the modern conception of evolution itself. The second is the notion of branching evolution, implying the common descent of all species of living things on earth from a single unique origin. Up until 1859, all evolutionary proposals, such as that of naturalist Jean-Baptiste Lamarck, instead endorsed linear evolution, a teleological march toward greater perfection that had been in vogue since Aristotle's concept of *Scala Naturae*, the chain of being. Darwin further noted that evolution must be gradual, with no major breaks or discontinuities. Finally, he reasoned that the mechanism of evolution was natural selection.

These four insights served as the foundation for Darwin's founding of a new branch of the philosophy of science, a philosophy of biology. Despite the passing of a century before this new branch of philosophy fully developed, its eventual form is based on Darwinian concepts. For example, Darwin introduced historicity into science. Evolutionary biology, in contrast with physics and chemistry, is a historical science—the evolutionist attempts to explain events and processes that have already taken place. Laws and experiments are inappropriate techniques for the explication of such events and processes. Instead one constructs a historical narrative, consisting of a tentative reconstruction of the particular scenario that led to the events one is trying to explain.

For example, three different scenarios have been proposed for the sudden extinction of the dinosaurs at the end of the Cretaceous: a devastating epidemic; a catastrophic change of climate; and the impact of an asteroid, known as the Alvarez theory. The first two narratives were ultimately refuted by evidence incompatible with them. All the known facts, however, fit the Alvarez theory, which is now widely accepted. The testing of historical narratives implies that the wide gap between science and the humanities that so troubled physicist C. P. Snow is actually nonexistent—by virtue of its methodology and its acceptance of the time factor that makes change possible, evolutionary biology serves as a bridge.

The discovery of natural selection, by Darwin and Alfred Russell Wallace, must itself be counted as an extraordinary philosophical advance. The principle remained unknown throughout the more than 2,000-year history of philosophy ranging from the Greeks to Hume, Kant and the Victorian era. The concept of natural selection had remarkable power for explaining directional and adaptive changes. Its nature is simplicity itself. It is not a force like the forces described in the laws of physics; its mechanism is simply the elimination of inferior individuals. This process of nonrandom elimination impelled Darwin's contemporary, philosopher Herbert Spencer, to describe evolution with the now familiar term "survival of the fittest." (This description was long ridiculed as circular reasoning: "Who are the fittest? Those who survive." In reality, a careful analysis can usually determine why certain individuals fail to thrive in a given set of conditions.)

The truly outstanding achievement of the principle of natural selection is that it makes unnecessary the invocation of "final causes"—that is, any teleological forces leading to a particular end. In fact, nothing is predetermined. Furthermore, the objective of selection even may change from one generation to the next, as environmental circumstances vary.

A diverse population is a necessity for the proper working of natural selection. (Darwin's success meant that typologists, for whom all members of a class are essentially identical, were left with an untenable viewpoint.) Because of the importance of variation, natural selection should be considered a two-step process: the production of abundant variation is followed by the elimination of inferior individuals. This latter step is directional. By adopting natural selection, Darwin settled the several-thousand-year-old argument among philosophers over chance or necessity. Change on the earth is the result of both, the first step being domi-nated by randomness, the second by necessity.

Darwin was a holist: for him the object, or target, of selection was primarily the individual as a whole. The geneticists, almost from 1900 on, in a rather reductionist spirit preferred to consider the gene the target of evolution. In the past 25 years, however, they have largely returned to the Darwinian view that the individual is the principal target.

For 80 years after 1859, bitter controversy raged as to which of four competing evolutionary theories was valid. "Transmutation" was the establishment of a new species or new type through a single mutation, or saltation. "Orthogenesis" held that intrinsic teleological tendencies led to transformation. Lamarckian evolution relied on the inheritance of acquired characteristics. And now there was Darwin's variational evolution, through natural selection. Darwin's theory clearly emerged as the victor during the evolutionary synthesis of the 1940s, when the new discoveries in genetics were married with taxonomic observations concerning systematics, the classification of organisms by their relationships. Darwinism is now almost unanimously accepted by knowledgeable evolutionists. In addition, it has become the basic component of the new philosophy of biology.

A most important principle of the new biological philosophy, undiscovered for almost a century after the publication of *On the Origin of Species*, is the dual nature of biological processes. These activities are governed both by the universal laws of physics and chemistry and by a genetic program, itself the result of natural selection, which has molded the genotype for millions of generations. The causal factor of the possession of a genetic program is unique to living organisms, and it is totally absent in the inanimate world. Because of the backward state of molecular and genetic knowledge in his time, Darwin was unaware of this vital factor.

Another aspect of the new philosophy of biology concerns the role of laws. Laws give way to concepts in Darwinism. In the physical sciences, as a rule, theories are based on laws; for example, the laws of motion led to the theory of gravitation. In evolutionary biology, however, theo-ries are largely based on concepts such as competition, female choice, selection, succession and dominance. These biological concepts, and the theories based on them, cannot be reduced to the laws and theories of the physical sciences. Darwin himself never stated this idea plainly. My assertion of Darwin's importance to modern thought is the result of an analysis of Darwinian theory over the past century. During this period, a pronounced change in the methodology of biology took place. This transformation was not caused exclusively by Darwin, but it was greatly strengthened by developments in evolutionary biology. Observation, comparison and classification, as well as the testing of competing historical narratives, became the methods of evolutionary biology, outweighing experimentation.

I do not claim that Darwin was single-handedly responsible for all the intellectual developments in this period. Much of it, like the refutation of French mathematician and physicist Pierre-Simon Laplace's determinism, was "in the air." But Darwin in most cases either had priority or promoted the new views most vigorously.

THE DARWINIAN ZEITGEIST

A 21st-century person looks at the world quite differently than a citizen of the Victorian era did. This shift had multiple sources, particularly the incredible advances in technology. But what is not at all appreciated is the great extent to which this shift in thinking indeed resulted from Darwin's ideas.

Remember that in 1850 virtually all leading scientists and philosophers were Christian men. The world they inhabited had been created by God, and as the natural theologians claimed, He had instituted wise laws that brought about the perfect adaptation of all organisms to one another and to their environment. At the same time, the architects of the scientific revolution had constructed a worldview based on physicalism (a reduction to spatiotemporal things or events or their properties), teleology, determinism and other basic principles. Such was the thinking of Western man prior to the 1859 publication of *On the Origin of*

Species. The basic principles proposed by Darwin would stand in total conflict with these prevailing ideas.

First, Darwinism rejects all supernatural phenomena and causations. The theory of evolution by natural selection explains the adaptedness and diversity of the world solely materialistically. It no longer requires God as creator or designer (although one is certainly still free to believe in God even if one accepts evolution). Darwin pointed out that creation, as described in the Bible and the origin accounts of other cultures, was contradicted by almost any aspect of the natural world. Every aspect of the "wonderful design" so admired by the natural theologians could be explained by natural selection. (A closer look also reveals that design is often not so wonderful—see "Evolution and the Origins of Disease," by Randolph M. Nesse and George C. Williams; SCIENTIFIC AMERICAN, November 1998). Eliminating God from science made room for strictly scientific explanations of all natural phenomena; it gave rise to positivism; it produced a powerful intellectual and spiritual revolution, the effects of which have lasted to this day.

Second, Darwinism refutes typology. From the time of the Pythagoreans and Plato, the general concept of the diversity of the world emphasized its invariance and stability. This viewpoint is called typology, or essentialism. The seeming variety, it was said, consisted of a limited number of natural kinds (essences or types), each one forming a class. The members of each class were thought to be identical, constant, and sharply separated from the members of other essences.

Variation, in contrast, is nonessential and accidental. A triangle illustrates essentialism: all triangles have the same fundamental characteristics and are sharply delimited against quadrangles or any other geometric figures. An intermediate between a triangle and a quadrangle is inconceivable. Typological thinking, therefore, is unable to accommodate variation and gives rise to a misleading conception of human races. For the typologist, Caucasians, Africans, Asians or Inuits are types that conspicuously differ from other human ethnic

groups. This mode of thinking leads to racism. (Although the ignorant misapplication of evolutionary theory known as "social Darwinism" often gets blamed for justifications of racism, adherence to the disproved essentialism preceding Darwin in fact can lead to a racist viewpoint.)

Darwin completely rejected typological thinking and introduced instead the entirely different concept now called population thinking. All groupings of living organisms, including humanity, are populations that consist of uniquely different individuals. No two of the six billion humans are the same. Populations vary not by their essences but only by mean statistical differences. By rejecting the constancy of populations, Darwin helped to introduce history into scientific thinking and to promote a distinctly new approach to explanatory interpretation in science.

Third, Darwin's theory of natural selection made any invocation of teleology unnecessary. From the Greeks onward, there existed a universal belief in the existence of a teleological force in the world that led to ever greater perfection. This "final cause" was one of the causes specified by Aristotle. After Kant, in the *Critique of Judgment*, had unsuccessfully attempted to describe biological phenomena with the help of a physicalist Newtonian explanation, he then invoked teleological forces. Even after 1859, teleological explanations (orthogenesis) continued to be quite popular in evolutionary biology. The acceptance of the *Scala Naturae* and the explanations of natural theology were other manifestations of the popularity of teleology. Darwinism swept such considerations away.

(The designation "teleological" actually applied to various different phenomena. Many seemingly end-directed processes in inorganic nature are the simple consequence of natural laws—a stone falls or a heated piece of metal cools because of laws of physics, not some end-directed process. Processes in living organisms owe their apparent goal-directedness to the operation of an inborn genetic or acquired program. Adapted systems, such as the heart or kidneys, may engage in activities that can be considered goal seeking, but the

systems themselves were acquired during evolution and are continuously fine-tuned by natural selection. Finally, there was a belief in cosmic teleology, with a purpose and predetermined goal ascribed to everything in nature. Modern science, however, is unable to substantiate the existence of any such cosmic teleology.)

Fourth, Darwin does away with determinism. Laplace notoriously boasted that a complete knowledge of the current world and all its processes would enable him to predict the future to infinity. Darwin, by comparison, accepted the universality of randomness and chance throughout the process of natural selection. (Astronomer and philosopher John Herschel referred to natural selection contemptuously as "the law of the higgledy-piggledy.") That chance should play an important role in natural processes has been an unpalatable thought for many physicists. Einstein expressed this distaste in his statement, "God does not play dice." Of course, as previously mentioned, only the first step in natural selection, the production of variation, is a matter of chance. The character of the second step, the actual selection, is to be directional.

Despite the initial resistance by physicists and philosophers, the role of contingency and chance in natural processes is now almost universally acknowledged. Many biologists and philosophers deny the existence of universal laws in biology and suggest that all regularities be stated in probabilistic terms, as nearly all so-called biological laws have exceptions. Philosopher of science Karl Popper's famous test of falsification therefore cannot be applied in these cases.

Fifth, Darwin developed a new view of humanity and, in turn, a new anthropocentrism. Of all of Darwin's proposals, the one his contemporaries found most difficult to accept was that the theory of common descent applied to Man. For the theologians and philosophers alike, Man was a creature above and apart from other living beings. Aristotle, Descartes and Kant agreed on this sentiment, no matter how else their thinking diverged. But biologists Thomas Huxley and Ernst Haeckel revealed through rigorous comparative anatomical study that humans and living apes clearly had common ancestry, an assessment that has never again been seriously questioned in science. The application of the theory of common descent to Man deprived man of his former unique position.

Ironically, though, these events did not lead to an end to anthropocentrism. The study of man showed that, in spite of his descent, he is indeed unique among all organisms. Human intelligence is unmatched by that of any other creature. Humans are the only animals with true language, including grammar and syntax. Only humanity, as Darwin emphasized, has developed genuine ethical systems. In addition, through high intelligence, language and long parental care, humans are the only creatures to have created a rich culture. And by these means, humanity has attained, for better or worse, an unprecedented dominance over the entire globe.

Sixth, Darwin provided a scientific foundation for ethics. The question is frequently raised—and usually rebuffed—as to whether evolution adequately explains healthy human ethics. Many wonder how, if selection rewards the individual only for behavior that enhances his own survival and reproductive success, such pure selfishness can lead to any sound ethics. The widespread thesis of social Darwinism, promoted at the end of the 19th century by Spencer, was that evolutionary explanations were at odds with the development of ethics.

We now know, however, that in a social species not only the individual must be considered—an entire social group can be the target of selection. Darwin applied this reasoning to the human species in 1871 in *The Descent of Man*. The survival and prosperity of a social group depends to a large extent on the harmonious cooperation of the members of the group, and this behavior must be based on altruism. Such altruism, by furthering the survival and prosperity of the group, also indirectly benefits the fitness of the group's individuals. The result amounts to selection favoring altruistic behavior.

Kin selection and reciprocal helpfulness in particular will be greatly favored in a social group. Such selection for altruism has been demonstrated in recent years to be widespread among many other social animals. One can then perhaps encapsulate the relation between ethics and evolution by saying that a propensity for altruism and harmonious cooperation in social groups *is* favored by natural selection. The old thesis of social Darwinism—strict selfishness—was based on an incomplete understanding of animals, particularly social species.

THE INFLUENCE OF NEW CONCEPTS

Let me now try to summarize my major findings. No educated person any longer questions the validity of the so-called theory of evolution, which we now know to be a simple fact. Likewise, most of Darwin's particular theses have been fully confirmed, such as that of common descent, the gradualism of evolution, and his explanatory theory of natural selection.

I hope I have successfully illustrated the wide reach of Darwin's ideas. Yes, he established a philosophy of biology by introducing the time factor, by demonstrating the importance of chance and contingency, and by showing that theories in evolutionary biology are based on concepts rather than laws. But furthermore—and this is perhaps Darwin's greatest contribution—he developed a set of new principles that influence the thinking of every person: the living world, through evolution, can be explained without recourse to supernaturalism; essentialism or typology is invalid, and we must adopt population thinking, in which all individuals are unique (vital for education and the refutation of racism); natural selection, applied to social groups, is indeed sufficient to account for the origin and maintenance of altruistic ethical systems; cosmic teleology, an intrinsic process leading life automati-

cally to ever greater perfection, is fallacious, with all seemingly teleological phenomena explicable by purely material processes; and determinism is thus repudiated, which places our fate squarely in our own evolved hands.

To borrow Darwin's phrase, there is grandeur in this view of life. New modes of thinking have been, and are being, evolved. Almost every component in modern man's belief system is somehow affected by Darwinian principles.

This article is based on the September 23, 1999, lecture that Mayr delivered in Stockholm on receiving the Crafoord Prize from the Royal Swedish Academy of Science.

FURTHER INFORMATION

DARWIN ON MAN: A PSYCHOLOGICAL STUDY OF SCIENTIFIC CREATIVITY. Second edition. Howard E. Gruber. University of Chicago Press, 1981.

ONE LONG ARGUMENT: CHARLES DARWIN AND THE GENESIS OF MODERN EVOLUTIONARY THOUGHT. Ernst Mayr. Harvard University Press, 1993.

CHARLES DARWIN: VOYAGING: A BIOGRAPHY. Janet Browne. Princeton University Press, 1996.

THE DESCENT OF MAN. Charles Darwin. Popular current edition. Prometheus Books, 1997.

THE ORIGIN OF SPECIES. Charles Darwin. Popular current edition. Bantam Classic, 1999.

ERNST MAYR is one of the towering figures in the history of evolutionary biology. Following his graduation from the University of Berlin in 1926, ornithological expeditions to New Guinea fueled his interest in theoretical evolutionary biology. Mayr emigrated to the U.S. in 1931 and in 1953 joined the faculty of Harvard University, where he is now Alexander Agassiz Professor of Zoology, Emeritus. His conception of rapid speciation of isolated populations formed the basis for the well-known neoevolutionary concept of punctuated equilibrium. The author of some of the 20th century's most influential volumes on evolution, Mayr is the recipient of numerous awards, including the National Medal of Science.

15

Answers to

Creationist

Nonsense

Opponents of evolution want to make a place for creationism
by tearing down real science, but their arguments don't hold up

By John Rennie

When Charles Darwin introduced the theory of evolution through natural selection 143 years ago, the scientists of the day argued over it fiercely, but the massing evidence from paleontology, genetics, zoology, molecular biology and other fields gradually established evolution's truth beyond reasonable doubt. Today that battle has been won everywhere—except in the public imagination.

Embarrassingly, in the 21st century, in the most scientifically advanced nation the world has ever known, creationists can still persuade politicians, judges and ordinary citizens that evolution is a flawed, poorly supported fantasy. They lobby for creationist ideas such as "intelligent design" to be taught as alternatives to evolution in science classrooms. As this article goes to press, the Ohio Board of Education is debating whether to mandate such a change. Some antievolutionists, such as Philip E. Johnson, a law professor at the University of California at Berkeley and author of *Darwin on Trial*, admit that they intend for intelligent-design theory to serve as a "wedge" for reopening science classrooms to discussions of God.

Besieged teachers and others may increasingly find themselves on the spot to defend evolution and refute creationism. The arguments that creationists use are typically specious and based on misunderstandings of (or outright lies about) evolution, but the number and diversity of the objections can put even well-informed people at a disadvantage.

To help with answering them, the following list rebuts some of the most common "scientific" arguments raised against evolution. It also directs readers to further sources for information and explains why creation science has no place in the classroom.

1. Evolution is only a theory. It is not a fact or a scientific law.

Many people learned in elementary school that a theory falls in the middle of a hierarchy of certainty—above a mere hypothesis but below a law. Scientists do not use the terms that way, however. According to the National Academy of Sciences (NAS), a scientific theory is "a well-substantiated explanation of some aspect of the natural world that can incorporate facts, laws, inferences, and tested hypotheses." No amount of validation changes a theory into a law, which is a descriptive generalization about nature. So when scientists talk about the theory of evolution—or the atomic theory or the theory of relativity, for that matter—they are not expressing reservations about its truth.

In addition to the *theory* of evolution, meaning the idea of descent with modification, one may also speak of the *fact* of evolution. The NAS defines a fact as "an observation that has been repeatedly confirmed and for all practical purposes is accepted as 'true.'" The fossil record and abundant other evidence testify that organisms have evolved through time. Although no one observed those transformations, the indirect evidence is clear, unambiguous and compelling.

All sciences frequently rely on indirect evidence. Physicists cannot see subatomic particles directly, for instance, so they

PATRICIA J. WYNNE

GALÁPAGOS FINCHES show adaptive beak shapes

verify their existence by watching for tell-tale tracks that the particles leave in cloud chambers. The absence of direct observation does not make physicists' conclusions less certain.

2. Natural selection is based on circular reasoning: the fittest are those who survive, and those who survive are deemed fittest.

"Survival of the fittest" is a conversational way to describe natural selection, but a more technical description speaks of differential rates of survival and reproduction. That is, rather than labeling species as more or less fit, one can describe how many offspring they are likely to leave under given circumstances. Drop a fast-breeding pair of small-beaked finches and a slower-breeding pair of large-beaked finches onto an island full of food seeds. Within a few generations the fast breeders may control more of the food resources. Yet if large beaks more easily crush seeds, the advantage may tip to the slow breeders. In a pioneering study of finches on the Galápagos Islands, Peter R. Grant of Princeton University observed these kinds of population shifts in the wild [see his article "Natural Selection and Darwin's Finches"; SCIENTIFIC AMERICAN, October 1991].

The key is that adaptive fitness can be defined without reference to survival: large beaks are better adapted for crushing seeds, irrespective of whether that trait has survival value under the circumstances.

3. Evolution is unscientific, because it is not testable or falsifiable. It makes claims about events that were not observed and can never be re-created.

This blanket dismissal of evolution ignores important distinctions that divide the field into at least two broad areas: microevolution and macroevolution. Microevolution looks at changes within species over time—changes that may be preludes to speciation, the origin of new species. Macroevolution studies how taxonomic groups above the level of species change. Its evidence draws frequently from the fossil record and DNA comparisons to reconstruct how various organisms may be related.

These days even most creationists acknowledge that microevolution has been upheld by tests in the laboratory (as in studies of cells, plants and fruit flies) and in the field (as in Grant's studies of evolving beak shapes among Galapagos finches). Natural selection and other mechanisms—such as chromosomal changes, symbiosis and hybridization—can drive profound changes in populations over time.

The historical nature of macroevolutionary study involves inference from fossils and DNA rather than direct observation. Yet in the historical sciences (which include astronomy, geology and archaeology, as well as evolutionary biology), hypotheses can still be tested by checking whether they accord with physical evidence and whether they lead to verifiable predictions about future discoveries. For instance, evolution implies that between the earliest-known ancestors of humans (roughly five million years old) and the appearance of anatomically modern humans (about 100,000 years ago), one should find a succession of hominid creatures with features progressively less apelike and more modern, which is indeed what the fossil record shows. But one should not—and does not—find modern human fossils embedded in strata from the Jurassic period (65 million years ago). Evolutionary biology routinely makes predictions far more refined and precise than this, and researchers test them constantly.

Evolution could be disproved in other ways, too. If we could document the spontaneous generation of just one complex life-form from inanimate matter, then at least a few creatures seen in the fossil record might have originated this way. If superintelligent aliens appeared and claimed credit for creating life on earth (or even particular species), the purely evolutionary explanation would be cast in doubt. But no one has yet produced such evidence.

It should be noted that the idea of falsifiability as the defining characteristic of science originated with philosopher Karl Popper in the 1930s. More recent elaborations on his thinking have expanded the narrowest interpretation of his principle precisely because it would eliminate too many branches of clearly scientific endeavor.

4. Increasingly, scientists doubt the truth of evolution.

No evidence suggests that evolution is losing adherents. Pick up any issue of a peer-reviewed biological journal, and you will find articles that support and extend evolutionary studies or that embrace evolution as a fundamental concept.

Conversely, serious scientific publications disputing evolution are all but nonexistent. In the mid-1990s George W. Gilchrist of the University of Washington surveyed thousands of journals in the primary literature, seeking articles on intelligent design or creation science. Among those hundreds of thousands of scientific reports, he found none. In the past two years, surveys done independently by Barbara Forrest of Southeastern Louisiana University and Lawrence M. Krauss of Case Western Reserve University have been similarly fruitless.

Creationists retort that a closed-minded scientific community rejects their evidence. Yet according to the editors of *Nature, Science* and other leading journals, few antievolution manuscripts are even submitted. Some antievolution authors have published papers in serious journals. Those papers, however, rarely attack evolution directly or advance creationist arguments; at best, they identify certain evolutionary problems as unsolved and difficult (which no one disputes). In short, creationists are not giving the scientific world good reason to take them seriously.

5. The disagreements among even evolutionary biologists show how little solid science supports evolution.

Evolutionary biologists passionately debate diverse topics: how speciation happens, the rates of evolutionary change, the ancestral relationships of birds and dinosaurs, whether Neandertals were a species apart from modern humans, and much more. These disputes are like those found in all other branches of science. Acceptance of evolution as a factual occurrence and a guiding principle is nonetheless universal in biology.

Unfortunately, dishonest creationists have shown a willingness to take scientists' comments out of context to exaggerate and distort the disagreements. Anyone acquainted with the works of paleontologist Stephen Jay Gould of Harvard University knows that in addition to co-authoring the punctuated-equilibrium model, Gould was one of the most eloquent defenders and articulators of evolution. (Punctuated equilibrium explains patterns in the fossil record by suggesting that most evolutionary changes occur within geologically brief intervals—which may nonetheless amount to hundreds of generations.) Yet creationists delight in dissecting out phrases from Gould's voluminous prose to make him sound as though he had doubted evolution, and they present punctuated equilibrium as though it allows new species to materialize overnight or birds to be born from reptile eggs.

When confronted with a quotation from a scientific authority that seems to question evolution, insist on seeing the statement in context. Almost invariably, the attack on evolution will prove illusory.

6. If humans descended from monkeys, why are there still monkeys?

This surprisingly common argument reflects several levels of ignorance about evolution. The first mistake is that evolution does not teach that humans descended from monkeys; it states that both have a common ancestor.

The deeper error is that this objection is tantamount to asking, "If children descended from adults, why are there still adults?" New species evolve by splintering off from established ones, when populations of organisms become isolated from the main branch of their family and acquire sufficient differences to remain forever distinct. The parent species may survive indefinitely thereafter, or it may become extinct.

7. Evolution cannot explain how life first appeared on earth.

The origin of life remains very much a mystery, but biochemists have learned about how primitive nucleic acids, amino acids and other building blocks of life could have formed and organized themselves into self-replicating, self-sustaining units, laying the foundation for cellular biochemistry. Astrochemical analyses hint that quantities of these compounds might have originated in space and fallen to earth in comets, a scenario that may solve the problem of how those constituents arose under the conditions that prevailed when our planet was young.

Creationists sometimes try to invalidate all of evolution by pointing to science's current inability to explain the origin of life. But even if life on earth turned out to have a non-evolutionary origin (for instance, if aliens introduced the first cells billions of years ago), evolution since then would be robustly confirmed by countless microevolutionary and macroevolutionary studies.

8. Mathematically, it is inconceivable that anything as complex as a protein, let alone a living cell or a human, could spring up by chance.

Chance plays a part in evolution (for example, in the random mutations that can give rise to new traits), but evolution does not depend on chance to create organisms, proteins or other entities. Quite the opposite: natural selection, the principal known mechanism of evolution, harnesses nonrandom change by preserving "desirable" (adaptive) features and eliminating "undesirable" (non-adaptive) ones. As long as the forces of selection stay constant, natural selection can push evolution in one direction and produce sophisticated structures in surprisingly short times.

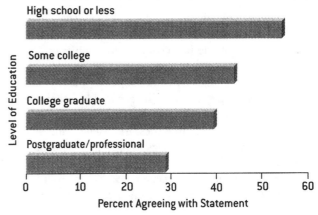

"GOD CREATED HUMANS IN THEIR PRESENT FORM WITHIN THE PAST 10,000 YEARS OR SO."

SOURCE: The Gallup Organization, 199 CLEO VILETT

As an analogy, consider the 13-letter sequence "TOBEOR-NOTTOBE." Those hypothetical million monkeys, each pecking out one phrase a second, could take as long as 78,800 years to find it among the 26^{13} sequences of that length. But in the 1980s Richard Hardison of Glendale College wrote a computer program that generated phrases randomly while preserving the positions of individual letters that happened to be correctly placed (in effect, selecting for phrases more like Hamlet's). On average, the program re-created the phrase in just 336 iterations, less than 90 seconds. Even more amazing, it could reconstruct Shakespeare's entire play in just four and a half days.

9. The Second Law of Thermodynamics says that systems must become more disordered over time. Living cells therefore could not have evolved from inanimate chemicals, and multicellular life could not have evolved from protozoa.

This argument derives from a misunderstanding of the Second Law. If it were valid, mineral crystals and snowflakes would also be impossible, because they, too, are complex structures that form spontaneously from disordered parts.

The Second Law actually states that the total entropy of a closed system (one that no energy or matter leaves or enters) cannot decrease. Entropy is a physical concept often casually described as disorder, but it differs significantly from the conversational use of the word.

More important, however, the Second Law permits parts of a system to decrease in entropy as long as other parts experience an offsetting increase. Thus, our planet as a whole can grow more complex because the sun pours heat and light onto it, and the greater entropy associated with the sun's nuclear fusion more than rebalances the scales. Simple organisms can fuel their rise toward complexity by consuming other forms of life and nonliving materials.

10. Mutations are essential to evolution theory, but mutations can only eliminate traits. They cannot produce new features.

On the contrary, biology has catalogued many traits produced by point mutations (changes at precise positions in an organism's DNA)—bacterial resistance to antibiotics, for example.

Mutations that arise in the homeobox (*Hox*) family of development-regulating genes in animals can also have complex effects. *Hox* genes direct where legs, wings, antennae and body segments should grow. In fruit flies, for instance, the mutation called *Antennapedia* causes legs to sprout where antennae should grow. These abnormal limbs are not functional, but their existence demonstrates that genetic mistakes can produce complex structures, which natural selection can then test for possible uses.

Moreover, molecular biology has discovered mechanisms for genetic change that go beyond point mutations, and these expand the ways in which new traits can appear. Functional modules within genes can be spliced together in novel ways.

Whole genes can be accidentally duplicated in an organism's DNA, and the duplicates are free to mutate into genes for new, complex features. Comparisons of the DNA from a wide variety of organisms indicate that this is how the globin family of blood proteins evolved over millions of years.

11. Natural selection might explain microevolution, but it cannot explain the origin of new species and higher orders of life.

Evolutionary biologists have written extensively about how natural selection could produce new species. For instance, in the model called allopatry, developed by Ernst Mayr of Harvard University, if a population of organisms were isolated from the rest of its species by geographical boundaries, it might be subjected to different selective pressures. Changes would accumulate in the isolated population. If those changes became so significant that the splinter group could not or routinely would not breed with the original stock, then the splinter group would be *reproductively isolated* and on its way toward becoming a new species.

Natural selection is the best studied of the evolutionary mechanisms, but biologists are open to other possibilities as well. Biologists are constantly assessing the potential of unusual genetic mechanisms for causing speciation or for producing complex features in organisms. Lynn Margulis of the University of Massachusetts at Amherst and others have persuasively argued that some cellular organelles, such as the energy-generating mitochondria, evolved through the symbiotic merger of ancient organisms. Thus, science welcomes the possibility of evolution resulting from forces beyond natural selection. Yet those forces must be natural; they cannot be attributed to the actions of mysterious creative intelligences whose existence, in scientific terms, is unproved.

12. Nobody has ever seen a new species evolve.

Speciation is probably fairly rare and in many cases might take centuries. Furthermore, recognizing a new species during a formative stage can be difficult, because biologists sometimes disagree about how best to define a species. The most widely used definition, Mayr's Biological Species Concept, recognizes a species as a distinct community of reproductively isolated populations—sets of organisms that normally do not or cannot breed outside their community. In practice, this standard can be difficult to apply to organisms isolated by distance or terrain or to plants (and, of course, fossils do not breed). Biologists therefore usually use organisms' physical and behavioral traits as clues to their species membership.

Nevertheless, the scientific literature does contain reports of apparent speciation events in plants, insects and worms. In most of these experiments, researchers subjected organisms to various types of selection—for anatomical differences, mating behaviors, habitat preferences and other traits—and found that they had created populations of organisms that did not breed with outsiders. For example, William R. Rice of the University of New Mexico and George W. Salt of the University of California at Davis demonstrated that if they sorted a group of fruit flies by their preference for certain environments and bred those flies separately over 35 generations, the resulting flies would refuse to breed with those from a very different environment.

13. Evolutionists cannot point to any transitional fossils—creatures that are half reptile and half bird, for instance.

Actually, paleontologists know of many detailed examples of fossils intermediate in form between various taxonomic groups. One of the most famous fossils of all time is *Archaeopteryx*, which combines feathers and skeletal structures peculiar to birds with features of dinosaurs. A flock's worth of other feathered fossil species, some more avian and some less, has also been found. A sequence of fossils spans the evolution of modern horses from the tiny *Eohippus*. Whales had four-legged ancestors that walked on land, and creatures known as *Ambulocetus* and *Rodhocetus* helped to make that transition [see "The Mammals That Conquered the Seas," by Kate Wong; SCIENTIFIC AMERICAN, May]. Fossil seashells trace the evolution of various mollusks through millions of years. Perhaps 20 or more hominids (not all of them our ancestors) fill the gap between Lucy the australopithecine and modern humans.

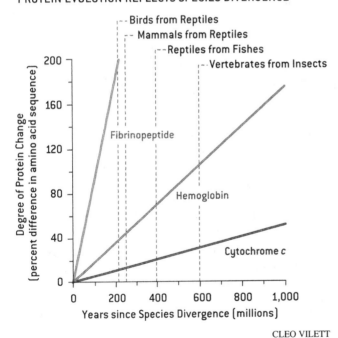

PROTEIN EVOLUTION REFLECTS SPECIES DIVERGENCE

CLEO VILETT

Creationists, though, dismiss these fossil studies. They argue that *Archaeopteryx* is not a missing link between reptiles and birds—it is just an extinct bird with reptilian features. They want evolutionists to produce a weird, chimeric monster that cannot be classified as belonging to any known group. Even if a creationist does accept a fossil as transitional between two species, he or she may then insist on seeing other fossils inter-

mediate between it and the first two. These frustrating requests can proceed ad infinitum and place an unreasonable burden on the always incomplete fossil record.

Nevertheless, evolutionists can cite further supportive evidence from molecular biology. All organisms share most of the same genes, but as evolution predicts, the structures of these genes and their products diverge among species, in keeping with their evolutionary relationships. Geneticists speak of the "molecular clock" that records the passage of time. These molecular data also show how various organisms are transitional within evolution.

14. Living things have fantastically intricate features—at the anatomical, cellular and molecular levels—that could not function if they were any less complex or sophisticated. The only prudent conclusion is that they are the products of intelligent design, not evolution.

This "argument from design" is the backbone of most recent attacks on evolution, but it is also one of the oldest. In 1802 theologian William Paley wrote that if one finds a pocket watch in a field, the most reasonable conclusion is that someone dropped it, not that natural forces created it there. By analogy, Paley argued, the complex structures of living things must be the handiwork of direct, divine invention. Darwin wrote *On the Origin of Species* as an answer to Paley: he explained how natural forces of selection, acting on inherited features, could gradually shape the evolution of ornate organic structures.

Generations of creationists have tried to counter Darwin by citing the example of the eye as a structure that could not have evolved. The eye's ability to provide vision depends on the perfect arrangement of its parts, these critics say. Natural selection could thus never favor the transitional forms needed during the eye's evolution—what good is half an eye? Anticipating this criticism, Darwin suggested that even "incomplete" eyes might confer benefits (such as helping creatures orient toward light) and thereby survive for further evolutionary refinement. Biology has vindicated Darwin: researchers have identified primitive eyes and light-sensing organs throughout the animal kingdom and have even tracked the evolutionary history of eyes through comparative genetics. (It now appears that in various families of organisms, eyes have evolved independently.)

Today's intelligent-design advocates are more sophisticated than their predecessors, but their arguments and goals are not fundamentally different. They criticize evolution by trying to demonstrate that it could nor account for life as we know it and then insist that the only tenable alternative is that life was designed by an unidentified intelligence.

15. Recent discoveries prove that even at the microscopic level, life has a quality of

OTHER RESOURCES FOR DEFENDING EVOLUTION

How to Debate a Creationist: 25 Creationists' Arguments and 25 Evolutionists' Answers. Michael Shermer. Skeptics Society, 1997. This well-researched refutation of creationist claims deals in more depth with many of the same scientific arguments raised here, as well as other philosophical problems. *Skeptic* magazine routinely covers creation/evolution debates and is a solid, thoughtful source on the subject: **www.skeptic.com**

Defending Evolution in the Classroom: A Guide to the Creation/Evolution Controversy. Brian J. Alters and Sandra M. Alters. Jones and Bartlett Publishers, 2001. This up-to-date overview of the creation/evolution controversy explores the issues clearly and readably, with a full appreciation of the cultural and religious influences that create resistance to teaching evolution. It, too, uses a question-and-answer format that should be particularly valuable for teachers.

Science and Creationism: A View from the National Academy of Sciences. Second edition. National Academy Press, 1999. This concise booklet has the backing of the country's top scientific authorities. Although its goal of making a clear, brief statement necessarily limits the detail with which it can pursue its arguments, the publication serves as handy proof that the scientific establishment unwaveringly supports evolution. It is also available at **www7.nationalacademies.org/evalution/**

The Triumph of Evolution and the Failure of Creationism. Niles Eldredge. W. H. Freeman and Company, 2000. The author, a leading contributor to evolution theory and a curator at the American Museum of Natural History in New York City, offers a scathing critique of evolution's opponents.

Intelligent Design Creationism and Its Critics. Edited by Robert T. Pennock. Bradford Books/MIT Press, 2001. For anyone who wishes to understand the "intelligent design" controversy in detail, this book is a terrific one-volume summary of the scientific, philosophical and theological issues. Philip E. Johnson, Michael J. Behe and William A. Dembski make the case for intelligent design in their chapters and are rebutted by evolutionists, including Pennock, Stephen Jay Gould and Richard Dawkins.

Talk.Origins archive (www.talkorigins.org). This wonderfully thorough online resource compiles useful essays and commentaries that have appeared in Usenet discussions about creationism and evolution. It offers detailed discussions (some of which may be too sophisticated for casual readers) and bibliographies relating to virtually any objection to evolution that creationists might raise.

National Center for Science Education Web site (www.ncseweb.org). The center is the only national organization that specializes in defending the teaching of evolution against creationist attacks. Offering resources for combating misinformation and monitoring antievolution legislation, it is ideal for staying current with the ongoing public debate.

PBS Web site for evolution (www.pbs.org/wgbh/evolution/). Produced as a companion to the seven-part television series *Evolution*, this site is an enjoyable guide to evolutionary science. It features multimedia tools for teaching evolution. The accompanying book, *Evolution*, by Carl Zimmer (HarperCollins, 2001), is also useful for explaining evolution to doubters.

---

complexity that could not have come about through evolution.

"Irreducible complexity" is the battle cry of Michael J. Behe of Lehigh University, author of *Darwin's Black Box: The Biochemical Challenge to Evolution*. As a household example of irreducible complexity, Behe chooses the mousetrap—a machine that could not function if any of its pieces were missing and whose pieces have no value except as parts of the whole. What is true of the mousetrap, he says, is even truer of the bacterial flagellum, a whiplike cellular organelle used for propulsion that operates like an outboard motor. The proteins that make up a flagellum are uncannily arranged into motor components, a universal joint and other structures like those that a human engineer might specify. The possibility that this intricate array could have arisen through evolutionary modification is virtually nil, Behe argues, and that bespeaks intelligent design. He makes similar points about the blood's clotting mechanism and other molecular systems.

Yet evolutionary biologists have answers to these objections. First, there exist flagellae with forms simpler than the one that

Behe cites, so it is not necessary for all those components to be present for a flagellum to work. The sophisticated components of this flagellum all have precedents elsewhere in nature, as described by Kenneth R. Miller of Brown University and others. In fact, the entire flagellum assembly is extremely similar to an organelle that *Yersinia pestis*, the bubonic plague bacterium, uses to inject toxins into cells.

The key is that the flagellum's component structures, which Behe suggests have no value apart from their role in propulsion, can serve multiple functions that would have helped favor their evolution. The final evolution of the flagellum might then have involved only the novel recombination of sophisticated parts that initially evolved for other purposes. Similarly, the blood-clotting system seems to involve the modification and elaboration of proteins that were originally used in digestion, according to studies by Russell F. Doolittle of the University of California at San Diego. So some of the complexity that Behe calls proof of intelligent design is not irreducible at all.

Complexity of a different kind—"specified complexity"—is the cornerstone of the intelligent-design arguments of William A. Dembski of Baylor University in his books *The Design In-*

ference and *No Free Lunch*. Essentially his argument is that living things are complex in a way that undirected, random processes could never produce. The only logical conclusion, Dembski asserts, in an echo of Paley 200 years ago, is that some superhuman intelligence created and shaped life.

Dembski's argument contains several holes. It is wrong to insinuate that the field of explanations consists only of random processes or designing intelligences. Researchers into nonlinear systems and cellular automata at the Santa Fe Institute and elsewhere have demonstrated that simple, undirected processes can yield extraordinarily complex patterns. Some of the complexity seen in organisms may therefore emerge through natural phenomena that we as yet barely understand. But that is far different from saying that the complexity could not have arisen naturally.

"CREATION SCIENCE" IS A CONTRADICTION IN TERMS. A central tenet of modern science is methodological naturalism—it seeks to explain the universe purely in terms of observed or testable natural mechanisms. Thus, physics describes the atomic nucleus with specific concepts governing matter and energy, and it tests those descriptions experimentally. Physicists introduce new particles, such as quarks, to flesh out their theories only when data show that the previous descriptions cannot adequately explain observed phenomena. The new particles do not have arbitrary properties, moreover—their definitions are tightly constrained, because the new particles must fit within the existing framework of physics.

In contrast, intelligent-design theorists invoke shadowy entities that conveniently have whatever unconstrained abilities are needed to solve the mystery at hand. Rather than expanding scientific inquiry, such answers shut it down. (How does one disprove the existence of omnipotent intelligences?)

Intelligent design offers few answers. For instance, when and how did a designing intelligence intervene in life's history? By creating the first DNA? The first cell? The first human? Was every species designed, or just a few early ones? Proponents of intelligent-design theory frequently decline to be pinned down on these points. They do not even make real attempts to reconcile their disparate ideas about intelligent design. Instead they pursue argument by exclusion—that is, they belittle evolutionary explanations as far-fetched or incomplete and then imply that only design-based alternatives remain.

Logically, this is misleading: even if one naturalistic explanation is flawed, it does not mean that all are. Moreover, it does not make one intelligent-design theory more reasonable than another. Listeners are essentially left to fill in the blanks for themselves, and some will undoubtedly do so by substituting their religious beliefs for scientific ideas.

Time and again, science has shown that methodological naturalism can push back ignorance, finding increasingly detailed and informative answers to mysteries that once seemed impenetrable: the nature of light, the causes of disease, how the brain works. Evolution is doing the same with the riddle of how the living world took shape. Creationism, by any name, adds nothing of intellectual value to the effort.

John Rennie is editor in chief of Scientific American.

Profile of an Anthropologist

No Bone Unturned

Patrick Huyghe

The research of some physical anthropologists and archaeologists involves the discovery and analysis of old bones (as well as artifacts and other remains). Most often these bones represent only part of a skeleton or maybe the mixture of parts of several skeletons. Often these remains are smashed, burned, or partially destroyed. Over the years, physical anthropologists have developed a remarkable repertoire of skills and techniques for teasing the greatest possible amount of information out of sparse material remains.

Although originally developed for basic research, the methods of physical anthropology can be directly applied to contemporary human problems…. In this profile, we look briefly at the career of Clyde C. Snow, a physical anthropologist who has put these skills to work in a number of different settings….

As you read this selection, ask yourself the following questions:

- Given what you know of physical anthropology, what sort of work would a physical anthropologist do for the Federal Aviation Administration?
- What is anthropometry? *How might anthropometric surveys of pilots and passengers help in the design of aircraft equipment?*
- What is forensic anthropology? *How can a biological anthropologist be an expert witness in legal proceedings?*

Clyde Snow is never in a hurry. He knows he's late. He's always late. For Snow, being late is part of the job. In fact, he doesn't usually begin to work until death has stripped some poor individual to the bone, and no one—neither the local homicide detectives nor the pathologists—can figure out who once gave identity to the skeletonized remains. No one, that is, except a shrewd, laconic, 60-year-old forensic anthropologist.

Snow strolls into the Cook County Medical Examiner's Office in Chicago on this brisk October morning wearing a pair of Lucchese cowboy boots and a three-piece pin-striped suit. Waiting for him in autopsy room 160 are a bunch of naked skeletons found in Illinois, Wisconsin, and Minnesota since his last visit. Snow, a native Texan who now lives in rural Oklahoma, makes the trip up to Chicago some six times a year. The first case on his agenda is a pale brown skull found in the garbage of an abandoned building once occupied by a Chicago cosmetics company.

Snow turns the skull over slowly in his hands, a cigarette dangling from his fingers. One often does. Snow does not seem overly concerned about mortality, though its tragedy surrounds him daily.

"There's some trauma here," he says, examining a rough edge at the lower back of the skull. He points out the area to Jim Elliott, a homicide detective with the Chicago police. "This looks like a chopping blow by a heavy bladed instrument. Almost like a decapitation." In a place where the whining of bone saws drifts through hallways and the sweet-sour smell of death hangs in the air, the word surprises no one.

Snow begins thinking aloud. "I think what we're looking at here is a female, or maybe a small male, about thirty to forty years old. Probably Asian." He turns the skull upside down, pointing out the degree of wear on the teeth. "This was somebody who lived on a really rough diet. We don't normally find this kind of dental wear in a modern Western population."

"How long has it been around?" Elliott asks.

Snow raises the skull up to his nose. "It doesn't have any decompositional odors," he says. He pokes a finger in the skull's nooks and crannies. "There's no soft tissue left. It's good and dry. And it doesn't show signs of having been buried. I would say that this has been lying around in an attic or a box for years. It feels like a souvenir skull," says Snow.

Souvenir skulls, usually those of Japanese soldiers, were popular with U.S. troops serving in the Pacific during World War II; there was also a trade in skulls during the Vietnam War years. On closer inspection, though, Snow begins to wonder about the skull's Asian origins—the broad nasal aperture and the jutting forth of the upper-tooth-bearing part of the face suggest Melanesian features. Sifting through the objects found in the abandoned building with the skull, he finds several loose-leaf albums of 35-millimeter transparencies documenting life among the highland tribes of New Guinea. The slides, shot by an anthropologist, include graphic scenes of ritual warfare. The skull, Snow concludes, is more likely to be a trophy from one of these tribal battles than the result of a local Chicago homicide.

"So you'd treat it like found property?" Elliott asks finally. "Like somebody's garage-sale property?"

"Exactly," says Snow.

Clyde Snow is perhaps the world's most sought-after forensic anthropologist. People have been calling upon him to identify skeletons for more than a quarter of a century. Every year he's involved in some 75 cases of identification, most of them without fanfare. "He's an old scudder who doesn't have to blow his own whistle," says Walter Birkby, a forensic anthropologist at the University of Arizona. "He know's he's good."

Yet over the years Snow's work has turned him into something of an unlikely celebrity. He has been called upon to identify the remains of the Nazi war criminal Josef Mengele, reconstruct the face of the Egyptian boy-king Tutankhamen, confirm the authenticity of the body autopsied as that of President John F. Kennedy, and examine the skeletal remains of General Custer's men at the battlefield of the Little Bighorn. He has also been involved in the grim task of identifying the bodies in some of the United States' worst airline accidents.

Such is his legend that cases are sometimes attributed to him in which he played no part. He did not, as the *New York Times* reported, identify the remains of the crew of the *Challenger* disaster. But the man is often the equal of his myth. For the past four years, setting his personal safety aside, Snow has spent much of his time in Argentina, searching for the graves and identities of some of the thousands who "disappeared" between 1976 and 1983, during Argentina's military regime.

Snow did not set out to rescue the dead from oblivion. For almost two decades, until 1979, he was a physical anthropologist at the Civil Aeromedical Institute, part of the Federal Aviation Administration in Oklahoma City. Snow's job was to help engineers improve aircraft design and safety features by providing them with data on the human frame.

One study, he recalls, was initiated in response to complaints from a flight attendants' organization. An analysis of accident patterns had revealed that inadequate restraints on flight attendants'

jump seats were leading to deaths and injuries and that aircraft doors weighing several hundred pounds were impeding evacuation efforts. Snow points out that ensuring the survival of passengers in emergencies is largely the flight attendants' responsibility. "If they are injured or killed in a crash, you're going to find a lot of dead passengers."

Reasoning that equipment might be improved if engineers had more data on the size and strength of those who use it, Snow undertook a study that required meticulous measurement. When his report was issued in 1975, Senator William Proxmire was outraged that $57,800 of the taxpayers' money had been spent to caliper 423 airline stewardesses from head to toe. Yet the study, which received one of the senator's dubious Golden Fleece Awards, was firmly supported by both the FAA and the Association of Flight Attendants. "I can't imagine," says Snow with obvious delight, "how much coffee Proxmire got spilled on him in the next few months."

It was during his tenure at the FAA that he developed an interest in forensic work. Over the years the Oklahoma police frequently consulted the physical anthropologist for help in identifying crime victims. "The FAA figured it was a kind of community service to let me work on these cases," he says.

The experience also helped to prepare him for the grim task of identifying the victims of air disasters. In December 1972, when a United Airlines plane crashed outside Chicago, killing 43 of the 61 people aboard (including the wife of Watergate conspirator Howard Hunt, who was found with $10,000 in her purse), Snow was brought in to help examine the bodies. That same year, with Snow's help, forensic anthropology was recognized as a specialty by the American Academy of Forensic Sciences. "It got a lot of anthropologists interested in forensics," he says, "and it made a lot of pathologists out there aware that there were anthropologists who could help them."

Each nameless skeleton poses a unique mystery for Snow. But some, like the second case awaiting him back in the autopsy room at the Cook County morgue, are more challenging than oth-

ers. This one is a real chiller. In a large cardboard box lies a jumble of bones along with a tattered leg from a pair of blue jeans, a sock shrunk tightly around the bones of a foot, a pair of Nike running shoes without shoelaces, and, inside the hood of a blue windbreaker, a mass of stringy, blood-caked hair. The remains were discovered frozen in ice about 20 miles outside Milwaukee. A rusted bicycle was found lying close by. Paul Hibbard, chief deputy medical examiner for Waukesha County, who brought the skeleton to Chicago, says no one has been reported missing.

Snow lifts the bones out of the box and begins reconstructing the skeleton on an autopsy table. "There are two hundred six bones and thirty-two teeth in the human body," he says, "and each has a story to tell." Because bone is dynamic, living tissue, many of life's significant events—injuries, illness, childbearing—leave their mark on the body's internal framework. Put together the stories told by these bones, he says, and what you have is a person's "osteobiography."

Snow begins by determining the sex of the skeleton, which is not always obvious. He tells the story of a skeleton that was brought to his FAA office in the late 1970s. It had been found along with some women's clothes and a purse in a local back lot, and the police had assumed that it was female. But when Snow examined the bones, he realized that "at six foot three, she would have probably have been the tallest female in Oklahoma."

Then Snow recalled that six months earlier the custodian in his building had suddenly not shown up for work. The man's supervisor later mentioned to Snow, "You know, one of these days when they find Ronnie, he's going to be dressed as a woman." Ronnie, it turned out, was a weekend transvestite. A copy of his dental records later confirmed that the skeleton in women's clothing was indeed Snow's janitor.

The Wisconsin bike rider is also male. Snow picks out two large bones that look something like twisted oysters—the innominates, or hipbones, which along with the sacrum, or lower backbone, form the pelvis. This pelvis is narrow and steep-walled like a male's, not broad and shallow like a female's. And the sciatic notch (the V-shaped space where the sciatic nerve passes through the hipbone) is narrow, as is normal in a male. Snow can also determine a skeleton's sex by checking the size of the mastoid processes (the bony knobs at the base of the skull) and the prominence of the brow ridge, or by measuring the head of an available limb bone, which is typically broader in males.

From an examination of the skull he concludes that the bike rider is "predominantly Caucasoid." A score of bony traits help the forensic anthropologist assign a skeleton to one of the three major racial groups: Negroid, Caucasoid, or Mongoloid. Snow notes that the ridge of the boy's nose is high and salient, as it is in whites. In Negroids and Mongoloids (which include American Indians as well as most Asians) the nose tends to be broad in relation to its height. However, the boy's nasal margins are somewhat smoothed down, usually a Mongoloid feature. "Possibly a bit of American Indian admixture," says Snow. "Do you have Indians in your area?" Hibbard nods.

Age is next. Snow takes the skull and turns it upside down, pointing out the basilar joint, the junction between the two major bones that form the underside of the skull. In a child the joint would still be open to allow room for growth, but here the joint has fused—something that usually happens in the late teen years. On the other hand, he says, pointing to the zigzagging lines on the dome of the skull, the cranial sutures are open. The cranial sutures, which join the bones of the braincase, begin to fuse and disappear in the mid-twenties.

Next Snow picks up a femur and looks for signs of growth at the point where the shaft meets the knobbed end. The thin plates of cartilage—areas of incomplete calcification—that are visible at this point suggest that the boy hadn't yet attained his full height. Snow double-checks with an examination of the pubic symphysis, the joint where the two hipbones meet. The ridges in this area, which fill in and smooth over in adulthood, are still clearly marked. He concludes that the skeleton is that of a boy between 15 and 20 years old.

"One of the things you learn is to be pretty conservative," says Snow. "It's very impressive when you tell the police, 'This person is eighteen years old,' and he turns out to be eighteen. The problem is, if the person is fifteen you've blown it—you probably won't find him. Looking for a missing person is like trying to catch fish. Better get a big net and do your own sorting."

Snow then picks up a leg bone, measures it with a set of calipers, and enters the data into a portable computer. Using the known correlation between the height and length of the long limb bones, he quickly estimates the boy's height. "He's five foot six and a half to five foot eleven," says Snow. "Medium build, not excessively muscular, judging from the muscle attachments that we see." He points to the grainy ridges that appear where muscle attaches itself to the bone. The most prominent attachments show up on the teenager's right arm bone, indicating right-handedness.

Then Snow examines the ribs one by one for signs of injury. He finds no stab wounds, cuts, or bullet holes, here or elsewhere on the skeleton. He picks up the hyoid bone from the boy's throat and looks for the tell-tale fracture signs that would suggest the boy was strangled. But, to Snow's frustration, he can find no obvious cause of death. In hopes of identifying the missing teenager, he suggests sending the skull, hair, and boy's description to Betty Pat Gatliff, a medical illustrator and sculptor in Oklahoma who does facial reconstructions.

Six weeks later photographs of the boy's likeness appear in the *Milwaukee Sentinel*. "If you persist long enough," says Snow, "eighty-five to ninety percent of the cases eventually get positively identified, but it can take anywhere from a few weeks to a few years."

Snow and Gatliff have collaborated many times, but never with more glitz than in 1983, when Snow was commissioned by Patrick Barry, a Miami orthopedic surgeon and amateur Egyptologist, to reconstruct the face of the Egyptian boy-king Tutankhamen. Normally a facial reconstruction begins with a skull, but since Tutankhamen's 3,000-year-old remains were in Egypt, Snow had to make do with the skull measurements from a 1925 postmortem and X-rays taken in 1975. A plaster model of the skull was made, and on the basis on Snow's report—"his skull is Caucasoid with some Negroid admixtures"—Gatliff put a face on it. What did Tutankhamen look like? Very much like the gold mask on his sarcophagus, says Snow, confirming that it was, indeed, his portrait.

Many cite Snow's use of facial reconstructions as one of his most important contributions to the field. Snow, typically self-effacing, says that Gatliff "does all the work." The identification of skeletal remains, he stresses, is often a collaboration between pathologists, odontologists, radiologists, and medical artists using a variety of forensic techniques.

One of Snow's last tasks at the FAA was to help identify the dead from the worst airline accident in U.S. history. On May 25, 1979, a DC-10 crashed shortly after takeoff from Chicago's O'Hare Airport, killing 273 people. The task facing Snow and more than a dozen forensic specialists was horrific. "No one ever sat down and counted," says Snow, "but we estimated ten thousand to twelve thousand pieces or parts of bodies." Nearly 80 percent of the victims were identified on the basis of dental evidence and fingerprints. Snow and forensic radiologist John Fitzpatrick later managed to identify two dozen others by comparing postmortem X-rays with X-rays taken during the victim's lifetime.

Next to dental records, such X-ray comparisons are the most common way of obtaining positive identifications. In 1978, when a congressional committee reviewed the evidence on John F. Kennedy's assassination, Snow used X-rays to show that the body autopsied at Bethesda Naval Hospital was indeed that of the late president and had not—as some conspiracy theorists believed—been switched.

The issue was resolved on the evidence of Kennedy's "sinus print," the scalloplike pattern on the upper margins of the sinuses that is visible in X-rays of the forehead. So characteristic is a person's sinus print that courts throughout the world accept the matching of antemortem and postmortem X-rays of the sinuses as positive identification.

Yet another technique in the forensic specialist's repertoire is photo superposition. Snow used it in 1977 to help identify the mummy of a famous Oklahoma outlaw named Elmer J. McCurdy, who was killed by a posse after holding up a train in 1911. For years the mummy had been exhibited as a "dummy" in a California funhouse—until it was found to have a real human skeleton inside it. Ownership of the mummy was eventually traced back to a funeral parlor in Oklahoma, where McCurdy had been embalmed and exhibited as "the bandit who wouldn't give up."

Using two video cameras and an image processor, Snow superposed the mummy's profile on a photograph of McCurdy that was taken shortly after his death. When displayed on a single monitor, the two coincided to a remarkable degree. Convinced by the evidence, Thomas Noguchi, then Los Angeles County corner, signed McCurdy's death certificate ("Last known occupation: Train robber") and allowed the outlaw's bones to be returned to Oklahoma for a decent burial.

It was this technique that also allowed forensic scientists to identify the remains of the Nazi "Angel of Death," Josef Mengele, in the summer of 1985. A team of investigators, including Snow and West German forensic anthropologist Richard Helmer, flew to Brazil after an Austrian couple claimed that Mengele lay buried in a grave on a São Paulo hillside. Tests revealed that the stature, age, and hair color of the unearthed skeleton were consistent with information in Mengele's SS files; yet without X-rays or dental records, the scientists still lacked conclusive evidence. When an image of the reconstructed skull was superposed on 1930s photographs of Mengele, however, the match was eerily compelling. All doubts were removed a few months later when Mengele's dental X-rays were tracked down.

In 1979 Snow retired from the FAA to the rolling hills of Norman, Oklahoma, where he and his wife, Jerry, live in a sprawling, early-1960s ranch house. Unlike his 50 or so fellow forensic anthropologists, most of whom are tied to academic positions, Snow is free to pursue his consultancy work full-time. Judging from the number of miles that he logs in the average month, Snow is clearly not ready to retire for good.

His recent projects include a reexamination of the skeletal remains found at the site of the Battle of the Little Bighorn, where more than a century ago Custer and his 210 men were killed by Sioux and Cheyenne warriors. Although most of the enlisted men's remains were moved to a mass grave in 1881, an excavation of the battlefield in the past few years uncovered an additional 375 bones and 36 teeth. Snow, teaming up again with Fitzpatrick, determined that these remains belonged to 34 individuals.

The historical accounts of Custer's desperate last stand are vividly confirmed by their findings. Snow identified one skeleton as that of a soldier between the ages of 19 and 23 who weighed around 150 pounds and stood about five foot eight. He'd sustained gunshot wounds to his chest and left forearm. Heavy blows to his head had fractured his skull and sheared off his teeth. Gashed thigh bones indicated that his body was later dismembered with an ax or hatchet.

Given the condition and number of the bodies, Snow seriously questions the accuracy of the identifications made by the original nineteenth-century burial crews. He doubts, for example, that the skeleton buried at West Point is General Custer's.

For the last four years Snow has devoted much of his time to helping two countries come to terms with the horrors of a much more recent past. As part of a group sponsored by the American Association for the Advancement of Science, he has been helping the Argentinian National Commission on Disappeared Persons to determine the fate of some of those who vanished during their country's harsh military rule: between 1976 and 1983 at least 10,000 people were systematically swept off the streets by roving death squads to be tortured, killed, and buried in unmarked graves. In December 1986, at the invitation of the Aquino government's Human Rights Commission, Snow also spent several weeks training Philippine scientists to investigate the disappearances that occurred under the Marcos regime.

But it is in Argentina where Snow has done the bulk of his human-rights work. He has spent more than 27 months in and around Buenos Aires, first training a small group of local medical and anthropology students in the techniques of forensic investigation, and later helping them carefully exhume and examine scores of the *desaparecidos*, or disappeared ones.

Only 25 victims have so far been positively identified. But the evidence has helped convict seven junta members and other high-ranking military and police officers. The idea is not necessarily to identify all 10,000 of the missing, says Snow. "If you have a colonel who ran a detention center where maybe five hundred people were killed, you don't have to nail them with five hundred deaths. Just one or two should be sufficient to get him convicted." Forensic evidence from Snow's team may be used to prosecute several other military officers, including General Suarez Mason. Mason is the former commander of the I Army Corps in Buenos Aires and is believed to be responsible for thousands of disappearances. He was recently extradited from San Francisco back to Argentina, where he is expected to stand trial this winter [1988].

The investigations have been hampered by a frustrating lack of antemortem information. In 1984, when commission lawyers took depositions from relatives and friends of the disappeared, they often failed to obtain such basic information as the victim's height, weight, or hair color. Nor did they ask for the missing person's X-rays (which in Argentina are given to the patient) or the address of the victim's dentist. The problem was compounded by the inexperience of those who carried out the first mass exhumations prior to Snow's arrival. Many of the skeletons were inadvertently destroyed by bulldozers as they were brought up.

Every unearthed skeleton that shows signs of gunfire, however, helps to erode the claim once made by many in the Argentinian military that most of the *desaparecidos* are alive and well and living in Mexico City, Madrid, or Paris. Snow recalls the case of a 17-year-old boy named Gabriel Dunayavich, who disappeared in the summer of 1976. He was walking home from a movie with his girlfriend when a Ford Falcon with no license plates snatched him off the street. The police later found his body and that of another boy and girl dumped by the roadside on the outskirts of Buenos Aires. The police went through the motions of an investigation, taking photographs and doing an autopsy, then buried the three teenagers in an unmarked grave.

A decade later Snow, with the help of the boy's family, traced the autopsy reports, the police photographs, and the grave of the three youngsters. Each of them had four or five closely spaced bullet wounds in the upper chest—the signature, says Snow, of an automatic weapon. Two also had wounds on their arms from bullets that had entered behind the elbow and exited from the forearm.

"That means they were conscious when they were shot," says Snow. "When a gun was pointed at them, they naturally raised their arm." It's details like these that help to authenticate the last moments of the victims and bring a dimension of reality to the judges and jury.

Each time Snow returns from Argentina he says that this will be the last time. A few months later he is back in Buenos Aires. "There's always more work to do," he says. It is, he admits quietly, "terrible work."

"These were such brutal, cold-blooded crimes," he says. "The people who committed them not only murdered; they had a system to eliminate all trace that their victims even existed."

Snow will not let them obliterate their crimes so conveniently. "There are human-rights violations going on all around the world," he says. "But to me murder is murder, regardless of the motive. I hope that we are sending a message to governments who murder in the name of politics that they can be held to account."

From *Discover* magazine, December 1988, pp. 51–56. © 1988 by Patrick Huyghe. Reprinted with permission of the author.

GO AHEAD,

KISS YOUR COUSIN

HECK, *MARRY* HER IF YOU WANT TO

By Richard Conniff

In Paris in 1876 a 31-year-old banker named Albert took an 18-year-old named Bettina as his wife. Both were Rothschilds, and they were cousins. According to conventional notions about inbreeding, their marriage ought to have been a prescription for infertility and enfeeblement.

In fact, Albert and Bettina went on to produce seven children, and six of them lived to be adults. Moreover, for generations the Rothschild family had been inbreeding almost as intensively as European royalty, without apparent ill effect. Despite his own limited gene pool, Albert, for instance, was an outdoorsman and the seventh person ever to climb the Matterhorn. The American du Ponts practiced the same strategy of cousin marriage for a century. Charles Darwin, the grandchild of first cousins, married a first cousin. So did Albert Einstein.

In our lore, cousin marriages are unnatural, the province of hillbillies and swamp rats, not Rothschilds and Darwins. In the United States they are deemed such a threat to mental health that 31 states have outlawed first-cousin marriages. This phobia is distinctly American, a heritage of early evolutionists with misguided notions about the upward march of human societies. Their fear was that cousin marriages would cause us to breed our way back to frontier savagery—or worse. "You can't marry your first cousin," a character declares in the 1982 play *Brighton Beach Memoirs*. "You get babies with nine heads."

So when a team of scientists led by Robin L. Bennett, a genetic counselor at the University of Washington and the president of the National Society of Genetic Counselors, announced that cousin marriages are not significantly riskier than any other

marriage, it made the front page of *The New York Times*. The study, published in the *Journal of Genetic Counseling* last year, determined that children of first cousins face about a 2 to 3 percent higher risk of birth defects than the population at large. To put it another way, first-cousin marriages entail roughly the same increased risk of abnormality that a woman undertakes when she gives birth at 41 rather than at 30. Banning cousin marriages makes about as much sense, critics argue, as trying to ban childbearing by older women.

THE MARRIAGE OF ALBERT ROTHSCHILD AND BETTINA ROTHSCHILD WAS THE RESULT OF FOUR GENERATIONS OF INBREEDING IN THE BANKING DYNASTY—A PRACTICE ADVOCATED BY THE FAMILY FOUNDER MAYER AMSCHEL ROTHSCHILD. HIS INTENTION WAS CERTAINLY A FRUITFUL ONE IF THE DARWINIAN MEASURE OF CAPITALISTIC SUCCESS IS THE PRESERVATION OF WEALTH.

But the nature of cousin marriage is far more surprising than recent publicity has suggested. A closer look reveals that moderate inbreeding has always been the rule, not the exception, for humans. Inbreeding is also commonplace in the natural world, and contrary to our expectations, some biologists argue that this

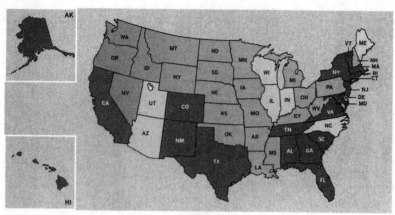

CAN YOU MARRY A COUSIN?

GLOBAL INBREEDING

MAPS BY MATT ZANG

(A) Laws governing the marriage of first cousins vary widely. In 24 states (medium grey), such marriages are illegal. In 19 states (dark grey), first cousins are permitted to wed. Seven states (light grey) allow first-cousin marriage but with conditions. Maine, for instance, requires genetic counseling; some states say yes only if one partner is sterile. North Carolina prohibits marriage only for double first cousins. Got that?

(B) Researchers who study inbreeding track consanguineous marriages—those between second cousins or closer. In dark grey countries, at least 20 percent and, in some cases, more than 50 percent of marriages fall into this category. Medium grey countries report 1 to 10 percent consanguinity; light grey-colored countries, less than 1 percent. Data is unavailable for white countries.

can be a very good thing. It depends in part on the degree of inbreeding.

The idea that inbreeding might sometimes be beneficial is clearly contrarian. So it's important to acknowledge first that inbreeding can sometimes also go horribly wrong—and in ways that, at first glance, make our stereotypes about cousin marriage seem completely correct.

A CLOSER LOOK REVEALS THAT MODERATE INBREEDING HAS ALWAYS BEEN THE RULE, NOT THE EXCEPTION, FOR HUMANS

In the Yorkshire city of Bradford, in England, for instance, a majority of the large Pakistani community can trace their origins to the village of Mirpur in Kashmir, which was inundated by a new dam in the 1960s. Cousin marriages have been customary in Kashmir for generations, and more than 85 percent of Bradford's Pakistanis marry their cousins. Local doctors are seeing sharp spikes in the number of children with serious genetic disabilities, and each case is its own poignant tragedy. One couple was recently raising two apparently healthy children. Then, when they were 5 and 7, both were diagnosed with neural degenerative disease in the same week. The children are now slowly dying. Neural degenerative diseases are eight times more common in Bradford than in the rest of the United Kingdom.

The great hazard of inbreeding is that it can result in the unmasking of deleterious recessives, to use the clinical language of geneticists. Each of us carries an unknown number of genes—an individual typically has between five and seven—capable of killing our children or grandchildren. These so-

called lethal recessives are associated with diseases like cystic fibrosis and sickle-cell anemia.

Most lethal genes never get expressed unless we inherit the recessive form of the gene from both our mother and father. But when both parents come from the same gene pool, their children are more likely to inherit two recessives.

So how do scientists reconcile the experience in Bradford with the relatively moderate level of risk reported in the *Journal of Genetic Counseling?* How did Rothschilds or Darwins manage to marry their cousins with apparent impunity? Above all, how could any such marriages ever possibly be beneficial?

The traditional view of human inbreeding was that we did it, in essence, because we could not get the car on Saturday night. Until the past century, families tended to remain in the same area for generations, and men typically went courting no more than about five miles from home—the distance they could walk out and back on their day off from work. As a result, according to Robin Fox, a professor of anthropology at Rutgers University, it's likely that 80 percent of all marriages in history have been between second cousins or closer.

Factors other than mere proximity can make inbreeding attractive. Pierre-Samuel du Pont, founder of an American dynasty that believed in inbreeding, hinted at these factors when he told his family: "The marriages that I should prefer for our colony would be between the cousins. In that way we should be sure of honesty of soul and purity of blood." He got his wish, with seven cousin marriages in the family during the 19th century. Mayer Amschel Rothschild, founder of the banking family, likewise arranged his affairs so that cousin marriages among his descendants were inevitable. His will barred female descendants from any direct inheritance. Without an inheritance, female Rothschilds had few possible marriage partners of the same religion and suitable eco-

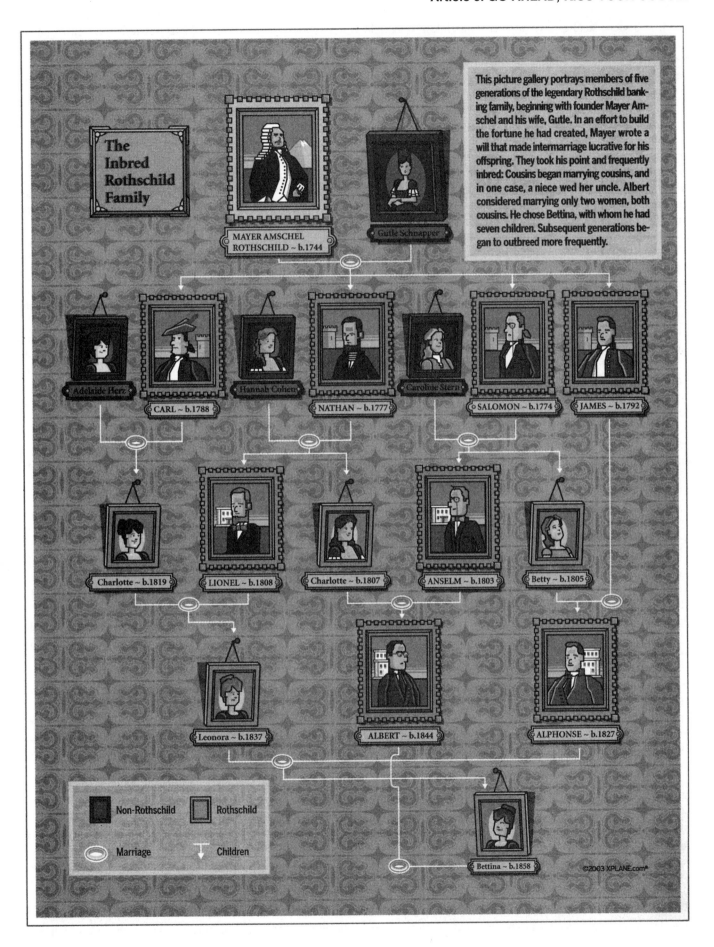

The Inbred Rothschild Family

This picture gallery portrays members of five generations of the legendary Rothschild banking family, beginning with founder Mayer Amschel and his wife, Gutle. In an effort to build the fortune he had created, Mayer wrote a will that made intermarriage lucrative for his offspring. They took his point and frequently inbred: Cousins began marrying cousins, and in one case, a niece wed her uncle. Albert considered marrying only two women, both cousins. He chose Bettina, with whom he had seven children. Subsequent generations began to outbreed more frequently.

MAYER AMSCHEL ROTHSCHILD ~ b.1744

Gutle Schnapper

Adelaide Herz

CARL ~ b.1788

Hannah Cohen

NATHAN ~ b.1777

Caroline Stern

SALOMON ~ b.1774

JAMES ~ b.1792

Charlotte ~ b.1819

LIONEL ~ b.1808

Charlotte ~ b.1807

ANSELM ~ b.1803

Betty ~ b.1805

Leonora ~ b.1837

ALBERT ~ b.1844

ALPHONSE ~ b.1827

Bettina ~ b.1858

Non-Rothschild   Rothschild

Marriage   Children

©2003 XPLANE.com®

nomic and social stature—except other Rothschilds. Rothschild brides bound the family together. Four of Mayer's granddaughters married grandsons, and one married her uncle. These were hardly people whose mate choice was limited by the distance they could walk on their day off.

Some families have traditionally chosen inbreeding as the best strategy for success because it offers at least three highly practical benefits. First, such marriages make it likelier that a shared set of cultural values will pass down intact to the children.

Second, cousin marriages make it more likely that spouses will be compatible, particularly in an alien environment. Such marriages may be even more attractive for Pakistanis in Bradford, England, than back home in Kashmir. Intermarriage decreases the divorce rate and enhances the independence of wives, who retain the support of familiar friends and relatives. Among the 19th-century du Ponts, for instance, women had an equal vote with men in family meetings.

Finally, marrying cousins minimizes the need to break up family wealth from one generation to the next. The rich have frequently chosen inbreeding as a means to keep estates intact and consolidate power.

Moderate inbreeding may also produce biological benefits. Contrary to lore, cousin marriages may do even better than ordinary marriages by the standard Darwinian measure of success, which is reproduction. A 1960 study of first-cousin marriages in 19th-century England done by C. D. Darlington, a geneticist at Oxford University, found that inbred couples produced twice as many great-grandchildren as did their outbred counterparts.

Consider, for example, the marriage of Albert and Bettina Rothschild. Their children were descended from a genetic pool of just 24 people (beginning with family founders Mayer Amschel and Gutle Rothschild), and more than three-fifths of them were born Rothschilds. In a family that had not inbred, the same children would have 38 ancestors. Because of inbreeding, they were directly descended no fewer than six times each from Mayer and Gutle Rothschild. If our subconscious Darwinian agenda is to get as much of our genome as possible into future generations, then inbreeding clearly provided a genetic benefit for Mayer and Gutle.

And for their descendants? How could the remarkably untroubled reproductive experience of intermarried Rothschilds differ so strikingly from that of intermarried families in Bradford?

The consequences of inbreeding are unpredictable and depend largely on what biologists call the founder effect: If the founding couple pass on a large number of lethal recessives, as appears to have happened in Bradford, these recessives will spread and double up through intermarriage. If, however, Mayer and Gutle Rothschild handed down a comparatively healthy genome, their descendants could safely intermarry for generations—at least until small deleterious effects inevitably began to pile up and produce inbreeding depression, a long-term decline in the well-being of a family or a species.

A founding couple can also pass on advantageous genes. Among animal populations, generations of inbreeding frequently lead to the development of coadapted gene complexes, suites of genetic traits that tend to be inherited together. These traits may confer special adaptations to a local environment, like resistance to disease.

The evidence for such benefits in humans is slim, perhaps in part because any genetic advantages conferred by inbreeding may be too small or too gradual to detect. Alan Bittles, a professor of human biology at Edith Cowan University in Australia, points out that there's a dearth of data on the subject of genetic disadvantages too. Not until some rare disorder crops up in a place like Bradford do doctors even notice intermarriage.

Something disturbingly eugenic about the idea of better-families-through-inbreeding also causes researchers to look away. Oxford historian Niall Ferguson, author of *The House of Rothschild,* speculates that that there may have been "a Rothschild 'gene for financial acumen,'" which intermarriage somehow helped to perpetuate. Perhaps it was that which made the Rothschilds truly exceptional." But he quickly dismisses this as "unlikely."

At the same time, humans are perfectly comfortable with the idea that inbreeding can produce genetic benefits for domesticated animals. When we want a dog with the points to take Best in Show at Madison Square Garden, we often get it by taking individuals displaying the desired traits and "breeding them back" with their close kin.

Researchers have observed that animals in the wild may also attain genetic benefits from inbreeding. Ten mouse colonies may set up housekeeping in a field but remain separate. The dominant male in each colony typically inbreeds with his kin. His genes rapidly spread through the colony—the founder effect again—and each colony thus becomes a little different from the others, with double recessives proliferating for both good and ill effects. When the weather changes or some deadly virus blows through, one colony may end up better adapted to the new circumstances than the other nine, which die out.

Inbreeding may help explain why insects can develop resistance almost overnight to pesticides like DDT: The resistance first shows up as a recessive trait in one obscure family line. Inbreeding, with its cascade of double recessives, causes the trait to be expressed in every generation of this family—and under the intense selective pressure of DDT, this family of resistant insects survives and proliferates.

THE OBVIOUS PROBLEM WITH THIS CONTRARIAN argument is that so many animals seem to go out of their way to avoid inbreeding. Field biologists have often observed that animals reared together from an early age become imprinted on one another and lack mutual sexual interest as adults; they have an innate aversion to homegrown romance.

But what they are avoiding, according to William Shields, a biologist at the State University of New York College of Environmental Science and Forestry at Syracuse, is merely incest, the most extreme form of inbreeding, not inbreeding itself. He argues that normal patterns of dispersal actually encourage inbreeding. When young birds leave the nest, for instance, they typically move four or five home ranges away, not 10 or 100; that is, they stay within breeding distance of their cousins. Intense loyalty to a home territory helps keep a population healthy, according to Shields, because it encourages "optimal inbreeding." This elusive ideal is the point at which a population gets the benefit of adaptations to local habitat—the co-adapted gene complexes—without the hazardous unmasking of recessive disorders.

GENETIC AND METABOLIC TESTS CAN NOW SCREEN FOR ABOUT 100 RECESSIVE DISORDERS

In some cases, outbreeding can be the real hazard. A study conducted by E. L. Brannon, an ecologist at the University of Idaho, looked at two separate populations of sockeye salmon, one breeding where a river entered a lake, the other where it exited. Salmon fry at the inlet evolved to swim downstream to the lake. The ones at the outlet evolved to swim upstream. When researchers crossed the populations, they ended up with salmon young too confused to know which way to go. In the wild, such a hybrid population might lose half or more of its fry and soon vanish.

It is, of course, a long way from sockeye salmon and inbred insects to human mating behavior. But Patrick Bateson, a professor of ethology at Cambridge University, argues that outbreeding has at times been hazardous for humans too. For instance, the size and shape of our teeth is a strongly inherited trait. So is jaw size and shape. But the two traits aren't inherited together. If a woman with small jaws and small teeth marries a man with big jaws and big teeth, their grandchildren may end up with a mouthful of gnashers in a Tinkertoy jaw. Before dentistry was commonplace, Bateson adds, "ill-fitting teeth were probably a serious cause of mortality because it increased the likelihood of abscesses in the mouth." Marrying a cousin was one way to avoid a potentially lethal mismatch.

Bateson suggests that while youngsters imprinting on their siblings lose sexual interest in one another they may also gain a search image for a mate—someone who's not a sibling but *like* a sibling. Studies have shown that people overwhelmingly choose spouses similar to themselves, a phenomenon called assortative mating. The similarities are social, psychological, and physical, even down to traits like earlobe length. Cousins, Bateson says, perfectly fit this human preference for "slight novelty."

So where does this leave us? No scientist is advocating intermarriage, but the evidence indicates that we should at least moderate our automatic disdain for it. One unlucky woman, whom Robin Bennett encountered in the course of her research, recalled the reaction when she became pregnant after living with her first cousin for two years. Her gynecologist professed horror, told her the baby "would be sick all the time," and advised her to have an abortion. Her boyfriend's mother, who was also her aunt, "went nuts, saying that our baby would be retarded." The woman had an abortion, which she now calls "the worst mistake of my life."

Science is increasingly able to help such people look at their own choices more objectively. Genetic and metabolic tests can now screen for about 10 recessive disorders. In the past, families in Bradford rarely recognized genetic origins of causes of death or patterns of abnormality. The likelihood of stigma within the community or racism from without also made people reluctant to discuss such problems. But new tests have helped change that. Last year two siblings in Bradford were hoping to intermarry their children despite a family history of thalassemia, a recessive blood disorder that is frequently fatal before the age of 30. After testing determined which of the children carried the thalassemia gene, the families were able to arrange a pair of carrier-to-noncarrier first-cousin marriages.

Such planning may seem complicated. It may even be the sort of thing that causes Americans, with their entrenched dread of inbreeding, to shudder. But the needs of both culture and medicine were satisfied, and an observer could only conclude that the urge to marry cousins must be more powerful, and more deeply rooted, than we yet understand.

Curse and Blessing of the Ghetto

Tay-Sachs disease is a choosy killer, one that for centuries targeted Eastern European Jews above all others. By decoding its lethal logic, we can learn a lot about how genetic diseases evolve— and how they can be conquered.

Jared Diamond

Marie and I hated her at first sight, even though she was trying hard to be helpful. As our obstetrician's genetics counselor, she was just doing her job, explaining to us the unpleasant results that might come out of the genetic tests we were about to have performed. As a scientist, though, I already knew all I wanted to know about Tay-Sachs disease, and I didn't need to be reminded that the baby sentenced to death by it could be my own.

Fortunately, the tests would reveal that my wife and I were not carriers of the Tay-Sachs gene, and our preparenthood fears on that matter at least could be put to rest. But at the time I didn't yet know that. As I glared angrily at that poor genetics counselor, so strong was my anxiety that now, four years later, I can still clearly remember what was going through my mind: If I were an evil deity, I thought, trying to devise exquisite tortures for babies and their parents, I would be proud to have designed Tay-Sachs disease.

Tay-Sachs is completely incurable, unpreventable, and preprogrammed in the genes. A Tay-Sachs infant usually appears normal for the first few months after birth, just long enough for the parents to grow to love him. An exaggerated "startle reaction" to sounds is the first ominous sign. At about six months the baby starts to lose control of his head and can't roll over or sit without support. Later he begins to drool, breaks out into unmotivated bouts of laughter, and suffers convulsions. Then his head grows abnormally large, and he becomes blind. Perhaps what's most frightening for the parents is that their baby loses all contact with his environment and becomes virtually a vegetable. By the child's third birthday, if he's still alive, his skin will turn yellow and his hands pudgy. Most likely he will die before he's four years old.

My wife and I were tested for the Tay-Sachs gene because at the time we rated as high-risk candidates, for two reasons. First, Marie was carrying twins, so we had double the usual chance to bear a Tay-Sachs baby. Second, both she and I are of Eastern European Jewish ancestry, the population with by far the world's highest Tay-Sachs frequency.

In peoples around the world Tay-Sachs appears once in every 400,000 births. But it appears a hundred times more frequently—about once in 3,600 births—among descendants of Eastern European Jews, people known as Ashkenazim. For descendants of most other groups of Jews—Oriental Jews, chiefly from the Middle East, or Sephardic Jews, from Spain and other Mediterranean countries—the frequency of Tay-Sachs disease is no higher than in non-Jews. Faced with such a clear correlation, one cannot help but wonder: What is it about this one group of people that produces such an extraordinarily high risk of this disease?

Finding the answer to this question concerns all of us, regardless of our ancestry. Every human population is especially susceptible to certain diseases, not only because of its life-style but also because of its genetic inheritance. For example, genes put European whites at high risk for cystic fibrosis, African blacks for sickle-cell disease, Pacific Islanders for diabetes—and Eastern European Jews for ten different diseases, including Tay-Sachs. It's not that Jews are notably susceptible to genetic diseases in general; but a combination of historical factors has led to Jews' being intensively studied, and so their susceptibilities are far better known than those of, say, Pacific Islanders.

Tay-Sachs exemplifies how we can deal with such diseases; it has been the object of the most successful screening program to date. Moreover, Tay-Sachs is helping us understand how ethnic diseases evolve. Within the past couple of years discoveries by molecular biologists have provided tantalizing clues to precisely how a deadly gene can persist and spread over the centuries. Tay-Sachs may be primarily a disease of Eastern European Jews, but through this affliction of one group of people, we gain a window on how our genes simultaneously curse and bless us all.

The disease's hyphenated name comes from the two physicians—British ophthalmologist W. Tay and New York neurologist B. Sachs—who independently first recognized the disease, in 1881 and 1887, respectively. By 1896 Sachs had seen enough cases to realize that the disease was most common among Jewish children.

Not until 1962, however, were researchers able to trace the cause of the affliction to a single biochemical abnormality: the excessive accumulation in nerve cells of a fatty substance called G_{M2} ganglioside. Normally G_{M2} ganglioside is present at only modest levels in cell membranes, because it is constantly being broken down as well as synthesized. The breakdown depends on the enzyme hexosaminidase A, which is found in the tiny structures within our cells known as lysosomes. In the unfortunate Tay-Sachs victims this enzyme is lacking, and without it the ganglioside piles up and produces all the symptoms of the disease.

We have two copies of the gene that programs our supply of hexosaminidase A, one inherited from our father, the other from our mother; each of our parents, in turn, has two copies derived from their own parents. As long as we have one good copy of the gene, we can produce enough hexosaminidase A to prevent a buildup of G_{M2} ganglioside and we won't get Tay-Sachs. This genetic disease is of the sort termed recessive rather than dominant—meaning that to get it, a child must inherit a defective gene not just from one parent but from both of them. Clearly, each parent must have had one good copy of the gene along with the defective copy—if either had had two defective genes, he or she would have died of the disease long before reaching the age of reproduction. In genetic terms the diseased child is homozygous for the defective gene and both parents are heterozygous for it.

None of this yet gives any hint as to why the Tay-Sachs gene should be most common among Eastern European Jews. To come to grips with that question, we must take a short detour into history.

From their biblical home of ancient Israel, Jews spread peacefully to other Mediterranean lands, Yemen, and India. They were also dispersed violently through conquest by Assyrians, Babylonians, and Romans. Under the Carolingian kings of the eighth and ninth centuries Jews were invited to settle in France and Germany as traders and financiers. In subsequent centuries, how-

ever, persecutions triggered by the Crusades gradually drove Jews out of Western Europe; the process culminated in their total expulsion from Spain in 1492. Those Spanish Jews—called Sephardim—fled to other lands around the Mediterranean. Jews of France and Germany—the Ashkenazim—fled east to Poland and from there to Lithuania and western Russia, where they settled mostly in towns, as businessmen engaged in whatever pursuit they were allowed.

There the Jews stayed for centuries, through periods of both tolerance and oppression. But toward the end of the nineteenth century and the beginning of the twentieth, waves of murderous anti-Semitic attacks drove millions of Jews out of Eastern Europe, with most of them heading for the United States. My mother's parents, for example, fled to New York from Lithuanian pogroms of the 1880s, while my father's parents fled from the Ukrainian pogroms of 1903–6. The more modern history of Jewish migration is probably well known to you all: most Jews who remained in Eastern Europe were exterminated during World War II, while most the survivors immigrated to the United States and Israel. Of the 13 million Jews alive today, more than three-quarters are Ashkenazim, the descendants of the Eastern European Jews and the people most at risk for Tay-Sachs.

Have these Jews maintained their genetic distinctness through the thousands of years of wandering? Some scholars claim that there has been so much intermarriage and conversion that Ashkenazic Jews are now just Eastern Europeans who adopted Jewish culture. However, modern genetic studies refute that speculation.

First of all, there are those ten genetic diseases that the Ashkenazim have somehow acquired, by which they differ both from other Jews and from Eastern European non-Jews. In addition, many Ashkenazic genes turn out to be ones typical of Palestinian Arabs and other peoples of the Eastern Mediterranean areas where Jews originated. (In fact, by genetic standards the current Arab-Israeli conflict is an internecine civil war.) Other Ashkenazic genes have indeed di-

verged from Mediterranean ones (including genes of Sephardic and Oriental Jews) and have evolved to converge on genes of Eastern European non-Jews subject to the same local forces of natural selection. But the degree to which Ashkenazim prove to differ genetically from Eastern European non-Jews implies an intermarriage rate of only about 15 percent.

Can history help explain why the Tay-Sachs gene in particular is so much more common in Ashkenazim than in their non-Jewish neighbors or in other Jews? At the risk of spoiling a mystery, I'll tell you now that the answer is yes, but to appreciate it, you'll have to understand the four possible explanations for the persistence of the Tay-Sachs gene.

First, new copies of the gene might be arising by mutation as fast as existing copies disappear with the death of Tay-Sachs children. That's the most likely explanation for the gene's persistence in most of the world, where the disease frequency is only one in 400,000 births—that frequency reflects a typical human mutation rate. But for this explanation to apply to the Ashkenazim would require a mutation rate of at least one per 3,600 births—far above the frequency observed for any human gene. Furthermore, there would be no precedent for one particular gene mutating so much more often in one human population than in others.

As a second possibility, the Ashkenazim might have acquired the Tay-Sachs gene from some other people who already had the gene at high frequency. Arthur Koestler's controversial book *The Thirteenth Tribe*, for example, popularized the view that the Ashkenazim are really not a Semitic people but are instead descended from the Khazar, a Turkic tribe whose rulers converted to Judaism in the eighth century. Could the Khazar have brought the Tay-Sachs gene to Eastern Europe? This speculation makes good romantic reading, but there is no good evidence to support it. Moreover, it fails to explain why deaths of Tay-Sachs children didn't eliminate the gene by natural selection in the past 1,200 years, nor how the Khazar acquired high frequencies of the gene in the first place.

The third hypothesis was the one preferred by a good many geneticists until recently. It invokes two genetic processes, termed the founder effect and genetic drift, that may operate in small populations. To understand these concepts, imagine that 100 couples settle in a new land and found a population that then increases. Imagine further that one parent among those original 100 couples happens to have some rare gene, one, say, that normally occurs at a frequency of one in a million. The gene's frequency in the new population will now be one in 200 as a result of the accidental presence of that rare founder.

Or suppose again that 100 couples found a population, but that one of the 100 men happens to have lots of kids by his wife or that he is exceptionally popular with other women, while the other 99 men are childless or have few kids or are simply less popular. That one man may thereby father 10 percent rather than a more representative one percent of the next generation's babies, and their genes will disproportionately reflect that man's genes. In other words, gene frequencies will have drifted between the first and second generation.

Through these two types of genetic accidents a rare gene may occur with an unusually high frequency in a small expanding population. Eventually, if the gene is harmful, natural selection will bring its frequency back to normal by killing off gene bearers. But if the resultant disease is recessive—if heterozygous individuals don't get the disease and only the rare, homozygous individuals die of it—the gene's high frequency may persist for many generations.

These accidents do in fact account for the astonishingly high Tay-Sachs gene frequency found in one group of Pennsylvania Dutch: out of the 333 people in this group, 98 proved to carry the Tay-Sachs gene. Those 333 are all descended from one couple who settled in the United States in the eighteenth century and had 13 children. Clearly, one of that founding couple must have carried the gene. A similar accident may explain why Tay-Sachs is also relatively common among French Canadians, who number 5 million today but are descended from fewer than 6,000 French immigrants who arrived in the New World between 1638 and 1759. In the two or three centuries since both these founding events, the high Tay-Sachs gene frequency among Pennsylvania Dutch and French Canadians has not yet had enough time to decline to normal levels.

The same mechanisms were one proposed to explain the high rate of Tay-Sachs disease among the Ashkenazim. Perhaps, the reasoning went, the gene just happened to be overrepresented in the founding Jewish population that settled in Germany or Eastern Europe. Perhaps the gene just happened to drift up in frequency in the Jewish populations scattered among the isolated towns of Eastern Europe.

It seems unlikely that genetic accidents would have pumped up the frequency of the same gene not once but twice in the same population.

But geneticists have long questioned whether the Ashkenazim population's history was really suitable for these genetic accidents to have been significant. Remember, the founder effect and genetic drift become significant only in small populations, and the founding populations of Ashkenazim may have been quite large. Moreover, Ashkenazic communities were considerably widespread; drift would have sent gene frequencies up in some towns but down in others. And, finally, natural selection has by now had a thousand years to restore gene frequencies to normal.

Granted, those doubts are based on historical data, which are not always as precise or reliable as one might want. But within the past several years the case against those accidental explanations for Tay-Sachs disease in the Ashkenazim has been bolstered by discoveries by molecular biologists.

Like all proteins, the enzyme absent in Tay-Sachs children is coded for by a piece of our DNA. Along that particular stretch of DNA there are thousands of different sites where a mutation could occur that would result in no enzyme and hence in the same set of symptoms. If molecular biologists had discovered that all cases of Tay-Sachs in Ashkenazim involved damage to DNA at the same site, that would have been strong evidence that in Ashkenazim the disease stems from a single mutation that has been multiplied by the founder effect or genetic drift—in other words, the high incidence of Tay-Sachs among Eastern European Jews is accidental.

In reality, though, several different mutations along this stretch of DNA have been identified in Ashkenazim, and two of them occur much more frequently than in non-Ashkenazim populations. It seems unlikely that genetic accidents would have pumped up the frequency of the same gene not once but twice in the same population.

And that's not the sole unlikely coincidence arguing against accidental explanations. Recall that Tay-Sachs is caused by the excessive accumulation of one fatty substance, G_{M2} ganglioside, from a defect in one enzyme, hexosaminidase A. But Tay-Sachs is one of ten genetic diseases characteristic of Ashkenazim. Among those other nine, two—Gaucher's disease and Niemann-Pick disease—result from the accumulation of two other fatty substances similar to G_{M2} ganglioside, as a result of defects in two other enzymes similar to hexosaminidase A. Yet our bodies contain thousands of different enzymes. It would have been an incredible roll of the genetic dice if, by nothing more than chance, Ashkenazim had independently acquired mutations in three closely related enzymes—and had acquired mutations in one of those enzymes twice.

All these facts bring us to the fourth possible explanation of why the Tay-Sachs gene is so prevalent among Ashkenazim: namely, that something about them favored accumulation of G_{M2} ganglioside and related fats.

For comparison, suppose that a friend doubles her money on one stock while you are getting wiped out with your investments. Taken alone, that could just mean she was lucky on that one occasion. But suppose that she doubles her money on each of two different stocks and at the same time rings up big profits in real estate while also making a killing in bonds. That implies more than lady luck; it suggests that something about your friend—like shrewd judgment—favors financial success.

What could be the blessings of fat accumulation in Eastern European Jews? At first this question sounds weird. After all, that fat accumulation was noticed only because of the curses it bestows: Tay-Sachs, Gaucher's, or Niemann-Pick disease. But many of our common genetic diseases may persist because they bring both blessings and curses (see "The Cruel Logic of Our Genes," *Discover*, November 1989). They kill or impair individuals who inherit two copies of the faulty gene, but they help those who receive only one defective gene by protecting them against other diseases. The best understood example is the sickle-cell gene of African blacks, which often kills homozygotes but protects heterozygotes against malaria. Natural selection sustains such genes because more heterozygotes than normal individuals survive to pass on their genes, and those extra gene copies offset the copies lost through the deaths of homozygotes.

So let us refine our question and ask, What blessing could the Tay-Sachs gene bring to those individuals who are heterozygous for it? A clue first emerged back in 1972, with the publication of the results of a questionnaire that had asked U.S. Ashkenzaic parents of Tay-Sachs children what their own Eastern European-born parents had died of. Keep in mind that since these unfortunate children had to be homozygotes, with two copies of the Tay-Sachs gene, all their parents had to be heterozygotes, with one copy, and half of the parents' parents also had to be heterozygotes.

As it turned out, most of those Tay-Sachs grandparents had died of the usual causes: heart disease, stroke, cancer, and diabetes. But strikingly, only one of the 306 grandparents had died of tuberculosis, even though TB was generally one of the big killers in these grandparents' time. Indeed, among the general population of large Eastern European cities in the early twentieth century, TB caused up to 20 percent of all deaths.

This big discrepancy suggested that Tay-Sachs heterozygotes might somehow have been protected against TB. Interestingly, it was already well known that Ashkenazim in general had some such protection: even when Jews and non-Jews were compared within the same European city, class, and occupational group (for example, Warsaw garment workers), Jews had only half the TB death rate of non-Jews, despite their being equally susceptible to infection. Perhaps, one could reason, the Tay-Sachs gene furnished part of that well-established Jewish resistance.

We're not a melting pot, and we won't be for a long time. Each ethnic group has some characteristic genes of its own, a legacy of its distinct history.

A second clue to a heterozygote advantage conveyed by the Tay-Sachs gene emerged in 1983, with a fresh look at the data concerning the distributions of TB and the Tay-Sachs gene within Europe. The statistics showed that the Tay-Sachs gene was nearly three times more frequent among Jews originating from Austria, Hungary, and Czechoslovakia—areas where an amazing 9 to 10 percent of the population were heterozygotes—than among Jews from Poland, Russia, and Germany. At the same time records from an old Jewish TB sanatorium in Denver in 1904 showed that among patients born in Europe between 1860 and 1910, Jews from Austria and Hungary were overrepresented.

Initially, in putting together these two pieces of information, you might be tempted to conclude that because the highest frequency of the Tay-Sachs gene appeared in the same geographic region that produced the most cases of TB, the gene in fact offers no protection whatsoever. Indeed, this was precisely the mistaken conclusion of many researchers who had looked at these data before. But you have to pay careful attention to the numbers here: even at its highest fre-

quency the Tay-Sachs gene was carried by far fewer people than would be infected by TB. What the statistics really indicate is that where TB is the biggest threat, natural selection produces the biggest response.

Think of it this way: You arrive at an island where you find that all the inhabitants of the north end wear suits of armor, while all the inhabitants of the south end wear only cloth shirts. You'd be pretty safe in assuming that warfare is more prevalent in the north—and that war-related injuries account for far more deaths there than in the south. Thus, if the Tay-Sachs gene does indeed lend heterozygotes some protection against TB, you would expect to find the gene most often precisely where you find TB most often. Similarly, the sickle-cell gene reaches its highest frequencies in those parts of Africa where malaria is the biggest risk.

But you may believe there's still a hole in the argument: If Tay-Sachs heterozygotes are protected against TB, you may be asking, why is the gene common just in the Ashkenazim? Why did it not become common in the non-Jewish populations also exposed to TB in Austria, Hungary, and Czechoslovakia?

At this point we must recall the peculiar circumstances in which the Jews of Eastern Europe were forced to live. They were unique among the world's ethnic groups in having been virtually confined to towns for most of the past 2,000 years. Being forbidden to own land, Eastern European Jews were not peasant farmers living in the countryside, but businesspeople forced to live in crowded ghettos, in an environment where tuberculosis thrived.

Of course, until recent improvements in sanitation, these towns were not very healthy places for non-Jews either. Indeed, their populations couldn't sustain themselves: deaths exceeded births, and the number of dead had to be balanced by continued emigration from the countryside. For non-Jews, therefore, there was no genetically distinct urban population. For ghetto-bound Jews, however, there could be no emigration from the countryside; thus the Jewish population was under the strongest selection to evolve genetic resistance to TB.

Those are the conditions that probably led to Jewish TB resistance, whatever particular genetic factors prove to underlie it. I'd speculate that G_{M2} and related fats accumulate at slightly higher-than-normal levels in heterozygotes, although not at the lethal levels seen in homozygotes. (The fat accumulation in heterozygotes probably takes place in the cell membrane, the cell's "armor.") I'd also speculate that the accumulation provides heterozygotes with some protection against TB, and that that's why the genes for Tay-Sachs, Gaucher's, and Niemann-Pick disease reached high frequencies in the Ashkenazim.

Having thus stated the case, let me make clear that I don't want to overstate it. The evidence is still speculative. Depending on how you do the calculation, the low frequency of TB deaths in Tay-Sachs grandparents either barely reaches or doesn't quite reach the level of proof that statisticians require to accept an effect as real rather than as one that's arisen by chance. Moreover, we have no idea of the biochemical mechanism by which fat accumulation might confer resistance against TB. For the moment, I'd say that the evidence points to some selective advantage of Tay-Sachs heterozygotes among the Ashkenazim, and that TB resistance is the only plausible hypothesis yet proposed.

For now Tay-Sachs remains a speculative model for the evolution of ethnic diseases. But it's already a proven model of what to do about them. Twenty years ago a test was developed to identify Tay-Sachs heterozygotes, based on their lower-than-normal levels of hexosaminidase A. The test is simple, cheap, and accurate: all I did was to donate a small sample of my blood, pay $35, and wait a few days to receive the results.

If that test shows that at least one member of a couple is not a Tay-Sachs heterozygote, then any child of theirs can't be a Tay-Sachs homozygote. If both parents prove to be heterozygotes, there's a one-in-four chance of their child being a homozygote; that can then be determined by other tests performed on the mother early in pregnancy. If the results are positive, it's early enough for her to abort, should she choose to. That critical bit of knowledge has enabled parents who had gone through the agony of bearing a Tay-Sachs baby and watching him die to find the courage to try again.

The Tay-Sachs screening program launched in the United States in 1971 was targeted at the high-risk population: Ashkenazic Jewish couples of childbearing age. So successful has this approach been that the number of Tay-Sachs babies born each year in this country has declined tenfold. Today, in fact, more Tay-Sachs cases appear here in non-Jews than in Jews, because only the latter couples are routinely tested. Thus, what used to be the classic genetic disease of Jews is so no longer.

There's also a broader message to the Tay-Sachs story. We commonly refer to the United States as a melting pot, and in many ways that metaphor is apt. But in other ways we're not a melting pot, and we won't be for a long time. Each ethnic group has some characteristic genes of its own, a legacy of its distinct history. Tuberculosis and malaria are not major causes of death in the United States, but the genes that some of us evolved to protect ourselves against them are still frequent. Those genes are frequent only in certain ethnic groups, though, and they'll be slow to melt through the population.

With modern advances in molecular genetics, we can expect to see more, not less, ethnically targeted practice of medicine. Genetic screening for cystic fibrosis in European whites, for example, is one program that has been much discussed recently; when it comes, it will surely be based on the Tay-Sachs experience. Of course, what that may mean someday is more anxiety-ridden parents-to-be glowering at more dedicated genetics counselors. It will also mean fewer babies doomed to the agonies of diseases we may understand but that we'll never be able to accept.

Contributing editor Jared Diamond is a professor of physiology at the UCLA School of Medicine.

The Saltshaker's Curse

Physiological adaptations that helped American blacks
survive slavery may now be predisposing
their descendants to hypertension

Jared Diamond

On the walls of the main corridor at UCLA Medical School hang thirty-seven photographs that tell a moving story. They are the portraits of each graduating class, from the year that the school opened (Class of 1955) to the latest crop (Class of 1991). Throughout the 1950s and early 1960s the portraits are overwhelmingly of young white men, diluted by only a few white women and Asian men. The first black student graduated in 1961, an event not repeated for several more years. When I came to UCLA in 1966, I found myself lecturing to seventy-six students, of whom seventy-four were white. Thereafter the numbers of blacks, Hispanics, and Asians exploded, until the most recent photos show the number of white medical students declining toward a minority.

In these changes of racial composition, there is of course nothing unique about UCLA Medical School. While the shifts in its student body mirror those taking place, at varying rates, in other professional groups throughout American society, we still have a long way to go before professional groups truly mirror society itself. But ethnic diversity among physicians is especially important because of the dangers inherent in a profession composed of white practitioners for whom white biology is the norm.

Different ethnic groups face different health problems, for reasons of genes as well as of life style. Familiar examples include the prevalence of skin cancer and cystic fibrosis in whites, stomach cancer and stroke in Japanese, and diabetes in Hispanics and Pacific islanders. Each year, when I teach a seminar course in ethnically varying disease patterns, these by-now-familiar textbook facts assume a gripping reality, as my various students choose to discuss some disease that affects themselves or their relatives. To read about the molecular biology of sickle-cell anemia is one thing. It's quite another thing when one of my students, a black man homozygous for the sickle-cell gene, describes the pain of his own sickling attacks and how they have affected his life.

Sickle-cell anemia is a case in which the evolutionary origins of medically important genetic differences among peoples are well understood. (It evolved only in malarial regions because it confers resistance against malaria.) But in many other cases the evolutionary origins are not nearly so transparent. Why is it, for example, that only some human populations have a high frequency of the Tay-Sachs gene or of diabetes?...

Compared with American whites of the same age and sex, American blacks have, on the average, higher blood pres-

sure, double the risk of developing hypertension, and nearly ten times the risk of dying of it. By age fifty, nearly half of U.S. black men are hypertensive. For a given age and blood pressure, hypertension more often causes heart disease and especially kidney failure and strokes in U.S. blacks than whites. Because the frequency of kidney disease in U.S. blacks is eighteen times that in whites, blacks account for about two-thirds of U.S. patients with hypertensive kidney failure, even though they make up only about one-tenth of the population. Around the world, only Japanese exceed U.S. blacks in their risk of dying from stroke. Yet it was not until 1932 that the average difference in blood pressure between U.S. blacks and whites was clearly demonstrated, thereby exposing a major health problem outside the norms of white medicine.

What is it about American blacks that makes them disproportionately likely to develop hypertension and then to die of its consequences? While this question is of course especially "interesting" to black readers, it also concerns all Americans, because other ethnic groups in the United States are not so far behind blacks in their risk of hypertension. If *Natural History* readers are a cross section of the United States, then about one-quarter of you now have high blood pressure, and more than half of you will die of a heart attack or stroke to which high blood pressure predisposes. Thus, we all have valid reasons for being interested in hypertension.

First, some background on what those numbers mean when your doctor inflates a rubber cuff about your arm, listens, deflates the cuff, and finally pronounces, "Your blood pressure is 120 over 80." The cuff device is called a sphygmomanometer, and it measures the pressure in your artery in units of millimeters of mercury (that's the height to which your blood pressure would force up a column of mercury in case, God forbid, your artery were suddenly connected to a vertical mercury column). Naturally, your blood pressure varies with each stroke of your heart, so the first and second numbers refer, respectively, to the peak pressure at each heartbeat (systolic pressure) and to the minimum pressure between beats (diastolic pressure). Blood pressure varies somewhat with position, activity, and anxiety level, so the measurement is usually made while you are resting flat on your back. Under those conditions, 120 over 80 is an average reading for Americans.

There is no magic cutoff between normal blood pressure and high blood pressure. Instead, the higher your blood pressure, the more likely you are to die of a heart attack, stroke, kidney failure, or ruptured aorta. Usually, a pressure reading higher than 140 over 90 is arbitrarily defined as constituting hypertension, but some people with lower readings will die of a stroke at age fifty, while others with higher readings will die in a car accident in good health at age ninety.

Why do some of us have much higher blood pressure than others? In about 5 percent of hypertensive patients there is an identifiable single cause, such as hormonal imbalance or use of oral contraceptives. In 95 percent of such cases, though, there is no such obvious cause. The clinical euphemism for our ignorance in such cases is "essential hypertension."

Nowadays, we know that there is a big genetic component in essential hypertension, although the particular genes involved have not yet been identified. Among people living in the same house-

hold, the correlation coefficient for blood pressure is 0.63 between identical twins, who share all of their genes. (A correlation coefficient of 1.00 would mean that the twins share identical blood pressures as well and would suggest that pressure is determined entirely by genes and not at all by environment.) Fraternal twins or ordinary siblings or a parent and child, who share half their genes and whose blood pressure would therefore show a correlation coefficient of 0.5 if purely determined genetically, actually have a coefficient of about 0.25. Finally, adopted siblings or a parent and adopted child, who have no direct genetic connection, have a correlation coefficient of only 0.05. Despite the shared household environment, their blood pressures are barely more similar than those of two people pulled randomly off the street. In agreement with this evidence for genetic factors underlying blood pressure itself, your risk of actually developing hypertensive disease increases from 4 percent to 20 percent to 35 percent if, respectively, none or one or both of your parents were hypertensive.

But these same facts suggest that environmental factors also contribute to high blood pressure, since identical twins have similar but not identical blood pressures. Many environmental or life style factors contributing to the risk of hypertension have been identified by epidemiological studies that compare hypertension's frequency in groups of people living under different conditions. Such contributing factors include obesity, high intake of salt or alcohol or saturated fats, and low calcium intake. The proof of this approach is that hypertensive patients who modify their life styles so as to minimize these putative factors often succeed in reducing their blood pressure. Patients are especially advised to reduce salt intake and stress, reduce intake of cholesterol and saturated fats and alcohol, lose weight, cut out smoking, and exercise regularly.

Here are some examples of the epidemiological studies pointing to these risk factors. Around the world, comparisons within and between populations show that both blood pressure and the frequency of hypertension increase hand in hand with salt intake. At the one ex-

treme, Brazil's Yanomamö Indians have the world's lowest-known salt consumption (somewhat above 10 milligrams per day!), lowest average blood pressure (95 over 61!), and lowest incidence of hypertension (no cases!). At the opposite extreme, doctors regard Japan as the "land of apoplexy" because of the high frequency of fatal strokes (Japan's leading cause of death, five times more frequent than in the United States), linked with high blood pressure and notoriously salty food. Within Japan itself these factors reach their extremes in Akita Prefecture, famous for its tasty rice, which Akita farmers flavor with salt, wash down with salty miso soup, and alternate with salt pickles between meals. Of 300 Akita adults studied, not one consumed less than five grams of salt daily, the average consumption was twenty-seven grams, and the most salt-loving individual consumed an incredible sixty-one grams—enough to devour the contents of the usual twenty-six-ounce supermarket salt container in a mere twelve days. The average blood pressure in Akita by age fifty is 151 over 93, making hypertension (pressure higher than 140 over 90) the norm. Not surprisingly, Akitas' frequency of death by stroke is more than double even the Japanese average, and in some Akita villages 99 percent of the population dies before age seventy.

Why salt intake often (in about 60 percent of hypertensive patients) leads to high blood pressure is not fully understood. One possible interpretation is that salt intake triggers thirst, leading to an increase in blood volume. In response, the heart increases its output and blood pressure rises, causing the kidneys to filter more salt and water under that increased pressure. The result is a new steady state, in which salt and water excretion again equals intake, but more salt and water are stored in the body and blood pressure is raised.

At this point, let's contrast hypertension with a simple genetic disease like Tay-Sachs disease. Tay-Sachs is due to a defect in a single gene; every Tay Sachs patient has a defect in that same gene. Everybody in whom that gene is defective is certain to die of Tay-Sachs, regardless of their life style or environment. In contrast, hypertension involves several different genes whose molecular products remain to be identified. Because there are many causes of raised blood pressure, different hypertensive patients may owe their condition to different gene combinations. Furthermore, whether someone genetically predisposed to hypertension actually develops symptoms depends a lot on life style. Thus, hypertension is not one of those uncommon, homogeneous, and intellectually elegant diseases that geneticists prefer to study. Instead, like diabetes and ulcers, hypertension is a shared set of symptoms produced by heterogeneous causes, all involving an interaction between environmental agents and a susceptible genetic background.

Since U.S. blacks and whites differ on the average in the conditions under which they live, could those differences account for excess hypertension in U.S. blacks? Salt intake, the dietary factor that one thinks of first, turns out on the average not to differ between U.S. blacks and whites. Blacks do consume less potassium and calcium, do experience more stress associated with more difficult socioeconomic conditions, have much less access to medical care, and are therefore much less likely to be diagnosed or treated until it is too late. Those factors surely contribute to the frequency and severity of hypertension in blacks.

However, those factors don't seem to be the whole explanation: hypertensive blacks aren't merely like severely hypertensive whites. Instead, physiological differences seem to contribute as well. On consuming salt, blacks retain it on average far longer before excreting it into the urine, and they experience a greater rise in blood pressure on a high-salt diet. Hypertension is more likely to be "salt-sensitive" in blacks than in whites, meaning that blood pressure is more likely to rise and fall with rises and falls in dietary salt intake. By the same token, black hypertension is more likely to be treated successfully by drugs that cause the kidneys to excrete salt (the so-called thiazide diuretics) and less likely to respond to those drugs that reduce heart rate and cardiac output (so-called beta blockers, such as propanolol). These facts suggest that there are some qualitative differences between the causes of black and white hypertension, with black hypertension more likely to involve how the kidneys handle salt.

Physicians often refer to this postulated feature as a "defect": for example, "kidneys of blacks have a genetic defect in excreting sodium." As an evolutionary biologist, though, I hear warning bells going off inside me whenever a seemingly harmful trait that occurs frequently in an old and large human population is dismissed as a "defect." Given enough generations, genes that greatly impede survival are extremely unlikely to spread, unless their net effect is to increase survival and reproductive success. Human medicine has furnished the best examples of seemingly defective genes being propelled to high frequency by counterbalancing benefits. For example, sickle-cell hemoglobin protects far more people against malaria than it kills of anemia, while the Tay-Sachs gene may have protected far more Jews against tuberculosis than it killed of neurological disease. Thus, to understand why U.S. blacks now are prone to die as a result of their kidneys' retaining salt, we need to ask under what conditions people might have benefited from kidneys good at retaining salt.

That question is hard to understand from the perspective of modern Western society, where saltshakers are on every dining table, salt (sodium chloride) is cheap, and our bodies' main problem is getting rid of it. But imagine what the world used to be like before saltshakers became ubiquitous. Most plants contain very little sodium, yet animals require sodium at high concentrations in all their extracellular fluids. As a result, carnivores readily obtain their needed sodium by eating herbivores, but herbivores themselves face big problems in acquiring that sodium. That's why the animals that one sees coming to salt licks are deer and antelope, not lions and tigers. Similarly, some human hunter-gatherers obtained enough salt from the meat that they ate. But when we began to take up farming ten thousand years ago, we either had to evolve kidneys superefficient at conserving salt or learn to extract salt at great effort or trade for it at great expense.

Examples of these various solutions abound. I already mentioned Brazil's Yanomamö Indians, whose staple food is low-sodium bananas and who excrete on the average only 10 milligrams of salt daily—barely one-thousandth the salt excretion of the typical American. A single Big Mac hamburger analyzed by *Consumer Reports* contained 1.5 grams (1,500 milligrams) of salt, representing many weeks of intake for a Yanomamö. The New Guinea highlanders with whom I work, and whose diet consists up to 90 percent of low-sodium sweet potatoes, told me of the efforts to which they went to make salt a few decades ago, before Europeans brought it as trade goods. They gathered leaves of certain plant species, burned them, scraped up the ash, percolated water through it to dissolve the solids, and finally evaporated the water to obtain small amounts of bitter salt.

Thus, salt has been in very short supply for much of recent human evolutionary history. Those of us with efficient kidneys able to retain salt even on a low-sodium diet were better able to survive our inevitable episodes of sodium loss (of which more in a moment). Those kidneys proved to be a detriment only when salt became routinely available, leading to excessive salt retention and hypertension with its fatal consequences. That's why blood pressure and the frequency of hypertension have shot up recently in so many populations around the world as they have made the transition from being self-sufficient subsistence farmers to members of the cash economy and patrons of supermarkets.

This evolutionary argument has been advanced by historian-epidemiologist Thomas Wilson and others to explain the current prevalence of hypertension in American blacks in particular. Many West African blacks, from whom most American blacks originated via the slave trade, must have faced the chronic problem of losing salt through sweating in their hot environment. Yet in West Africa, except on the coast and certain inland areas, salt was traditionally as scarce for African farmers as it has been for Yanomamö and New Guinea farmers. (Ironically, those Africans who sold other Africans as slaves often took payment in salt traded from the Sahara.) By this argument, the genetic basis for hypertension in U.S. blacks was already widespread in many of their West African ancestors. It required only the ubiquity of saltshakers in twentieth-century America for that genetic basis to express itself as hypertension. This argument also predicts that as Africa's life style becomes increasingly Westernized, hypertension could become as prevalent in West Africa as it now is among U.S. blacks. In this view, American blacks would be no different from the many Polynesian, Melanesian, Kenyan, Zulu, and other populations that have recently developed high blood pressure under a Westernized life style.

But there's an intriguing extension to this hypothesis, proposed by Wilson and physician Clarence Grim, collaborators at the Hypertension Research Center of Drew University in Los Angeles. They suggest a scenario in which New World blacks may now be at more risk for hypertension than their African ancestors. That scenario involves very recent selection for super-efficient kidneys, driven by massive mortality of black slaves from salt loss.

Grim and Wilson's argument goes as follows. Black slavery in the Americas began about 1517, with the first imports of slaves from West Africa, and did not end until Brazil freed its slaves barely a century ago in 1888. In the course of the slave trade an estimated 12 million Africans were brought to the Americas. But those imports were winnowed by deaths at many stages, from an even larger number of captives and exports.

First, slaves captured by raids in the interior of West Africa were chained together, loaded with heavy burdens, and marched for one or two months, with little food and water, to the coast. About 25 percent of the captives died en route. While awaiting purchase by slave traders, the survivors were held on the coast in hot, crowded buildings called barracoons, where about 12 percent of them died. The traders went up and down the coast buying and loading slaves for a few weeks or months until a ship's cargo was full (5 percent more died). The dreaded Middle Passage across the Atlantic killed 10 percent of the slaves, chained together in a hot, crowded, unventilated

hold without sanitation. (Picture to yourself the result of those toilet "arrangements.") Of those who lived to land in the New World, 5 percent died while awaiting sale, and 12 percent died while being marched or shipped from the sale yard to the plantation. Finally, of those who survived, between 10 and 40 percent died during the first three years of plantation life, in a process euphemistically called seasoning. At that stage, about 70 percent of the slaves initially captured were dead, leaving 30 percent as seasoned survivors.

Even the end of seasoning, however, was not the end of excessive mortality. About half of slave infants died within a year of birth because of the poor nutrition and heavy workload of their mothers. In plantation terminology, slave women were viewed as either "breeding units" or "work units," with a built-in conflict between those uses: "These Negroes breed the best, whose labour is least," as an eighteenth-century observer put it. As a result, many New World slave populations depended on continuing slave imports and couldn't maintain their own numbers because death rates exceeded birth rates. Since buying new slaves cost less than rearing slave children for twenty years until they were adults, slave owners lacked economic incentive to change this state of affairs.

Recall that Darwin discussed natural selection and survival of the fittest with respect to animals. Since many more animals die than survive to produce offspring, each generation becomes enriched in the genes of those of the preceding generation that were among the survivors. It should now be clear that slavery represented a tragedy of unnatural selection in humans on a gigantic scale. From examining accounts of slave mortality, Grim and Wilson argue that death was indeed selective: much of it was related to unbalanced salt loss, which quickly brings on collapse. We think immediately of salt loss by sweating under hot conditions: while slaves were working, marching, or confined in unventilated barracoons or ships' holds. More body salt may have been spilled with vomiting from seasickness. But the biggest salt loss at every stage was from diarrhea due to crowding and lack of san-

itation—ideal conditions for the spread of gastrointestinal infections. Cholera and other bacterial diarrheas kill us by causing sudden massive loss of salt and water. (Picture your most recent bout of *turista*, multiplied to a diarrheal fluid output of twenty quarts in one day, and you'll understand why.) All contemporary accounts of slave ships and plantation life emphasized diarrhea, or "fluxes" in eighteenth-century terminology, as one of the leading killers of slaves.

Grim and Wilson reason, then, that slavery suddenly selected for superefficient kidneys surpassing the efficient kidneys already selected by thousands of years of West African history. Only those slaves who were best able to retain salt could survive the periodic risk of high salt loss to which they were exposed. Salt supersavers would have had the further advantage of building up, under normal conditions, more of a salt reserve in their body fluids and bones, thereby enabling them to survive longer or more frequent bouts of diarrhea. Those superkidneys became a disadvantage only when modern medicine began to reduce diarrhea's lethal impact, thereby transforming a blessing into a curse.

Thus, we have two possible evolutionary explanations for salt retention by New World blacks. One involves slow selection by conditions operating in Africa for millennia; the other, rapid recent selection by slave conditions within the past few centuries. The result in either case would make New World blacks more susceptible than whites to hypertension, but the second explanation would, in addition, make them more susceptible than African blacks. At present, we don't know the relative importance of these two explanations. Grim and Wilson's provocative hypothesis is likely to stimulate medical and physiological comparisons of American blacks with African blacks and thereby to help resolve the question.

While this piece has focused on one medical problem in one human population, it has several larger morals. One, of course, is that our differing genetic heritages predispose us to different diseases, depending on the part of the world where our ancestors lived. Another is that our genetic differences reflect not only ancient conditions in different parts of the world but also recent episodes of migration and mortality. A well-established example is the decrease in the frequency of the sickle-cell hemoglobin gene in U.S. blacks compared with African blacks, because selection for resistance to malaria is now unimportant in the United States. The example of black hypertension that Grim and Wilson discuss opens the door to considering other possible selective effects of the slave experience. They note that occasional periods of starvation might have selected slaves for superefficient sugar metabolism, leading under modern conditions to a propensity for diabetes.

Finally, consider a still more universal moral. Almost all people alive today exist under very different conditions from those under which every human lived 10,000 years ago. It's remarkable that our old genetic heritage now permits us to survive at all under such different circumstances. But our heritage still catches up with most of us, who will die of life style related diseases such as cancer, heart attack, stroke, and diabetes. The risk factors for these diseases are the strange new conditions prevailing in modern Western society. One of the hardest challenges for modern medicine will be to identify for us which among all those strange new features of diet, life style, and environment are the ones getting us into trouble. For each of us, the answers will depend on our particular genes, hence on our ancestry. Only with such individually tailored advice can we hope to reap the benefits of modern living while still housed in bodies designed for life before saltshakers.

Jared Diamond is a professor of physiology at UCLA Medical School.

Reprinted with permission from *Natural History,* October 1991, pp. 20, 22–26. © 1991 by Natural History Magazine, Inc.

Of Mice, Men, and Genes

The best-laid plans o' DNA gang aft agley.

By Robert M. Sapolsky

Don't you love urban legends, those outrageous stories everyone believes? There are academicians who study urban legends for a living; they catalogue them, track their origins in Norse mythology, get into arguments at conferences about them. But amid all that intellectualizing, it's just plain fascinating to hear some of the made-up stuff that lots of people fall for. There's the endlessly repeated one about the poodle stuffed into a microwave to get dried off, or the classic about the scuba diver who gets scooped up along with a lot of water into the giant bucket of a fire-fighting plane, then is dropped onto a forest fire. And there's the one about the woman who leaves groceries in her car on a sweltering day: a tube of cookie dough explodes from the heat just as she gets back in, splattering the back of her head, and she's convinced she's been shot and the dough is her splattered brains.

And then there's the one about a bunch of scientists who sequenced the human genome: they can explain everything about you; all they have to do is look it up in the sequence of your genes. But it just ain't so: we're back in the domain of urban legend.

Why are people such suckers for the idea that genes are the be-all and end-all? The tendency is particularly bad right now. Not only has the human genome recently been (mostly) sequenced, but we've also just come off the golden anniversary of the discovery of the structure of DNA. The celebrations have been replete with religious imagery about the genetic code as holy grail, the Code of Codes. And this imagery even gets trotted out by biologists, people who get paid to know better.

And biologists really should know better, because they've had the sobering concept of "gene-environment interaction" hammered into their heads for much of their lives. (In fact, "gene-environment interaction" is probably one of the first utterances most biologists made as infants, along with "doggie, doggie come.") The trouble is, it is a phrase so often repeated that it has become as reflexive and ingrained—and, ultimately, ignored—as the words to "Elmo's Song."

The idea that genes and environment interact can mean a number of things. At the least, it means that people who get into black-and-white arguments about nature versus nurture are a century out of date. Of more relevance, it means that though genes can (indirectly) instruct cells, organs, and organisms about how to function in the environment, the environment can also regulate which genes become active at particular times. Of greatest relevance here, though, is that the thing a particular gene most proximally produces—a particular protein—can function quite differently in different environments. So, in theory, you might have a gene that in one environment causes you to grow antlers and, in another, causes you to fly south for the winter.

For folks who still want to fight the nature-nurture wars, the question up for debate becomes: OK, just how powerful are these gene-environment interactions? At one extreme are those who scoff at contrasts as gaping as the one between growing antlers and flying south. In their view, a gene does

Beatrix Potter: Hunca Munca (from The Tale of Two Bad Mice), 1904

something or other, and the environment perhaps alters how fast or how strong or how long the gene does that something or other. But none of those environmental influences lead to dramatically different effects. Framed in the context of genes and disease, it's like saying, Yeah, how windy it is may alter the precise speed with which the anvil drops from a ten-story building and lands on your toe, but who cares about that environmental interaction with the anvil? And at the other extreme are those who assert that interactions can be of huge consequence—say, if what is dropping is a feather and not an anvil.

And so the scientists happily argue and experiment away, squandering tax dollars that could otherwise go for Halliburton contracts. Amid these debates, it's useful to be reminded just how powerful gene-environment interactions can be. Two recent studies provide some terrific examples.

The first study investigated the effects of one of the subtlest, least appreciated environments: the prenatal one. For many years, strains of laboratory rodents have been bred for various traits—one strain gets a type of diabetes, another strain gets hypertension, and so on. Each strain is developed by inbreeding generation after generation of animals with some trait, until all the members of the strain are as close as possible to being genetically identical—like clones of one another. If all the members of that strain show the trait, regardless of which laboratory they're raised in, there's some reason to think that the animals are subject to a strong genetic influence.

All the inbreeding is then followed by an experiment known as a "cross-fostering study," regarded as critical for detecting a genetic influence. Suppose all the mice of the Coke strain grow up preferring Coke to Pepsi, and all the mice of the Pepsi strain grow up displaying the opposite persuasion. Take some Coke-strain mice at birth and let Pepsi-strain moms raise them in a Pepsi-strain colony. If the Coke-strain mice still grow up craving Coke, the typical interpretation is that you've found a behavior that strongly resists environmental influence; score one for nature over nurture. But are cross-fostering experiments the last word?

That's where one of the new studies comes in. Carried out by Darlene Francis, a neurobiologist at Emory University in Atlanta, and her colleagues, it was published in the prestigious journal *Nature Neuroscience*. The investigators looked at two mouse strains that differ across an array of behavior patterns. To simplify a bit, one strain is more anxious and skittish than the other. Compared with the more "relaxed" strain, the "timid" strain is slower to enter a scary or novel environment, and timid-strain mice have more trouble learning during a stressful task than relaxed-strain mice do.

Environmental influences don't begin at birth: the prenatal environment also interacts with genes.

Geneticists who study mice had known about those differences for a long time. They had also confirmed, apparently, that the differences were largely governed by genetics. True, there was some evidence that relaxed-strain mothers are more nurturing than timid-strain moms, licking and grooming their pups more. That evidence had raised the possibility that mothering style caused the differences between the two strains. But then the acid test

Walking in the Rain, *an American postcard from the early twentieth century*

had been performed: relaxed-strain mice that were raised from birth by timid-strain moms grew up to be just as relaxed as any other member of their strain.

But Francis and her team went a step further. With the same kind of technology used by clinics performing in vitro fertilization, the investigators cross-fostered mice as embryos. Specifically, they implanted fertilized eggs from relaxed-strain parents into timid-strain females, which then carried the relaxed-strain embryos to term. They also did the key control: they implanted relaxed-strain eggs into relaxed-strain females just in case the process of in vitro fertilization and implantation distorted the results). After they were born, some relaxed-strain pups were raised by timid-strain moms, and others by relaxed-strain ones. (If all this isn't confusing enough, at least thank Francis and her colleagues for not bothering to implant fertilized timid-strain eggs into relaxed-strain females.)

And the result? When the supposedly genetically hardwired relaxed-strain mice went through both fetal development and early puphood with timid-strain moms, they grew up to be just as timid as any other timid-strain mice. Same genes, different environment, different outcome.

This result raises two points. First, environmental influences don't begin at birth. Some factor or factors in the environment of a timid-strain mouse mother during her pregnancy—her level of stress, perhaps, or the nutrition she gets—is affecting the anxiety levels and learning abilities of her offspring, even as adults. The mechanisms may have to do with alterations in their brain structure, hormone profiles, or metabolism. In fact, some of the same effects have already been documented in people. The second point? Relaxed-strain mice aren't relaxed only because of their genes; their fetal and neonatal environments are crucial factors.

A finding like this one could give panic attacks to mouse mothers the world over: Remember the time we got all stressed-out when we were pregnant? Remember that other time we got irritable with our newborn pup? One of them could be the reason the kid won't get into the best college. But such worries are far afield, of course, from human concerns. And that's where the other study comes in.

The second recent study is a landmark paper, published in the equally prestigious journal *Science*, by Avshalom Caspi, a psychiatrist at King's College, London, and his colleagues. These investigators have been doing work that puts to shame those studies that come out of watching some fruit fly with a twenty-four-hour life span. Caspi and company have been following a population of more than a thousand New Zealand kids, beginning at age three and continuing well into adulthood, nigh onto a quarter century. Among the things they've examined is who, as a young adult, suffers from clinical depression. That topic, by the way, is a useful one to get some insight about—given that depression can be life-threatening and afflicts between 5 and 20 percent of us.

Caspi's team examined patterns of depression in their subjects and discovered that it has something to do with possessing a certain variant of a gene. That's a nice finding, of course, but what makes it really exciting is that the gene in question is not just any random gene. It has already been implicated in biochemical theories about depression, coding for a protein that helps regulate how much serotonin gets into neurons. Serotonin is a neurotransmitter, one of scores of different kinds of neurotransmitter in the brain, but it is the one responsive to antidepressant drugs such as Prozac, Paxil, and Zoloft (collectively known as "selective serotonin re-uptake inhibitors"—SSRIs).

The serotonin-regulating gene—which for reasons not worth going into is called *5-HTT*—comes in two different "flavors." Both flavors code for the same kind of protein, but the two flavors differ in how much of the protein gets produced. Individuals can have two copies of either flavor (one from each parent) or one copy of both. At least some nonhuman primates can as well. Studies had already shown that a rhesus monkey's *5-HTT* makeup affects how readily the animal deals with stress.

So Caspi and his colleagues tabulated the two *5-HTT* gene flavors and how they correlated with the incidence of depression in their pool of New Zealand subjects. And what they discovered is worth stating carefully. Did they demonstrate that genes of a certain flavor actually cause depression? No. Did they show that having a certain *5-HTT* makeup significantly increases a person's risk of depression? Not really.

What they showed was that the *5-HTT* genes you inherit greatly increase your risk of depression, but only in a certain environment. What

kind of environment? One with a history of major stressful events and traumas in childhood or early adulthood (such as the death of a loved one, the loss of a job, a serious illness). Those in their study with a "bad" *5-HTT* profile, who also suffered major stressful events, had almost twice the risk of depression, and nearly four times the risk of suicide or suicidal thoughts, as those with the "best" profile. But those who were spared a history of major stresses were no worse off for having a "bad" *5-HTT* profile. (Completing this picture is work by a group at the University of Wurzburg, in Germany, showing that stress hormones regulate the activity of the *5-HTT* gene, and do so differently, according to its flavor.)

What lessons lurk here? Obviously, beware of simple explanations; it is rare that nature is parsimonious.

And keep genes in their proper place. Sometimes genetics is about inevitability. If you have the mutation for Huntington's Disease, for instance, there's a 100 percent chance you're going to have this awful neurological disease by middle age: no two ways about it. But genes are more often about vulnerabilities and potentials than they are about destiny.

What all this highfalutin molecular biology should teach us is that we can't just throw up our hands and say: "His genes made him do it." We all have a responsibility to create environments that interact benignly with our genes.

ROBERT M. SAPOLSKY is a professor of biological sciences and neurology at Stanford University. He is the author of A Primate's Memoir: A Neuroscientist's Unconventional Life among the Baboons. *His most recent article for* Natural History, *"The Pleasure (and Pain) of 'Maybe'" (September 2003), has been nominated for the 2004 National Magazine Award for Essays.*

What you can learn from
drunk
monkeys

A remarkable NIH study says you're just as likely to become an alcoholic from a bad childhood as from bad genes

Being alone is not normal for rhesus monkeys, and being a loner means a monkey will most likely have a taste for alcohol. Likewise, innate sociability is key to understanding chronic alcoholism among humans, argues NIH researcher Dee Higley: "People become alcoholics not because they feel bad but because they have social problems."

BY MEREDITH F. SMALL

I AM STANDING IN AN ANIMAL RE-search lab dressed entirely in blue paper—paper shower cap, paper shirt and pants, even blue paper shoes. My face is covered with a plastic shield, and my hands are gloved. This getup is required because I am holding a newborn rhesus monkey, a tiny ball of fur with button-brown eyes and hair that sticks straight up off the top of its head. The baby wiggles around in my hands, grabs my thumbs, and makes "coo-coo" noises that are heartbreakingly endearing. I look into his eyes and think that this little guy might just be the cutest thing I've ever seen. Harder to deal with is the reality that this research monkey may become a chronic alcoholic. Even more disturbing is the idea that his future alcoholism is not rooted in bad genes alone. Instead, a contrived unhappy childhood could push him toward the bottle.

For the past 15 years, a National Institutes of Health research team led by psychologist Dee Higley has been raising rhesus monkeys to develop an animal model for chronic alcoholism. Higley has discovered that although genes mat-ter when it comes to the risk of alcoholism, attachment to a mother and a normal early social life also have a major impact. When monkeys are removed from their mothers at birth and never allowed to bond with a parent, when they have to rely on peers rather than mom for social lessons, they often end up social zeros with a taste for booze. And if they have a genetic history that makes them vulnerable to alcohol abuse, a bad childhood will be just enough to tip the balance and turn them into chronic alcohol abusers.

The complex influences of genes and experience on alcohol consumption in monkeys places Higley smack in the middle of the debate about the etiology of human alcoholism. Is alcoholism a disease, an illness beyond our control, as we have been led to believe? Or is it a product of society, of upbringing, something we might be able to change?

ALCOHOL IS THE MOST WIDELY used and accepted psychoactive drug in the world. Alcohol abuse is devastating to individual health, and it casts a wide net of pain across families and society.

The National Council on Alcoholism and Drug Dependence claims that more than 13 million American adults are alcoholics, and another 76 million have been affected by an alcoholic in the family. Drinking is also implicated in many crimes, including assault, rape, and homicide. In all, alcohol contributes to an estimated 100,000 deaths annually.

Two-thirds of the population drink, but half of all booze is consumed by only 10 percent of the people in this country. Clearly, some drinkers are prone to alcohol abuse, while others can party occasionally with restraint. So why is it that some people just can't stay on this side of the buzz?

Until Victorian times alcoholism was considered a moral issue—only the weak-willed succumbed. But when physicians introduced the idea that excess alcohol consumption might be a sickness, the disease model for alcoholism became fashionable. There was hope in this diagnosis: If alcoholism is a disease, there must be a treatment and a possible cure. The disease model led to the establishment in 1935 of Alcoholics Anonymous, an organization founded largely on the premise that alcoholism is a progressive, biologically based illness.

Today most people believe that abusive drinking is a physical or mental condition that is biologically predestined. Based on twin and adoption studies, there indeed appears to be some genetic influence on the pattern of alcoholism. In a study published in 1998, Marc Schuckit of the University of California at San Diego found that 40 percent of college-age children of alcoholics have a low reaction to alcohol, compared with only 10 percent of the children of nonalcoholics. Presumably, the low reaction says something about the biology of these individuals, a biology they inherited from their parents. More tellingly, follow-up studies revealed that those with a low reaction were more likely to become alcoholics by age 35.

Monkeys growing up without parents around tend to consume enormous amounts of alcohol

---

Research also indicates there is a relationship between alcoholism and genetic deficiencies in the opioid and dopamine receptors in the brain. Kenneth Blum of the University of Texas Health Science Center and Ernest Noble of the University of California at Los Angeles reported in the 1990s that they had discovered a form of the gene for a dopamine receptor that could derail the normal pleasure pathway and push people to become addicted to alcohol, cigarettes, or food.

But not all children who grow up with the suspected genes for drinking do so, and sometimes someone with no family history of alcoholism suddenly becomes a drunk. Clearly, genes alone don't explain why some people are more at risk than others. Now some researchers have begun to suspect that alcoholism lies in social and psychological influences that mold a personality already susceptible to mind-altering substances.

DEE HIGLEY AND I ARE STROLLING by a row of outdoor cages at the National

Institutes of Health Animal Care Center in Poolesville, Maryland. Higley, 48, a tall man with a buzz cut and a warm smile, looks like an academic version of Gene Hackman on a good day. In front of each cage, he asks me, "Who do you think are the chronic drinkers?" Even with 20 or so adult rhesus monkeys per cage, it's easy to see which animals have been imbibing that day. Just like the regulars at a local bar, some animals are draped across each other or lounging about alone, too blitzed to groom themselves or run about like the teetotalers. Some monkeys hungrily suck a red or green liquid that flows from a contraption on the side of the cage. Higley says both liquids are laced with an artificial sweetener, but only one is 8.5 percent alcohol. The alcohol is available five days a week for an hour a day. I'm looking at the end of happy hour.

Based on the consumption patterns of 300 animals, Higley has found that monkeys soon establish a routine. Some regularly abstain, some imbibe occasionally, and 10 to 20 percent of the animals consume at a rate that matches human alcoholism. Higley has come to the startling conclusion that how the monkeys are treated as infants can predict which will be at risk.

At the Animal Care Center, some newborn monkeys are removed from their mothers and hand reared for a month. The youngsters are then placed in a larger cage with little ones their age to form a peer group. Other babies born at the same time are allowed to stay with mom for seven months and then put with peers; they provide the normal controls for the study. At 4 years of age, the beginning of adulthood for rhesus monkeys, they're all offered a drink. "Those that grow up without parents around just consume enormous amounts of alcohol—about double what the mother-reared monkeys do," says Higley. "And they are more likely to get intoxicated on a daily basis. They also show a number of other kinds of behaviors that are characteristic of human alcoholics." In other words, they not only drink like alcoholics, they act like alcoholics.

In 1987 psychiatrist Robert Cloninger theorized that alcoholism could be traced to two different personality types that

correspond to specific drinking patterns. Type I alcoholics, Cloninger suggested, are people emotionally dependent on others and afraid of risk. They typically start drinking in adulthood as social drinkers and end up addicted; drinking for them is a sedative against anxiety. In contrast, type II alcoholics begin drinking early and hard in their adolescence, seeking out alcohol as they seek out other risky situations. Unlike type I alcoholics, their drinking is not about curbing anxiety but a desire for the euphoria of a high combined with an inability to stop once they start. Type IIs typically have little impulse control. And type IIs are almost exclusively male.

Higley has found the same distinctive types of drinkers in monkey groups. Some monkeys are constantly anxious and love to drink, like human type I alcoholics. Others echo the human type II alcoholics—they are anxious, yet they like to take risks, have little impulse control, and are aggressive and antisocial. One big difference between the monkey type IIs and their human counterparts is that female rhesus monkeys are just as likely as males to be impulsive risk takers who turn to the bottle.

"I suspect culture produces the [gender] difference in humans," Higley says. "Women growing up in human society are told that drinking a lot is something that you shouldn't do." But female monkeys are free to be impulsive and drink as much as they want without being admonished to act like ladies.

Higley has also found that impulsive behavior and drinking have an enduring biological basis. Although there are probably many neurotransmitters responsible for appreciating alcohol, serotonin seems to be especially predictive in monkeys. In humans, a low level of serotonin activity is implicated in depression, obsessive-compulsive disorders, eating disorders, and suicide. "Serotonin is, in a sense, the brakes of the brain," Higley points out. "It regulates what we do with our emotions, what we do with our motivations, what we do with our behavior." Without decent serotonin activity, we lose control of our impulses.

Back at Higley's office, our paper clothes shed, Higley rocks back in his chair and offers a twist on the old joke about two guys in a bar: "Two guys walk into a bar, one with high serotonin and one with low serotonin. They start drinking, and then in comes another guy who is aggressive and drunk. He rudely grabs a pretty girl they've been talking with. The high-serotonin male decides to walk away. The low-serotonin guy plows right in, and before long he's in the middle of a fight. The difference is in the braking, the stopping."

For the monkeys in Higley's lab, serotonin seems to have the same influence. Those with low levels of a spinal-fluid marker for serotonin activity called 5-hydroxyindoleacetic acid, or 5-HIAA, are the ones with little impulse control and the urge to drink and drink. Higley has also found the same serotonin-impulse control relationship in groups of free-ranging rhesus monkeys living on an island off the coast of South Carolina. Along with primatologist Patrick Mehlman, Higley discovered that male monkeys with lots of fight scars had low serotonin function. Over a three-year period, these males turned out to be the guys who not only started fights but also readily jumped into everyone else's conflicts, and they typically were the ones involved in fights that escalated out of control.

"When monkeys raised without their mothers reach adolescence, they are happy to drink from a bottle that is laced with a winelike solution," Dee Higley says. Some monkeys will drink until they pass out.

Like the low-serotonin males in Higley's lab, the scarred males on the island appear to be social losers. They migrated to new groups much sooner than other males and spent most of their time alone. And they also ended up dead more often. Eleven migrating males died during Higley and Mehlman's study, and 10 of those 11 came from the low-serotonin group.

The free-ranging monkeys were never exposed to alcohol, but Higley is

confident that given the chance, the low-serotonin males would become classic type II alcoholics. "There is a certain impulsive quality about them," he says. "They leap from branch to branch rather than proceeding with caution, they threaten those higher in rank, with no chance of winning. They don't look at the consequences of their behavior."

The best childhood in the world won't necessarily make up for low serotonin activity

---

And the researchers can follow this pattern linking low serotonin and impulsive behavior over generations. "In the lab, we have a rhesus named Devil Monkey. He and his offspring tend to get in more fights, be loners in their social groups, and consume more alcohol," Higley says. Devil Monkey runs his group like a dictator and has a long history of aggression toward others. He has the lowest serotonin levels Higley has ever seen, and his offspring also have low levels.

In contrast, the members of a family headed by a congenial monkey named Redford are quite different. "All his offspring seem to be invulnerable to early negative experiences. Despite their social groups, they aren't anxious and don't get in many fights," says Higley. Members of the Redford clan tend to have normal or high levels of serotonin, and they don't drink as much.

But Higley's observations of monkeys in the lab also suggest that decent parenting can prevent some monkeys born with low levels of serotonin from being pushed toward alcohol. The key seems to be an early attachment to mom. "From attentive mothers, little monkeys get 'wait' signals, and they get discipline," says Higley. "Peer-reared monkeys don't get those stop signals; when peer groups have conflict, it's resolved by brute force. There are no mothers to regulate negotiation, so these monkeys don't know how to resolve social problems." Many of the peer-raised monkeys grow up to be drinkers.

Still, neither genes nor environment make the outcome certain. The best

childhood in the world won't necessarily make up for a genetic blueprint for low serotonin activity and a history of family alcoholism. And some monkeys with the genes for adequate serotonin activity might be buffered against an abnormal childhood, but that buffer goes only so far. When a less-vulnerable, mother-raised monkey is uprooted and left alone in a cage for several days, shaking her monkey world to the core, she's much more likely to drink until she has returned to the group.

JUST LIKE HUMANS, THE MONKEYS in Higley's study are set up by their genes and then rocked by experience. All the biological influences are presumably inherited, but so far no one can point to specific genes, or a single biological process, that accurately predicts alcoholism. In fact, most researchers who believe in the disease model say that genes can explain only half the risk. If half of the vulnerability is due to family upbringing and life experience, can chronic alcoholism really be called a disease?

Psychologist Stanton Peele suggests that we may have carried that model too far. At his Web site, and in various articles and books, Peele argues that no one has conclusively shown that there is a biological basis to alcoholism or any other addiction. Instead, Peele believes that personal and social expectations torque biological tendencies to such a degree that any study seeking to identify genetic underpinnings is suspect.

Look at what people do, he suggests. Not everyone who is anxious or impulsive is a problem drinker, and many people who are hard-core alcoholics stop drinking without treatment. There is data to back up that view. In 1992 the National Institute on Alcohol Abuse and Alcoholism interviewed 4,542 adults who at some time in their lives had been alcohol dependent according to diagnostic criteria used by the American Psychiatric Association. At the time of the study, 28 percent were still heavy drinkers, but 22 percent had given up alcohol and 50 percent drank in moderation. Therefore, roughly three-quarters of these people would no longer be considered alcoholics. Interestingly, those who were treated for alcohol abuse didn't fare any better on average than those who had no treatment.

"Natural remission is overwhelming in its importance," Peele says. "And yet it is systematically ignored by researchers." If alcoholism is a disease, how can so many people cure themselves?

Peele also points to the low rate of alcoholism and alcohol-related problems among Asians. Normally, alcohol is broken down by the enzyme alcohol dehydrogenase (ADH), which in turn produces acetaldehyde, a toxic compound that can cause high blood pressure, skin flushing, and vomiting. Most people get rid of acetaldehyde with another enzyme called aldehyde hydrogenase (ALDH2). But about 10 percent of Asians have a genetic variant of this enzyme that is inactive; as a result, they feel sick when they drink and rarely become alcoholics. Another 40 percent of the Asian population is heterozygous for this genetic variant; members of this group feel the high from alcohol faster than those with the more common form of the enzyme and tend to drink less.

Researchers have assumed that biology alone is at work here, but Peele wonders about those Asians who have the normal enzyme but also choose to drink in moderation or not at all. And he wonders why people would avoid alcohol just because it takes smaller quantities for them to feel the effects. Being biologically sensitive to alcohol has certainly not prevented other ethnic groups, such as Native Americans, from having alcohol problems.

Peele suggests that the difference may be cultural values, not biology. When cultures disdain drunkenness, those sanctions alone may be the more powerful preventative factor. "The [biological] theories can't make sense of the most obvious aspect of human addiction and self abuse—natural remission and value choices," he says. "Nonetheless, the researchers pursue them madly."

HIGLEY, OF COURSE, IS KEENLY aware of the social context of alcohol abuse. "You don't wake up with a set of genes as a new infant and end up an alcoholic," he says. "It's the interaction with the environment that's going to determine what you become."

Higley also speaks from personal experience, because alcoholism has touched his family. "My grandfather died of alcoholism," he says. "He literally froze to death in the snow in an alcoholic stupor. He died before I was even born, but there's no question that it had a tremendous impact on the family."

Watching monkeys, as well as charting his own relationship with alcohol, has convinced Higley of the curative power of family. He offers a simple explanation for why his genes did not push him down a path of alcohol abuse: "I grew up in Utah," he says, laughing. "I know nothing about alcohol. I'm a Mormon."

From *Discover*, July 2002, pp. 41-44. © 2002 by Meredith F. Small. Reprinted by permission of the author.

UNIT 2
Primates

Unit Selections

10. **What Are Friends For?**, Barbara Smuts
11. **Fossey in the Mist**, Robert M. Sapolsky
12. **The Mind of the Chimpanzee**, Jane Goodall
13. **Got Culture?**, Craig Stanford
14. **Dim Forest, Bright Chimps**, Christophe Boesch and Hedwige Boesch-Achermann
15. **Rethinking Primate Aggression**, Richard Conniff
16. **Disturbing Behaviors of the Orangutan**, Anne Nacey Maggioncalda and Robert M. Sapolsky
17. **Are We in Anthropodenial?**, Frans de Waal

Key Points to Consider

• Why is friendship important to olive baboons? What implications does this have for the origins of pair-bonding in hominid evolution?

• How is it possible to objectively study and assess emotional and mental states of nonhuman primates?

• What are the implications for human evolution of tool use, social hunting, and food sharing among Ivory Coast chimpanzees?

• Should chimpanzee behavioral patterns be classified as "cultural?"

• Are primates naturally aggressive?

• Why is the mountain gorilla in danger of extinction?

• Why is orangutan rape very different from human rape?

• Are we in anthropodenial? Explain your answer.

 **Links: www.dushkin.com/online/**
These sites are annotated in the World Wide Web pages.

African Primates at Home
http://www.indiana.edu/~primate/primates.html
Electronic Zoo/NetVet-Primate Page
http://netvet.wustl.edu/primates.htm
Laboratory Primate Newsletter
http://www.brown.edu/Research/Primate/other.html

Primates are fun. They are active, intelligent, colorful, emotionally expressive, and unpredictable. In other words, observing them is like holding up an opaque mirror to ourselves. The image may not be crystal-clear or, indeed, what some would consider flattering, but it is certainly familiar enough to be illuminating.

Primates are, of course, but one of many orders of mammals that adaptively radiated into the variety of ecological niches vacated at the end of the Age of Reptiles about 65 million years ago. Whereas some mammals took to the sea (cetaceans), and some took to the air (chiroptera, or bats), primates are characterized by an arboreal or forested adaptation. While some mammals can be identified by their food-getting habits, such as the meat-eating carnivores, primates have a penchant for eating almost anything and are best described as omnivorous. In taking to the trees, primates did not simply develop a full-blown set of distinguishing characteristics that set them off easily from other orders of mammals, the way the rodent order can be readily identified by its gnawing set of front teeth. Rather, each primate seems to represent degrees of anatomical, biological, and behavioral characteristics on a continuum of progress with respect to the particular traits we humans happen to be interested in.

None of this is meant to imply, of course, that the living primates are our ancestors. Since the prosimians, monkeys, and apes are our contemporaries, they are no more our ancestors than we are theirs, and, as living end-products of evolution, we have all descended from a common stock in the distant past. So, if we are interested primarily in our own evolutionary past, why study primates at all? Because, by the criteria we have set up as significant milestones in the evolution of humanity, an inherent reflection of our own bias, primates have not evolved as far as we have. They and their environments, therefore, may represent glimmerings of the evolutionary stages and ecological circumstances through which our own ancestors may have gone. What we stand to gain, for instance, is an educated guess as to how our own ancestors might have appeared and behaved as semi-erect creatures before becoming bipedal. Aside from being a pleasure to observe, then, living primates can teach us something about our past.

Another reason for studying primates is that they allow us to test certain notions too often taken for granted. For instance, Barbara Smuts, in "What Are Friends For?" reveals that friendship bonds, as illustrated by the olive baboons of East Africa, have little if anything to do with a sexual division of labor or even sexual exclusivity between a pair-bonded male and female. Smuts challenges the traditional male-oriented idea that primate societies are dominated solely by males for males.

This unit demonstrates that relationships between the sexes are subject to wide variation, that the answers obtained depend upon the questions asked, and that we have to be very careful in making inferences about human beings from any one particular primate study. We may, if we are not careful, draw conclusions that say more about our own skewed perspectives than about that which we claim to understand. See "Disturbing Behaviors of the Orangutan" for an example of this point. Still another benefit of primate field research is that it provides us with perspectives that the bones and stones of the fossil hunters will never reveal: a sense of the richness and variety of social patterns that must have existed in the primate order for many tens of millions of years. (See Robert Sapolsky's report, "Fossey in the Mist," and Jane Goodall's "The Mind of the Chimpanzee.")

Even if we had the physical remains of the earliest hominids in front of us, which we do not have, there is no way such evidence could thoroughly answer the questions that physical anthropologists care most deeply about: How did these creatures move about and get their food? Did they cooperate and share? On what levels did they think and communicate? Did they have a sense of family, let alone a sense of self? In one way or another, all of the previously mentioned articles on primates relate to these issues, as do some of the subsequent ones on the fossil evidence. But what sets off this unit from the others is how some of the authors attempt to deal with these matters head-on, even in the absence of direct fossil evidence. Christophe Boesch and Hedwige Boesch-Achermann, in "Dim Forest, Bright Chimps," indicate that some aspects of "hominization" (the acquisition of such humanlike qualities as cooperative hunting and food sharing) actually may have begun in the African rain forest rather than in the dry savanna, as has usually been proposed. They base their suggestions on some remarkable first-hand observations of forest-dwelling chimpanzees.

As he shows that chimpanzee behavior may vary according to local circumstances, just as we know human behavior does, Craig Stanford, in "Got Culture?" also makes a strong case for such differences to be classified as cultural.

Recent research has shown some striking resemblances between apes and humans, hinting that such qualities might have been characteristic of our common ancestor. Following this line of reasoning, Frans de Waal (in "Rethinking Primate Aggression" and "Are We in Anthropodenial?") argues that we can make educated guesses as to the mental and physical processes of our hominid predecessors.

Taken collectively, the articles in this section show how far anthropologists are willing to go to construct theoretical formulations based upon limited data. Although making so much out of so little may be seen as a fault and may generate irreconcilable differences among theorists, a readiness to entertain new ideas should be welcomed for what it is—a stimulus for more intensive and meticulous research.

What Are Friends For?

Among East African baboons, friendship means companions, health, safety...
and, sometimes, sex

Barbara Smuts

Virgil, a burly adult male olive baboon, closely followed Zizi, a middle-aged female easily distinguished by her grizzled coat and square muzzle. On her rump Zizi sported a bright pink swelling, indicating that she was sexually receptive and probably fertile. Virgil's extreme attentiveness to Zizi suggested to me—and all rival males in the troop—that he was her current and exclusive mate.

Zizi, however, apparently had something else in mind. She broke away from Virgil, moved rapidly through the troop, and presented her alluring sexual swelling to one male after another. Before Virgil caught up with her, she had managed to announce her receptive condition to several of his rivals. When Virgil tried to grab her, Zizi screamed and dashed into the bushes with Virgil in hot pursuit. I heard sounds of chasing and fighting coming from the thicket. Moments later Zizi emerged from the bushes with an older male named Cyclops. They remained together for several days, copulating often. In Cyclops's presence, Zizi no longer approached or even glanced at other males.

Primatologists describe Zizi and other olive baboons (*Papio cynocephalus anubis*) as promiscuous, meaning that both males and females usually mate with several members of the opposite sex within a short period of time. Promiscuous mating behavior characterizes many of the larger, more familiar primates, including chimpanzees, rhesus macaques, and gray langurs, as well as olive, yellow, and chacma baboons, the three subspecies of savanna baboon. In colloquial usage, promiscuity often connotes wanton and random sex, and several early studies of primates supported this stereotype. However, after years of laboriously recording thousands of copulations under natural conditions, the Peeping Toms of primate fieldwork have shown that, even in promiscuous species, sexual pairings are far from random.

Some adult males, for example, typically copulate much more often than others. Primatologists have explained these differences in terms of competition: the most dominant males monopolize females and prevent lower-ranking rivals from mating. But exceptions are frequent. Among baboons, the exceptions often involve scruffy, older males who mate in full view of younger, more dominant rivals.

A clue to the reason for these puzzling exceptions emerged when primatologists began to question an implicit assumption of the dominance hypothesis—that females were merely passive objects of male competition. But what if females were active arbiters in this system? If females preferred some males over others and were able to express these preferences, then models of mating activity based on male dominance alone would be far too simple.

Once researchers recognized the possibility of female choice, evidence for it turned up in species after species. The story of Zizi, Virgil, and Cyclops is one of hundreds of examples of female primates rejecting the sexual advances of particular males and enthusiastically cooperating with others. But what is the basis for female choice? Why might they prefer some males over others?

This question guided my research on the Eburru Cliffs troop of olive baboons, named after one of their favorite sleeping sites, a sheer rocky outcrop rising several hundred feet above the floor of the Great Rift Valley, about 100 miles northwest of Nairobi, Kenya. The 120 members of Eburru Cliffs spent their days wandering through open grassland studded with occasional acacia thorn trees. Each night they retired to one of a dozen sets of cliffs that provided protection from nocturnal predators such as leopards.

Most previous studies of baboon sexuality had focused on females who, like Zizi, were at the peak of sexual receptivity. A female baboon does not mate when she is pregnant or lactating, a period of abstinence lasting about eighteen months. The female then goes into estrus, and for about two weeks out of every thirty-five-day cycle, she mates. Toward the end of this two-week period she may ovulate, but usually the female undergoes four or five estrous cycles before she conceives. During pregnancy, she once again resumes a chaste existence. As a result, the typical female baboon is sexually active for less than 10 percent of her adult life. I thought that by focusing on the other 90 percent, I might learn something new. In particular, I suspected that routine, day-to-day relationships between males and pregnant or lactating (nonestrous) females might provide clues to female mating preferences.

Nearly every day for sixteen months, I joined the Eburru Cliffs baboons at their sleeping cliffs at dawn and traveled several miles with them while they foraged for roots, seeds, grass, and occasionally, small prey items, such as baby gazelles or hares (see "Predatory Baboons of Kekopey," *Natural History*, March 1976). Like all savanna baboon troops, Eburru Cliffs functioned as a cohesive unit organized around a core of related females, all of whom were born in the troop. Unlike the females, male savanna baboons leave their natal troop to join another where they may remain for many years, so most of the Eburru Cliffs adult males were immigrants. Since membership in the troop remained relatively constant during the period of my study, I learned to identify each individual. I relied on differences in size, posture, gait, and especially, facial features. To the practiced observer, baboons look as different from one another as human beings do.

As soon as I could recognize individuals, I noticed that particular females tended to turn up near particular males again and again. I came to think of these pairs as friends. Friendship among animals is not a well-documented phenomenon, so to convince skeptical colleagues that baboon friendship was real, I needed to develop objective criteria for distinguishing friendly pairs.

I began by investigating grooming, the amiable simian habit of picking through a companion's fur to remove dead skin and ectoparasites (see "Little Things That Tick Off Baboons," *Natural History*, February 1984). Baboons spend much more time grooming than is necessary for hygiene, and previous research had indicated that it is a good measure of social bonds.

Although eighteen adult males lived in the troop, each nonestrous female performed most of her grooming with just one, two, or occasionally three males. For example, of Zizi's twenty-four grooming bouts with males, Cyclops accounted for thirteen, and a second male, Sherlock, accounted for all the rest. Different females tended to favor different males as grooming partners.

Another measure of social bonds was simply who was observed near whom. When foraging, traveling, or resting, each pregnant or lactating female spent a lot of time near a few males and associated with the others no more often than expected by chance. When I compared the identities of favorite grooming partners and frequent companions, they overlapped almost completely. This enabled me to develop a formal definition of friendship: any male that scored high on both grooming and proximity measures was considered a friend.

Virtually all baboons made friends; only one female and three males who had most recently joined the troop lacked such companions. Out of more than 600 possible adult female-adult male pairs in the troop, however, only about one in ten qualified as friends; these really were special relationships.

Several factors seemed to influence which baboons paired up. In most cases, friends were unrelated to each other, since the male had immigrated from another troop. (Four friendships, however, involved a female and an adolescent son who had not yet emigrated. Unlike other friends, these related pairs never mated.) Older females tended to be friends with older males; younger females with younger males. I witnessed occasional May–December romances, usually involving older females and young adult males. Adolescent males and females were strongly rule-bound, and with the exception of mother-son pairs, they formed friendships only with one another.

Regardless of age or dominance rank, most females had just one or two male friends. But among males, the number of female friends varied greatly from none to eight. Although high-ranking males enjoyed priority of access to food and sometimes mates, dominant males did not have more female friends than low-ranking males. Instead it was the older males who had lived in the troop for many years who had the most friends. When a male had several female friends, the females were often closely related to one another. Since female baboons spend a lot of time near their kin, it is probably easier for a male to maintain bonds with several related females at once.

When collecting data, I focused on one nonestrous female at a time and kept track of her every movement toward or away from any male; similarly, I noted every male who moved toward or away from her. Whenever the female and male moved close enough to exchange intimacies, I wrote down exactly what happened. When foraging together, friends tended to remain a few yards apart. Males more often wandered away from females than the reverse, and females, more often than males, closed the gap. The female behaved as if she wanted to keep the male within calling distance, in case she needed his protection. The male, however, was more likely to make approaches that brought them within actual touching distance. Often, he would plunk himself down right next to his friend and ask her to groom him by holding a pose with exaggerated stillness. The female sometimes responded by grooming, but more often, she exhibited the most reliable sign of true intimacy: she ignored her friend and simply continued whatever she was doing.

In sharp contrast, when a male who was not a friend moved close to a female, she dared not ignore him. She stopped whatever she was doing and held still, often glancing surreptitiously at the intruder. If he did not move away, she sometimes lifted her tail and presented her rump. When a female is not in estrus, this is a gesture of appeasement, not sexual enticement. Immediately after this respectful acknowledgement of his presence, the female would slip away. But such tense interactions with nonfriend males were rare, because females usually moved away before the males came too close.

These observations suggest that females were afraid of most of the males in their troop, which is not surprising: male baboons are twice the size of females, and their canines are longer and sharper than those of a lion. All Eburru Cliffs males directed both mild and severe aggression toward females. Mild aggression, which usually involved threats and chases but no body contact, occurred most often during feeding competition or when the male redirected aggression toward a female after losing a fight with another male. Females and juveniles showed aggression toward other females and juveniles in similar circumstances and occasionally inflicted superficial wounds. Severe aggression by males, which involved body contact and sometimes biting, was less common and also more puzzling, since there was no apparent cause.

An explanation for at least some of these attacks emerged one day when I was watching Pegasus, a young adult male, and his friend Cicily, sitting together in the middle of a small clearing. Cicily moved to the edge of the clearing to feed, and a higher-ranking female, Zora, suddenly attacked her. Pegasus stood up and looked as if he were about to intervene when both females disappeared into the bushes. He sat back down, and I remained with him. A full ten minutes later, Zora appeared at the edge of the clearing; this was the first time she had come into view since her attack on Cicily. Pegasus instantly pounced on Zora, repeatedly grabbed her neck in his mouth and lifted her off the ground, shook her whole body, and then dropped her. Zora screamed continuously and tried to escape. Each time, Pegasus caught her and continued his brutal attack. When hc finally released her five minutes later she had a deep canine gash on the palm of her hand that made her limp for several days.

This attack was similar in form and intensity to those I had seen before and labeled "unprovoked." Certainly, had I come upon the scene after Zora's aggression toward Cicily, I would not have understood why Pegasus attacked Zora. This suggested that some, perhaps many, severe attacks by males actually represented punishment for actions that had occurred some time before.

Whatever the reasons for male attacks on females, they represent a serious threat. Records of fresh injuries indicated that Eburru Cliffs adult females received canine slash wounds from males at the rate of one for every female each year, and during my study, one female died of her injuries. Males probably pose an even greater threat to infants. Although only one infant was killed during my study, observers in Botswana and

Tanzania have seen recent male immigrants kill several young infants.

Protection from male aggression, and from the less injurious but more frequent aggression of other females and juveniles, seems to be one of the main advantages of friendship for a female baboon. Seventy times I observed an adult male defend a female or her offspring against aggression by another troop member, not infrequently a high-ranking male. In all but six of these cases, the defender was a friend. Very few of these confrontations involved actual fighting; no male baboon, subordinate or dominant, is anxious to risk injury by the sharp canines of another.

Males are particularly solicitous guardians of their friends' youngest infants. If another male gets too close to an infant or if a juvenile female plays with it too roughly, the friend may intervene. Other troop members soon learn to be cautious when the mother's friend is nearby, and his presence provides the mother with a welcome respite from the annoying pokes and prods of curious females and juveniles obsessed with the new baby. Male baboons at Gombe Park in Tanzania and Amboseli Park in Kenya have also been seen rescuing infants from chimpanzees and lions. These several forms of male protection help to explain why females in Eburru Cliffs stuck closer to their friends in the first few months after giving birth than at any other time.

The male-infant relationship develops out of the male's friendship with the mother, but as the infant matures, this new bond takes on a life of its own. My co-worker Nancy Nicolson found that by about nine months of age, infants actively sought out their male friends when the mother was a few yards away, suggesting that the male may function as an alternative caregiver. This seemed to be especially true for infants undergoing unusually early or severe weaning. (Weaning is generally a gradual, prolonged process, but there is tremendous variation among mothers in the timing and intensity of weaning. See "Mother Baboons," *Natural History*, September 1980). After being rejected by the mother, the crying infant often approached the male friend and sat huddled

against him until its whimpers subsided. Two of the infants in Eburru Cliffs lost their mothers when they were still quite young. In each case, their bond with the mother's friend subsequently intensified, and—perhaps as a result—both infants survived.

A close bond with a male may also improve the infant's nutrition. Larger than all other troop members, adult males monopolize the best feeding sites. In general, the personal space surrounding a feeding male is inviolate, but he usually tolerates intrusions by the infants of his female friends, giving them access to choice feeding spots.

Although infants follow their male friends around rather than the reverse, the males seem genuinely attached to their tiny companions. During feeding, the male and infant express their pleasure in each other's company by sharing spirited, antiphonal grunting duets. If the infant whimpers in distress, the male friend is likely to cease feeding, look at the infant, and grunt softly, as if in sympathy, until the whimpers cease. When the male rests, the infants of his female friends may huddle behind him, one after the other, forming a "train," or, if feeling energetic, they may use his body as a trampoline.

When I returned to Eburru Cliffs four years after my initial study ended, several of the bonds formed between males and the infants of their female friends were still intact (in other cases, either the male or the infant or both had disappeared). When these bonds involved recently matured females, their long-time male associates showed no sexual interest in them, even though the females mated with other adult males. Mothers and sons, and usually maternal siblings, show similar sexual inhibitions in baboons and many other primate species.

The development of an intimate relationship between a male and the infant of his female friend raises an obvious question: Is the male the infant's father? To answer this question definitely we would need to conduct genetic analysis, which was not possible for these baboons. Instead, I estimated paternity probabilities from observations of the temporary (a few hours or days) exclusive mating relationships, or consortships, that estrous females form with a series of different males. These estimates were apt to be fairly accurate, since changes in the female's sexual swelling allow one to pinpoint the timing of conception to within a few days. Most females consorted with only two or three males during this period, and these males were termed likely fathers.

In about half the friendships, the male was indeed likely to be the father of his friend's most recent infant, but in the other half he was not—in fact, he had never been seen mating with the female. Interestingly, males who were friends with the mother but not likely fathers nearly always developed a relationship with her infant, while males who had mated with the female but were not her friend usually did not. Thus friendship with the mother, rather than paternity, seems to mediate the development of male-infant bonds. Recently, a similar pattern was documented for South American capuchin monkeys in a laboratory study in which paternity was determined genetically.

These results fly in the face of a prominent theory that claims males will invest in infants only when they are closely related. If males are not fostering the survival of their own genes by caring for the infant, then why do they do so? I suspected that the key was female choice. If females preferred to mate with males who had already demonstrated friendly behavior, then friendships with mothers and their infants might pay off in the future when the mothers were ready to mate again.

To find out if this was the case, I examined each male's sexual behavior with females he had befriended before they resumed estrus. In most cases, males consorted considerably more often with their friends than with other females. Baboon females typically mate with several different males, including both friends and nonfriends, but prior friendship increased a male's probability of mating with a female above what it would have been otherwise.

This increased probability seemed to reflect female preferences. Females occasionally overtly advertised their disdain for certain males and their desire for others. Zizi's behavior, described above,

is a good example. Virgil was not one of her friends, but Cyclops was. Usually, however, females expressed preferences and aversions more subtly. For example, Delphi, a petite adolescent female, found herself pursued by Hector, a middle-aged adult male. She did not run away or refuse to mate with him, but whenever he wasn't watching, she looked around for her friend Homer, an adolescent male. When she succeeded in catching Homer's eye, she narrowed her eyes and flattened her ears against her skull, the friendliest face one baboon can send another. This told Homer she would rather be with him. Females expressed satisfaction with a current consort partner by staying close to him, initiating copulations, and not making advances toward other males. Baboons are very sensitive to such cues, as indicated by an experimental study in which rival hamadryas baboons rarely challenged a male-female pair if the female strongly preferred her current partner. Similarly, in Eburru Cliffs, males were less apt to challenge consorts involving a pair that shared a long-term friendship.

Even though females usually consorted with their friends, they also mated with other males, so it is not surprising that friendships were most vulnerable during periods of sexual activity. In a few cases, the female consorted with another male more often than with her friend, but the friendship survived nevertheless. One female, however, formed a strong sexual bond with a new male. This bond persisted after conception, replacing her previous friendship. My observations suggest that adolescent and young adult females tend to have shorter, less stable friendships than do older females. Some friendships, however, last a very long time. When I returned to Eburru Cliffs six years after my study began, five couples were still together. It is possible that friendships occasionally last for life (baboons probably live twenty to thirty years in the wild), but it will require longer studies, and some very patient scientists to find out.

By increasing both the male's chances of mating in the future and the likelihood that a female's infant will survive, friendship contributes to the reproductive success of both partners. This

clarifies the evolutionary basis of friendship-forming tendencies in baboons, but what does friendship mean to a baboon? To answer this question we need to view baboons as sentient beings with feelings and goals not unlike our own in similar circumstances. Consider, for example, the friendship between Thalia and Alexander.

The affair began one evening as Alex and Thalia sat about fifteen feet apart on the sleeping cliffs. It was like watching two novices in a singles bar. Alex stared at Thalia until she turned and almost caught him looking at her. He glanced away immediately, and then she stared at him until his head began to turn toward her. She suddenly became engrossed in grooming her toes. But as soon as Alex looked away, her gaze returned to him. They went on like this for more than fifteen minutes, always with split-second timing. Finally, Alex managed to catch Thalia looking at him. He made the friendly eyes-narrowed, ears-back face and smacked his lips together rhythmically. Thalia froze, and for a second she looked into his eyes. Alex approached, and Thalia, still nervous, groomed him. Soon she calmed down, and I found them still together on the cliffs the next morning. Looking back on this event months later, I realized that it marked the beginning of their friendship. Six years later, when I returned to Eburru Cliffs, they were still friends.

If flirtation forms an integral part of baboon friendship, so does jealousy. Overt displays of jealousy, such as chasing a friend away from a potential rival, occur occasionally, but like humans, baboons often express their emotions in more subtle ways. One evening a colleague and I climbed the cliffs and settled down near Sherlock, who was friends with Cybelle, a middle-aged female still foraging on the ground below the cliffs. I observed Cybelle while my colleague watched Sherlock, and we kept up a running commentary. As long as Cybelle was feeding or interacting with females, Sherlock was relaxed, but each time she approached another male, his body would stiffen, and he would stare intently at the scene below. When Cybelle presented politely to a male who had recently tried to befriend her, Sherlock even made threatening sounds under his breath. Cybelle was not in estrus at the time, indicating that male baboon jealousy extends beyond the sexual arena to include affiliative interactions between a female friend and other males.

Because baboon friendships are embedded in a network of friendly and antagonistic relationships, they inevitably lead to repercussions extending beyond the pair. For example, Virgil once provoked his weaker rival Cyclops into a fight by first attacking Cyclops's friend Phoebe. On another occasion, Sherlock chased Circe, Hector's best friend, just after Hector had chased Antigone, Sherlock's friend.

In another incident, the prime adult male Triton challenged Cyclops's possession of meat. Cyclops grew increasingly tense and seemed about to abandon the prey to the younger male. Then Cyclops's friend Phoebe appeared with her infant Phyllis. Phyllis wandered over to Cyclops. He immediately grabbed her, held her close, and threatened Triton away from the prey. Because any challenge to Cyclops now involved a threat to Phyllis as well, Triton risked being mobbed by Phoebe and her relatives and friends. For this reason, he backed down. Males frequently use the infants of their female friends as buffers in this way. Thus, friendship involves costs as well as benefits because it makes the participants vulnerable to social manipulation or redirected aggression by others.

Finally, as with humans, friendship seems to mean something different to each baboon. Several females in Eburru Cliffs had only one friend. They were devoted companions. Louise and Pandora, for example, groomed their friend Virgil and no other male. Then there was Leda, who, with five friends, spread herself more thinly than any other female. These contrasting patterns of friendship were associated with striking personality differences. Louise and Pandora were unobtrusive females who hung around quietly with Virgil and their close relatives. Leda seemed to be everywhere at once, playing with infants, fighting with juveniles, and making friends with males. Similar differences were apparent among the males. Some devoted a great deal of time and energy to cultivating friendships with females, while others focused more on challenging other males. Although we probably will never fully understand the basis of these individual differences, they contribute immeasurably to the richness and complexity of baboon society.

Male-female friendships may be widespread among primates. They have been reported for many other groups of savanna baboons, and they also occur in rhesus and Japanese Macaques, capuchin monkeys, and perhaps in bonobos (pygmy chimpanzees). These relationships should give us pause when considering popular scenarios for the evolution of male-female relationships in humans. Most of these scenarios assume that, except for mating, males and females had little to do with one another until the development of a sexual division of labor, when, the story goes, females began to rely on males to provide meat in exchange for gathered food. This, it has been argued, set up new selection pressures favoring the development of long-term bonds between individual males and females, female sexual fidelity, and as paternity certainty increased, greater male investment in the offspring of these unions. In other words, once women began to gather and men to hunt, presto—we had the nuclear family.

This scenario may have more to do with cultural biases about women's economic dependence on men and idealized views of the nuclear family than with the actual behavior of our hominid ancestors. The nonhuman primate evidence challenges this story in at least three ways.

First, long-term bonds between the sexes can evolve in the absence of a sexual division of labor of food sharing. In our primate relatives, such relationships rest on exchanges of social, not economic, benefits.

Second, primate research shows that highly differentiated, emotionally intense male-female relationships can occur without sexual exclusivity. Ancestral men and women may have experienced intimate friendships long before they invented marriage and norms of sexual fidelity.

Third, among our closest primate relatives, males clearly provide mothers and infants with social benefits even when they are unlikely to be the fathers of those infants. In return, females provide a variety of benefits to the friendly males, including acceptance into the group and, at least in baboons, increased mating opportunities in the future. This suggests that efforts to reconstruct the evolution of hominid societies may have overemphasized what the female must supposedly do (restrict her mating to just one male) in order to obtain male parental investment.

Maybe it is time to pay more attention to what the male must do (provide benefits to females and young) in order to obtain female cooperation. Perhaps among our ancestors, as in baboons today, sex and friendship went hand in hand. As for marriage—well, that's another story.

Fossey in the Mist

'MY WORK IN THE BUSH AS A PRIMATOLOGIST ALWAYS makes me think of someone whose unlikely job would be to collect snowflakes, then rush into a warm room and observe their unique patterns under a microscope before they melt and are never seen again. This is an account of my time of Africa's Mt. Karisimbi, where the snowflakes are the rarest and nearest to melting....'

By Robert M. Sapolsky

OH, WHAT NEW CAN I SAY ABOUT Dian Fossey? She's been featured in in books, enshrined in the movies. She was clearly the stuff of legend. She was a large, imposing, awkward woman who looked not one bit like Sigourney Weaver, who played her in the 1988 film *Gorillas in the Mist*. By chance, the mother of a member of my lab at Stanford University went to high school with Fossey in the late 1940s; she related that Fossey was already difficult, withdrawn, marked. I saw Fossey's yearbook photo. At age 17, she had the hunted, unhappy look of the high-school weirdo destined to become either a reclusive field biologist or a serial murderer.

At a relatively late age, Fossey fell in love with the ideas of Africa and of the mountain gorilla—the largest and last-discovered great ape by Western man, studied in the field only once, cloaked in legend and misconception. Without any formal training, she make up her mind to go to Africa and live with them. In 1963, she encountered Louis Leakey, the famed paleontologist and sponsor of female primatologists, and convinced him to send her to the rain forest of the Virunga mountains to study the gorillas for a short stretch. She stayed on for decades.

She immersed herself utterly in the gorillas, broke all the objective rules about not touching them, not interacting with them, and managed to observe astounding things about their behavior. In the process, she became more reclusive, more difficult, drove away possible collaborators and colleagues. She did little science of note beyond observing amazing things by sheer dint of her persistence, was openly contemptuous of most scientists doing fieldwork, and clearly wanted little more than to be a gorilla herself. I could understand the last. As a child, something primal had clicked in me the first time I stood before the mountain gorilla diorama at the American Museum of Natural History in New York City, and I had set on a path to become a primatologist.

Fossey fought with the poachers and the tribesmen, and the rangers who led the tourists that she loathed

---

I met Fossey once, as an undergrad at Harvard, in the mid-1970s. Gorillas resonated emotionally with me in an extraordinary way (although eventually I would study baboons), and Fossey was one of the humans I most admired. I thought I would swoon with pleasure at meeting her.

Fossey was in Cambridge against her will, forced by her funding sources to act like a proper citizen of the scientific community. It was an evening seminar in the living room of the senior primatology professor, and it was jammed. Quickly, one had the sickened, guilty, voyeuristic sense of watching a bear forced to perform in some medieval circus. She sat with her knees drawn up to her chest, and then suddenly burst out, pacing back and forth in front of the room, bent so that her hands hung near her knees. She mostly talked to herself, in a monotone, and nearly yelled at people when they asked questions. Once, she did yell. One professor had his young kid sitting on his lap, the kid making occasional sounds typical of a four-year-old, and suddenly Fossey stopped, pointed, and said "Child, shut thy mouth or I will shut it for you."

I was mesmerized and more than a little bit horrified. Afterward, I went up to her and asked the question I had been preparing since I was 10: Could I go to Rwanda as her research assistant and devote my life to the gorillas? She scowled at me, said yes, and told me to write to her. I returned to my dorm in a transcendent euphoria and sent her that letter by midnight. She never answered. I later learned that this was her standard way of dealing with the acolytes and petitioners; say yes to anything, tell them to write, never answer.

Soon after that, her difficulties began. The rain forest of Rwanda were inhabited by Batwa tribesmen, hunter-gatherers who lived by catching forest bucks with snares, Inevitably, a gorilla would

step on a snare now and then and be trapped. Gangrene, death. The best evidence indicates that these first deaths were accidental. Fossey freaked. She began to fight the tribesmen, destroying their snares, their source of food. And they began to fight back. Soon they were killing her gorillas intentionally, dumping their decapitated bodies on the path to her cabin, high up in the volcanoes, while she, in turn, kidnapped those tribesmen's children.

Fossey, in a turnaround, became extroverted. She ran around the world lecturing about the killings of her animals and demanding help. She opened the field site to students, collaborators—so long as they would fight the gorilla killers. Before long, there was a split in the conservation community. Some said, yes, let's pour money in there, but not to her. She is too inflammatory, too provocative. Get her out of there, and pour money into the dirt-poor Rwandan game park service to get some rangers up there, armed, to make the place a real wildlife preserve. The other half said, give her money, give her guns. If there are going to be any gorillas surviving, it will be because of her. Who else cares?

The former group prevailed. Money poured into the Digit Fund, named for her most beloved animal, whose butchered body was left for her to find. A real, functioning, protective park service was established. Enough interest was gener-

ated to start gorilla-watching tourism that has continued to fund the park and the local economy. The gorillas started to do better, perhaps increasing in numbers.

And Fossey was sent away. Some sort of visiting adjunct professorship was rigged up for her at Cornell, where, by most reports, she sank into depression and alcoholism.

Against everyone's pleading, she returned to Rwanda and her gorillas. She fought with the poachers, with the rangers who led the tourists that she loathed, with the agricultural tribesmen whose slash-and-burning was decimating the remnants of the rain forest, fought with the government. Her health was destroyed by drinking, chain-smoking and emphysema, and by trying to live in humid, high-altitude conditions. She could barely walk, had to be carried up to her cabin. That's where she was murdered one night in late December 1985. The government lamely and unconvincingly blamed an American grad student and condemned him to death in absentia after making sure he had left the country, and everyone felt sure it was poachers or government rangers.

The funeral service was held near her cabin, a week after Christmas, and was conducted by a missionary who said, "Last week the world did honor to a long-ago event that changed its history.... the coming of the Lord to Earth.... We see at our feet here a parable of that magnifi-

cent condescension—Dian Fossey, born to a home of comfort and privilege that she left by her own choice to live among a race facing extinction.... And if you think that the distance Christ had to come to take the likeness of man is not so great as that from man to gorilla, then you don't know men. Or gorillas. Or God." And, as per her wish, she was buried in the graveyard of her slain gorillas, next to Digit.

NINE MONTHS AFTER FOSSEY'S murder I flew with two friends from Kenya, where I had been studying baboons for eight years, to Kigali, Rwanda's capital. It was a country of staggering population density. As we headed toward the gorillas, we passed endless hills with endless terraces and endless farms, every inch under cultivation, up to the very west, the very last edge of the country. There, forming the border between Zaire (now the Democratic Republic of the Congo) to the west and Uganda to the east, are the Ruwenzoris, the famed Mountains of the Moon, which are followed to the south by the Virungas, a ribbon of mammoth volcanoes between Congo and Rwanda. The peaks there rise up more than 14,000 feet, rugged, jutting, one after another after another, snow on top spilling into the Congo, wild rain forest below. And because they are too steep for even the desperate farmers to try to squeeze food out of, on the saddles and slopes survive the last mountain gorillas on Earth.

We splurged and stayed in the only real hotel in Ruhengeri, the town at the entrance to the park. It was ramshackle old jobbie, dripping with colonial nostalgia. We slept fitfully, feeling the volcanoes hovering over us, and were agitatedly ready by dawn. We hiked up with park rangers, the men who find the gorilla groups each day for the 18 tourists allowed in to see the three groups on display. The rangers were silent men who moved with smooth, frictionless gestures.

We set off through the farm fields, already angled steeply where they weren't terraced, weaving our way through huts and rows of corn until we reached a wall of bamboo with a slight forest path through it. We plunged in, winding up steep unstable slopes thick with bamboo and moss-covered hagenia trees that have always looked silly to me unless they are shrouded in mist. Higher, onto a saddle of one of the volcanoes, a view of forest ahead of us, a small lake, fields of bushes. Onward, the rangers macheteing a way through fields of stinging nettles. Clouds and mist and chills and heat, somehow all simultaneously. Sweating and shivering. Sliding down a deep ravine, clambering the way back up to other side, more nettles, more bamboo.

A few hours had passed yet the rangers continued their silent, coordinated movement. One would examine some broken bamboo shoots, another would sniff the flattened grass around there. Gorillas, but from yesterday, they concluded. Another hour. Misty rain, but somehow warmer. More nettles. Something resembling a real path and a flattened clump of grass to the left of it. Large, fibrous, shredded turds in the middle, the type you would expect from a pro football player gone vegetarian. The gorilla. Fresh, late night's nest.

Pushing ahead, tired and excited and impatient. Down another ravine, and one of the rangers hears a murmur up the other side. We stopped, silent, willing to invent the sound to convince ourselves that they were close, and suddenly, we heard the unmistakable murmur, deep, throaty, slow-motion, paternal. We rushed, tiptoed up the other side, and, on top of the ridge, I saw my first wild mountain gorillas.

When tribesmen's snares accidentally killed some gorillas, Fossey freaked and began destroying the traps. Soon the hunters were killing gorillas intentionally, dumping the bodies near her cabin. She in turn kidnapped their children

---

It was a group of perhaps a dozen. A prime-aged male—a silverback. Some females with infants, a few lurking younger males, some adolescents. The silverback played with the kids. The mothers fed, lumbering about with the infants carried dorsal. The two young males spent most of an hour wrestling, rolling around with each other, mouthing each other in restrained bites. They'd pant as they rolled and tickled each other, get exhausted from the excitement, and have to retreat to separate corners to catch their breaths. Refreshed, one would pound its chest and they'd launch themselves at each other again. At one point, both ambled over to sit next to me and stare, one leaning in so close that the rangers forced me to lean back. They had a comforting, musty, damp smell to them, like opening a trunk from the mildewed corners of a cellar that contains forgotten beloved objects.

I had a flood of thoughts and feelings. At the first sight, I thought, "Now my eyes will well up with tears," but I was too intent on watching for that to happen. I wondered what my social rank would be if I had wound up a mountain gorilla. I was mesmerized by their eyes; their faces seemed less emotionally expressive than those of chimps or even baboons, but their eyes, you wanted to go swimming in. I tried not to make eye contact, not only because it's bad field technique and discomforts primates, but because the act would make me want to confess to unlikely crimes. I found myself with the barely controllable urge to scream, or to gibber dangerously among them, or to rudely kiss one, so that they would stomp me to death then and there and stop my suspense.

That night, sleeping in my tent on the mountain's slopes, I had a dream that summarized my feelings far better than I could when awake. It was a dream so tender, so ludicrously sentimental, so full of beliefs that I do not have when awake, that I still marvel at it. I dreamt that God and angels and seraphs and devils all existed, in a very literal way, each with potential strengths and frailties much like our own. And I dreamt that the rain forests of the Mountains of the Moon were where God placed the occasional angel born with Down syndrome.

MY FRIENDS LEFT THE NEXT DAY. I stayed another week, going back to the gorillas repeatedly. It was heaven, but with each day, I felt more depressed. The gorillas were wondrous, but the weight of what was gone, removed, unmentioned, unanswered, irrevocable, became heavier. I felt it in the park headquarters, where the posters on the park's history made more mention of 19th-century Belgian colonials than of Fossey. With the rangers, who would say, yes, we knew Fossey, and then change the subject. With the gorillas, where you would watch a mother hold her child and nibble at bamboo, and all the while hear the farmers, their chickens, the school kids, 200 yards down the slope, where the slash-and-burning had finally stopped. On the miles and miles of empty rain forests paths aching with no more gorillas. And finally, from atop the nearly 15,000-foot Mt. Karisimbi, the highest point in the range, where I climbed to peer down and discover that the massive, endless, magisterial, mythic Virungas were nearly gone, a tiny narrow ribbon of forest engulfed by the infinity of terraces spreading from Rwanda to Uganda.

It was on top of that mountain that the week finally got to me and I had a night of African paranoia. You weren't allowed to hike alone in the range. Instead, a ranger had to be hired as a guide. Hauling to the top of the highest volcano around was clearly not their idea of fun, and the most junior of the rangers was given the task. From previous days of hanging around the rangers, I had noticed him and already had a dislike for him; even the other rangers seemed to ostracize him. He was a sullen, sloe-eyed kid, with a face like a mask and a tense air of violence about him. He mostly sat off on the side of the camp and seemed to get into a lot of monosyllabic arguments when he did interact.

As we started hiking, my dislike for my guide began to build. I could elicit nothing more than grunts out of him, as I tried in French, Swahili, English, my 20 words of Kirwanda. I slipped and fell on a wet rock at one point, and he laughed; it had a sneering, dismissive whine to it. Once, he flung stones at grazing forest bucks, probably both to hurt them and to deprive me of the view.

Our dislike for each other simmered. Somehow, these mutual feelings evolved, wordlessly, into competition. We began to hike faster, moving more relentlessly, until we were racing up the mountain, seeing who would first ask to rest. We pushed harder and harder, through the rain forest, montane forest, patchy woodland, open moorland where we sank to our knees in mud, to stark open rock with patches of frost, from 7,000 to 14,000 feet. The air got thinner, I felt an edge of altitude sickness, my vision got blurry, my chest throbbed. He climbed these mountains for a living, and I had the heavier pack, but sheer anger let me keep pace with him. "*Fatigué?*" he would ask in French and I would gasp, "*Non.*" Once, he spoke his longest pronouncement: "*Je pense tu es fatigué. Tu es mzee* [Swahili for old man]." I nearly sprinted after him, hoping to kill him. At one triumphant point, I got ahead for a minute, and was able to whisper the same breathless "*Fatigué?*" to him, while he gasped, "*Non.*"

We reached our goal, a corrugated metal shelter near the rim of the crater, just as an ice storm let loose. We lay in there, gasping, as the storm closed in and

pounded on the metal. And there we stayed, from mid-afternoon until the next morning. We ate a bit, rice and French bread, but everything tends to taste sickening at that altitude. Your eyes throb, your head hurts constantly, your chest aches with each breath. At that altitude, my resting heart rate is usually about 110, which means you wake from presumably relaxing sleep already feeling like you've been climbing stairs.

We lay on the wooden floor, as far away from each other as the small shelter would allow. I tried to play the recorder, but didn't have the breath; instead, I mostly thought about gorillas. He muttered to himself and scraped his name, *Bonaventre*, into the metal with his machete, all the while smoking in our closed hut at 14,000 feet.

So the hours passed, until sometime around nightfall, as I still lay there with my eyeballs throbbing, it occurred to me for the first time to become afraid. Fossey was murdered just nine months before on this mountain. Not only was it probably a ranger who did it (I had now decided), but it was probably this kid with the very same machete he was now holding. And tonight was almost certainly my night to get it. I was suddenly terribly frightened, near to panic. I desperately wanted to escape. I struggled to control my breathing, thought to cry out for help. I lay awake most of the night, with my pocketknife opened at my side, and truly thought I was going to die. The ranger, meanwhile, spent the night talking in his sleep—mutterings, and harsh muffled barks.

At dawn, I felt foolish and angry and relieved and lucky. We struggled up the ice-coated rocks and were at the summit by 7:00. He sat, looked impatient, and kicked at rocks. I looked out over Rwanda, Uganda, Zaire, and tried to imagine that it was once all rain forest full with gorillas. He clearly wanted us to head down immediately; I could have stayed there forever. He was saved from

that fate, as the clouds rolled in, obscuring all view and forcing us down.

We ran over the ice-covered rocks. We ran through the near frozen mud fields of the moorland down past the groves of trees and the rain forest and past the bamboo. And as we came to the saddle of the mountain, coming down a different path than we had taken up yesterday, the ranger slowed down. He didn't seem tired, and I couldn't imagine he was slowing out of concern for me. He suddenly seemed cautious, even uncomfortable. It was the nearest I could detect to an emotion on his face.

The forest had opened a bit, there were longer views, and a beautiful stream running alongside our path. We were walking slowly now, the ground was level. We crossed the stream on a log. Another minute walking, and the grove of trees near us parted. And then, with no warning, we were standing in front of Fossey's cabin.

It was plain, small, boarded. A Rwandan flag was flying over it. I walked over toward it, and the ranger motioned me away. I walked closer, and this silent kid told me in French, in Swahili, even in broken but understandable English, that it was not allowed. I walked past the cabin, and for the moment before he forced me away, I stood at the grave of Fossey and the other primates.

FOSSEY, FOSSEY, YOU CRANKY difficult strong-arming self-destructive misanthrope, mediocre scientist, deceiver of earnest college students, probable cause of more deaths of the gorillas than if you had never set foot in Rwanda, Fossey, you pain-in-the-ass saint, I do not believe in prayers or souls, but I will pray for your soul, I will remember you for all of my days, in gratitude for that moment by the graves when all I felt was the pure, cleansing sadness of returning home and finding nothing but ghosts.

From *A Primate's Memoir* by Robert M. Sapolsky. Copyright © 2001 by Robert M. Sapolsky. Reprinted by permission of Scribner, an imprint of Simon & Schuster, Inc.

The Mind of the Chimpanzee

Jane Goodall

Often I have gazed into a chimpanzee's eyes and wondered what was going on behind them. I used to look into Flo's, she so old, so wise. What did she remember of her young days? David Greybeard had the most beautiful eyes of them all, large and lustrous, set wide apart. They somehow expressed his whole personality, his serene self-assurance, his inherent dignity—and, from time to time, his utter determination to get his way. For a long time I never liked to look a chimpanzee straight in the eye—I assumed that, as is the case with most primates, this would be interpreted as a threat or at least as a breach of good manners. No so. As long as one looks with gentleness, without arrogance, a chimpanzee will understand, and may even return the look. And then—or such is my fantasy—it is as though the eyes are windows into the mind. Only the glass is opaque so that the mystery can never be fully revealed.

I shall never forget my meeting with Lucy, an eight-year-old home-raised chimpanzee. She came and sat beside me on the sofa and, with her face very close to mine, searched in my eyes—for what? Perhaps she was looking for signs of mistrust, dislike, or fear, since many people must have been somewhat disconcerted when, for the first time, they came face to face with a grown chimpanzee. Whatever Lucy read in my eyes clearly satisfied her for she suddenly put one arm round my neck and gave me a generous and very chimp-like kiss, her mouth wide open and laid over mine. I was accepted.

For a long time after that encounter I was profoundly disturbed. I had been at Gombe for about fifteen years then and I was quite familiar with chimpanzees in the wild. But Lucy, having grown up as a human child, was like a changeling, her essential chimpanzeeness overlaid by the various human behaviours she had acquired over the years. No longer purely chimp yet eons away from humanity, she was man-made, some other kind of being. I watched, amazed, as she opened the refrigerator and various cupboards, found bottles and a glass, then poured herself a gin and tonic. She took the drink to the TV, turned the set on, flipped from one channel to another then, as though in disgust, turned it off again. She selected a glossy magazine from the table and, still carrying her drink, settled in a comfortable chair. Occasionally, as she leafed through the magazine she identified something she saw, using the signs of ASL, the American Sign Language used by the deaf. I, of course, did not understand, but my hostess, Jane Temerlin (who was also Lucy's 'mother'), translated: 'That dog,' Lucy commented, pausing at a photo of a small white poodle. She turned the page. 'Blue,' she declared, pointing then signing as she gazed at a picture of a lady advertising some kind of soap powder and wearing a brilliant blue dress. And finally, after some vague hand movements—perhaps signed mutterings—'This Lucy's, this mine,' as she closed the magazine and laid it on her lap. She had just been taught, Jane told me, the use of the possessive pronouns during the thrice weekly ASL lessons she was receiving at the time.

The book written by Lucy's human 'father,' Maury Temerlin, was entitled *Lucy, Growing Up Human*. And in fact, the chimpanzee is more like us than is any other living creature. There is close resemblance in the physiology of our two species and genetically, in the structure of the DNA, chimpanzees and humans differ by only just over one per cent. This is why medical research uses chimpanzees as experimental animals when they need substitutes for humans in the testing of some drug or vaccine. Chimpanzees can be infected with just about all known human infectious diseases including those, such as hepatitis B and AIDS, to which other non-human animals (except gorillas, orangutans and gibbons) are immune. There are equally striking similarities between humans and chimpanzees in the anatomy and wiring of the brain and nervous system, and—although many scientists have been reluctant to admit to this—in social behaviour, intellectual ability, and the emotions. The notion of an evolutionary continuity in physical structure from prehuman ape to modern man has long been morally acceptable to most scientists. That the same might hold good for mind was generally considered an absurd hypothesis—particularly by those who used, and often misused, animals in their laboratories. It is, after all, convenient to believe that the creature you are using, while it may react in disturbingly human-like ways, is, in fact, merely a mindless and, above all, unfeeling, 'dumb' animal.

When I began my study at Gombe in 1960 it was not permissible—at least not in ethological circles—to talk about an animal's mind. Only humans had minds. Nor was it quite proper to talk about animal personality. Of course everyone knew that they *did* have their own unique characters—everyone who had ever owned a dog or other pet was aware of that. But ethologists, striving to make theirs a 'hard' science, shied away from the task of trying to explain such things objectively. One respected ethologist, while acknowledging that there was 'variability between individual animals,' wrote that it was best that this fact be 'swept under the carpet.' At that time ethological carpets fairly bulged with all that was hidden beneath them.

How naive I was. As I had not had an undergraduate science education I didn't realize that animals were not supposed to have personalities, or to think, or to feel emotions or pain. I had no idea that it would have been more appropriate to assign each of the chimpanzees a number rather than a name when I got to know him or her. I didn't realize that it was not scientific to discuss behaviour in terms of motivation or purpose. And no one had told me that terms such as *childhood* and *adolescence* were uniquely human phases of the life cycle, culturally determined, not to be used when referring to young chimpanzees. Not knowing, I freely made use of all those forbidden terms and concepts in my initial attempt to describe, to the best of my ability, the amazing things I had observed at Gombe.

I shall never forget the response of a group of ethologists to some remarks I made at an erudite seminar. I described how Figan, as an adolescent, had learned to stay behind in camp after senior males had left, so that we could give him a few bananas for himself. On the first occasion he had, upon seeing the fruits, uttered loud, delighted food calls: whereupon a couple of the older males had charged back, chased after Figan, and taken his bananas. And then, coming to the point of the story, I explained how, on the next occasion, Figan had actually suppressed his calls. We could hear little sounds, in his throat, but so quiet that none of the others could have heard them. Other young chimps, to whom we tried to smuggle fruit without the knowledge of their elders, never learned such self-control. With shrieks of glee they would fall to, only to be robbed of their booty when the big males charged back.

I had expected my audience to be as fascinated and impressed as I was. I had hoped for an exchange of views about the chimpanzee's undoubted intelligence. Instead there was a chill silence, after which the chairman hastily changed the subject. Needless to say, after being thus snubbed, I was very reluctant to contribute any comments, at any scientific gatherings, for a very long time. Looking back, I suspect that everyone was interested, but it was, of course, not permissible to present a mere 'anecdote' as evidence for anything.

The editorial comments on the first paper I wrote for publication demanded that every *he* or *she* be replaced with *it*, and every *who* be replaced with *which*. Incensed, I, in my turn, crossed out the *its* and *whichs* and scrawled back the original pronouns. As I had no desire to carve a niche for myself in the world of science, but simply wanted to go on living among and learning about chimpanzees, the possible reaction of the editor of the learned journal did not trouble me. In fact I won that round: the paper when finally published did confer upon the chimpanzees the dignity of their appropriate genders and properly upgraded them from the status of mere 'things' to essential Beingness.

However, despite my somewhat truculent attitude, I did want to learn, and I was sensible of my incredible good fortune in being admitted to Cambridge. I wanted to get my PhD, if only for the sake of Louis Leakey and the other people who had written letters in support of my admission. And how lucky I was to have, as my supervisor, Robert Hinde. Not only because I thereby benefitted from his brilliant mind and clear thinking, but also because I doubt that I could have found a teacher more suited to my particular needs and personality. Gradually he was able to cloak me with at least some of the trappings of a scientist. Thus although I continued to hold to most of my convictions—that animals had personalities; that they could feel happy or sad or fearful; that they could feel pain; that they could strive towards planned goals and achieve greater success if they were highly motivated—I soon realized that these personal convictions were, indeed, difficult to prove. It was best to be

circumspect—at least until I had gained some credentials and credibility. And Robert gave me wonderful advice on how best to tie up some of my more rebellious ideas with scientific ribbon. 'You can't *know* that Fifi was jealous,' had admonished on one occasion. We argued a little. And then: 'Why don't you just say *If Fifi were a human child we would say she was jealous.*' I did.

It is not easy to study emotions even when the subjects are human. I know how I feel if I am sad or happy or angry, and if a friend tells me that he is feeling sad, happy or angry, I assume that his feelings are similar to mine. But of course I cannot know. As we try to come to grips with the emotions of beings progressively more different from ourselves the task, obviously, becomes increasingly difficult. If we ascribe human emotions to non-human animals we are accused of being anthropomorphic—a cardinal sin in ethology. But is it so terrible? If we test the effect of drugs on chimpanzees because they are biologically so similar to ourselves, if we accept that there are dramatic similarities in chimpanzee and human brain and nervous system, is it not logical to assume that there will be similarities also in at least the more basic feelings, emotions, moods of the two species?

In fact, all those who have worked long and closely with chimpanzees have no hesitation in asserting that chimps experience emotions similar to those which in ourselves we label pleasure, joy, sorrow, anger, boredom and so on. Some of the emotional states of the chimpanzee are so obviously similar to ours that even an inexperienced observer can understand what is going on. An infant who hurls himself screaming to the ground, face contorted, hitting out with his arms at any nearby object, banging his head, is clearly having a tantrum. Another youngster, who gambols around his mother, turning somersaults, pirouetting and, every so often, rushing up to her and tumbling into her lap, patting her or pulling her hand towards him in a request for tickling, is obviously filled with *joie de vivre*. There are few observers who would not unhesitatingly ascribe his behaviour to a happy, carefree state of well-being. And one cannot watch chimpanzee infants for long without realizing that they have the same emotional need for affection and reassurance as human children. An adult male, reclining in the shade after a good meal, reaching benignly to play with an infant or idly groom an adult female, is clearly in a good mood. When he sits with bristling hair, glaring at his subordinates and threatening them, with irritated gestures, if they come too close, he is clearly feeling cross and grumpy. We make these judgements because the similarity of so much of a chimpanzee's behaviour to our own permits us to empathize.

It is hard to empathize with emotions we have not experienced. I can image, to some extent, the pleasure of a female chimpanzee during the act of procreation. The feelings of her male partner are beyond my knowledge—as are those of the human male in the same context. I have spent countless hours watching mother chimpanzees interacting with their infants. But not until I had an infant of my own did I begin to understand the basic, powerful instinct of mother-love. If someone accidentally did something to frighten Grub, or threaten his well-being in any way, I felt a surge of quite irrational anger. How much more easily could I then understand the feelings of the chimpanzee mother who furiously waves her arm and barks in threat at an individual who approaches her infant too closely, or at a playmate who inadvertently hurts her child. And it was not until I knew the numbing grief that gripped me after the death of my second husband that I could even begin to appreciate the despair and sense of loss that can cause young chimps to pine away and die when they lose their mothers.

Empathy and intuition can be of tremendous value as we attempt to understand certain complex behavioral interactions, provided that the behaviour, as it occurs, is recorded precisely and objectively. Fortunately I have seldom found it difficult to record facts in an orderly manner even during times of powerful emotional involvement. And "knowing" intuitively how a chimpanzee is feeling—after an attack, for example—may help one to understand what happens next. We should not be afraid at least to try to make use of our

close evolutionary relationship with the chimpanzees in our attempts to interpret complex behaviour.

Today, as in Darwin's time, it is once again fashionable to speak of and study the animal mind. This change came about gradually, and was, at least in part, due to the information collected during careful studies of animal societies in the field. As these observations became widely known, it was impossible to brush aside the complexities of social behaviour that were revealed in species after species. The untidy clutter under the ethological carpets was brought out and examined, piece by piece. Gradually it was realized that parsimonious explanations of apparently intelligent behaviours were often misleading. This led to a succession of experiments that, taken together, clearly prove that many intellectual abilities that had been thought unique to humans were actually present, though in a less highly developed form, in other, non-human beings. Particularly, of course, in the non-human primates and especially in chimpanzees.

When first I began to read about human evolution, I learned that one of the hallmarks of our own species was that we, and only we, were capable of making tools. *Man the Toolmaker* was an oft-cited definition—and this despite the careful and exhaustive research of Wolfgang Kohler and Robert Yerkes on the tool-using and tool-making abilities of chimpanzees. Those studies, carried out independently in the early twenties, were received with scepticism. Yet both Kohler and Yerkes were respected scientists, and both had a profound understanding of chimpanzee behaviour. Indeed, Kohler's descriptions of the personalities and behaviour of the various individuals in his colony, published in his book *The Mentality of Apes*, remain some of the most vivid and colourful ever written. And his experiments, showing how chimpanzees could stack boxes, then climb the unstable constructions to reach fruit suspended from the ceiling, or join two short sticks to make a pole long enough to rake in fruit otherwise out of reach, have become classic, appearing in almost all textbooks dealing

with intelligent behaviour in non-human animals.

By the time systematic observations of tool-using came from Gombe those pioneering studies had been largely forgotten. Moreover, it was one thing to know that humanized chimpanzees in the lab could use implements: it was quite another to find that this was a naturally occurring skill in the wild. I well remember writing to Louis about my first observations, describing how David Greybeard not only used bits of straw to fish for termites but actually stripped leaves from a stem and thus *made* a tool. And I remember too receiving the now oft-quoted telegram he sent in response to my letter: "Now we must redefine *tool*, redefine *Man*, or accept chimpanzees as humans."

There were initially, a few scientists who attempted to write off the termiting observations, even suggesting that I had taught the chimps! By and large, though, people were fascinated by the information and by the subsequent observations of the other contexts in which the Gombe chimpanzees used objects as tools. And there were only a few anthropologists who objected when I suggested that the chimpanzees probably passed their tool-using traditions from one generation to the next, through observations, imitation and practice, so that each population might be expected to have its own unique tool-using culture. Which, incidentally, turns out to be quite true. And when I described how one chimpanzee, Mike, spontaneously solved a new problem by using a tool (he broke off a stick to knock a banana to the ground when he was too nervous to actually take it from my hand) I don't believe there were any raised eyebrows in the scientific community. Certainly I was not attacked viciously, as were Kohler and Yerkes, for suggesting that humans were not the only beings capable of reasoning and insight.

The mid-sixties saw the start of a project that, along with other similar research, was to teach us a great deal about the chimpanzee mind. This was Project Washoe, conceived by Trixie and Allen Gardner. They purchased an infant chimpanzee and began to teach her the signs of ASL, the American Sign Language used by the deaf. Twenty years earlier another husband and wife team, Richard and Cathy Hayes, had tried, with an almost total lack of success, to teach a young chimp, Vikki, to talk. The Hayes's undertaking taught us a lot about the chimpanzee mind, but Vikki, although she did well in IQ tests, and was clearly an intelligent youngster, could not learn human speech. The Gardners, however, achieved spectacular success with their pupil, Washoe. Not only did she learn signs easily, but she quickly began to string them together in meaningful ways. It was clear that each sign evoked, in her mind, a mental image of the object it represented. If, for example, she was asked, in sign language, to fetch an apple, she would go and locate an apple that was out of sight in another room.

Other chimps entered the project, some starting their lives in deaf signing families before joining Washoe. And finally Washoe adopted an infant, Loulis. He came from a lab where no thought of teaching signs had ever penetrated. When he was with Washoe he was given no lessons in language acquisition—not by humans, anyway. Yet by the time he was eight years old he had made fifty-eight signs in their correct contexts. How did he learn them? Mostly, it seems, by imitating the behaviour of Washoe and the other three signing chimps, Dar, Moja and Tatu. Sometimes, though, he received tuition from Washoe herself. One day, for example, she began to swagger about bipedally, hair bristling, signing *food! food! food!* in great excitement. She had seen a human approaching with a bar of chocolate. Loulis, only eighteen months old, watched passively. Suddenly Washoe stopped her swaggering, went over to him, took his hand, and moulded the sign for *food* (fingers pointing towards mouth). Another time, in a similar context, she made the sign for *chewing gum*—but with *her* hand on *his* body. On a third occasion Washoe, apropos of nothing, picked up a small chair, took it over to Loulis, set it down in front of him, and very distinctly made the *chair* sign three times, watching him closely as she did so. The two food signs became incorporated into Loulis's vocabulary but the sign for chair did not. Obviously the priorities of a young

chimp are similar to those of a human child!

When news of Washoe's accomplishments first hit the scientific community it immediately provoked a storm of bitter protest. It implied that chimpanzees were capable of mastering a human language, and this, in turn, indicated mental powers of generalization, abstraction and concept-formation as well as an ability to understand and use abstract symbols. And these intellectual skills were surely the prerogatives of *Homo sapiens*. Although there were many who were fascinated and excited by the Gardners' findings, there were many more who denounced the whole project, holding that the data was suspect, the methodology sloppy, and the conclusions not only misleading, but quite preposterous. The controversy inspired all sorts of other language projects. And, whether the investigators were sceptical to start with and hoped to disprove the Gardners' work, or whether they were attempting to demonstrate the same thing in a new way, their research provided additional information about the chimpanzee's mind.

And so, with new incentive, psychologists began to test the mental abilities of chimpanzees in a variety of different ways; again and again the results confirmed that their minds are uncannily like our own. It had long been held that only humans were capable of what is called 'cross-modal transfer of information'—in other words, if you shut your eyes and someone allows you to feel a strangely shaped potato, you will subsequently be able to pick it out from other differently shaped potatoes simply by looking at them. And vice versa. It turned out that chimpanzees can 'know' with their eyes what they 'feel' with their fingers in just the same way. In fact, we now know that some other non-human primates can do the same thing. I expect all kinds of creatures have the same ability.

Then it was proved, experimentally and beyond doubt, that chimpanzees could recognize themselves in mirrors—that they had, therefore, some kind of self-concept. In fact, Washoe, some years previously, had already demonstrated the ability when she spontane-

ously identified herself in the mirror, staring at her image and making her name sign. But that observation was merely anecdotal. The proof came when chimpanzees who had been allowed to play with mirrors were, while anaesthetized, dabbed with spots of odourless paint in places, such as the ears or the top of the head, that they could see only in the mirror. When they woke they were not only fascinated by their spotted images, but immediately investigated, with their fingers, the dabs of paint.

The fact that chimpanzees have excellent memories surprised no one. Everyone, after all, has been brought up to believe that 'an elephant never forgets' so why should a chimpanzee be any different? The fact that Washoe spontaneously gave the name-sign of Beatrice Gardner, her surrogate mother, when she saw her after a separation of eleven years was no greater an accomplishment than the amazing memory shown by dogs who recognize their owners after separations of almost as long—and the chimpanzee has a much longer life span than a dog. Chimpanzees can plan ahead, too, at least as regards the immediate future. This, in fact, is well illustrated at Gombe, during the termiting season: often an individual prepares a tool for use on a termite mound that is several hundred yards away and absolutely out of sight.

This is not the place to describe in detail the other cognitive abilities that have been studied in laboratory chimpanzees. Among other accomplishments chimpanzees possess pre-mathematical skills: they can, for example, readily differentiate between *more* and *less*. They can classify things into specific categories according to a given criterion—thus they have no difficulty in separating a pile of food into *fruits* and *vegetables* on one occasion, and, on another, dividing the same pile of food into *large* versus *small* items, even though this requires putting some vegetables with some fruits. Chimpanzees who have been taught a language can combine signs creatively in order to describe objects for which they have no symbol. Washoe, for example, puzzled her caretakers by asking, repeatedly, for a *rock berry*. Eventually it transpired that she was referring to Brazil nuts which she had encountered for the first time a while before. Another language-trained chimp described a cucumber as a *green banana*, and another referred to an Alka-Seltzer as a *listen drink*. They can even invent signs. Lucy, as she got older, had to be put on a leash for her outings. One day, eager to set off but having no sign for *leash*, she signalled her wishes by holding a crooked index finger to the ring on her collar. This sign became part of her vocabulary. Some chimpanzees love to draw, and especially to paint. Those who have learned sign language sometimes spontaneously label their works, 'This [is] apple'—or bird, or sweetcorn, or whatever. The fact that the paintings often look, to our eyes, remarkably unlike the objects depicted by the artists either means that the chimpanzees are poor draughtsmen or that we have much to learn regarding ape-style representational art!

People sometimes ask why chimpanzees have evolved such complex intellectual powers when their lives in the wild are so simple. The answer is, of course, that their lives in the wild are not so simple! They use—and need—all their mental skills during normal day-to-day life in their complex society. They are always having to make choices—where to go, or with whom to travel. They need highly developed social skills—particularly those males who are ambitious to attain high positions in the dominance hierarchy. Low-ranking chimpanzees must learn deception—to conceal their intentions or to do things in secret—if they are to get their way in the presence of their superiors. Indeed, the study of chimpanzees in the wild suggests that their intellectual abilities evolved, over the millennia, to help them cope with daily life. And now, the solid core of data concerning chimpanzee intellect collected so carefully in the lab setting provides a background against which to evaluate the many examples of intelligent, rational behaviour that we see in the wild.

It is easier to study intellectual prowess in the lab where, through carefully devised tests and judicious use of rewards, the chimpanzees can be encouraged to exert themselves, to stretch their minds to the limit. It is more meaningful to study the subject in the wild, but much harder. It is more meaningful because we can better understand the environmental pressures that led to the evolution of intellectual skills in chimpanzee societies. It is harder because, in the wild, almost all behaviours are confounded by countless variables; years of observing, recording and analysing take the place of contrived testing; sample size can often be counted on the fingers of one hand; the only experiments are nature's own, and only time— eventually—may replicate them.

In the wild a single observation may prove of utmost significance, providing a clue to some hitherto puzzling aspect of behaviour, a key to the understanding of, for example, a changed relationship. Obviously it is crucial to see as many incidents of this sort as possible. During the early years of my study at Gombe it became apparent that one person alone could never learn more than a fraction of what was going on in a chimpanzee community at any given time. And so, from 1964 onwards, I gradually built up a research team to help in the gathering of information about the behaviour of our closest living relatives.

Got Culture?

by Craig Stanford

ON MY FIRST TRIP TO EAST AFRICA in the early 1990s, I stood by a dusty, dirt road hitchhiking. I had waited hours in rural Tanzania for an expected lift from a friend who had never shown up, leaving me with few options other than the kindness of strangers. I stood with my thumb out, but the cars and trucks roared by me, leaving me caked in paprika-red dust. I switched to a palm-down gesture I had seen local people using to get lifts. Voilà; on the first try a truck pulled over and I hopped in. A conversation in Kiswahili with the truck driver ensued and I learned my mistake. Hitchhiking with your thumb upturned may work in the United States, but in Africa the gesture can be translated in the way that Americans understand the meaning of an extended, declarative middle finger. Not exactly the best way to persuade a passing vehicle to stop. The universally recognized symbol for needing a lift is not so universal.

Much of culture is the accumulation of thousands of such small differences. Put a suite of traditions together—religion, language, ways of dress, cuisine and a thousand other features—and you have a culture. Of course cultures can be much simpler too. A group of toddlers in a day care center possesses its own culture, as does a multi-national corporation, suburban gardeners, inner-city gang members. Many elements of a culture are functional and hinged to individual survival: thatched roof homes from the tropics would work poorly in Canada, nor would harpoons made for catching seals be very useful in the Sahara. But other features are purely symbolic. Brides in Western culture wear white to symbolize sexual purity. Brides in Hindu weddings wear crimson, to symbolize sexual purity. Whether white or red is more pure is nothing more than a product of the long-term memory and mindset of the two cultures. And the most symbolic of cultural traditions, the one that has always been considered the bailiwick of humanity only, is language. The words "white" and "red" have an entirely arbitrary relationship to the colors themselves. They are simply code names.

Arguing about how to define culture has long been a growth industry among anthropologists. We argue about culture the way the Joint Chiefs of Staff argue about national security: as though our lives depended on it. But given that culture requires symbolism and some linguistic features, can we even talk about culture in other animals?

In 1996 I was attending a conference near Rio de Janeiro when the topic turned to culture.[1] As a biological anthropologist with a decade of field research on African great apes, I offered my perspective on the concept of culture. Chimpanzees, I said with confidence, display a rich cultural diversity. Recent years have shown that each wild chimpanzee population is more than just a gene pool. It is also a distinct culture, comprising a unique assortment of learned traditions in tool use, styles of grooming and hunting, and other features of the sort that can only be seen in the most socially sophisticated primates. Go from one forest to another and you will run into a new culture, just as walking between two human villages may introduce you to tribes who have different ways of building boats or celebrating marriages.

At least that's what I meant to say. But I had barely gotten the word "culture" past my lips when I was made to feel the full weight of my blissful ignorance. The cultural anthropologists practically leaped across the seminar table to berate me for using the words "culture" and "chimpanzee" in the same sentence. I had apparently set off a silent security alarm, and the culture-theory guards came running. How dare you, they said, use a human term like "cultural diversity" to describe what chimpanzees do? Say "behavioral variation," they demanded. "Apes are mere animals, and culture is something that only the human animal can claim. Furthermore, not only can humans alone claim culture, culture alone can explain humanity." It became clear to me that culture, as understood by most anthropologists, is a human concept, and many passionately want it to stay that way. When I asked if this was not just a semantic difference—what are cultural traditions if not learned behavioral variations?—they replied that culture is symbolic, and what animals do lacks symbolism.

When Jane Goodall first watched chimpanzees make simple stick tools to probe into termite mounds, it became clear that tool cultures are not unique to human societies. Of course many animals use tools. Sea otters on the California coast forage for abalones, which they place on their chests and hammer open with stones. Egyptian vultures use stones to break the eggs of ostriches. But these are simple, relatively inflexible lone behaviors. Only among chimpanzees do we see elaborate forms of tools made and used in variable ways, and also see distinct chimp tool cultures across Africa. In Gombe National Park in Tanzania, termite mounds of red earth rise 2 meters high and shelter millions of the almond-colored insects. Chimpanzees pore over the mounds, scratching at plugged tunnels until they find portals into the mound's interior. They will gently insert a twig or blade of grass into a tunnel until the soldier termites latch onto the tools with their powerful mandibles, then they'll withdraw the probe from the mound. With dozens of soldier and worker termites clinging ferociously to the twig, the chimpanzee draws the stick between her lips and reaps a nutritious bounty.

Less than 100 kilometers away from Gombe's termite-fishing apes is another culture. Chimpanzees in Mahale National Park live in a forest that is home to most of the same species of termites, but they practically never use sticks to eat them. If Mahale chimpanzees forage for termites at all, they use their fingers to crumble apart soil and pick out their insect snacks. However, Mahale chimpanzees love to eat ants. They climb up the straight-sided trunks of great trees and poke Gombe-like probes into holes to obtain woodboring species. As adept as Gombe chimpanzees are at fishing for termites, they practically never fish for these ants, even though both the ants and termites occur in both Gombe and Mahale.[2]

Segue 2,000 kilometers westward, to a rainforest in Côte d'Ivoire. In a forest filled with twigs, chimpanzees do not use stick tools. Instead, chimpanzees in Taï National Park and other forests in western Africa use hammers made of rock and wood. Swiss primatologists Christophe and Hedwige Boesch and their colleagues first reported the use of stone tools by chimpanzees twenty years ago.[3] Their subsequent research showed that Taï chimpanzees collect hammers when certain species of nut-bearing trees are in fruit. These hammers are not modified in any way as the stone tools made by early humans were; they are hefted, however, and appraised for weight and smashing value before being carried back to the nut tree. A nut is carefully positioned in a depression in the tree's aboveground root

buttresses (the anvil) and struck with precision by the tool-user. The researchers have seen mothers instructing their children on the art of tool use, by assisting them in placing the nut in the anvil in the proper way.

So chimpanzees in East Africa use termite- and ant-fishing tools, and West African counterparts use hammers, but not vice versa. These are subsistence tools; they were almost certainly invented for food-getting. Primatologist William McGrew of Miami University of Ohio has compared the tool technologies of wild chimpanzees with those of traditional human hunter-gatherer societies. He found that in at least some instances, the gap between chimpanzee technology and human technology is not wide. The now-extinct aboriginal Tasmanians, for example, possessed no complex tools or weapons of any kind. Though they are an extreme example, the Tasmanians illustrate that human culture need not be technologically complex.[4]

As McGrew first pointed out, there are three likeliest explanations for the differences we see among the chimpanzee tool industries across Africa.[5] The first is genetic: perhaps there are mutations that arise in one population but not others that govern tool making. This seems extremely unlikely, just as we would never argue that Hindu brides wear red while Western brides wear white due to a genetic difference between Indians and Westerners. The second explanation is ecological: maybe the environment in which the chimpanzee population lives dictates patterns of tool use. Maybe termite-fishing sticks will be invented in places where there are termites and sticks but not rocks and nuts, and hammers invented in the opposite situation. But a consideration of each habitat raises doubts. Gombe is a rugged, rock-strewn place where it is hard to find a spot to sit that is not within arm's reach of a few stones, but Gombe chimpanzees do not use stone tools. The West African chimpanzees who use stone tools live, by contrast, in lowland rainforests that are nearly devoid of rocks. Yet they purposely forage to find them. The tool-use pattern is exactly the opposite of what we would expect if environment and local availability accounted for differences

among chimpanzee communities in tool use.

British psychologist Andrew Whiten and his colleagues recently conducted the first systematic survey of cultural differences in tool use among the seven longest-term field studies, representing more than a century and a half of total observation time. They found thirty-nine behaviors that could not be explained by environmental factors at the various sites.[6] Alone with humans in the richness of their behavior repertoire, chimpanzee cultures show variations that can only be ascribed to learned traditions. These traditions, passed from one generation to the next through observation and imitation, are a simple version of human culture.

But wait. I said earlier that human culture must have a symbolic element. Tools that differ in form and function, from sticks to hammers to sponges made of crushed leaves, are all utterly utilitarian. They tell us much about the environment in which they are useful but little about the learned traditions that led to their creation. Human artifacts, on the other hand, nearly always contain some purely symbolic element, be it the designs carved into a piece of ancient pottery or the "Stanley" logo on my new claw hammer. Is there anything truly symbolic in chimpanzee culture, in the human sense of an object or behavior that is completely detached from its use?

Male chimpanzees have various ways of indicating to a female that they would like to mate. At Gombe, one such courtship behavior involves rapidly shaking a small bush or branch several times, after which a female in proximity will usually approach the male and present her swelling to him. But in Mahale, males have learned to use leaves in their courtship gesture. A male plucks a leafy stem from a nearby plant and noisily uses his teeth and fingers to tear off its leaves. Leaf-clipping is done mainly in the context of wanting to mate with a particular female, and appears to function as a purely symbolic signal of sexual desire (it could also be a gesture of frustration). A second leafy symbol is leaf-grooming. Chimpanzees pick leaves and intently groom them with their fingers, as seriously as though they were grooming another chimpanzee. And this may be the function; leaf-grooming may signal a desire for real grooming from a social partner. Since the signal for grooming involves grooming, albeit of another object, this gesture is not symbolic in the sense that leaf-clipping is. But its distribution across Africa is equally spotty; leaf-grooming is commonly practiced in East African chimpanzee cultures but is largely absent in western Africa.[7]

These two cases of potentially symbolic behavior may not seem very impressive. After all, the briefest consideration of human culture turns up a rich array of symbolism, from language to the arts. But are all human cultures highly symbolic? If we use language and other forms of symbolic expression as the criterion for culture, then how about a classroom full of two-year-old toddlers in a day care center? They communicate by a very simple combination of gestures and half-formed sentences. Toddlers have little symbolic communication or appreciation for art and are very little different from chimpanzees in their cultural output. We grant them human qualities because we know they will mature into symbol-using, linguistically expert adults, leaving chimpanzees in the dust. But this is no reason to consider them on a different plane from the apes when both are fifteen months old.

Chimpanzee societies are based on learned traditions passed from mother to child and from adult males to eager wannabe males. These traditions vary from place to place. This is culture. Culture is not limited, however, to those few apes that are genetically 99 percent human. Many primates show traditions. These are usually innovations by younger members of a group, which sweep rapidly through the society and leave it just slightly different than before. Japanese primatologists have long observed such traditions among the macaques native to their island nation. Researchers long ago noticed that a new behavior had arisen in one population of Japanese macaque monkeys living on Koshima Island just offshore the mainland. The monkeys were regularly tossed sweet potatoes, rice and other local treats by the locals. One day Imo, a young female in the group, took her potato and carried it to the sea, where she washed it with salty brine before eating it. This behavior rap-

idly spread throughout the group, a nice example of innovation happening in real time so that researchers could observe the diffusion. Later, other monkeys invented the practice of scooping up rice offered them with the beach sand it was scattered on, throwing both onto the surf and then scraping up the grains that floated while the sand sank.

At a supremely larger scale, such innovations are what human cultural differences are all about. Of course, only in human cultures do objects such as sweet potatoes take on the kind of symbolic meaning that permits them to stand for other objects and thus become a currency. Chimpanzees lack the top-drawer cognitive capacity needed to invent such a currency. Or do they? Wild chimpanzees hunt for a part of their living. All across equatorial Africa, meat-eating is a regular feature of chimpanzee life, but its style and technique vary from one forest to another. In Taï National Park in western Africa, hunters are highly cooperative; Christophe Boesch has reported specific roles such as ambushers and drivers as part of the apes' effort to corral colobus monkeys in the forest canopy.[8] At Gombe in East Africa, meanwhile, hunting is like a baseball game; a group sport performed on an individual basis. This difference may be environmentally influenced; perhaps the high canopy rain forest at Taï requires cooperation more than the broken, low canopy forest at Gombe. There is a culture of hunting in each forest as well, in which young and eager male wannabes copy the predatory skills of their elders. At Gombe, for instance, chimpanzees relish wild pigs and piglets in addition to monkeys and small antelope. At Taï, wild pigs are ignored even when they stroll in front of a hunting party.

There is also a culture of sharing the kill. Sharing of meat is highly nepotistic at Gombe; sons who make the kill share with their mothers and brothers but snub rival males. They also share preferentially with females who have sexual swellings, and with high-ranking females. At Taï, the captor shares with the other members of the hunting party whether or not they are allies or relatives; a system of reciprocity seems to be in place in which the golden rule works. I have argued that

since the energy and time that chimpanzees spend hunting is rarely paid back by the calories, protein and fat gotten from a kill, we should consider hunting a social behavior done at least partly for its own sake.[9] When chimpanzees barter a limited commodity such as meat for other services—alliances, sex, grooming—they are engaging in a very simple and primitive form of a currency exchange. Such an exchange relies on the ability of the participants to remember the web of credits and debts owed one another and to act accordingly. It may be that the two chimpanzee cultures 2,000 kilometers apart have developed their distinct uses of meat as a social currency. In one place meat is used as a reward for cooperation, in the other as a manipulative tool of nepotism. Such systems are commonplace in all human societies, and their roots may be seen in chimpanzees' market economy, too.[10]

I have not yet considered one obvious question. If tool use and other cultural innovations can be so valuable to chimpanzees, why have they not arisen more widely among primates and other big-brained animals? Although chimpanzees are adept tool-users, their very close relatives the bonobos are not. Bonobos do a number of very clever things—dragging their hands beside them as they wade through streams to catch fish is one notable example—but they are not accomplished technicians. Gorillas don't use tools at all, and orangutans have only recently been observed to occasionally use sticks as probing tools in their rainforest canopy world.[11]

Other big-brained animals fare even worse. Wild elephants don't use their wonderfully dexterous trunks to manipulate tools in any major way, although when you're strong enough to uproot trees you may not have much use for a pokey little probe. Dolphins and whales, cognitively gifted though they may be, lack the essential anatomical ingredient for tool manufacture—a pair of nimble hands. Wild bottlenose dolphins have been observed to carry natural sponges about on their snouts to ferret food from the sea bottom, the only known form of cetacean tool use.[12] But that may be the limit of how much a creature that lacks any grasping appendages can manipulate its surroundings.

So to be a cultural animal, it is not enough to be big-brained. You must have the anatomical prerequisites for tool cultures to develop. Even if these are in place, there is no guarantee that a species will generate a subsistence culture in the form of tools. Perhaps environmental necessity dictates which ape species use tools and which don't, except it is hard to imagine that bonobos have much less use for tools than chimpanzees do. There is probably a strong element of chance involved. The chance that a cultural tradition—tool use, hunting style or grooming technique—will develop may be very small in any given century or millennium. Once innovated, the chance that the cultural trait will disappear—perhaps due to the death of the main practitioners from whom everyone learned the behavior—may conversely be great. Instead of a close fit between the environment and the cultural traditions that evolve in it—which many scholars believe explains cultural diversity in human societies— the roots of cultural variation may be much more random. A single influential individual who figures out how to make a better mousetrap, so to speak, can through imitation spread his mousetrap through the group and slowly into other groups.

We tend to think of cultural traditions as highly plastic and unstable compared to biological innovation. It takes hundreds of generations for natural selection to bring about biological change, whereas cultural change can happen in one lifetime, even in a few minutes. Because we live in a culture in which we buy the newest cell phone and the niftiest handheld computer—we fail to appreciate how conservative traditions like tool use can be. *Homo erectus*, with a brain nearly the size of our own, invented a teardrop-shaped stone tool called a hand axe 1.5 million years ago. It was presumably used for butchering carcasses, though some archaeologists think it may have also been a weapon. Whatever its purpose, more than a million years later those same stone axes were still being manufactured and used. Fifty thousand generations passed without a significant change in the major piece of material culture in a very big-brained and intelligent human species. *That's* conservatism and it offers us two lessons. First, if it ain't broke don't fix it: when a traditional way of making a tool works and the environment is not throwing any curves your way, there may be no pressure for a change. Second, we see a human species vastly more intelligent than an ape (*Homo erectus*' neocortical brain volume was a third smaller than a modern human's, but two and a half times larger than a chimpanzee's) whose technology didn't change at all. This tells us that innovations, once made, may last a very long time without being either extinguished or improved upon. It suggests that chimpanzee tool cultures may have been in place for all of the 5 million years since their divergence from our shared ancestor.

The very word *culture*, as William McGrew has pointed out, was invented for humans, and this has long blinded cultural theorists to a more expansive appreciation of the concept. Whether apes have culture or not is not really the issue. The heart of the debate is whether scholars who study culture and consider it their intellectual territory will accept a more expansive definition. In purely academic arguments like this one, the power lies with the party who owns the key concepts of the discipline. They define concepts however they choose, and the choice is usually aimed at fencing off their intellectual turf from all others.

Primatologists are latecomers to the table of culture, and they have had to wait their turn before being allowed to sit. We should be most interested in what the continuum of intelligence tells us about the roots of human behavior, not whether what apes do or don't do fits any particular, rigid definition of culture. When it comes to human practices, from building boats to weddings to choosing mates, we should look at the intersections of our biology and our culture for clues about what has made us who we are.

NOTES

1. *Changing Views of Primate Societies: The Role of Gender and Nationality*, June 1996, sponsored by the Wenner-Gren Foundation for Anthropological Research.
2. For an enlightening discussion of cross-cultural differences in chimpanzee tool use, see almost anything William McGrew has written, but especially McGrew (1992).
3. See Boesch and Boesch (1989).
4. Again, see McGrew (1992).
5. McGrew (1979)
6. Whiten *et al.* (1999) combined data from seven long-term chimpanzees studies to produce the most systematic examination of cultural variation in these apes.
7. For further discussion of chimpanzee symbolic behavior in the wild, see Goodall (1986), Wrangham *et al.* (1994) and McGrew et al. (1996).
8. See Boesch and Boesch (1989).
9. See Stanford (1999, 2001).
10. See de Waal (1996) and Stanford (2001).
11. For the first report of systematic tool use by wild orangutans, see van Schaik *et al.* (1996).
12. See Smolker *et al.* (1997).

From *Significant Others*, 2001, pp. 109-119. © 2001 by Craig Stanford. Reprinted by permission of Basic Books, a member of Perseus Books, L.L.C.

Dim Forest, Bright Chimps

*In the rain forest of Ivory Coast, chimpanzees meet
the challenge of life by hunting cooperatively
and using crude tools*

**Christophe Boesch and
Hedwige Boesch-Achermann**

Taï National Park, Ivory Coast, December 3, 1985. Drumming, barking, and screaming, chimps rush through the undergrowth, little more than black shadows. Their goal is to join a group of other chimps noisily clustering around Brutus, the dominant male of this seventy-member chimpanzee community. For a few moments, Brutus, proud and self-confident, stands fairly still, holding a shocked, barely moving red colobus monkey in his hand. Then he begins to move through the group, followed closely by his favorite females and most of the adult males. He seems to savor this moment of uncontested superiority, the culmination of a hunt high up in the canopy. But the victory is not his alone. Cooperation is essential to capturing one of these monkeys, and Brutus will break apart and share this highly prized delicacy with most of the main participants of the hunt and with the females. Recipients of large portions will, in turn, share more or less generously with their offspring, relatives, and friends.

In 1979, we began a long-term study of the previously unknown chimpanzees of Taï National Park, 1,600 square miles of tropical rain forest in the Republic of the Ivory Coast (Côte d'Ivoire). Early on, we were most interested in the chimps' use of natural hammers—branches and stones—to crack open the five species of hard-shelled nuts that are abundant here. A sea otter lying on its back, cracking an abalone shell with a rock, is a familiar picture, but no primate had ever before been observed in the wild using stones as hammers. East Africa's savanna chimps, studied for decades by Jane Goodall in Gombe, Tanzania, use twigs to extract ants and termites from their nests or honey from a bees' nest, but they have never been seen using hammerstones.

As our work progressed, we were surprised by the many ways in which the life of the Taï forest chimpanzees differs from that of their savanna counterparts, and as evidence accumulated, differences in how the two populations hunt proved the most intriguing. Jane Goodall had found that chimpanzees hunt monkeys, antelope, and wild pigs, findings confirmed by Japanese biologist Toshida Nishida, who conducted a long-term study 120 miles south of Gombe, in the Mahale Mountains. So we were not surprised to discover that the Taï chimps eat meat. What intrigued us was the degree to which they hunt cooperatively. In 1953 Raymond Dart proposed that group hunting and cooperation were key ingredients in the evolution of *Homo sapiens*. The argument has been modified consid-erably since Dart first put it forward, and group hunting has also been observed in some social carnivores (lions and African wild dogs, for instance), and even some birds of prey. Nevertheless, many anthropologists still hold that hunting cooperatively and sharing food played a central role in the drama that enabled early hominids, some 1.8 million years ago, to develop the social systems that are so typically human.

We hoped that what we learned about the behavior of forest chimpanzees would shed new light on prevailing theories of human evolution. Before we could even begin, however, we had to habituate a community of chimps to our presence. Five long years passed before we were able to move with them on their daily trips through the forest, of which "our" group appeared to claim some twelve square miles. Chimpanzees are alert and shy animals, and the limited field of view in the rain forest—about sixty-five feet at best—made finding them more difficult. We had to rely on sound, mostly their vocalizations and drumming on trees. Males often drum regularly while moving through the forest: pant-hooting, they draw near a big buttress tree; then, at full speed they fly over the buttress, hitting it repeatedly with their hands and feet. Such drumming may resound more than half a mile in the forest. In the beginning, our ignorance about how they moved and who was drumming led to failure more often than not, but eventually we learned that the dominant males drummed during the day to let other group members know the direction of travel. On some days, however, intermittent drumming about dawn was the only signal for the whole day. If we were out of earshot at the time, we were often reduced to guessing.

During these difficult early days, one feature of the chimps' routine proved to be our salvation: nut cracking is a noisy business. So noisy, in fact, that in the early days of French colonial rule, one officer apparently even proposed the theory that some unknown tribe was forging iron in the impenetrable and dangerous jungle.

Guided by the sounds made by the chimps as they cracked open nuts, which they often did for hours at a time, we were gradually able to get within sixty feet of the animals. We still seldom saw the chimps themselves (they fled if we came too close), but even so, the evidence left after a session of nut cracking taught us a great deal about what types of nuts they were eating, what sorts of hammer and anvil tools they were using, and—thanks to the very distinctive noise a nut makes when it finally splits open— how many hits were needed to crack a nut and how many nuts could be opened per minute.

After some months, we began catching glimpses of the chimpanzees before they fled, and after a little more time, we were able to draw close enough to watch them at work. The chimps gather nuts from the ground. Some nuts are tougher to crack than others. Nuts of the *Panda oleosa* tree are the most demanding, harder than any of the foods processed by present-day hunter-gatherers and breaking open only when a force of 3,500 pounds is applied. The stone hammers used by the Taï chimps range from stones of ten ounces to granite blocks of four to forty-five pounds. Stones of any size, however, are a rarity in the forest and are seldom conveniently placed near a nut-bearing tree. By observing closely, and in some cases imitating the way the chimps handle hammerstones,

we learned that they have an impressive ability to find just the right tool for the job at hand. Taï chimps could remember the positions of many of the stones scattered, often out of sight, around a panda tree. Without having to run around rechecking the stones, they would select one of appropriate size that was closest to the tree. These mental abilities in spatial representation compare with some of those of nine-year-old humans.

To extract the four kernels from inside a panda nut, a chimp must use a hammer with extreme precision. Time and time again, we have been impressed to see a chimpanzee raise a twenty-pound stone above its head, strike a nut with ten or more powerful blows, and then, using the same hammer, switch to delicate little taps from a height of only four inches. To finish the job, the chimps often break off a small piece of twig and use it to extract the last tiny fragments of kernel from the shell. Intriguingly, females crack panda nuts more often than males, a gender difference in tool use that seems to be more pronounced in the forest chimps than in their savanna counterparts.

After five years of fieldwork, we were finally able to follow the chimpanzees at close range, and gradually, we gained insights into their way of hunting. One morning, for example, we followed a group of six male chimps on a three-hour patrol that had taken them into foreign territory to the north. (Our study group is one of five chimpanzee groups more or less evenly distributed in the Taï forest.) As always during these approximately monthly incursions, which seem to be for the purpose of territorial defense, the chimps were totally silent, clearly on edge and on the lookout for trouble. Once the patrol was over, however, and they were back within their own borders, the chimps shifted their attention to hunting. They were after monkeys, the most abundant mammals in the forest. Traveling in large, multi-species groups, some of the forest's ten species of monkeys are more apt than others to wind up as a meal for the chimps. The relatively sluggish and large (almost thirty pounds) red colobus monkeys are the chimps' usual fare. (Antelope also live in the forest, but in our ten years at Taï, we have never

seen a chimp catch, or even pursue, one. In contrast, Gombe chimps at times do come across fawns, and when they do, they seize the opportunity—and the fawn.)

The six males moved on silently, peering up into the vegetation and stopping from time to time to listen for the sound of monkeys. None fed or groomed; all focused on the hunt. We followed one old male, Falstaff, closely, for he tolerates us completely and is one of the keenest and most experienced hunters. Even from the rear, Falstaff set the pace; whenever he stopped, the others paused to wait for him. After thirty minutes, we heard the unmistakable noises of monkeys jumping from branch to branch. Silently, the chimps turned in the direction of the sounds, scanning the canopy. Just then, a diana monkey spotted them and gave an alarm call. Dianas are very alert and fast; they are also about half the weight of colobus monkeys. The chimps quickly gave up and continued their search for easier, meatier prey.

Shortly after, we heard the characteristic cough of a red colobus monkey. Suddenly Rousseau and Macho, two twenty-year-olds, burst into action, running toward the cough. Falstaff seemed surprised by their precipitousness, but after a moment's hesitation, he also ran. Now the hunting barks of the chimps mixed with the sharp alarm calls of the monkeys. Hurrying behind Falstaff, we saw him climb up a conveniently situated tree. His position, combined with those of Schubert and Ulysse, two mature chimps in their prime, effectively blocked off three of the monkeys' possible escape routes. But in another tree, nowhere near any escape route and thus useless, waited the last of the hunters, Kendo, eighteen years old and the least experienced of the group. The monkeys, taking advantage of Falstaff's delay and Kendo's error, escaped.

The six males moved on and within five minutes picked up the sounds of another group of red colobus. This time, the chimps approached cautiously, nobody hurrying. They screened the canopy intently to locate the monkeys, which were still unaware of the approaching danger. Macho and Schubert chose two adjacent trees, both full of monkeys, and started climbing very quietly, taking care not to move any branches. Meanwhile, the other four chimps blocked off anticipated escape routes. When Schubert was halfway up, the monkeys finally detected the two chimps. As we watched the colobus monkeys take off in literal panic, the appropriateness of the chimpanzees' scientific name—*Pan* came to mind: with a certain stretch of the imagination, the fleeing monkeys could be shepherds and shepherdesses frightened at the sudden appearance of Pan, the wild Greek god of the woods, shepherds, and their flocks.

Taking off in the expected direction, the monkeys were trailed by Macho and Schubert. The chimps let go with loud hunting barks. Trying to escape, two colobus monkeys jumped into smaller trees lower in the canopy. With this, Rousseau and Kendo, who had been watching from the ground, sped up into the trees and tried to grab them. Only a third of the weight of the chimps, however, the monkeys managed to make it to the next tree along branches too small for their pursuers. But Falstaff had anticipated this move and was waiting for them. In the following confusion, Falstaff seized a juvenile and killed it with a bite to the neck. As the chimps met in a rush on the ground, Falstaff began to eat, sharing with Schubert and Rousseau. A juvenile colobus does not provide much meat, however, and this time, not all the chimps got a share. Frustrated individuals soon started off on another hunt, and relative calm returned fairly quickly: this sort of hunt, by a small band of chimps acting on their own at the edge of their territory, does not generate the kind of high excitement that prevails when more members of the community are involved.

So far we have observed some 200 monkey hunts and have concluded that success requires a minimum of three motivated hunters acting cooperatively. Alone or in pairs, chimps succeed less than 15 percent of the time, but when three or four act as a group, more than half the hunts result in a kill. The chimps seem well aware of the odds; 92 percent of all the hunts we observed were group affairs.

Gombe chimps also hunt red colobus monkeys, but the percentage of group hunts is much lower: only 36 percent. In addition, we learned from Jane Goodall that even when Gombe chimps do hunt in groups, their strategies are different. When Taï chimps arrive under a group of monkeys, the hunters scatter, often silently, usually out of sight of one another but each aware of the others' positions. As the hunt progresses, they gradually close in, encircling the quarry. Such movements require that each chimp coordinate his movements with those of the other hunters, as well as with those of the prey, at all times.

Coordinated hunts account for 63 percent of all those observed at Taï but only 7 percent of those at Gombe. Jane Goodall says that in a Gombe group hunt, the chimpanzees typically travel together until they arrive at a tree with monkeys. Then, as the chimps begin climbing nearby trees, they scatter as each pursues a different target. Goodall gained the impression that Gombe chimps boost their success by hunting independently but simultaneously, thereby disorganizing their prey; our impression is that the Taï chimps owe their success to being organized themselves.

Just why the Gombe and Taï chimps have developed such different hunting strategies is difficult to explain, and we plan to spend some time at Gombe in the hope of finding out. In the meantime, the mere existence of differences is interesting enough and may perhaps force changes in our understanding of human evolution. Most currently accepted theories propose that some three million years ago, a dramatic climate change in Africa east of the Rift Valley turned dense forest into open, drier habitat. Adapting to the difficulties of life under these new conditions, our ancestors supposedly evolved into cooperative hunters and began sharing food they caught. Supporters of this idea point out that plant and animal remains indicative of dry, open environments have been found at all early hominid excavation sites in Tanzania, Kenya, South Africa, and Ethiopia. That the large majority of apes in Africa today live west of the Rift Valley appears to many anthropologists to lend further support to the idea that a change in environment caused the common ancestor of apes and humans to evolve along a different line from those remaining in the forest.

Our observations, however, suggest quite another line of thought. Life in dense, dim forest may require more sophisticated behavior than is commonly assumed: compared with their savanna relatives, Taï chimps show greater complexity in both hunting and tool use. Taï chimps use tools in nineteen different ways and have six different ways of making them, compared with sixteen uses and three methods of manufacture at Gombe.

Anthropologist colleagues of mine have told me that the discovery that some chimpanzees are accomplished users of hammerstones forces them to look with a fresh eye at stone tools turned up at excavation sites. The important role played by female Taï chimps in tool use also raises the possibility that in the course of human evolution, women may have been decisive in the development of many of the sophisticated manipulative skills characteristic of our species. Taï mothers also appear to pass on their skills by actively teaching their offspring. We have observed mothers providing their young with hammers and then stepping in to help when the inexperienced youngsters encounter difficulty. This help may include carefully showing how to position the nut or hold the hammer properly. Such behavior has never been observed at Gombe.

Similarly, food sharing, for a long time said to be unique to humans, seems more general in forest than in savanna chimpanzees. Taï chimp mothers share with their young up to 60 percent of the nuts they open, at least until the latter become sufficiently adept, generally at about six years old. They also share other foods acquired with tools, including honey, ants, and bone marrow. Gombe mothers share such foods much less often, even with their infants. Taï chimps also share meat more frequently than do their Gombe relatives, sometimes dividing a chunk up and giving portions away, sometimes simply allowing beggars to grab pieces.

Any comparison between chimpanzees and our hominid ancestors can only be suggestive, not definitive. But our studies lead us to believe that the process of hominization may have begun independently of the drying of the environment. Savanna life could even have delayed the process; many anthropologists have been struck by how slowly hominid-associated remains, such as the hand ax, changed after their first appearance in the Olduvai age.

Will we have the time to discover more about the hunting strategies or other, perhaps as yet undiscovered abilities of these forest chimpanzees? Africa's tropical rain forests, and their inhabitants, are threatened with extinction by extensive logging, largely to provide the Western world with tropical timber and such products as coffee, co-

coa, and rubber. Ivory Coast has lost 90 percent of its original forest, and less than 5 percent of the remainder can be considered pristine. The climate has changed dramatically. The harmattan, a cold, dry wind from the Sahara previously unknown in the forest, has now swept through the Taï forest every year since 1986. Rainfall has diminished; all the rivulets in our study region are now dry for several months of the year.

In addition, the chimpanzee, biologically very close to humans, is in demand for research on AIDS and hepatitis vaccines. Captive-bred chimps are available, but they cost about twenty times more than wild-caught animals. Chimps

taken from the wild for these purposes are generally young, their mothers having been shot during capture. For every chimp arriving at its sad destination, nine others may well have died in the forest or on the way. Such priorities—cheap coffee and cocoa and chimpanzees—do not do the economies of Third World countries any good in the long run, and they bring suffering and death to innocent victims in the forest. Our hope is that Brutus, Falstaff, and their families will survive, and that we and others will have the opportunity to learn about them well into the future. But there is no denying that modern times work against them and us.

Rethinking Primate Aggression

Researcher Frans de Waal shows that apes (and humans) get along better than we thought

Richard Conniff

ONE AFTERNOON in the 1970s, at a zoo in the Netherlands, a burly, dopey-faced chimpanzee named Nikkie, a veteran of the Holiday on Ice Revue, chased another male named Luit around their compound. Chimpanzee males have five times the upper body strength of a college football player, and roughly the same sense of decorum. So other chimps leaped for safety as the two combatants kicked up clouds of dust. You could hear their screaming at the far end of the zoo. Nikkie and Luit ended up in the bare branches of a dead oak tree, safely separated, panting as they gradually calmed down.

This raucous confrontation fit the conventional thinking of 30 years ago perfectly. In a lingering echo of World War II violence, many biologists saw higher primates, including humans, as natural-born "killer apes," their lives defined largely by competition, territoriality and dominance. But the biologist looking on that afternoon at the Arnhem zoo, a soft-spoken young Dutchman named Frans de Waal, perceived something different. About ten minutes after the fight, Nikkie, the alpha male in the group, reached out his arm toward Luit, fingers extended, palm upward, in an offering of peace. De Waal snapped a photograph and watched as the two apes descended to the fork of the tree, where they kissed and embraced, then groomed each other.

Most researchers would have consigned that moment to oblivion trader some dusty academic category like "post-conflict interaction." Discussing animals in language that hinted of emotion was heresy then. But de Waal described what had happened between Nikkie and Luit with the same word he would have used after a fight between his own brothers: it was a "reconciliation." Moreover, he went on to argue that chimps are champions of reconciliation. If they could seem like "killer apes," it was far more accurate to describe them as natural-born peacemakers.

This arresting new view of primate behavior, and de Waal's gift for writing about it gracefully in a series of popular books, have placed him among the leaders of a quiet revolution in our ideas about the animal world and about ourselves. Harvard University biologist E. O. Wilson credits de Waal with "moving the great apes closer to the human level than could have been imagined as recently as two decades ago."

Anthropologist Sarah Blaffer Hrdy, once a skeptic, now calls herself one of de Waal's "biggest fans" and says his description of the tactics primate societies use to stay together "in spite of their dominance-seeking and even murderous tendencies was terribly important, most especially if we want to understand humans." It's a measure of de Waal's influence beyond the scientific community that his book *Chimpanzee Politics* has been singled out as recommended reading in Congress, and his laboratory in Atlanta has been visited (though with unknown effect) by the richest alpha male in the world, Microsoft chairman Bill Gates.

By watching animal groups in captivity for thousands of hours, de Waal helped show just how narrow and misguided the "killer ape" stereotype really was. His research has also helped correct popular misconceptions about what "Darwinian" behavior means, particularly the "selfish gene" idea that we are born ruthless and, except for human culture, would probably stay that way

De Waal has argued, on the contrary, that morality is a part of our innate biological heritage. In his 1996 book, *Good Natured*, he didn't quite say that we are born to be good, merely that being good—being cooperative and conciliatory is the likeliest way to thrive in a social group, whether it's a bridge club, a stock brokerage house or a chimpanzee troop. According to de Waal, chimps, like humans, live by a highly developed set of social rules. They display a keen sense of fairness in their daily give-and-take, an appetite for punishing individuals who misbehave, empathy for victims of injustice, an interest in peacemaking after conflict and, above all, an abiding concern with the maintenance of good relations in the community. De Waal believes this is the rudimentary basis for morality, which may thus date back more than five million years, to the time when chimpanzees and humans shared a common ape ancestor.

Other researchers have since found forms of reconciliation in far more distantly related species, from hyenas to fish. Moreover, when neuroscientists have conducted imaging studies on human subjects, they have found that moral questions light up some of the most primitive emotion centers of the brain. "Morality is not a superficial thing that we added on very late in our evolution," de Waal says. "It relates to very old affectionate and affiliative tendencies that we have as a species, and that we share with all sorts of animals."

De Waal's latest book, *My Family Album: Thirty Years of Primate Photography* (University of California Press), is a tour through the rich array of community-oriented behaviors he has witnessed among apes and monkeys. It's also an introduction to the individual chimps, bonobos, capuchin monkeys and macaques who taught de Waal to see these behaviors. "I follow their social lives," de Waal writes, "the way people follow soap operas."

As in a good soap opera, chimpanzee life is anything but gentle, and, his interest in peacemaking notwithstanding, that suits de Waal just fine. On this lazy spring afternoon, he sits watching his study animals from a boxy yellow tower beside an open-air compound, part of the Yerkes National Primate Research Center at Emory University in Atlanta, where de Waal is a psychology professor. Below, one chimp strolls past another and deals out a slap that would send a football tackle to the emergency room. A second chimp casually sits on a subordinate. Others hurl debris, charge, bluff and displace one another. One chimp lets out an outraged *waaa!* and others join in till the screaming swirls up into a cacophony, then dies away.

De Waal, now 55, going gray at the temples, in round, wire-rimmed glasses and a "Save the Congo" T-shirt, smiles down on the apparent chaos. "Growing up in a family of six boys, I never looked at aggression and conflict as particularly disturbing," he says. "That's maybe a difference I have with people who are always depicting aggression as nasty and negative and bad. I just shrug my shoulders and say, 'Well, it's a little fight. As long as they don't kill each other....'" And killing members of their own troop is something chimpanzees rarely do. Their lives are more like one of those marriages where husband and wife are always squabbling, and always making up.

De Waal got his start in biology as a child wandering the polders, or flooded lowlands, in the Netherlands, and bringing home stickleback fish and dragonfly larvae to raise in jars and buckets. His mother indulged this interest, despite her own aversion to seeing animals in captivity. (She was the child of a pet shop owner and joked that the gene had skipped a generation.) When her fourth son briefly considered studying physics in college, she nudged him toward biology. De Waal wound up studying jackdaws, members of the crow family, which rived around (and sometimes in) his residence. Jackdaws were among the main study animals for de Waal's early hero,

Konrad Lorenz, whose book *On Aggression* was one of the most influential biological works of the 1960s.

Like many students then, de Waal wore his hair long, and sported a disreputable-looking fur-fringed jacket, with the result that he flunked a crucial oral exam. The chairman of the panel said, "If you don't have a tie on, what can you expect?" De Waal was furious, but during the next six months preparing for his makeup exam, he got his first chance to do behavioral work with chimpanzees. This time he passed the exam, then threw himself full-time into captive primate studies. Eventually he obtained three different degrees at three different universities in Holland, including a PhD in primatology. He continued his research with chimps at the Arnhem zoo, then spent ten years studying macaques as a staff member at a primate center in Madison, Wisconsin. Since 1991, he has divided his time between research at Yerkes and teaching at Emory.

At Yerkes, the chimpanzee compound for de Waal's main study group, FS1, is an area of dirt and grass half again as large as a basketball court, enclosed by steel walls and fencing. The chimps lounge around on plastic drums, sections of culvert pipe and old tires. Dividing walls angle across the open space, giving the chimps a chance to get away from one another. (The walls, says de Waal, "let subordinates copulate without getting caught by the alpha.") Toys include an old telephone book, which the chimpanzees like to shred as a form of amusement.

It is, de Waal acknowledges, a completely artificial environment. Unlike chimps in the wild, his charges don't spend seven hours a day foraging across their home range, they face no competition from outside groups, there are no immigrants or emigrants, and because of a worldwide surplus of captive chimps, birth control is mandatory. Captivity also reduces the power difference between males and females; females who live together defend one other against male aggression. "But the basic psychology of the chimpanzee and the basic behavioral repertoire are still there," he says.

Captive studies also offer one crucial advantage: "You have control and you can see more," says de Waal. In wild studies, it's often a matter of luck whether you find the animals in the first place, "and it's tricky to see when they have a fight, because they tend to run into the underbrush. So to follow what happens after a fight is almost an impossibility." Students of captives used to say that research in the wild was anecdotal and unscientific; the wild researchers in turn said captive work had nothing to do with how animals really live. But the two sides now often collaborate. "I look at it that we need both," says de Waal.

He points out some of the characters in FS1, his mild Dutch accent rendering Rhett as "Rat" and Peony as "Penny." The alpha male in the group is a bristling middleweight named Bjorn. "He's a very hyped-up mean male who has come to the top, I think, by fighting dirty." Within the group, rival males generally fight by something like Queensberry rules. But not Bjorn: "He makes injuries in the belly, in the scrotum, in the throat, places that are potentially dangerous."

These tactics naturally make Bjorn an unpopular alpha. He faces constant pressure from his closest rival, a larger male named Socko, short for Socrates. Nobody else much likes Bjorn either, and they show it by the pant-grunts with which subordinates acknowledge another chimp's superior status. "Bjorn has to work for his pant-grunts," says de Waal. "Socko gets his for free." As in most human groups, regime change is a tantalizing possibility, and de Waal notes, a little hopefully, that Socko's kid brother Klaus is almost at an age when the two siblings might form a coalition to oust Bjorn from power.

To the newcomer, all this tends to look like an indecipherable tumult of hairy beasts "chaotically charging around uttering ear-piercing screams," in de Waal's words. It is a little startling to see an observation get recorded, via Palm Pilot, as an equation like this:

31 a4 71 ao w, 036.979
82 a4 31 a4 d, 037.461

Translated, this means that Socko (animal 31) trampled or bit (that's an a4, on a scale of antagonistic incidents from zero to six) the subordinate male named Rhett (71), resulting in a win (w), at about 37 minutes into the observation period. Bjorn (82) came charging to the rescue with an attack on Socko, who smacked Bjorn right back with an a4. It's a measure of Bjorn's unpopularity that Rhett responded to this attack by siding with his assailant, Socko, leading to a draw (d). The conflict resolved itself 45 minutes later when Socko began to groom Rhett, with Bjorn promptly joining in. Then Bjorn groomed Socko, with Rhett joining in.

The statistical technique is not that different from taking a football game—more hairy beasts chaotically charging around uttering ear-piercing screams—and logging it into record books as a neat set of numbers. It allows de Waal to sort through the 4,000 or so antagonistic episodes he has recorded over the years to find out how often Bjorn and Socko have fought, how supporting characters shifted loyalties, who won and whether they reconciled. The statistics turn animal-watching into science, providing a database to test theories.

As with sports, you can always argue about what the statistics mean, and some scientists believe de Waal overstates the case for peacemaking. "I think he is not fully aware of the importance of unreconciled aggressive interactions in the wild—or he chooses not to recognize them," says Richard Wrangham, whose book *Demonic Males* uses ape behavior to explore the origins of human violence. When chimps quarrel in the wild, he says, they reconcile less than 13 percent of the time, only about a third as often as de Waal reports in captivity. This may be because the combatants can get away from each other in the wild, or because, for strategic reasons, they choose not to reconcile. But Wrangham promptly adds the conciliatory note

that he "totally admires" de Waal for having demonstrated that primate life isn't exclusively about waging war, nor about making peace. "If you know chimps, you know they do both."

Indeed, despite the combative nature of academic life, de Waal manages to remain widely liked even among fellow primatologists, possibly because his own behavior is so conciliatory and easygoing. He drives out to the Yerkes field station in an avocado green 1970 Pontiac Catalina, a big boat of a car that he calls "an immigrant type of infatuation." (His other car is a more conventional 2001 Toyota.) He speaks English to his students, French at home, German to colleagues passing through, and Dutch to his chimpanzees. He and his wife, Catherine Marin, who was born in the Loire Valley and teaches French at Georgia Tech, live in a wooded area outside Atlanta. They are both workaholics and made a conscious decision not to have children. But they keep goldfish ponds, birdbaths, hummingbird stations and aquariums around the house. De Waal also bakes bread, and plays Bach and improvised blues on the piano. His upbringing has made him a joker, which he describes as a good survival strategy when you are the fourth son and have no hope of becoming the alpha.

His work has always been distinguished, says *The Naked Ape* author Desmond Morris, by a rare "combination of objectivity and imagination." De Waal knows the names of his chimps, their friends and family, their rivals, their characteristic facial expressions and vocalizations, their quirks of personality. He does not worry about the old rule in Western science against attributing feelings, thoughts or even individuality to mere animals. Rather, he writes of animals and humans sharing a "vast common ground" of behaviors. "Instead of being tied to how we are unlike any animal, human identity should be built around how we are animals that have taken certain capacities a significant step farther."

Back when de Waal started out, the ban on "anthropomorphism" was intended to discourage naively projecting human states of mind onto animals. But the intended objectivity was often an illusion. Scientists were happy to describe two chimps as "rivals," according to de Waal, but balked at the idea that chimps could also sometimes be friends. (The word "affiliative" seemed to come more readily to their lips.) They projected their own interest in aggression onto their study animals. (In fact, it turns out, chimps and most other primates spend only about 5 percent of their day in aggressive encounters.) Worse, says de Waal, the underlying idea of an absolute divide between the behaviors of animals and humans was paralyzing, a kind of "anthropodenial." It turned the animals into robots, "blind actors in a play" that only we understood.

But in real life, animals don't act that way. At the Arnhem zoo, for example, one of de Waal's favorite chimps was a deposed alpha named Yeroen whose blustering shows of dominance no longer impressed because he needed to sit down afterward "with eyes shut, panting heavily." Yeroen was enough of a schemer to play the younger males off one another and hang on as a king-maker. He allied himself with Nikkie, helping him to become the alpha. In repayment, Nikkie indulged the old fox's sexual forays with females in the group, a privilege the alpha would normally try to preserve for himself. To keep the boss on edge, Yeroen would sometimes side with Nikkie's rival Luit. Yeroen was anything but a blind actor in this drama.

De Waal came to view chimpanzee life mainly as an endless round of challenges, fights, coalition-building and brokering of favors. He had witnessed the treetop reconciliation between Nikkie and Luit, and he had an idea that peacemaking behaviors were essential to hold the group together through all this maneuvering. But the maneuvering still dominated his thinking. "Whole passages of Machiavelli seem to be directly applicable to chimpanzee behaviour," he wrote in *Chimpanzee Politics*, an account of his years at Arnhem.

If Machiavelli's *The Prince* had been the first book to frankly describe the power motives and manipulations among the human elite, *Chimpanzee Politics*, published in 1982, was the first to show that these behaviors were embedded in our animal evolution. De Waal wrote that his work at Arnhem had taught him "that the roots of politics are older than humanity." It wasn't a case of projecting human patterns onto chimpanzees: "The reverse is nearer the truth; my knowledge and experience of chimpanzee behaviour has led me to look at humans in another light."

The idea of chimpanzee politics naturally attracted the interest of reporters, who asked questions like "Who do you consider to be the biggest chimpanzee in our present government?" De Waal declined to make such a comparison. "People do it to mock the politicians," he remarked, "but I feel they insult my chimps." On the other hand, politicians themselves have sometimes seen a resemblance.

When he became speaker of the U.S. House of Representatives in 1995, Newt Gingrich placed *Chimpanzee Politics* on his list of recommended reading for incoming Republicans. Gingrich himself proved adept at fierce infighting, but seems not to have paid as much attention to the parts of the book about reconciliation. He eventually had to resign from Congress after the Republicans suffered massive losses in the 1998 elections.

De Waal, by contrast, went on after *Chimpanzee Politics* to emphasize peacemaking. What struck him as he watched his chimpanzees was that serious injuries rarely occurred during fights within the group. Nikkie and Luit, for instance, never exchanged an actual blow during their brawl before Nikkie's gesture of Peace in the oak tree; their only physical contact occurred as part of the reconciliation. Likewise, Bjorn may bite in the wrong places, but he never unleashes the deadly force chimpanzee males can deploy against outsiders. When de Waal was starting out, the best explanation for such restraint came from an eminent evolutionary biologist who concluded "with a lot of fancy mathematics" that animals generally

don't try to kill one another because if they did, their rivals might kill them. "It was so simplistic and so limiting in perspective," says de Waal. "It didn't talk about animals liking each other or needing each other or living together. It just talked about fear of injury."

De Waal came to believe that his chimps lived according to a loose system of favors given and received, what evolutionary biologists called reciprocal altruism. The idea that primates may have evolved for this sort of altruism also gave de Waal the means to counter one of the most pervasive concepts in modern biology. In his influential 1976 book, *The Selfish Gene*, Oxford evolutionist Richard Dawkins argued that we are little more than a product of our genes and that these genes have survived by being as ruthlessly competitive as Chicago gangsters. This became one of the most misinterpreted ideas of the 1980s and '90s and, like "survival of the fittest" in the age of the robber barons, helped to rationalize an era of flamboyantly selfish misbehavior. In fairness, Dawkins didn't intend it that way. "Let us try to teach generosity and altruism," he wrote, "because we are born selfish."

The animal who first made de Waal see the importance of cooperation was a big, lumbering old female chimp named Mama with an "enquiring and all-comprehending" gaze. She once broke up a fight between two warring males by embracing them, one in each arm. Another time she went up to a screaming male and put her finger in his mouth, a gesture of reassurance. Then she turned to his rival and called him over for a kiss, after which the two combatants embraced. "These males are very tense and they're dominant and strong and aggressive," says de Waal. "So to step in and bring them together is a risky business. To me, it means that she cares about relationships in her community. Chimpanzees have something like 'community concern.' They live in a group and they have to get along, and their life is going to be better if their community is better. That's the selfish motive. But this is also the basis of our moral systems: Our life will be better if our community functions better."

Below de Waal's tower at that moment, Bjorn and Socko are embracing like old pals. It is feeding time, and the Yerkes staff often serves a meal in two or three bundles, to study how factors like friendship or rank affect the tricky business of sharing food among the 20 or so chimps in the compound. So the moment is fraught with excitement and anxiety. Much as two humans declare their good intentions with a handshake—a literal clasping of weapon hands—the chimps make obvious gestures of nonaggression. Bjorn is allowing Socko to gnaw on the back of his wrist, and Socko is letting Bjorn mock-bite his shoulder. They slap each other on the back affectionately and dance up and down. Then Bjorn, Socko and Klaus, the three top males, join together in a huddle. It is not quite grace before dinner. But it is not all that different either. The chimps are so intent on defusing the tension of the moment that they completely miss the first round of sugarcane and don't seem to care.

Lest this display of community concern seem a little too rosy, de Waal points out another character in FSI. "Georgia's over here," he says, indicating a 15-year-old female indistinguishable to a newcomer from all the other females. "She's a very mischievous, troublemaking chimp." One of Georgia's favorite tricks as a youngster was to run to the spigot and collect a mouthful of water when she saw visitors arrive at the FSI compound. Then she would mingle among the other chimps, lips sealed, doing her best to look like a dumb ape, a blind actor. If the unwary visitors eventually came close enough, Georgia gleefully squirted them, to general shrieking and laughter from the other chimpanzees.

Since Darwin first suggested it almost 150 years ago, the human connection to animals, and particularly animals like Georgia, has often seemed like an affront to our dignity. For some religious denominations, it was an assault on the doctrine of human supremacy But when de Waal talks about the primates he has known, it seems reasonable to take comfort in the connection. Beneath the veneer of civilization, we humans are not necessarily killer apes, nor have we evolved to be as ruthless as Al Capone. We are simply social primates, endlessly working out the business of living together. It is difficult business because, like chimpanzees, we are a quarrelsome species. But if de Waal is right, peace may also come to us more naturally than we imagine because of our long evolutionary history of empathy, reconciliation, cooperation and morality.

Even that reprobate Georgia shows signs of reforming. She is a mother now herself and eager to tit into the give-and-take of the community. She has figured out that the man in the yellow tower wields some influence in her world and greets him lavishly, if only for strategic reasons. She no longer spits at guests. She is still not a perfect lady, just a pretty good chimp figuring out how to get along in her world. It is easy to understand why de Waal calls such creatures family.

RICHARD CONNIFF *is at work on an account of Homo sapiens in the workplace. The photographs are from Frans de Waal's recent book,* My Family Album: Thirty Years of Primate Photography.

Disturbing Behaviors of the ORANGUTAN

Studies of these great apes show that some males pursue an unexpected and disquieting evolutionary strategy

By Anne Nacey Maggioncalda and Robert M. Sapolsky

The orangutan is one of humankind's closest relatives. One of the four great apes (the other three are gorillas, chimpanzees and bonobos), *Pongo pygmaeus* is exquisitely adapted for life in the forest canopies of the Southeast Asian islands of Borneo and Sumatra. With their long arms and hooklike hands, orangutans are adept at swinging from tree to tree in search of tropical fruits. They are among the most solitary of large primates and the only great apes found outside Africa. Orangutans are also notable for the striking size difference between male and females: the average weight of an adult male (about 90 kilograms, or 198 pounds) is more than twice that of a female.

An adult male orangutan is an impressive sight. The animal has a pair of wide cheek pads, called flanges, and a well-developed throat sac used for emitting loud cries known as long calls. The mature male also has long, brightly colored hair on its body and face. These are secondary sexual characteristics, the flamboyant signals that male orangutans flaunt to proclaim their fertility and fitness to the opposite sex. The features emerge during orangutan adolescence: males reach puberty at around seven to nine years of age, then spend a few years in a far-from-impressive "subadult" stage, during which they are about the same size as mature females. The males reach their adult size and develop secondary sexual traits by ages 12 to 14. Or at least that's what primate researchers used to think.

As stable social groups of orangutans were established in zoos, however, it became clear that an adolescent male could remain a subadult, in a state of arrested development, until his late teens. In the 1970s, studies of orangutans in the rain forests of Southeast Asia by Biruté M.F. Galdikas of Simon Fraser University in British Columbia and others produced the same finding: sometimes males were arrested adolescents for a decade or more, about half their potential reproductive lives. Variability of this magnitude is fascinating—it is like finding a species in which pregnancy could last anywhere from six months to five years.

Biologists are keenly interested in studying cases of arrested development because they often shed light on the processes of growth and maturation. In some instances, the cause of arrested development is a genetic disorder; for example, a mutation in the receptor for a growth factor in humans results in a form of dwarfism. Environmental factors can also slow or halt an organism's development. For instance, food shortages delay maturation in humans and many other animals. This response is logical from an evolutionary standpoint—if it is unclear whether you will survive another week, it makes no sense to waste calories by adding bone mass or developing secondary sexual characteristics. Gymnasts and ballet dancers who exercise to extremes and anorexics who starve themselves sometimes experience delayed onset of puberty.

Among male orangutans, though, the cause of arrested development seems to lie in the animals' *social* environment. The presence of dominant adult males appears to delay the maturation of adolescent males in the same vicinity. Until recently, researchers believed that they were observing a stress-induced pathology—that is, the adolescent orangutans stopped developing because the adult males bullied and frightened them. Over the past few years, however, we have conducted studies suggesting that arrested development among orangutans is not a pathology but an adaptive evolutionary strategy. The arrested adolescent males are capable of impregnating females, and by staying small and immature (in terms of secondary sexual features) they minimize the amount of food they need and lower the risk of serious conflict with adult males. But the strategy of these arrested adolescents has a disquieting aspect: they copulate forcibly with females. In other words, they rape.

Measuring Stress

THE FIRST INVESTIGATIONS into this subject focused on groups of captive orangutans. Terry L. Maple of Zoo Atlanta and other zoo biologists found that adolescent males remained developmentally arrested as long as there was a mature male in their enclosure. If the researchers removed that dominant male, the adolescents soon began to develop into adults. This kind of social regulation had been observed previously in other species. Among mandrill monkeys, for instance, socially dominant males develop dramatic secondary sexual characteristics, such as large testes and high testosterone levels, whereas subordinate males do not. In tree shrews and many rodent species, puberty is delayed in the subordinate animals. In another example, elephant poaching in certain areas of Africa has recently produced orphaned males that grew up in a fairly unsocialized manner. When in "musth"—a male elephant's mating period—these animals become quite aggressive and dangerous. Some zoologists have reported an effective solution: introducing older, more dominant males into the region, which results in social suppression of musth in the rogue males.

In all these cases, researchers have generally agreed that the stress of being subordinate accounts for the developmental arrest. During a typical period of stress for a mammal—say, a sprint across the savanna to escape a predator—energy is mobilized to power the muscles. As part of this process, a variety of long-term building projects in the body are inhibited, including growth, tissue repair and reproductive functions. It is the logic of triage: the animal concentrates on survival during the emergency and resumes long-term tasks later, if there is a later. But when an animal undergoes chronic stress, such as that caused by social subordination, the triaging can have adverse consequences, such as decreased growth, lower levels of sex hormones, reduced fertility and delayed puberty. In humans, severe and prolonged psychological stress can cause growth to stop in children, a rare syndrome called psychogenic dwarfism.

At first glance, adolescent male orangutans also appear to be under chronic stress. Adult male orangutans are extremely aggressive to adolescents, particularly within the confines of a zoo. In the wild, orangutan males are dispersed and solitary, belligerently defending a large territory that encompasses several females' territories—sort of a scattered harem. But even there, adolescents are well aware of the threatening presence of a mature male. One signal is a musky odorant that adult males spread about their territories. In addition, mature male orangutans announce their presence by performing long calls; John C. Mitani of the University of Michigan has found that these resonant cries can travel for miles.

Researchers had made little effort, however, to test the hypothesis that the stress of being near a dominant male induces

hormonal changes that arrest development in adolescents. In 1989 we began looking for a way to examine the hormones of arrested adolescent orangutans to determine whether these animals were indeed under chronic stress. Ideally one would want to measure the levels of relevant hormones in the orangutans' blood, but this was impossible to do, for ethical and practical reasons. So we took advantage of the fact that the average levels of various hormones in the animals' blood are reflected in a fairly parallel fashion in their urine. Getting urine from wild animals would be immensely difficult, so we studied captive populations. Thanks to the generous help of zookeepers, curators and veterinarians at 13 zoos, we obtained more than 1,000 urine samples from 28 male orangutans, along with information on their developmental status (juvenile, arrested adolescent, developing adolescent or adult), housing, diet, medical history and growth records. In collaboration with Nancy Czekala of the Center for Reproduction of Endangered Species at the San Diego Zoo, we measured the levels of nine hormones, comparing animals in different developmental stages.

First we focused on growth hormone, which is crucial for normal maturation. Among the juveniles, arrested adolescents and adults, growth hormone levels in the urine were low and extremely similar, within 15 percent of one another. In contrast, adolescent males that were maturing into adults had growth hormone levels approximately three times as high. This result basically served as an internal control, showing that the external assessments of an animal's development stage closely matched the hormonal profile relevant to growth. In other words, adolescent males going through a developmental spurt in terms of appearance—growing larger, increasing the size of their cheek flanges, and so on—were experiencing hormonal changes as well.

We then considered hormones that respond to stress. Probably the best known is adrenaline (also called epinephrine), which plays a central role in energy mobilization. Epinephrine, unfortunately, cannot be measured accurately in urine. We could, however, determine levels of another key class of stress hormones called the glucocorticoids, which can suppress growth, tissue repair and reproduction. In addition, we measured the levels of prolactin, a stress-indicative hormone that can inhibit reproduction.

This is where we got a surprise. Glucocorticoid levels did not differ among juveniles, arrested adolescents and adults. Prolactin levels did nor differ either. But adolescents going through the developmental spurt had glucocorticoid and prolactin levels roughly double those of the other groups. It wasn't the developmentally arrested adolescents who seemed to be stressed—it was the *developing* adolescents.

We got another surprise when we examined reproductive hormones in these animals. As expected, adolescent males who were developing secondary sexual characteristics had hormonal profiles implying an active gonadal system. Developing males had higher levels of testosterone and luteinizing hormone (which stimulates the release of testosterone) than did the arrested adolescents. But the levels of these hormones in arrested adolescents were equivalent to those seen in adults. Moreover, arrested males had levels of follicle-stimulating hormone

(FSH), which stimulates sperm maturation in males, equal to those of developing adolescents or adult males. And other investigators have found that arrested adolescents have mature functional sperm and that their testes are the same size as those of developing adolescents.

Evolutionary Strategies

THESE FINDINGS OVERTURNED some long-held assumptions about orangutans. Apparently, arrested adolescents are neither stressed nor reproductively suppressed. What is going on? It turns out that there is more than one way for a male orangutan to improve his chances of reproducing.

A cornerstone of modern evolutionary theory is that animal behavior has evolved not for the good of the species or the social group but to maximize the number of gene copies passed on by an individual and its close relatives. For a longtime, the study of primates was dominated by simplistic models of how animals achieve this goal. According to these models, male behavior consists of virtually nothing but aggression and competition to gain access to females. If only one female is sexually receptive in a group with many males, this competition would result in the highest-ranking male mating with her; if two females are receptive, the males ranking first and second in the hierarchy would mate with them, and so on.

But this kind of behavior is rarely seen among social primates. Instead male primates can choose alternative strategies to maximize their reproductive success. Why should there be alternatives? Because the seemingly logical strategy—developing powerful muscles and dramatic secondary sexual characteristics to excel at male-male competition—has some serious drawbacks. In many species, maintaining those secondary characteristics requires elevated testosterone levels, which have a variety of adverse effects on health. The aggression that comes with such a strategy is not great for health either.

Furthermore, increased body mass means greater metabolic demands and more pressure for successful food acquisition. During famines, the bigger primates are less likely to survive. For an arboreal species such as the orangutan, the heavier body of the mature male also limits which trees and branches can be accessed for food. And the development of secondary sexual characteristics makes a male more conspicuous, both to predators and to other males that view those characteristics as a challenge.

The competition between adult males and developing adolescents probably explains the elevated levels of stress hormones in the latter. In the eyes of an adult male orangutan, a developing male is soon to be a challenger, so naturally he becomes a prime target for aggression. The same pattern is seen among horses and various other social ungulates: it is not until the young males start developing secondary sexual characteristics that the unrelated dominant males begin to harass them into leaving the group. Another example comes from work by one of us (Sapolsky) with wild baboons. Some socially subordinate male baboons have much higher glucocorticoid levels than do the dominant animals, primarily because these subordinates are actively challenging the high-ranking males.

In contrast, the key impression that a developmentally arrested male communicates to an adult male is lack of threat or challenge, because the immature male looks like a kid. Arrested male orangutans are apparently inconspicuous enough to be spared a certain amount of social stress. What is more, the "low profile" of these animals may actually give them a competitive advantage when it comes to reproduction. In many primate species, the low-ranking males are actually doing a fair share of the mating. Genetic paternity testing of these primates has shown that the subordinate males are quite successful in passing on their genes. This finding extends to orangutans: studies of zoo populations have proved that arrested males mate and that these matings are fertile. More recently Sri Suci Utami of Utrecht University in the Netherlands has shown that arrested adolescents fathered approximately half of the orangutan babies at her Sumatran study site.

Why are these low-ranking males taking part in so many matings? In some primate species, such as the savanna baboon, the females can decide with whom they will mate, and they frequently choose males who exhibit strong male-female affiliation and parental behavior rather than male-male competition. Even when dominant male baboons stand guard to prevent low-ranking males from mating, the females often initiate surreptitious matings—sometimes referred to as "stolen copulations"—with the subordinates. For low-ranking male baboons, the strategy of pursuing affiliative "friendships" with females is a viable one because it avoids the metabolic costs, injuries and stress of male-male competition.

But arrested male orangutans do not engage in long-term affiliative relationships with females, although an arrested male may sometimes accompany a female for several days as she roams through the forest. Furthermore, the great majority of adult female orangutans are sexually receptive only to mature males. So how do the arrested males mate? Observations of orangutans both in the wild and in captive populations have indicated that the arrested males forcibly copulate with females. Rape is an apt term for these copulations: the adult females usually resist the arrested adolescents fiercely, biting the males whenever they can and emitting loud, guttural sounds (called rape grunts) that are heard only under these circumstances. Adult males sometimes rape, too, but not nearly as often as the arrested males. In a study conducted in Borneo during the early 1980s, Mitani and his field assistants observed 151 copulations by arrested males; 144 of the matings were forced.

Thus, two reproductive strategies appear to have evolved for adolescent male orangutans. If no fully mature males are nearby, the adolescent will most likely develop quickly in the hopes of attracting female attention. When adult males are present, however, a strategy of arrested development has its advantages. If the social environment changes—say, if the nearby adult males die off or migrate—the arrested males will rapidly develop secondary sexual features and change their behavior patterns. Researchers are now trying to determine exactly how the presence or absence of adult males triggers hormonal changes in the adolescents.

Unpleasant Findings

WHAT ARE THE LESSONS we can learn from the male orangutan? First, a situation that seems stressful from a human's perspective may not necessarily be so. Second, the existence of alternative reproductive strategies shows that the optimal approach can vary dramatically in different social and ecological settings. There is no single blueprint for understanding the evolution of behavior. Third, although the recognition of alternative strategies built around female choice has generally met with a receptive audience among scientists, the rape-oriented strategy of arrested male orangutans is not so pleasing. But the study of primates has demonstrated time and again that the behavior of these animals is far from Disney-esque. Just consider the strategic infanticide of langur monkeys or the organized aggression—sometimes called genocide—between groups of chimpanzee males.

One must be cautious, however, in trying to gain insights into human behavior by extrapolating from animal studies. There is a temptation to leap to a wrongheaded conclusion: because forcible copulation occurs in orangutans and something similar occurs in humans, rape has a natural basis and is therefore unstoppable. This argument ignores the fact that the orangutan is the only nonhuman primate to engage in forcible copulation as a routine means of siring offspring. Furthermore, close observations of orangutan rape show that it is very different from human rape: for example, researchers have never seen a male orangutan injure a female during copulation in an apparently intentional manner. Most important, the orangutan's physiology, life history and social structure are completely unlike those of any other primate. Orangutans have evolved a unique set of adaptations to survive in their environment, and hence it would be the height of absurdity to draw simpleminded parallels between their behaviors and those of humans.

MORE TO EXPLORE

Reflections of Eden: My Years with the Orangutans of Borneo. Biruté M. F. Galdikas. Back Bay Books, 1996.

Reproductive Hormone Profiles in Captive Male Orangutans: Implications for Understanding Developmental Arrest. Anne N. Maggioncalda, Robert M. Sapolsky and Nancy M. Czekala in *American Journal of Physical Anthropology*, Vol. 109, No. 1, pages 19–32; May 1999.

Orangutans: Wizards of the Forest. Anne E. Russon. Firefly Books, 2000.

Male Orangutan Subadulthood: A New Twist on the Relationship between Chronic Stress and Developmental Arrest. Anne N. Maggioncalda, Nancy M. Czekala and Robert M. Sapolsky in *American Journal of Physical Anthropology*, Vol. 118, No.1, pages 25–32; May 2002.

More information on orangutans is available at the Web sites of the Orangutan Foundation international (**www.orangutan.org**), the Balikpapan Orangutan Society (**www.orangutan.com**) and the Orangutan Network (**www.orangutannetwork.net**).

ANNE NACEY MAGGIONCALDA and *ROBERT M. SAPOLSKY* have been studying the evolution of male orangutan reproductive strategies for more than a decade. Maggioncalda, who received a Ph.D. in biological anthropology and anatomy from Duke University in 1995, is a lecturer in the department of anthropological sciences and the program in human biology at Stanford University and in the department of anatomy at the Stanford University School of Medicine. Sapolsky, who earned a Ph.D. in neuroendocrinology from the Rockefeller University in 1984, is professor of biological sciences and neurology at Stanford and a research associate at the National Museums of Kenya. His research interests include neuron death, gene therapy and the physiology of primates.

COMMENTARY

Are We in Anthropodenial?

By Frans de Waal

WHEN GUESTS ARRIVE AT THE Yerkes Regional Primate Research Center in Georgia, where I work, they usually pay a visit to the chimpanzees. And often, when she sees them approaching the compound, an adult female chimpanzee named Georgia will hurry to the spigot to collect a mouthful of water. She'll then casually mingle with the rest of the colony behind the mesh fence, and not even the sharpest observer will notice anything unusual. If necessary, Georgia will wait minutes, with her lips closed, until the visitors come near. Then there will be shrieks, laughs, jumps—and sometimes falls—when she suddenly sprays them.

I have known quite a few apes that are good at surprising people, naive and otherwise. Heini Hediger, the great Swiss zoo biologist, recounts how he—being prepared to meet the challenge and paying attention to the ape's every move—got drenched by an experienced chimpanzee. I once found myself in a similar situation with Georgia; she had taken a drink from the spigot and was sneaking up to me. I looked her straight in the eye and pointed my finger at her, warning in Dutch, "I have seen you!" She immediately stepped back, let some of the water dribble from her mouth, and swallowed the rest. I certainly do not wish to claim that she understands Dutch, but she must have sensed that I knew what she was up to, and that I was not going to be an easy target.

To endow animals with human emotions has long been a scientific taboo. But if we do not, we risk missing something fundamental, about both animals and us.

Now, no doubt even a casual reader will have noticed that in describing Georgia's actions, I've implied human qualities such as intentions, the ability to interpret my own awareness, and a tendency toward mischief. Yet scientific tradition says I should avoid such language—I am committing the sin of anthropomorphism, of turning nonhumans into humans. The word comes from the Greek, meaning "human form," and it was the ancient Greeks who first gave the practice a bad reputation. They did not have chimpanzees in mind: the philosopher Xenophanes objected to Homer's poetry because it treated Zeus and the other gods as if they were people. How could we be so arrogant, Xenophanes asked, as to think that the gods should look like us? If horses could draw pictures, he suggested mockingly, they would no doubt make their gods look like horses.

Nowadays the intellectual descendants of Xenophanes warn against perceiving animals to be like ourselves. There are, for example, the behaviorists, who follow psychologist B. F. Skinner in viewing the actions of animals as responses shaped by rewards and punishments rather than the result of internal decision making, emotions, or intentions. They would say that Georgia was not "up to" anything when she sprayed water on her victims. Far from planning and executing a naughty plot, Georgia merely fell for the irresistible reward of human surprise and annoyance. Whereas any person acting like her would be scolded, arrested, or held accountable, Georgia is somehow innocent.

Behaviorists are not the only scientists who have avoided thinking about the inner life of animals. Some sociobiologists—researchers who look for the roots of behavior in evolution—depict animals as "survival machines" and "pre-programmed robots" put on Earth to serve their "selfish" genes. There is a certain metaphorical value to these concepts, but is has been negated by the misunderstanding they've created. Such language can give the impression that only genes are entitled to an inner life. No more delusively anthropomorphizing idea has been put forward since the pet-rock craze of the 1970s. In fact, during evolution, genes—a mere batch of molecules—simply multiply at different rates, depending on the traits they produce in an individual. To say that genes are selfish is like saying a snowball growing in size as it rolls down a hill is greedy for snow.

Logically, these agnostic attitudes toward a mental life in animals can be valid only if they're applied to our own species as well. Yet it's uncommon to find researchers who try to study human behavior as purely a matter of reward and punishment. Describe a person as having intentions, feelings, and thoughts and you most likely won't encounter much resistance. Our own familiarity with our inner lives overrules whatever some school of thought might claim about us. Yet despite this double standard toward behavior in humans and animals, modern biology leaves us no choice other than to conclude that we *are* animals. In terms of anatomy, physiology, and neurology we are really no more exceptional than, say, an elephant or a platypus is in its own way. Even such presumed hallmarks of humanity as warfare, politics, culture, morality, and language may not be completely unprecedented. For example, different groups of wild chimpanzees employ different technologies—some fish for termites with sticks, others crack nuts with stones—that are transmitted from one generation to the next through a process reminiscent of human culture.

Given these discoveries, we must be very careful not to exaggerate the uniqueness of our species. The ancients apparently never gave much thought to this practice, the opposite of anthropomorphism, and so we lack a word for it. I will call it anthropodenial: a blindness to the human-like characteristics of other animals, or the animal-like characteristics of ourselves.

Those who are in anthropodenial try to build a brick wall to separate humans from the rest of the animal kingdom. They carry on the tradition of René Descartes, who declared that while humans possessed souls, animals were mere automatons. This produced a serious dilemma when Charles Darwin came along: If we descended from such automatons, were we not automatons ourselves? If not, how did we get to be so different?

Each time we must ask such a question, another brick is pulled out of the di-

viding wall, and to me this wall is beginning to look like a slice of Swiss cheese. I work on a daily basis with animals from which it is about as hard to distance yourself as from "Lucy," the famed 3.2-million-year-old fossil australopithecine. If we owe Lucy the respect of an ancestor, does this not force a different look at the apes? After all, as far as we can tell, the most significant difference between Lucy and modern chimpanzees is found in their hips, not their craniums.

As SOON AS WE ADMIT THAT ANIMALS are far more like our relatives than like machines, then anthropodenial becomes impossible and anthropomorphism becomes inevitable—and scientifically acceptable. But not *all* forms of anthropomorphism, of course. Popular culture bombards us with examples of animals being humanized for all sorts of purposes, ranging from education to entertainment to satire to propaganda. Walt Disney, for example, made us forget that Mickey is a mouse, and Donald a duck. George Orwell laid a cover of human societal ills over a population of livestock. I was once struck by an advertisement for an oil company that claimed its propane saved the environment, in which a grizzly bear enjoying a pristine landscape had his arm around his mate's shoulders. In fact, bears are nearsighted and do not form pair-bonds, so the image says more about our own behavior than theirs.

Perhaps that was the intent. The problem is, we do not always remember that, when used in this way, anthropomorphism can provide insight only into human affairs and not into the affairs of animals. When my book *Chimpanzee Politics* came out in France, in 1987, my publisher decided (unbeknownst to me) to put François Mitterrand and Jacques Chirac on the cover with a chimpanzee between them. I can only assume he wanted to imply that these politicians acted like "mere" apes. Yet by doing so he went completely against the whole point of my book, which was not to ridicule people but to show that chimpanzees live in complex societies full of

alliances and power plays that in some ways mirror our own.

You can often hear similar attempts at anthropomorphic humor in the crowds that form around the monkey exhibit at a typical zoo. Isn't it interesting that antelopes, lions, and giraffes rarely elicit hilarity? But people who watch primates end up hooting and yelling, scratching themselves in exaggeration, and pointing at the animals while shouting, "I had to look twice, Larry. I thought it was you!" In my mind, the laughter reflects anthropodenial: it is a nervous reaction caused by an uncomfortable resemblance.

That very resemblance, however, can allow us to make better use of anthropomorphism, but for this we must view it as a means rather than an end. It should not be our goal to find some quality in an animal that is precisely equivalent to an aspect of our own inner lives. Rather, we should use the fact that we are similar to animals to develop ideas we can test. For example, after observing a group of chimpanzees at length, we begin to suspect that some individuals are attempting to "deceive" others—by giving false alarms to distract unwanted attention from the theft of food or from forbidden sexual activity. Once we frame the observation in such terms, we can devise testable predictions. We can figure out just what it would take to demonstrate deception on the part of chimpanzees. In this way, a speculation is turned into a challenge.

Naturally, we must always be on guard. To avoid making silly interpretations based on anthropomorphism, one must always interpret animal behavior in the wider context of a species' habits and natural history. Without experience with primates, one could imagine that a grinning rhesus monkey must be delighted, or that a chimpanzee running toward another with loud grunts must be in an aggressive mood. But primatologists know from many hours of observation that rhesus monkeys bare their teeth when intimidated, and that chimpanzees often grunt when they meet and embrace. In other words, a grinning rhesus monkey signals submission, and a chimpanzee's grunting often serves as a greeting. A careful observer may thus arrive at an informed anthropomorphism that is at odds with extrapolations from human behavior.

One must also always be aware that some animals are more like ourselves than others. The problem of sharing the experiences of organisms that rely on different senses is a profound one. It was expressed most famously by the philosopher Thomas Nagel when he asked, "What is it like to be a bat?" A bat perceives its world in pulses of reflected sound, something we creatures of vision would have a hard time imagining. Perhaps even more alien would be the experience of an animal such as the star-nosed mole. With 22 pink, writhing tentacles around its nostrils, it is able to feel microscopic textures on small objects in the mud with the keenest sense of touch of any animal on Earth.

Humans can barely imagine a star-nosed mole's *Umwelt*—a German term for the environment as perceived by the animal. Obviously, the closer a species is to us, the easier it is to enter its *Umwelt*. This is why anthropomorphism is not only tempting in the case of apes but also hard to reject on the grounds that we cannot know how they perceive the world. Their sensory systems are essentially the same as ours.

LAST SUMMER, AN APE SAVED A three-year-old boy. The child, who had fallen 20 feet into the primate exhibit at Chicago's Brookfield Zoo, was scooped up and carried to safety by Binti Jua, an eight-year-old western lowland female gorilla. The gorilla sat down on a log in a stream, cradling the boy in her lap and patting his back, and then carried him to one of the exhibit doorways before laying him down and continuing on her way.

Binti became a celebrity overnight, figuring in the speeches of leading politicians who held her up as an example of much-needed compassion. Some scientists were less lyrical, however. They cautioned that Binti's motives might have been less noble than they appeared, pointing out that this gorilla had been raised by people and had been taught parental skills with a stuffed animal. The whole affair might have been one of a confused maternal instinct, they claimed.

Bonobos have been known to assist companions new to their quarters in zoos, taking them by the hand to guide them through the maze of corridors connecting parts of their building.

The intriguing thing about this flurry of alternative explanations was that nobody would think of raising similar doubts when a person saves a dog hit by a car. The rescuer might have grown up around a kennel, have been praised for being kind to animals, have a nurturing personality, yet we would still see his behavior as an act of caring. Whey then, in Binti's case, was her background held against her? I am not saying that I know what went through Binti's head, but I do know that no one had prepared her for this kind of emergency and that it is unlikely that, with her own 17-month-old infant on her back, she was "maternally confused." How in the world could such a highly intelligent animal mistake a blond boy in sneakers and a red T-shirt for a juvenile gorilla? Actually, the biggest surprise was how surprised most people were. Students of ape behavior did not feel that Binti had done anything unusual. Jörg Hess, a Swiss gorilla expert, put it most bluntly, "The incident can be sensational only for people who don't know a thing about gorillas."

Binti's action made a deep impression mainly because it benefited a member of our own species, but in my work on the evolution of morality and empathy, I have encountered numerous instances of animals caring for one another. For example, a chimpanzee consoles a victim after a violent attack, placing an arm around him and patting his back. And bonobos (or pygmy chimpanzees) have been known to assist companions new to their quarters in zoos, taking them by the hand to guide them through the maze of corridors connecting parts of their building. These kinds of cases don't reach the newspapers but are consistent with Binti's assistance to the unfortunate boy and the idea that apes have a capacity for sympathy.

The traditional bulwark against this sort of cognitive interpretation is the principle of parsimony—that we must make as few assumptions as possible when trying to construct a scientific explanation, and that assuming an ape is capable of something like sympathy is too great a leap. But doesn't that same principle of parsimony argue against assuming a huge cognitive gap when the evolutionary distance between humans and apes is so small? If two closely related species act in the same manner, their underlying mental processes are probably the same, too. The incident at the Brookfield Zoo shows how hard it is to avoid anthropodenial and anthropomorphism at the same time: in trying to avoid thinking of Binti as a human being, we run straight into the realization that Binti's actions make little sense if we refuse to assume intentions and feelings.

In the end we must ask: What kind of risk we are willing to take—the risk of underestimating animal mental life or the risk of overestimating it? There is no simple answer. But from an evolutionary perspective, Binti's kindness, like Georgia's mischief, is most parsimoniously explained in the same way we explain our own behavior—as the result of a complex, and familiar, inner life.

FRANS DE WAAL is a professor of psychology at Emory University and research professor at the Yerkes Regional Primate Research Center in Atlanta. He is the author of several books, including Chimpanzee Politics *and* Good Natured: The Origins of Right and Wrong in Humans and Other Animals. *His latest book, in collaboration with acclaimed wildlife photographer Frans Lanting, is* Bonobo: The Forgotten Ape, *published by the University of California Press (1997).*

UNIT 3
Sex and Society

Unit Selections

Key Points to Consider

• How does human sexuality differ from that of other creatures?

• What implications does bonobo sexual behavior have for understanding human evolution?

• How do social bonds provide females with protection against abusive males?

 **Links: www.dushkin.com/online/**
These sites are annotated in the World Wide Web pages.

American Anthropologist
http://www.aaanet.org/aa/index.htm
American Scientist
http://www.amsci.org/amsci.html
Bonobo Sex and Society
http://songweaver.com/info/bonobos.html

Any account of hominid evolution would be remiss if it did not at least attempt to explain that most mystifying of all human experiences—our sexuality.

No other aspect of our humanity—whether it be upright posture, tool-making ability, or intelligence in general—seems to elude our intellectual grasp at least as much as it dominates our subjective consciousness. While we are a long way from reaching a consensus as to why it arose and what it is all about, there is widespread agreement that our very preoccupation with sex is in itself one of the hallmarks of being human. Even as we experience it and analyze it, we exalt it and condemn it. Beyond seemingly irrational fixations, however, there is the further tendency to project our own values upon the observations we make and the data we collect.

There are many who argue quite reasonably that the human bias has been more male- than female-oriented and that the recent "feminization" of anthropology has resulted in new kinds of research and refreshingly new theoretical perspectives. (See "A Woman's Curse?" by Meredith Small.) Not only should we consider the source when evaluating the old theories, so goes the reasoning, but we should also welcome the source when considering the new. To take one example, traditional theory would

have predicted that wherever male primates are larger than females, the size difference will be a major factor in sexual coercion. In actuality, says Barbara Smuts in "Apes of Wrath," such coercion is reduced in those primate species in which females are able to form alliances against male aggression. That this is not so, that making love can be more important than making war, and that females do not necessarily have to live in fear of competitive males, just goes to show that, even among monkeys, nothing can be taken for granted.

Finally, there is the question of the social significance of sexuality in humans. In the essay "Mothers and Others" by Sarah Blaffer Hrdy, the point is made that reproductive success often depends upon how much assistance the mother gets from others, including adult males and older children. In "What's Love Got to Do With It?" Meredith Small shows that the chimp-like bonobos of Zaire use sex to reduce tensions and cement social relations and, in so doing, have achieved a high degree of equality between the sexes. Whether we see parallels in the human species, says Small, depends on our willingness to interpret bonobo behavior as a "modern version of our own ancestors' sex play," and this, in turn, may depend on our prior theoretical commitments.

Mothers and Others

From queen bees to elephant matriarchs, many animal mothers are assisted by others in rearing off-spring. Anthropologist Sarah Blaffer Hrdy maintains that our human ancestors, too, were "Cooperative Breeders"—A mode of life that enabled them to thrive in many new environments. Today, argues Hrdy, our continued ability to raise emotionally healthy children may well depend on how well we understand the cooperative aspect of our evolutionary heritage.

By Sarah Blaffer Hrdy

Mother apes—chimpanzees, gorillas, orangutans, humans—dote on their babies. And why not? They give birth to an infant after a long gestation and, in most cases, suckle it for years. With humans, however, the job of providing for a juvenile goes on and on. Unlike all other ape babies, ours mature slowly and reach independence late. A mother in a foraging society may give birth every four years or so, and her first few children remain dependent long after each new baby arrives; among nomadic foragers, grown-ups may provide food to children for eighteen or more years. To come up with the 10–13 million calories that anthropologists such as Hillard Kaplan calculate are needed to rear a young human to independence, a mother needs help.

So how did our prehuman and early human ancestresses living in the Pleistocene Epoch (from 1.6 million until roughly 10,000 years ago) manage to get those calories? And under what conditions would natural selection allow a female ape to produce babies so large and slow to develop that they are beyond her means to rear on her own?

The old answer was that fathers helped out by hunting. And so they do. But hunting is a risky occupation, and fathers may die or defect or take up with other females. And when they do, what then? New evidence from surviving traditional cultures suggests that mothers in the Pleistocene may have had a significant degree of help—from men who thought they just might have been the fathers, from grandmothers and great-aunts, from older children.

These helpers other than the mother, called allomothers by sociobiologists, do not just protect and provision youngsters. In groups such as the Efe and Aka Pygmies of central Africa, allomothers actually hold children and carry them about. In these tight-knit communities of communal foragers—within which men, women, and children still hunt with nets, much as humans are thought to have done tens of thousands of years ago—siblings, aunts, uncles, fathers, and grandmothers hold newborns on the first day of life. When University of New Mexico anthropologist Paula Ivey asked an Efe woman, "Who cares for babies?" the immediate answer was, "We all do!" By three weeks of age, the babies are in contact with allomothers 40 percent of the time. By eighteen weeks, infants actually spend more time with allomothers than with their gestational mothers. On average, Efe babies have fourteen different caretakers, most of whom are close kin. According to Washington State University anthropologist Barry Hewlett, Aka babies are within arm's reach of their fathers for more than half of every day.

Accustomed to celebrating the antiquity and naturalness of mother-centered models of child care, as well as the nuclear family in which the mother nurtures while the father provides, we Westerners tend to regard the practices of the Efe and the Aka as exotic. But to sociobiologists, whose stock in trade is comparisons across species, all this helping has a familiar ring. It's called cooperative breeding. During the past quarter century, as anthropologists and sociobiologists started to compare notes, one of the spectacular surprises has been how much allomaternal care goes on, not just within various human societies but among animals generally. Evidently, diverse organisms have converged on cooperative breeding for the best of evolutionary reasons.

A broad look at the most recent evidence has convinced me that cooperative breeding was the strategy that permitted our own ancestors to produce costly, slow-maturing infants at shorter intervals, to take advantage of new kinds of resources in habitats other than the mixed savanna-woodland of tropical Africa, and to spread more widely and swiftly than any primate had before. We already know that animal mothers who delegate some of the costs of infant care to others are thereby freed to produce more or larger young or to breed more frequently. Consider the case of silver-backed jackals. Patricia Moehlman, of the World Conservation Union, has shown that for every extra helper bringing back food, jackal parents rear one extra pup per litter. Cooperative breeding also helps various species expand into habitats in which they would normally not be able to rear any young at all. Florida scrub-jays, for example, breed in an exposed landscape where unrelenting predation from hawks and snakes usually precludes the fledging of young; survival in this habitat is possible only because older siblings help guard and feed the young. Such cooperative arrangements permit animals as different as naked mole rats (the social insects of the mammal world) and wolves to move into new habitats and sometimes to spread over vast areas.

When animal mothers delegate some infant-care costs to others, they can produce more or larger young and raise them in less-than-ideal habitats.

What does it take to become a cooperative breeder? Obviously, this lifestyle is an option only for creatures capable of living in groups. It is facilitated when young but fully mature individuals (such as young Florida scrub-jays) do not or cannot immediately leave their natal group to breed on their own and instead remain among kin in their natal location. As with delayed maturation, delayed dispersal of young means that teenagers, "spinster" aunts, real and honorary uncles will be on hand to help their kin rear young. Flexibility is another criterion for cooperative breeders. Helpers must be ready to shift to breeding mode should the opportunity arise. In marmosets and tamarins—the little South American monkeys that are, besides us, the only full-fledged cooperative breeders among primates—a female has to be ready to be a helper this year and a mother the next. She may have one mate or several. In canids such as wolves or wild dogs, usually only the dominant, or alpha, male and female in a pack reproduce, but younger group members hunt with the mother and return to the den to regurgitate predigested meat into the mouths of her pups. In a fascinat-

ing instance of physiological flexibility, a subordinate female may actually undergo hormonal transformations similar to those of a real pregnancy: her belly swells, and she begins to manufacture milk and may help nurse the pups of the alpha pair. Vestiges of cooperative breeding crop up as well in domestic dogs, the distant descendants of wolves. After undergoing a pseudopregnancy, my neighbors' Jack Russell terrier chased away the family's cat and adopted and suckled her kittens. To suckle the young of another species is hardly what Darwinians call an adaptive trait (because it does not contribute to the surrogate's own survival). But in the environment in which the dog family evolved, a female's tendency to respond when infants signaled their need—combined with her capacity for pseudopregnancy—would have increased the survival chances for large litters born to the dominant female.

According to the late W.D. Hamilton, evolutionary logic predicts that an animal with poor prospects of reproducing on his or her own should be predisposed to assist kin with better prospects so that at least some of their shared genes will be perpetuated. Among wolves, for example, both male and female helpers in the pack are likely to be genetically related to the alpha litter and to have good reasons for not trying to reproduce on their own: in a number of cooperatively breeding species (wild dogs, wolves, hyenas, dingoes, dwarf mongooses, marmosets), the helpers do try, but the dominant female is likely to bite their babies to death. The threat of coercion makes postponing ovulation the better part of valor, the least-bad option for females who must wait to breed until their circumstances improve, either through the death of a higher-ranking female or by finding a mate with an unoccupied territory.

One primate strategy is to line up extra fathers. Among common marmosets and several species of tamarins, females mate with several males, all of which help rear her young. As primatologist Charles T. Snowdon points out, in three of the four genera of Callitrichidae (*Callithrix*, *Saguinus*, and *Leontopithecus*), the more adult males the group has available to help, the more young survive.

Among many of these species, females ovulate just after giving birth, perhaps encouraging males to stick around until after babies are born. (In cotton-top tamarins, males also undergo hormonal changes that prepare them to care for infants at the time of birth.) Among cooperative breeders of certain other species, such as wolves and jackals, pups born in the same litter can be sired by different fathers.

Human mothers, by contrast, don't ovulate again right after birth, nor do they produce offspring with more than one genetic father at a time. Ever inventive, though, humans solve the problem of enlisting help from several adult males by other means. In some cultures, mothers rely on a peculiar belief that anthropologists call partible paternity—the notion that a fetus is built up by contributions of semen from all the men with whom women have had sex in the ten months or so prior to giving birth. Among the Canela, a matrilineal tribe in Brazil studied for many years by William Crocker of the Smithsonian Institution, publicly sanctioned intercourse between women and men other than their husbands—sometimes many men—takes place during villagewide ceremonies. What might lead to marital disaster elsewhere works among the Canela because the men believe in partible paternity. Across a broad swath of South America—from Paraguay up into Brazil, westward to Peru, and northward to Venezuela—mothers rely on this convenient folk wisdom to line up multiple honorary fathers to help them provision both themselves and their children. Over hundreds of generations, this belief has helped children thrive in a part of the world where food sources are unpredictable and where husbands are as likely as not to return from the hunt empty-handed.

The Bari people of Venezuela are among those who believe in shared paternity, and according to anthropologist Stephen Beckerman, Bari children with more than one father do especially well. In Beckerman's study of 822 children, 80 percent of those who had both a "primary" father (the man married to their mother) and a "secondary" father survived to age fifteen, compared with 64 percent survival for those with a primary father alone. Not surprisingly, as soon as a Bari woman suspects she is pregnant, she accepts sexual advances from the more successful fishermen or hunters in her group. Belief that fatherhood can be shared draws more men into the web of possible paternity, which effectively translates into more food and more protection.

One primate strategy is to line up extra "fathers." In some species of marmosets, females mate with several males, all of which help her raise her young.

But for human mothers, extra mates aren't the only source of effective help. Older children, too, play a significant role in family survival. University of Nebraska anthropologists Patricia Draper and Raymond Hames have just shown that among !Kung hunters and gatherers living in the Kalahari Desert, there is a significant correlation between how many children a parent successfully raises and how many older siblings were on hand to help during that person's own childhood.

Older matrilineal kin may be the most valuable helpers of all. University of Utah anthropologists Kristen Hawkes and James O'Connell and their UCLA colleague Nicholas Blurton Jones, who have demonstrated the important food-gathering role of older women among Hazda hunter-gatherers in Tanzania, delight in explaining that since human life spans may extend for a few decades after menopause, older women become available to care for—and to provide vital food for—children born to younger kin. Hawkes, O'Connell, and Blurton Jones further believe that dating from the earliest days of Homo erectus, the survival of weaned children during food shortages may have depended on tubers dug up by older kin.

At various times in human history, people have also relied on a range of customs, as well as on coercion, to line up allomaternal assistance—for example,

by using slaves or hiring poor women as wet nurses. But all the helpers in the world are of no use if they're not motivated to protect, carry, or provision babies. For both humans and nonhumans, this motivation arises in three main ways: through the manipulation of information about kinship; through appealing signals coming from the babies themselves; and, at the heart of it all, from the endocrinological and neural processes that induce individuals to respond to infants' signals. Indeed, all primates and many other mammals eventually respond to infants in a nurturing way if exposed long enough to their signals. Trouble is, "long enough" can mean very different things in males and females, with their very different response thresholds.

For decades, animal behaviorists have been aware of the phenomenon known as priming. A mouse or rat encountering a strange pup is likely to respond by either ignoring the pup or eating it. But presented with pup after pup, rodents of either sex eventually become sensitized to the baby and start caring for it. Even a male may gather pups into a nest and lick or huddle over them. Although nurturing is not a routine part of a male's repertoire, when sufficiently primed he behaves as a mother would. Hormonal change is an obvious candidate for explaining this transformation. Consider the case of the cooperatively breeding Florida scrub-jays studied by Stephan Schoech, of the University of Memphis. Prolactin, a protein hormone that initiates the secretion of milk in female mammals, is also present in male mammals and in birds of both sexes. Schoech showed that levels of prolactin go up in a male and female jay as they build their nest and incubate eggs and that these levels reach a peak when they feed their young. Moreover, prolactin levels rise in the jays' nonbreeding helpers and are also at their highest when they assist in feeding nestlings.

As it happens, male, as well as immature and nonbreeding female, primates can respond to infants' signals, although quite different levels of exposure and stimulation are required to get them going. Twenty years ago, when elevated prolactin levels were first reported in

common marmoset males (by Alan Dixson, for *Callithrix jacchus*), many scientists refused to believe it. Later, when the finding was confirmed, scientists assumed this effect would be found only in fathers. But based on work by Scott Nunes, Jeffrey Fite, Jeffrey French, Charles Snowdon, Lucille Roberts, and many others—work that deals with a variety of species of marmosets and tamarins—we now know that all sorts of hormonal changes are associated with increased nurturing in males. For example, in the tufted-eared marmosets studied by French and colleagues, testosterone levels in males went down as they engaged in caretaking after the birth of an infant. Testosterone levels tended to be lowest in those with the most paternal experience.

Genetic relatedness alone, in fact, is a surprisingly unreliable predictor of love. What matters are cues from infants and how we process these cues emotionally.

The biggest surprise, however, has been that something similar goes on in males of our own species. Anne Storey and colleagues in Canada have reported that prolactin levels in men who were living with pregnant women went up toward the end of the pregnancy. But the most significant finding was a 30 percent drop in testosterone in men right after the birth. (Some endocrinologically literate wags have proposed that this drop in testosterone levels is due to sleep deprivation, but this would probably not explain the parallel testosterone drop in marmoset males housed with parturient females.) Hormonal changes during pregnancy and lactation are, of course, indisputably more pronounced in mothers than in the men consorting with them, and no one is suggesting that male consorts are equivalent to mothers. But both sexes are surprisingly susceptible to infant signals—explaining why fathers, adoptive parents, wet nurses, and day-care workers can become deeply involved with the infants they care for.

Genetic relatedness alone, in fact, is a surprisingly unreliable predictor of love. What matters are cues from infants and how these cues are processed emotionally. The capacity for becoming emotionally hooked—or primed—also explains how a fully engaged father who is in frequent contact with his infant can become more committed to the infant's well-being than a detached mother will.

But we can't forget the real protagonist of this story: the baby. From birth, newborns are powerfully motivated to stay close, to root—even to creep—in quest of nipples, which they instinctively suck on. These are the first innate behaviors that any of us engage in. But maintaining contact is harder for little humans to do than it is for other primates. One problem is that human mothers are not very hairy, so a human mother not only has to position the baby on her breast but also has to keep him there. She must be motivated to pick up her baby even *before* her milk comes in, bringing with it a host of hormonal transformations.

Within minutes of birth, human babies can cry and vocalize just as other primates do, but human newborns can also read facial expressions and make a few of their own. Even with blurry vision, they engage in eye-to-eye contact with the people around them. Newborn babies, when alert, can see about eighteen inches away. When people put their faces within range, babies may reward this attention by looking back or even imitating facial expressions. Orang and chimp babies, too, are strongly attached to and interested in their mothers' faces. But unlike humans, other ape mothers and infants do not get absorbed in gazing deeply into each other's eyes.

To the extent that psychiatrists and pediatricians have thought about this difference between us and the other apes, they tend to attribute it to human mental agility and our ability to use language. Interactions between mother and baby, including vocal play and babbling, have been interpreted as protoconversations: revving up the baby to learn to talk. Yet even babies who lack face-to-face stimulation—babies born blind, say—learn to talk. Furthermore, humans are not the

only primates to engage in the continuous rhythmic streams of vocalization known as babbling. Interestingly, marmoset and tamarin babies also babble. It may be that the infants of cooperative breeders are specially equipped to communicate with caretakers. This is not to say that babbling is not an important part of learning to talk, only to question which came first—babbling so as to develop into a talker, or a predisposition to evolve into a talker because among cooperative breeders, babies that babble are better tended and more likely to survive.

If humans evolved as cooperative breeders, the degree of a human mother's commitment to her infant should be linked to how much social support she herself can expect. Mothers in cooperatively breeding primate species can afford to bear and rear such costly offspring as they do only if they have help on hand. Maternal abandonment and abuse are very rarely observed among primates in the wild. In fact, the only primate species in which mothers are anywhere near as likely to abandon infants at birth as mothers in our own species are the other cooperative breeders. A study of cotton-top tamarins at the New England Regional Primate Research Center showed a 12 percent chance of abandonment if mothers had older siblings on hand to help them rear twins, but a 57 percent chance when no help was available. Overburdened mothers abandoned infants within seventy-two hours of birth.

This new way of thinking about our species' history, with its implications for children, has made me concerned about the future. So far, most Western researchers studying infant development have presumed that living in a nuclear family with a fixed division of labor (mom nurturing, dad providing) is the normal human adaptation. Most contemporary research on children's psychosocial development is derived from John Bowlby's theories of attachment and has focused on such variables as how available and responsive the mother is, whether the father is present or absent, and whether the child is in the mother's care or in day care. Sure enough, studies done with this model in mind always

show that children with less responsive mothers are at greater risk.

In cooperative breeders, the degree of a mother's commitment to her infant should correlate with how much social support she herself can expect.

It is the baby, first and foremost, who senses how available and how committed its mother is. But I know of no studies that take into account the possibility that humans evolved as cooperative breeders and that a mother's responsiveness also happens to be a good indicator of her social supports. In terms of developmental outcomes, the most relevant factor might not be how securely or insecurely attached to the mother the baby is—the variable that developmental psychologists are trained to measure—but rather how secure the baby is in relation to all the people caring for him or her. Measuring attachment this way might help explain why even children whose relations with their mother suggest they are at extreme risk manage to do fine because of the interventions of a committed father, an older sibling, or a there-when-you-need-her grandmother.

The most comprehensive study ever done on how nonmaternal care affects kids is compatible with both the hypothesis that humans evolved as cooperative breeders and the conventional hypothesis that human babies are adapted to be reared exclusively by mothers. Undertaken by the National Institute of Child Health and Human Development (NICHD) in 1991, the seven-year study included 1,364 children and their families (from diverse ethnic and economic backgrounds) and was conducted in ten different U.S. locations. This extraordinarily ambitious study was launched because statistics showed that 62 percent of U.S. mothers with children under age six were working outside the home and that the majority of them (willingly or unwillingly) were back at work within three to five months of giving birth. Because this was an entirely new social phenomenon, no one really knew what the NICHD's research would reveal.

The study's main finding was that both maternal and hired caretakers' sensitivity to infant needs was a better predictor of a child's subsequent development and behavior (such traits as social "compliance," respect for others, and self-control were measured) than was actual time spent apart from the mother. In other words, the critical variable was not the continuous presence of the mother herself but rather how secure infants felt when cared for by someone else. People who had been convinced that babies need full-time care from mothers to develop normally were stunned by these results, while advocates of day care felt vindicated. But do these and other, similar findings mean that day care is not something we need to worry about anymore?

Not at all. We should keep worrying. The NICHD study showed only that day care was better than mother care if the mother was neglectful or abusive. But excluding such worst-case scenarios, the study showed no detectable ill effects from day care only when infants had a secure relationship with parents to begin with (which I take to mean that babies felt wanted) and only when the day care was of high quality. And in this study's context, "high quality" meant that the facility had a high ratio of caretakers to babies, that it had the same caretakers all the time, and that the caretakers were sensitive to infants' needs—in other words, that the day care staff acted like committed kin.

Bluntly put, this kind of day care is almost impossible to find. Where it exists at all, it's expensive. Waiting lists are long, even for cheap or inadequate care. The average rate of staff turnover in day care centers is 30 percent per year, primarily because these workers are paid barely the minimum wage (usually less, in fact, than parking-lot attendants). Furthermore, day care tends to be age-graded, so even at centers where staff members stay put, kids move annually to new teachers. This kind of day care is unlikely to foster trusting relationships.

What conclusion can we draw from all this? Instead of arguing over "mother care" versus "other care," we need to make day care better. And this is where I

think today's evolution-minded researchers have something to say. Impressed by just how variable child-rearing conditions can be in human societies, several anthropologists and psychologists (including Michael Lamb, Patricia Draper, Henry Harpending, and James Chisholm) have suggested that babies are up to more than just maintaining the relationship with their mothers. These researchers propose that babies actually monitor mothers to gain information about the world they have been born into. Babies ask, in effect, Is this world filled with people who are going to provide for me and help me survive? Can I count on them to care about me? If the answer to those questions is yes, they begin to sense that developing a conscience and a capacity for compassion would be a great idea. If the answer is no, they may then be asking, Can I not afford to count on others? Would I be better off just grabbing what I need, however I can? In this case, empathy, or thinking about others' needs, would be more of a hindrance than a help.

For a developing baby and child, the most practical way to behave might vary drastically, depending on whether the mother has kin who help, whether the father is around, whether foster parents are well-meaning or exploitative. These factors, however unconsciously perceived by the child, affect important developmental decisions. Being extremely self-centered or selfish, being oblivious to others or lacking in conscience—traits that psychologists and child-development theorists may view as pathological—are probably quite adaptive traits for an individual who is short on support from other group members.

If I am right that humans evolved as cooperative breeders, Pleistocene babies whose mothers lacked social support and were less than fully committed to infant care would have been unlikely to survive. But once people started to settle down—10,000 or 20,000 or perhaps 30,000 years ago—the picture changed. Ironically, survival chances for neglected children increased. As people lingered longer in one place, eliminated predators, built walled houses, stored food—not to mention inventing things such as rubber nipples and pasteurized

milk—infant survival became decoupled from continuous contact with a caregiver.

Since the end of the Pleistocene, whether in preindustrial or industrialized environments, some children have been surviving levels of social neglect that previously would have meant certain death. Some children get very little attention, even in the most benign of contemporary homes. In the industrialized world, children routinely survive caretaking practices that an Efe or a !Kung mother would find appallingly negligent. In traditional societies, no decent mother leaves her baby alone at any time, and traditional mothers are shocked to learn that Western mothers leave infants unattended in a crib all night.

> *In effect, babies ask: Is this world filled with people who are going to provide for me and help me survive? Can I count on them to care about me?*

Without passing judgment, one may point out that only in the recent history of humankind could infants deprived of supportive human contact survive to reproduce themselves. Certainly there are a lot of humanitarian reasons to worry about this situation: one wants each baby, each child, to be lovingly cared for. From my evolutionary perspective, though, even more is at stake.

Even if we manage to survive what most people are worrying about—global warming, emergent diseases, rogue viruses, meteorites crashing into earth—will we still be human thousands of years down the line? By that I mean human in the way we currently define ourselves. The reason our species has managed to survive and proliferate to the extent that 6 billion people currently occupy the planet has to do with how readily we can learn to cooperate when we want to. And our capacity for empathy is one of the things that made us good at doing that.

At a rudimentary level, of course, all sorts of creatures are good at reading intentions and movements and anticipating what other animals are going to do. Predators from gopher snakes to lions have to be able to anticipate where their quarry will dart. Chimps and gorillas can figure out what another individual is likely to know or not know. But compared with that of humans, this capacity to entertain the psychological perspective of other individuals is crude.

During early childhood, through relationships with mothers and other caretakers, individuals learn to look at the world from someone else's perspective.

The capacity for empathy is uniquely well developed in our species, so much so that many people (including me) believe that along with language and symbolic thought, it is what makes us human. We are capable of compassion, of understanding other people's "fears and motives, their longings and griefs and vanities," as novelist Edmund White puts it. We spend time and energy worrying about people we have never even met, about babies left in dumpsters, about the existence of more than 12 million AIDS orphans in Africa.

Psychologists know that there is a heritable component to emotional capacity and that this affects the development of compassion among individuals. By fourteen months of age, identical twins (who share all genes) are more alike in how they react to an experimenter who pretends to painfully pinch her finger on a clipboard than are fraternal twins (who share only half their genes). But empathy also has a learned component, which has more to do with analytical skills. During the first years of life, within the context of early relationships with mothers and other committed caretakers, each individual learns to look at the world from someone else's perspective.

And this is why I get so worried. Just because humans have evolved to be smart enough to chronicle our species' histories, to speculate about its origins, and to figure out that we have about 30,000 genes in our genome is no reason to assume that evolution has come to a standstill. As gene frequencies change, natural selection acts on the outcome, the expression of those genes. No one doubts, for instance, that fish benefit from being able to see. Yet species reared in total darkness—as are the small, cave-dwelling characin of Mexico—fail to develop their visual capacity. Through evolutionary time, traits that are unexpressed are eventually lost. If populations of these fish are isolated in caves long enough, youngsters descended from those original populations will no longer be able to develop eyesight at all, even if reared in sunlight.

If human compassion develops only under particular rearing conditions, and if an increasing proportion of the species survives to breeding age without developing compassion, it won't make any difference how useful this trait was among our ancestors. It will become like sight in cave-dwelling fish.

No doubt our descendants thousands of years from now (should our species survive) will still be bipedal, symbol-generating apes. Most likely they will be adept at using sophisticated technologies. But will they still be human in the way we, shaped by a long heritage of cooperative breeding, currently define ourselves?

This article was adapted from "Cooperation, Empathy, and the Needs of Human Infants," a Tanner Lecture delivered at the University of Utah. It is used with the permission of the Tanner Lectures on Human Values, a Corporation, University of Utah, Salt Lake City.

A Woman's Curse?

Why do cultures the world over treat menstruating women as taboo?
An anthropologist offers a new answer—and a challenge to Western
ideas about contraception

By Meredith F. Small

THE PASSAGE FROM GIRLHOOD TO womanhood is marked by a flow of blood from the uterus. Without elaborate ceremony, often without discussion, girls know that when they begin to menstruate, their world is changed forever. For the next thirty years or so, they will spend much energy having babies, or trying not to, reminded at each menstruation that either way, the biology of reproduction has a major impact on their lives.

Anthropologists have underscored the universal importance of menstruation by documenting how the event is interwoven into the ideology as well as the daily activities of cultures around the world. The customs attached to menstruation take peculiarly negative forms: the so-called menstrual taboos. Those taboos may prohibit a woman from having sex with her husband or from cooking for him. They may bar her from visiting sacred places or taking part in sacred activities. They may forbid her to touch certain items used by men, such as hunting gear or weapons, or to eat certain foods or to wash at certain times. They may also require that a woman paint her face red or wear a red hip cord, or that she segregate herself in a special hut while she is menstruating. In short, the taboos set menstruating women apart from the rest of their society, marking them as impure and polluting.

Anthropologists have studied menstrual taboos for decades, focusing on the negative symbolism of the rituals as a cultural phenomenon. Perhaps, suggested one investigator, taking a Freudian perspective, such taboos reflect the anxiety that men feel about castration, an anxiety that would be prompted by women's genital bleeding. Others have suggested that the taboos serve to prevent menstrual odor from interfering with hunting, or that they protect men from microorganisms that might otherwise be transferred during sexual intercourse with a menstruating woman. Until recently, few investigators had considered the possibility that the taboos—and the very fact of menstruation—might instead exist because they conferred an evolutionary advantage.

In the mid-1980s the anthropologist Beverly I. Strassmann of the University of Michigan in Ann Arbor began to study the ways men and women have evolved to accomplish (and regulate) reproduction. Unlike traditional anthropologists, who focus on how culture affects human behavior, Strassmann was convinced that the important role played by biology was being neglected. Menstruation, she suspected, would be a key for observing and understanding the interplay of biology and culture in human reproductive behavior.

To address the issue, Strassmann decided to seek a culture in which making babies was an ongoing part of adult life. For that she had to get away from industrialized countries, with their bias toward contraception and low birthrates. In a "natural-fertility population," she reasoned, she could more clearly see the connection between the physiology of women and the strategies men and women use to exploit that physiology for their own reproductive ends.

Strassmann ended up in a remote corner of West Africa, living in close quarters with the Dogon, a traditional society whose indigenous religion of ancestor worship requires that menstruating women spend their nights at a small hut. For more than two years Strassmann kept track of the women staying at the hut, and she confirmed the menstruations by testing urine samples for the appropriate hormonal changes. In so doing, she amassed the first long-term data describing how a traditional society appropriates a physiological event—menstruation—and refracts that event through a prism of behaviors and beliefs.

What she found explicitly challenges the conclusions of earlier investigators about the cultural function of menstrual taboos. For the Dogon men, she discovered, enforcing visits to the menstrual hut serves to channel parental resources into the upbringing of their own children. But more, Strassmann, who also had training as a reproductive physiologist, proposed a new theory of why menstruation itself evolved as it did—and again, the answer is essentially a story of conserving resources. Finally, her observations pose provocative questions about women's health in industrialized societies, raising serious doubts about the tactics favored by Western medicine for developing contraceptive technology.

Menstruation is the visible stage of the ovarian cycle, orchestrated primarily by hormones secreted by the ovaries: progesterone and a family of hormones called estrogens. At the beginning of each cycle (by convention, the first day of a woman's period) the levels of the estrogens begin to rise. After about five days, as their concentrations increase, they cause the blood- and nutrient-rich inner lining of the uterus, called the endometrium, to thicken and acquire a densely branching network of blood vessels. At about the middle of the cycle, ovulation takes place, and an egg makes its way from one of the two ovaries down one of the paired fallopian tubes to the uterus. The follicle from which the egg was released in the ovary now begins to secrete progesterone as well as estrogens, and the progesterone causes the endometrium to swell and become even richer with blood vessels—in short, fully ready for a pregnancy, should conception take place and the fertilized egg become implanted.

If conception does take place, the levels of estrogens and progesterone continue to rise throughout the pregnancy. That keeps the endometrium thick enough to support the quickening life inside the uterus. When the baby is born and the new mother begins nursing, the estrogens and progesterone fall to their initial levels, and lactation hormones keep them suppressed. The uterus thus lies quiescent until frequent lactation ends, which triggers the return to ovulation.

If conception does not take place after ovulation, all the ovarian hormones also drop to their initial levels, and menstruation—the shedding of part of the uterine lining—begins. The lining is divided into three layers: a basal layer that is constantly maintained, and two superficial layers, which shed and regrow with each menstrual cycle. All mammals undergo cyclical changes in the state of the endometrium. In most mammals the sloughed-off layers are resorbed into the body if fertilization does not take place. But in some higher primates, including

humans, some of the shed endometrium is not resorbed. The shed lining, along with some blood, flows from the body through the vaginal opening, a process that in humans typically lasts from three to five days.

Of course, physiological facts alone do not explain why so many human groups have infused a bodily function with symbolic meaning. And so in 1986 Strassmann found herself driving through the Sahel region of West Africa at the peak of the hot season, heading for a sandstone cliff called the Bandiagara Escarpment, in Mali. There, permanent Dogon villages of mud or stone houses dotted the rocky plateau. The menstrual huts were obvious: round, low-roofed buildings set apart from the rectangular dwellings of the rest of the village.

The Dogon are a society of millet and onion farmers who endorse polygyny, and they maintain their traditional culture despite the occasional visits of outsiders. In a few Dogon villages, in fact, tourists are fairly common, and ethnographers had frequently studied the Dogon language, religion and social structure before Strassmann's arrival. But her visit was the first time someone from the outside wanted to delve into an intimate issue in such detail.

It took Strassmann a series of hikes among villages, and long talks with male elders under the thatched-roof shelters where they typically gather, to find the appropriate sites for her research. She gained permission for her study in fourteen villages, eventually choosing two. That exceptional welcome, she thinks, emphasized the universality of her interests. "I'm working on all the things that really matter to [the Dogon]—fertility, economics—so they never questioned my motives or wondered why I would be interested in these things," she says. "It seemed obvious to them." She set up shop for the next two and a half years in a stone house in the village, with no running water or electricity. Eating the daily fare of the Dogon, millet porridge, she and a research assistant began to integrate themselves into village life, learning the language, getting to know people and tracking visits to the menstrual huts.

Following the movements of menstruating women was surprisingly easy. The menstrual huts are situated outside the walled compounds of the village, but in full view of the men's thatched-roof shelters. As the men relax under their shelters, they can readily see who leaves the huts in the morning and returns to them in the evening. And as nonmenstruating women pass the huts on their way to and from the fields or to other compounds, they too can see who is spending the night there. Strassmann found that when she left her house in the evening to take data, any of the villagers could accurately predict whom she would find in the menstrual huts.

The huts themselves are cramped, dark buildings—hardly places where a woman might go to escape the drudgery of work or to avoid an argument with her husband or a co-wife. The huts sometimes become so crowded that some occupants are forced outside—making the women even more conspicuous. Although babies and toddlers can go with their mothers to the huts, the women consigned there are not allowed to spend time with the rest of their families. They must cook with special pots, not their usual household possessions. Yet they are still expected to do their usual jobs, such as working in the fields.

Why, Strassmann wondered, would anyone put up with such conditions?

The answer, for the Dogon, is that a menstruating woman is a threat to the sanctity of religious altars, where men pray and make sacrifices for the protection of their fields, their families and their village. If menstruating women come near the altars, which are situated both indoors and outdoors, the Dogon believe that their aura of pollution will ruin the altars and bring calamities upon the village. The belief is so ingrained that the women themselves have internalized it, feeling its burden of responsibility and potential guilt. Thus violations of the taboo are rare, because a menstruating woman who breaks the rules knows that she is personally responsible if calamities occur.

NEVERTHELESS, STRASSMANN STILL thought a more functional explanation for menstrual taboos might also exist, one closely related to reproduction. As she was well aware, even before her studies among the Dogon, people around the world have a fairly sophisticated view of how reproduction works. In general, people everywhere know full well that menstruation signals the absence of a pregnancy and the possibility of another one. More precisely, Strassmann could frame her hypothesis by reasoning as follows: Across cultures, men and women recognize that a lack of menstrual cycling in a woman implies she is either pregnant, lactating or menopausal. Moreover, at least among natural-fertility cultures that do not practice birth control, continual cycles during peak reproductive years imply to people in those cultures that a woman is sterile. Thus, even though people might not be able to pinpoint ovulation, they can easily identify whether a woman will soon be ready to conceive on the basis of whether she is menstruating. And that leads straight to Strassmann's insightful hypothesis about the role of menstrual taboos: information about menstruation can be a means of tracking paternity.

"There are two important pieces of information for assessing paternity," Strassmann notes: timing of intercourse and timing of menstruation. "By forcing women to signal menstruation, men are trying to gain equal access to one part of that critical information." Such information, she explains, is crucial to Dogon men, because they invest so many resources in their own offspring. Descent is marked through the male line; land and the food that comes from the land is passed down from fathers to sons. Information about paternity is thus crucial to a man's entire lineage. And because each man has as many as four wives, he cannot possibly track them all. So forcing women to signal their menstrual periods, or lack thereof, helps men avoid cuckoldry.

TO TEST HER HYPOTHESIS, STRASSmann tracked residence in the menstrual huts for 736 consecutive days, collecting data on 477 complete cycles. She noted who was at each hut and how long each woman stayed. She also collected urine from ninety-three women over a ten-week period, to check the correlation between residence in the menstrual hut and the fact of menstruation.

The combination of ethnographic records and urinalyses showed that the Dogon women mostly play by the rules. In 86 percent of the hormonally detected menstruations, women went to the hut. Moreover, none of the tested women went to the hut when they were not menstruating. In the remaining 14 percent of the tested menstruations, women stayed home from the hut, in violation of the taboo, but some were near menopause and so not at high risk for pregnancy. More important, none of the women who violated the taboo did it twice in a row. Even they were largely willing to comply.

Thus, Strassmann concluded, the huts do indeed convey a fairly reliable signal, to men and to everyone else, about the status of a woman's fertility. When she leaves the hut, she is considered ready to conceive. When she stops going to the hut, she is evidently pregnant or menopausal. And women of prime reproductive age who visit the hut on a regular basis are clearly infertile.

It also became clear to Strassmann that the Dogon do indeed use that information to make paternity decisions. In several cases a man was forced to marry a pregnant woman, simply because everyone knew that the man had been the woman's first sexual partner after her last visit to the menstrual hut. Strassmann followed one case in which a child was being brought up by a man because he was the mother's first sexual partner after a hut visit, even though the woman soon married a different man. (The woman already knew she was pregnant by the first man at the time of her marriage, and she did not visit the menstrual hut before she married. Thus the truth was obvious to everyone, and the real father took the child.)

In general, women are cooperative players in the game because without a man, a woman has no way to support herself or her children. But women follow the taboo reluctantly. They complain about going to the hut. And if their husbands convert from the traditional religion of the Dogon to a religion that does not impose menstrual taboos, such as Is-

lam or Christianity, the women quickly cease visiting the hut. Not that such a religious conversion quells a man's interest in his wife's fidelity: far from it. But the rules change. Perhaps the sanctions of the new religion against infidelity help keep women faithful, so the men can relax their guard. Or perhaps the men are willing to trade the reproductive advantages of the menstrual taboo for the economic benefits gained by converting to the new religion. Whatever the case, Strassmann found an almost perfect correlation between a husband's religion and his wives' attendance at the hut. In sum, the taboo is established by men, backed by supernatural forces, and internalized and accepted by women until the men release them from the belief.

BUT BEYOND THE CULTURAL MACHInations of men and women that Strassmann expected to find, her data show something even more fundamental—and surprising—about female biology. On average, she calculates, a woman in a natural-fertility population such as the Dogon has only about 110 menstrual periods in her lifetime. The rest of the time she will be prepubescent, pregnant, lactating or menopausal. Women in industrialized cultures, by contrast, have more than three times as many cycles: 350 to 400, on average, in a lifetime. They reach menarche (their first menstruation) earlier—at age twelve and a half, compared with the onset age of sixteen in natural-fertility cultures. They have fewer babies, and they lactate hardly at all. All those factors lead women in the industrialized world to a lifetime of nearly continuous menstrual cycling.

The big contrast in cycling profiles during the reproductive years can be traced specifically to lactation. Women in more traditional societies spend most of their reproductive years in lactation amenorrhea, the state in which the hormonal changes required for nursing suppress ovulation and inhibit menstruation. And it is not just that the Dogon bear more children (eight to nine on average); they also nurse each child on demand rather than in scheduled bouts, all through the night as well as the day, and intensely enough that ovulation simply stops for about twenty months per child. Women in industrialized societies typically do not breast-feed as intensely (or at all), and rarely breast-feed each child for as long as the Dogon women do. (The average for American women is four months.)

The Dogon experience with menstruation may be far more typical of the human condition over most of evolutionary history than is the standard menstrual experience in industrialized nations. If so, Strassmann's findings alter some of the most closely held beliefs about female biology. Contrary to what the Western medical establishment might think, it is not particularly "normal" to menstruate each month. The female body, according to Strassmann, is biologically designed to spend much more time in lactation amenorrhea than in menstrual cycling. That in itself suggests that oral contraceptives, which alter hormone levels to suppress ovulation and produce a bleeding, could be forcing a continual state of cycling for which the body is ill-prepared. Women might be better protected against reproductive cancers if their contraceptives mimicked lactation amenorrhea and depressed the female reproductive hormones, rather than forcing the continual ebb and flow of menstrual cycles.

Strassmann's data also call into question a recently popularized idea about menstruation: that regular menstrual cycles might be immunologically beneficial for women. In 1993 the controversial writer Margie Profet, whose ideas about evolutionary and reproductive biology have received vast media attention, proposed in *The Quarterly Review of Biology* that menstruation could have such an adaptive value. She noted that viruses and bacteria regularly enter the female body on the backs of sperm, and she hypothesized that the best way to get them out is to flush them out. Here, then, was a positive, adaptive role for something unpleasant, an evolutionary reason for suffering cramps each month. Menstruation, according to Profet, had evolved to rid the body of pathogens. The "anti-pathogen" theory was an exciting hypothesis, and it

helped win Profet a MacArthur Foundation award. But Strassmann's work soon showed that Profet's ideas could not be supported because of one simple fact: under less-industrialized conditions, women menstruate relatively rarely.

Instead, Strassmann notes, if there is an adaptive value to menstruation, it is ultimately a strategy to conserve the body's resources. She estimates that maintaining the endometrial lining during the second half of the ovarian cycle takes substantial metabolic energy. Once the endometrium is built up and ready to receive a fertilized egg, the tissue requires a sevenfold metabolic increase to remain rich in blood and ready to support a pregnancy. Hence, if no pregnancy is forthcoming, it makes a lot of sense for the body to let part of the endometrium slough off and then regenerate itself, instead of maintaining that rather costly but unneeded tissue. Such energy conservation is common among vertebrates: male rhesus monkeys have shrunken testes during their nonbreeding season, Burmese pythons shrink their guts when they are not digesting, and hibernating animals put their metabolisms on hold.

Strassmann also suggests that periodically ridding oneself of the endometrium could make a difference to a woman's long-term survival. Because female reproductive hormones affect the brain and other tissues, the metabolism of the entire body is involved during cycling. Strassmann estimates that by keeping hormonal low through half the cycle, a woman can save about six days' worth of energy for every four nonconceptive cycles. Such caloric conservation might have proved useful to early hominids who lived by hunting and gathering, and even today it might be helpful for women living in less affluent circumstances than the ones common in the industrialized West.

BUT PERHAPS THE MOST PROVOCATIVE implications of Strassmann's work have to do with women's health. In 1994 a group of physicians and anthropologists pub-

lished a paper, also in *The Quarterly Review of Biology*, suggesting that the reproductive histories and lifestyles of women in industrialized cultures are at odds with women's naturally evolved biology, and that the differences lead to greater risks of reproductive cancers. For example, the investigators estimated that women in affluent cultures may have a hundredfold greater risk of breast cancer than do women who subsist by hunting and gathering. The increased risk is probably caused not only by low levels of exercise and a high-fat diet, but also by a relatively high number of menstrual cycles over a lifetime. Repeated exposure to the hormones of the ovarian cycle—because of early menarche, late menopause, lack of pregnancy and little or no breast-feeding—is implicated in other reproductive cancers as well.

Those of us in industrialized cultures have been running an experiment on ourselves. The body evolved over millions of years to move across the landscape looking for food, to live in small kin-based groups, to make babies at intervals of four years or so and to invest heavily in each child by nursing intensely for years. How many women now follow those traditional patterns? We move little, we rely on others to get our food, and we rarely reproduce or lactate. Those culturally initiated shifts in lifestyles may pose biological risks.

Our task is not to overcome that biology, but to work with it. Now that we have a better idea of how the female body was designed, it may be time to rework our lifestyles and change some of our expectations. It may be time to borrow from our distant past or from our contemporaries in distant cultures, and treat our bodies more as nature intended.

MEREDITH F. SMALL is a professor of anthropology at Cornell University in Ithaca, New York. Her latest book, OUR BABIES, OURSELVES: HOW BIOLOGY AND CULTURE SHAPE THE WAY WE PARENT, was published in May 1998 [see Laurence A. Marschall's review in Books in Brief, November/December 1998].

Reprinted by permission of *The Sciences*, January/February 1999, pp. 24–29. © 1999 by the New York Academy of Science. Individual subscriptions are $28 per year. Write to: The Sciences, 2 East 63rd Street, New York, NY 10021.

What's Love Got to Do With It?

Sex Among Our Closest Relatives Is a Rather Open Affair

Meredith F. Small

Maiko and Lana are having sex. Maiko is on top, and Lana's arms and legs are wrapped tightly around his waist. Lina, a friend of Lana's, approaches from the right and taps Maiko on the back, nudging him to finish. As he moves away, Lina enfolds Lana in her arms, and they roll over so that Lana is now on top. The two females rub their genitals together, grinning and screaming in pleasure.

This is no orgy staged for an X-rated movie. It doesn't even involve people—or rather, it involves them only as observers. Lana, Maiko, and Lina are bonobos, a rare species of chimplike ape in which frequent couplings and casual sex play characterize every social relationship—between males and females, members of the same sex, closely related animals, and total strangers. Primatologists are beginning to study the bonobos' unrestrained sexual behavior for tantalizing clues to the origins of our own sexuality.

In reconstructing how early man and woman behaved, researchers have generally looked not to bonobos but to common chimpanzees. Only about 5 million years ago human beings and chimps shared a common ancestor, and we still have much behavior in common: namely, a long period of infant dependency, a reliance on learning what to eat

and how to obtain food, social bonds that persist over generations, and the need to deal as a group with many everyday conflicts. The assumption has been that chimp behavior today may be similar to the behavior of human ancestors.

Bonobo behavior, however, offers another window on the past because they, too, shared our 5-million-year-old ancestor, diverging from chimps just 2 million years ago. Bonobos have been less studied than chimps for the simple reason that they are difficult to find. They live only on a small patch of land in Zaire, in central Africa. They were first identified, on the basis of skeletal material, in the 1920s, but it wasn't until the 1970s that their behavior in the wild was studied, and then only sporadically.

Bonobos, also known as pygmy chimpanzees, are not really pygmies but welterweights. The largest males are as big as chimps, and the females of the two species are the same size. But bonobos are more delicate in build, and their arms and legs are long and slender.

On the ground, moving from fruit tree to fruit tree, bonobos often stand and walk on two legs—behavior that makes them seem more like humans than chimps. In some ways their sexual behavior seems more human as well, suggesting that in the sexual arena, at least,

bonobos are the more appropriate ancestral model. Males and females frequently copulate face-to-face, which is an uncommon position in animals other than humans. Males usually mount females from behind, but females seem to prefer sex face-to-face. "Sometimes the female will let a male start to mount from behind," says Amy Parish, a graduate student at the University of California at Davis who's been watching female bonobo sexual behavior in several zoo colonies around the world. "And then she'll stop, and of course he's really excited, and then she continues face-to-face." Primatologists assume the female preference is dictated by her anatomy: her enlarged clitoris and sexual swellings are oriented far forward. Females presumably prefer face-to-face contact because it feels better.

> *"Sex is fun. Sex makes them feel good and keeps the group together."*

Like humans but unlike chimps and most other animals, bonobos separate sex from reproduction. They seem to treat sex as a pleasurable activity, and they rely on it as a sort of social glue, to make or break all sorts of relationships. "Ancestral humans behaved like this," proposes Frans de Waal, an ethologist at the Yerkes Regional Primate Research Center at Emory University. "Later, when we developed the family system, the use of sex for this sort of purpose became more limited, mainly occurring within families. A lot of the things we see, like pedophilia and homosexuality, may be leftovers that some now consider unacceptable in our particular society."

Depending on your morals, watching bonobo sex play may be like watching humans at their most extreme and perverse. Bonobos seem to have sex more often and in more combinations than the average person in any culture, and most of the time bonobo sex has nothing to do with making babies. Males mount females and females sometimes mount them back; females rub against other females just for fun; males stand rump to rump and press their scrotal areas together. Even juveniles participate by rubbing their genital areas against adults, although ethologists don't think that males actually insert their penises into juvenile females. Very young animals also have sex with each other: little males suck on each other's penises or French-kiss. When two animals initiate sex, others freely join in by poking their fingers and toes into the moving parts.

One thing sex does for bonobos is decrease tensions caused by potential competition, often competition for food. Japanese primatologists observing bonobos in Zaire were the first to notice that when bonobos come across a large fruiting tree or encounter piles of provisioned sugarcane, the sight of food triggers a binge of sex. The atmosphere of this sexual free-for-all is decidedly friendly, and it eventually calms the group down. "What's striking is how rapidly the sex drops off," says Nancy Thompson-Handler of the State University of New York at Stony Brook, who has observed bonobos at a site in Zaire called Lomako. "After ten minutes, sexual behavior decreases by fifty percent." Soon the group turns from sex to feeding.

But it's tension rather than food that causes the sexual excitement. "I'm sure the more food you give them, the more

sex you'll get," says De Waal. "But it's not really the food, it's competition that triggers this. You can throw in a cardboard box and you'll get sexual behavior." Sex is just the way bonobos deal with competition over limited resources and with the normal tensions caused by living in a group. Anthropologist Frances White of Duke University, a bonobo observer at Lomako since 1983, puts it simply: "Sex is fun. Sex makes them feel good and therefore keeps the group together."

"Females rule the business. It's a good species for feminists, I think."

Sexual behavior also occurs after aggressive encounters, especially among males. After two males fight, one may reconcile with his opponent by presenting his rump and backing up against the other's testicles. He might grab the penis of the other male and stroke it. It's the male bonobo's way of shaking hands and letting everyone know that the conflict has ended amicably.

Researchers also note that female bonobo sexuality, like the sexuality of female humans, isn't locked into a monthly cycle. In most other animals, including chimps, the female's interest in sex is tied to her ovulation cycle. Chimp females sport pink swellings on their hind ends for about two weeks, signaling their fertility, and they're only approachable for sex during that time. That's not the case with humans, who show no outward signs that they are ovulating, and can mate at all phases of the cycle. Female bonobos take the reverse tack, but with similar results. Their large swellings are visible for weeks before and after their fertile periods, and there is never any discernibly wrong time to mate. Like humans, they have sex whether or not they are ovulating.

What's fascinating is that female bonobos use this boundless sexuality in all their relationships. "Females rule the business—sex and food," says De Waal. "It's a good species for feminists, I think." For instance, females regularly

use sex to cement relationships with other females. A genital-genital rub, better known as GG-rubbing by observers, is the most frequent behavior used by bonobo females to reinforce social ties or relieve tension. GG-rubbing takes a variety of forms. Often one female rolls on her back and extends her arms and legs. The other female mounts her and they rub their swellings right and left for several seconds, massaging their clitorises against each other. GG-rubbing occurs in the presence of food because food causes tension and excitement, but the intimate contact has the effect of making close friends.

Sometimes females would rather GG-rub with each other than copulate with a male. Parish filmed a 15-minute scene at a bonobo colony at the San Diego Wild Animal Park in which a male, Vernon, repeatedly solicited two females, Lisa and Loretta. Again and again he arched his back and displayed his erect penis—the bonobo request for sex. The females moved away from him, tactfully turning him down until they crept behind a tree and GG-rubbed with each other.

Unlike most primate species, in which males usually take on the dangerous task of leaving home, among bonobos females are the ones who leave the group when they reach sexual maturity, around the age of eight, and work their way into unfamiliar groups. To aid in their assimilation into a new community, the female bonobos make good use of their endless sexual favors. While watching a bonobo group at a feeding tree, White saw a young female systematically have sex with each member before feeding. "An adolescent female, presumably a recent transfer female, came up to the tree, mated with all five males, went into the tree, and solicited GG-rubbing from all the females present," says White.

Once inside the new group, a female bonobo must build a sisterhood from scratch. In groups of humans or chimps, unrelated females construct friendships through the rituals of shopping together or grooming. Bonobos do it sexually. Although pleasure may be the motivation

HIDDEN HEAT

Standing upright is not a position usually—or easily—associated with sex. Among people, at least, anatomy and gravity prove to be forbidding obstacles. Yet our two-legged stance may be the key to a distinctive aspect of human sexuality: the independence of women's sexual desires from a monthly calendar.

Males in the two species most closely related to us, chimpanzees and bonobos, don't spend a lot of time worrying, "Is she interested or not?" The answer is obvious. When ovulatory hormones reach a monthly peak in female chimps and bonobos, and their eggs are primed for fertilization, their genital area swells up, and both sexes appear to have just one thing on their mind. "These animals really turn on when this happens. Everything else is dropped," says primatologist Frederick Szalay of Hunter College in New York.

Women, however, don't go into heat. And this departure from our relatives' sexual behavior has long puzzled researchers. Clear signals of fertility and the willingness to do something about it bring major evolutionary advantages: ripe eggs lead to healthier pregnancies, which leads to more of your genes in succeeding generations, which is what evolution is all about. In addition, male chimps give females that are waving these red flags of fertility first chance at high-protein food such as meat.

So why would our ancestors give this up? Szalay and graduate student Robert Costello have a simple explanation. Women gave heat up, they say, because our ancestors stood up. Fossil footprints indicate that somewhere around 3.5 million years ago hominids—non-ape primates—began walking on two legs. "In hominids, something dictated getting up. We don't know what it was," Szalay says. "But once it did, there was a problem with the signaling system." The problem was that it didn't work. Swollen genital areas that were visible when their owners were down on all fours became hidden between the legs. The mating signal was lost.

"Uprightness meant very tough times for females working with the old ovarian cycle," Szalay says. Males wouldn't notice them, and the swellings themselves, which get quite large, must have made it hard for two-legged creatures to walk around.

Those who found a way out of this quandary, Szalay suggests, were females with small swellings but with a little less hair on their rears and a little extra fat. It would have looked a bit like the time-honored mating signal. They got more attention, and produced more offspring. "You don't start a completely new trend in signaling," Szalay says. "You have a little extra fat, a little nakedness to mimic the ancestors. If there was an ever-so-little advantage because, quite simply, you look good, it would be selected for."

And if a little nakedness and a little fat worked well, Szalay speculates, then a lot of both would work even better. "Once you start a trend in sexual signaling, crazy things happen," he notes. "It's almost like: let's escalate, let's add more. That's what happens in horns with sheep. It's a particular part of the body that brings an advantage." In a few million years human ancestors were more naked than ever, with fleshy rears not found in any other primate. Since these features were permanent, unlike the monthly ups and downs of swellings, sex was free to become a part of daily life.

It's a provocative notion, say Szalay's colleagues, but like any attempt to conjure up the past from the present, there's no real proof of cause and effect. Anthropologist Helen Fisher of the American Museum of Natural History notes that Szalay is merely assuming that fleshy buttocks evolved because they were sex signals. Yet their mass really comes from muscles, which chimps don't have, that are associated with walking. And anthropologist Sarah Blaffer Hrdy of the University of California at Davis points to a more fundamental problem: our ancestors may not have had chimplike swellings that they needed to dispense with. Chimps and bonobos are only two of about 200 primate species, and the vast majority of those species don't have big swellings. Though they are our closest relatives, chimps and bonobos have been evolving during the last 5 million years just as we have, and swollen genitals may be a recent development. The current unswollen human pattern may be the ancestral one.

"Nobody really knows what happened," says Fisher. "Everybody has an idea. You pays your money and you takes your choice."

—Joshua Fischman

behind a female-female assignation, the function is to form an alliance.

These alliances are serious business, because they determine the pecking order at food sites. Females with powerful friends eat first, and subordinate females may not get any food at all if the resource is small. When times are rough, then, it pays to have close female friends. White describes a scene at Lomako in which an adolescent female, Blanche, benefited from her established friendship with Freda. "I was following Freda and her boyfriend, and they found a tree that they didn't expect to be there. It was a small tree, heavily in fruit with one of their favorites. Freda went straight up the tree and made a food call to Blanche. Blanche came tearing over—she was quite far away—and went tearing up the tree to join Freda, and they GG-rubbed like crazy."

Alliances also give females leverage over larger, stronger males who otherwise would push them around. Females have discovered there is strength in numbers. Unlike other species of primates, such as chimpanzees or baboons (or, all too often, humans), where tensions run high between males and females, bonobo females are not afraid of males, and the sexes mingle peacefully. "What is consistently different from chimps," says Thompson-Handler, "is the composition of parties. The vast majority are mixed, so there are males and females of all different ages."

Female bonobos cannot be coerced into anything, including sex. Parish recounts an interaction between Lana and a male called Akili at the San Diego Wild Animal Park. "Lana had just been introduced into the group. For a long time she lay on the grass with a huge swelling. Akili would approach her with a big erection and hover over her. It would have been easy for him to do a mount. But he wouldn't. He just kept trying to catch her eye, hovering around her, and she would scoot around the ground, avoiding him. And then he'd try again. She went around full circle." Akili was big enough to force himself on her. Yet he refrained.

In another encounter, a male bonobo was carrying a large clump of branches. He moved up to a female and presented his erect penis by spreading his legs and arching his back. She rolled onto her back and they copulated. In the midst of their joint ecstasy, she reached out and grabbed a branch from the male. When he pulled back, finished and satisfied, she moved away, clutching the branch to her chest. There was no tension between them, and she essentially traded copulation for food. But the key here is that the male allowed her to move away with the branch—it didn't occur to him to threaten her, because their status was virtually equal.

Although the results of sexual liberation are clear among bonobos, no one is sure why sex has been elevated to such a high position in this species and why it is restricted merely to reproduction among chimpanzees. "The puzzle for me," says De Waal, "is that chimps do all this bonding with kissing and embracing, with body contact. Why do bonobos do it in a sexual manner?" He speculates that the use of sex as a standard way to underscore relationships began between adult males and adult females as an extension of the mating process and later spread to all members of the group. But no one is sure exactly how this happened.

It is also unclear whether bonobo sexually became exaggerated only after their split from the human lineage or whether the behavior they exhibit today is the modern version of our common ancestor's sex play. Anthropologist Adrienne Zihlman of the University of California at Santa Cruz, who has used the evidence of fossil bones to argue that our earliest known non-ape ancestors, the australopithecines, had body proportions similar to those of bonobos, says, "The path of evolution is not a straight line from either species, but what I think is important is that the bonobo information gives us more possibilities for looking at human origins."

Some anthropologists, however, are reluctant to include the details of bonobo life, such as wide-ranging sexuality and a strong sisterhood, into scenarios of human evolution. "The researchers have all these commitments to male dominance [as in chimpanzees], and yet bonobos have egalitarian relationships," says De Waal. "They also want to see humans as unique, yet bonobos fit very nicely into many of the scenarios, making humans appear less unique."

Our divergent, non-ape path has led us away from sex and toward a culture that denies the connection between sex and social cohesion. But bonobos, with their versatile sexuality, are here to remind us that our heritage may very well include a primordial urge to make love, not war.

Apes of Wrath

Barbara Smuts

Nearly 20 years ago I spent a morning dashing up and down the hills of Gombe National Park in Tanzania, trying to keep up with an energetic young female chimpanzee, the focus of my observations for the day. On her rear end she sported the small, bright pink swelling characteristic of the early stages of estrus, the period when female mammals are fertile and sexually receptive. For some hours our run through the park was conducted in quiet, but then, suddenly, a chorus of male chimpanzee pant hoots shattered the tranquility of the forest. My female rushed forward to join the males. She greeted each of them, bowing and then turning to present her swelling for inspection. The males examined her perfunctorily and resumed grooming one another, showing no further interest.

Some female primates use social bonds to escape male aggression. Can women?

At first I was surprised by their indifference to a potential mate. Then I realized that it would be many days before the female's swelling blossomed into the large, shiny sphere that signals ovulation. In a week or two, I thought, these same males will be vying intensely for a chance to mate with her.

The attack came without warning. One of the males charged toward us, hair on end, looking twice as large as my small female and enraged. As he rushed by he picked her up, hurled her to the ground, and pummeled her. She cringed and screamed. He ran off, rejoining the other males seconds later as if nothing

had happened. It was not so easy for the female to return to normal. She whimpered and darted nervous glances at her attacker, as if worried that he might renew his assault.

In the years that followed I witnessed many similar attacks by males against females, among a variety of Old World primates, and eventually I found this sort of aggression against females so puzzling that I began to study it systematically—something that has rarely been done. My long-term research on olive baboons in Kenya showed that, on average, each pregnant or lactating female was attacked by an adult male about once a week and seriously injured about once a year. Estrous females were the target of even more aggression. The obvious question was, Why?

In the late 1970s, while I was in Africa among the baboons, feminists back in the United States were turning their attention to male violence against women. Their concern stimulated a wave of research documenting disturbingly high levels of battering, rape, sexual harassment, and murder. But although scientists investigated this kind of behavior from many perspectives, they mostly ignored the existence of similar behavior in other animals. My observations over the years have convinced me that a deeper understanding of male aggression against females in other species can help us understand its counterpart in our own.

Researchers have observed various male animals—including insects, birds, and mammals—chasing, threatening, and attacking females. Unfortunately, because scientists have rarely studied such aggression in detail, we do not know exactly how common it is. But the males of many of these species are most aggressive toward potential mates,

which suggests that they sometimes use violence to gain sexual access.

Jane Goodall provides us with a compelling example of how males use violence to get sex. In her 1986 book, *The Chimpanzees of Gombe*, Goodall describes the chimpanzee dating game. In one of several scenarios, males gather around attractive estrous females and try to lure them away from other males for a one-on-one sexual expedition that may last for days or weeks. But females find some suitors more appealing than others and often resist the advances of less desirable males. Males often rely on aggression to counter female resistance. For example, Goodall describes how Evered, in "persuading" a reluctant Winkle to accompany him into the forest, attacked her six times over the course of five hours, twice severely.

Sometimes, as I saw in Gombe, a male chimpanzee even attacks an estrous female days before he tries to mate with her. Goodall thinks that a male uses such aggression to train a female to fear him so that she will be more likely to surrender to his subsequent sexual advances. Similarly, male hamadryas baboons, who form small harems by kidnapping child brides, maintain a tight rein over their females through threats and intimidation. If, when another male is nearby, a hamadryas female strays even a few feet from her mate, he shoots her a threatening stare and raises his brows. She usually responds by rushing to his side; if not, he bites the back of her neck. The neck bite is ritualized—the male does not actually sink his razor-sharp canines into her flesh—but the threat of injury is clear. By repeating this behavior hundreds of times, the male lays claim to particular females months or even years before mating with them. When a female comes into estrus, she solicits sex only from her harem master, and other males rarely challenge his sexual rights to her.

In some species, females remain in their birth communities their whole lives, joining forces with related females to defend vital food resources against other females

These chimpanzee and hamadryas males are practicing sexual coercion: male use of force to increase the chances that a female victim will mate with him, or to decrease the chances that she will mate with someone else. But sexual coercion is much more common in some primate species than in others. Orangutans and chimpanzees are the only nonhuman primates whose males in the wild force females to copulate, while males of several other species, such as vervet monkeys and bonobos (pygmy chimpanzees), rarely if ever try to coerce females sexually. Between the two extremes lie many species, like hamadryas baboons, in which males do not force copulation but nonetheless use threats and intimidation to get sex.

These dramatic differences between species provide an opportunity to investigate which factors promote or inhibit sexual coercion. For example, we might expect to find more of it in species in which males are much larger than females—and we do. However, size differences between the sexes are far from the whole story. Chimpanzee and bonobo males both have only a slight size advantage, yet while male chimps frequently resort to force, male bonobos treat the fair sex with more respect. Clearly, then, although size matters, so do other factors. In particular, the social relationships females form with other females and with males appear to be as important.

In some species, females remain in their birth communities their whole lives, joining forces with related females

to defend vital food resources against other females. In such "female bonded" species, females also form alliances against aggressive males. Vervet monkeys are one such species, and among these small and exceptionally feisty African monkeys, related females gang up against males. High-ranking females use their dense network of female alliances to rule the troop; although smaller than males, they slap persistent suitors away like annoying flies. Researchers have observed similar alliances in many other female-bonded species, including other Old World monkeys such as macaques, olive baboons, patas and rhesus monkeys, and gray langurs; New World monkeys such as the capuchin; and prosimians such as the ring-tailed lemur.

Females in other species leave their birth communities at adolescence and spend the rest of their lives cut off from their female kin. In most such species, females do not form strong bonds with other females and rarely support one another against males. Both chimpanzees and hamadryas baboons exhibit this pattern, and, as we saw earlier, in both species females submit to sexual control by males.

Some of the factors that influence female vulnerability to male sexual coercion in different species may also help explain such variation among different groups in the same species.

This contrast between female-bonded species, in which related females gang together to thwart males, and non-female-bonded species, in which they don't, breaks down when we come to the bonobo. Female bonobos, like their close relatives the chimpanzees, leave their kin and live as adults with unrelated females. Recent field studies show that these unrelated females hang out together and engage in frequent homoerotic behavior, in which they embrace face-to-face and rapidly rub their genitals together; sex

seems to cement their bonds. Examining these studies in the context of my own research has convinced me that one way females use these bonds is to form alliances against males, and that, as a consequence, male bonobos do not dominate females or attempt to coerce them sexually. How and why female bonobos, but not chimpanzees, came up with this solution to male violence remains a mystery.

Female primates also use relationships with males to help protect themselves against sexual coercion. Among olive baboons, each adult female typically forms long-lasting "friendships" with a few of the many males in her troop. When a male baboon assaults a female, another male often comes to her rescue; in my troop, nine times out of ten the protector was a friend of the female's. In return for his protection, the defender may enjoy her sexual favors the next time she comes into estrus. There is a dark side to this picture, however. Male baboons frequently threaten or attack their female friends—when, for example, one tries to form a friendship with a new male. Other males apparently recognize friendships and rarely intervene. The female, then, becomes less vulnerable to aggression from males in general, but more vulnerable to aggression from her male friends.

As a final example, consider orangutans. Because their food grows so sparsely adult females rarely travel with anyone but their dependent offspring. But orangutan females routinely fall victim to forced copulation. Female orangutans, it seems, pay a high price for their solitude.

Some of the factors that influence female vulnerability to male sexual coercion in different species may also help explain such variation among different groups in the same species. For example, in a group of chimpanzees in the Taï Forest in the Ivory Coast, females form closer bonds with one another than do females at Gombe. Taï females may consequently have more egalitarian relationships with males than their Gombe counterparts do.

Such differences between groups especially characterize humans. Among the South American Yanomamö, for instance, men frequently abduct and rape women from neighboring villages and severely beat their wives for suspected adultery. However, among the Aka people of the Central African Republic, male aggression against women has never been observed. Most human societies, of course, fall between these two extremes.

How are we to account for such variation? The same social factors that help explain how sexual coercion differs among nonhuman primates may deepen our understanding of how it varies across different groups of people. In most traditional human societies, a woman leaves her birth community when she marries and goes to live with her husband and his relatives. Without strong bonds to close female kin, she will probably be in danger of sexual coercion. The presence of close female kin, though, may protect her. For example, in a community in Belize, women live near their female relatives. A man will sometimes beat his wife if he becomes jealous or suspects her of infidelity, but when this happens, onlookers run to tell her female kin. Their arrival on the scene, combined with the presence of other glaring women, usually shames the man enough to stop his aggression.

Even in societies in which women live away from their families, kin may provide protection against abusive husbands, though how much protection varies dramatically from one society to the next. In some societies a woman's kin, including her father and brothers, consistently support her against an abusive husband, while in others they rarely help her. Why?

The key may lie in patterns of male-male relationships. Alliances between males are much more highly developed in humans than in other primates, and men frequently rely on such alliances to compete successfully against other men. They often gain more by supporting their male allies than they do by supporting female kin. In addition, men often use their alliances to defeat rivals and abduct or rape their women, as painfully illustrated

by recent events in Bosnia. When women live far from close kin, among men who value their alliances with other men more than their bonds with women, they may be even more vulnerable to sexual coercion than many nonhuman primate females.

Even in societies in which women live away from their families, kin may provide protection against abusive husbands.

Like nonhuman primate females, many women form bonds with unrelated males who may protect them from other males. However, reliance on men exacts a cost—women and other primate females often must submit to control by their protectors. Such control is more elaborate in humans because allied men agree to honor one another's proprietary rights over women. In most of the world's cultures, marriage involves not only the exclusion of other men from sexual access to a man's wife—which protects the woman against rape by other men—but also entails the husband's right to complete control over his wife's sexual life, including the right to punish her for real or suspected adultery, to have sex with her whenever he wants, and even to restrict her contact with other people, especially men.

In modern industrial society, many men—perhaps most—maintain such traditional notions of marriage. At the same time, many of the traditional sources of support for women, including censure of abusive husbands by the woman's kinfolk or other community members, are eroding as more and more people end up without nearby kin or long-term neighbors. The increased vulnerability of women isolated from their birth communities, however, is not just a by-product of modern living. Historically, in highly patriarchal societies like those found in China and northern India, married

women lived in households ruled by their husband's mother and male kin, and their ties with their own kin were virtually severed. In these societies, today as in the past, the husband's female kin often view the wife as a competitor for resources. Not only do they fail to support her against male coercive control, but they sometimes actively encourage it. This scenario illustrates an important point: women do not invariably support other women against men, in part because women may perceive their interests as best served through alliances with men, not with other women. When men have most of the power and control most of the resources, this looks like a realistic assessment.

Decreasing women's vulnerability to sexual coercion, then, may require fundamental changes in social alliances. Women gave voice to this essential truth with the slogan SISTERHOOD IS POWERFUL—a reference to the importance of women's ability to cooperate with unrelated women as if they were indeed sisters. However, among humans, the male-dominant social system derives support from political, economic, legal, and ideological institutions that other primates can't even dream of. Freedom from male control—including male sexual coercion—therefore requires women to form alliances with one another (and with like-minded men) on a scale beyond that shown by nonhuman primates and humans in the past. Although knowledge of other primates can provide inspiration for this task, its achievement depends on the uniquely human ability to envision a future different from anything that has gone before.

Barbara Smuts is a professor of psychology and anthropology at the University of Michigan. She has been doing fieldwork in animal behavior since the early 1970s, studying baboons, chimps, and dolphins. "In my work I combine research in animal behavior with an abiding interest in feminist perspectives on science," says Smuts. She is the author of Sex and Friendship in Baboons.

UNIT 4

The Fossil Evidence

Unit Selections

Key Points to Consider

- When and where did our ancestors split off from the apes?

- Under what circumstances did bipedalism evolve?

- What is the "man the hunter" hypothesis, and how might the "scavenging theory" better suit the early hominid data?

- How would you draw the early hominid family tree?

- When, where and why did *Homo erectus* evolve? Is it one species or two? Explain your reasoning.

- Did Eugene Dubois really find the "missing link"?

- Was "Peking Man" a cannibal, a hunter, or the hunted?

 **Links: www.dushkin.com/online/**
These sites are annotated in the World Wide Web pages.

The African Emergence and Early Asian Dispersals of the Genus *Homo*
http://www.uiowa.edu/~bioanth/homo.html

Anthropology, Archaeology, and American Indian Sites on the Internet
http://dizzy.library.arizona.edu/library/teams/sst/anthro/

Long Foreground: Human Prehistory
http://www.wsu.edu/gened/learn-modules/top_longfor/lfopen-index.html

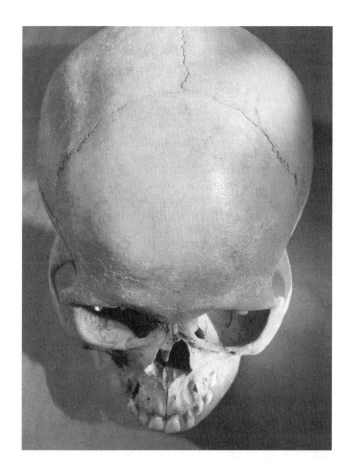

A primary focal point of this book, as well as of the whole of biological anthropology, is the search for and interpretation of fossil evidence for hominid (meaning human or humanlike) evolution. Paleoanthropologists are those who carry out this task by conducting the painstaking excavations and detailed analyses that serve as a basis for understanding our past. (See "Chasing Dubois's Ghost" for an account of one of the earliest examples of this type of endeavor.) Every fragment found is cherished like a ray of light that may help to illuminate the path taken by our ancestors in the process of becoming "us". At least, that is what we would like to believe. In reality, each discovery leads to further mystery, and for every fossil-hunting paleoanthropologist who thinks his or her find supports a particular theory, there are many others anxious to express their disagreement. (See "Hunting the First Hominid" and "*Erectus* Rising.")

How wonderful it would be, we sometimes think in moments of frustration over inconclusive data, if the fossils would just speak for themselves, and every primordial piece of humanity were to carry with it a self-evident explanation for its place in the evolutionary story. Paleoanthropology would then be more a quantitative problem of amassing enough material to reconstruct our ancestral development than a qualitative problem of interpreting what it all means. It would certainly be a simpler process, but would it be as interesting?

Most scientists tolerate, welcome, or even (dare it be said?) thrive on controversy, recognizing that diversity of opinion refreshes the mind, rouses students, and captures the imagination of the general public. After all, where would paleoanthropology be without the gadflies, the near-mythic heroes, and, lest we forget, the research funds they generate? Consider, for example, the issue of the differing roles played by males and females in the transition to humanity and all that it implies with regard to bipedalism, tool making, and the origin of the family. Did bipedalism really evolve in the grasslands? (See "Food for Thought.") Should the primary theme of human evolution be summed up as "man the hunter" or "woman the gatherer"?

Not all the research and theoretical speculation taking place in the field of paleoanthropology is so controversial. Most scientists, in fact, go about their work quietly and methodically, generating hypotheses that are much less explosive and yet have the cumulative effect of enriching our understanding of the details of human evolution. Thus, in "The Scavenging of 'Peking Man'," we get a new interpretation of old evidence. In "Scavenger Hunt," Pat Shipman tells how modern technology, in the form of the scanning electron microscope, combined with meticulous detailed analysis of cut marks on fossil animal bones, can help us better understand the locomotor and food-getting adaptations of our early hominid ancestors. In one stroke, Shipman is able to challenge the traditional "man the hunter" theme that has pervaded most early hominid research and writing and to simultaneously set forth an alternative hypothesis that will, in turn, inspire further research.

As we mull over the controversies outlined in this unit, we should not take them as reflecting an inherent weakness of the field of paleoanthropology, but rather as symbolic of its strength: the ability and willingness to scrutinize, question, and reflect (seemingly endlessly) on every bit of evidence.

Contrary to the way that the creationists would have it, an admission of doubt is not an expression of ignorance but simply a frank recognition of the imperfect state of our knowledge. If we are to increase our understanding of ourselves, we must maintain an atmosphere of free inquiry without preconceived notions and an unquestioning commitment to a particular point of view.

To paraphrase anthropologist Ashley Montagu, *whereas creationism seeks certainty without proof, science seeks proof without certainty.*

HUNTING THE FIRST HOMINID

by Pat Shipman

Self-centeredly, human beings have always taken an exceptional interest in their origins. Each discovery of a new species of hominid—both our human ancestors and the near-relatives arising after the split from the gorilla-chimp lineage—is reported with great fanfare, even though the First Hominid remains elusive. We hope that, when our earliest ancestor is finally captured, it will reveal the fundamental adaptations that make us *us*.

There is no shortage of ideas about the essential nature of the human species and the basic adaptations of our kind. Some say hominids are fundamentally thinkers; others favor tool-makers or talkers; still others argue that hunting, scavenging or bipedal walking made hominids special. Knowing what the First Hominid looked like would add some meat to a soup flavored with speculation and prejudice.

Genetic and molecular studies provide one sort of insight, showing what sort of *stuff* we are made of, and that it is only slightly different stuff from that which makes up the apes (gorillas, chimps, orangutans and gibbons). From the molecular differences among the genes of humans and apes, geneticists estimate the time when each of the various ape and hominid lineages diverged from the common stem. The result is a sort of hairy Y diagram, with multiple branches instead of simply two as is usual on a Y. Each terminus represents a living species; each branching point or node represents the appearance of some new evolutionary trait, such as new molecules, new genes, new shapes or new proportions of limb, skull and tooth. Unfortunately, this way of diagramming the results tends to lull us into thinking (falsely) that all the evolutionary changes occurred at those nodes, and none along the branches.

Such studies omit a crucial part of our history: the extinct species. Only the fossil record contains evidence, in context, of the precise pathway that evolution took. In this technological age, when sophisticated instrumentation and gee-whiz algorithms seem downright necessary, the most basic information about the evolution of our lineage still comes from branches of science that operate in rather old-fashioned ways. The primary discoveries in paleontology (the study of old things), pale oanthropology (the study of old humans) and archaeology (the study of the old stuff that old humans leave around) still rely on the efforts of handful of investigators who slog around on foot or excavate in desolate landscapes. Fancy equipment can't replace eyes and brains, although instrumentation plays a crucial role in the dating an analysis of fossil remains.

Finding the evolutionary origin of hominids is little like stalking big game. Paleoanthropologist struggle to establish when and where their quarry was last seen and what it was like—hoping to follow its tracks backward in time. (*Why* hominids or any other group arose is such a metaphysical question that most paleoanthropologists run away screaming when it is asked.)

When the first hominid slinked through the underbush has been estimated from molecular clock and confirmed by radiometric dates. These line of evidence converge on a period between 5 million and 7 million years ago as the time when primitive, perhaps vaguely apelike species evolved some definitive new adaptation that transformed it into the First Hominid. But like the point of inflection on a line graph, the first species in any new lineage is only readily apparent after the fact. The emergence of the first hominid was probably not obvious in prospect but only now, in retrospect—in the context of the entire evolutionary record of the hominids—when the long-term evolutionary trends can be seen.

Where this dangerous creature once lived has to be Africa, since both our closest living relatives (chimpanzees and gorillas) and all early hominids (older than about 2 million years ago) are African.

What to Look For?

What happened, exactly, and to *whom*, remain to be discovered. Two newly discovered fossil species have each been proposed to be the First Hominid. This circumstance raises a significant issue: How would we know the First Hominid if we saw it?

Making a list of key features that differentiate apes from people is not difficult, but misleading. It is absurd to expect that all of these differences arose simultaneously during a single evolutionary event represented by the final fork on the hairy Y diagram. The first ape on the gorilla-chimp lineage was neither a gorilla nor a chimpanzee, for modem gorillas and chimps have had at least 5 million years to evolve in isolation before arriving at their modem form. In the same way the First Hominid on our lineage was not a human and did not possess all of the characteristics of modem humans.

Using a hairy Y diagram, we can limit the number of contenders for the essential or basal hominid adaptation:

—Hominids might be essentially bipeds. All known hominids are bipedal; no apes are.

—Wishful thinking aside, hominids are not simply brainy apes. Alas, until about 2 million years ago no hominid had a brain larger than an ape's relative to its body size.

—Hominids might be apelike creatures that have lost their sexual dimorphism. Sexual dimorphism is exhibited as male-female differences that are not related to reproduction. For example, male orangs are typically much larger than females and have longer canine teeth that hone sharper with wear. The fossil record shows that hominids lost their dental sexual dimorphism first, since all known hominids have small and flat-wearing canines. In contrast, sexual dimorphism in body size persisted in hominids until about 2 million years ago, when the genus *Homo* first appeared.

—Thick dental enamel may be a key hominid trait. All hominids have thick enamel, whereas all fossil and living apes (except those in the orangutan lineage) have thin enamel. Because the fossil record of apes is so poor, we do not know whether the primitive condition for apes and hominids was thick or thin enamel. Indeed, how enamel thickness is to be measured and evaluated has generated many pages of debate.

—Hominids are hand-graspers or manipulators (from the Latin for hand, *manus*), whereas apes are foot-graspers. These differences are reflected in the sharp contrasts in the hand and foot anatomy of apes and humans. Apes have divergent big toes and long, curved toe bones for holding onto branches; their thumbs are short and cannot be opposed to the other fingers for skillful manipulation. Human beings are the opposite, with long, opposable thumbs and big toes that are closely aligned with the remaining short, straight toes. Human feet are nearly useless for grasping but are well adapted to bipedalism. An intermediate condition occurs in early hominids such as Lucy (the best-known individual of *Australopithecus afarensis*), who had opposable thumbs and numerous adaptations to bipedalism, and yet retained rather long and curved toes. Lucy and probably other types of *Australopithecus* were walkers, hand-graspers *and* somewhat compromised foot-graspers.

A description of our desired prey, then, might read like this:

> An ape-brained and small-canined creature, with dental enamel of unknown thickness. Large if male but smaller if female. May be spotted climbing adeptly in trees or walking bipedally on the ground. Last seen in Africa between 5 million and 7 million years ago.

From this description, can we identify the First Hominid? Well, no—not yet.

A Tale of Two Trophies

Yohannes Haile-Selassie of the University of California, Berkeley, described a likely contender from Ethiopia in July of 2001. His material comes from Ethiopian sediments between 5.2 million and 5.8 million years old and is called *Ardipithecus ramidus kadabba*, a new subspecies. *Ardipithecus* means "root ape" in the Mar language, and the species has been explicitly proposed to be a "root species" ancestral to all later hominids.

Haile-Selassie's specimens include more than 20 teeth, some associated with a mandible or lower jaw; substantial pieces of two left humeri, or upper arm bones; a partial ulna from the same forearm as one humerus; a partial clavicle or collarbone; a half of one finger bone; and a complete toe bone.

No ironclad evidence of bipedality in any *Ardipithecus* specimen has yet been published. In this collection, the only evidence about habitual patterns of locomotion comes from the single toe bone. Its weight-bearing surface faces downward as in bipeds, not inward as in apes. Any jury might be suspicious that *Ardipithecus* was bipedal, but none of the really telltale body parts—pelvis, complete femur, tibia, or ankle bones—has yet been recovered. The preserved bones of the arm, finger and shoulder closely resemble those of Lucy and may have been used in grasping and tree-climbing. *Ardipithecus* is as yet too poorly known for its relative brain size or sexual dimorphism in body size to be assessed.

The other candidate that has already been bagged is a 6 million-year-old find from the Tugen Hills of Kenya called *Orrorin tugenensis*. Its generic name is derived from the Tugen language and means "original man"—a claim as bold as "root ape." Found by a joint French-Kenyan team headed by Brigitte Senut of the Centre nationale de la recherche scientifique, the *Orrorin* fossils include a few teeth, some embedded in a jaw fragment; a partial humerus; a finger bone; and substantial parts of three femurs, or thigh bones.

The femurs, which might provide definitive evidence of bipedality, are incomplete. The sole evidence for bipedality lies in the head of the femur in *Orrorin*, which is proportionately larger than Lucy's. One reason to evolve a large-headed femur is to dissipate the forces produced by bipedalism. The team concludes that *Orrorin* evolved bipedalism separately from Lucy (and from other species of *Australopithecus*), making *Orrorin* the only known ancestor of *Homo*. *Australopithecus* is displaced to an extinct side-branch of the hominid lineage.

Their surprising conclusion is not universally accepted. Skeptics reply that the femoral differences between *Orrorin* and *Australopithecus* might disappear if *Orrorin*'s femur were compared with that of a large male individual rather than with the diminutive Lucy.

As in *Ardipithecus*, the bones from the upper limb of *Orrorin* show tree-climbing adaptations. Neither relative brain size nor body size dimorphism can be evaluated in *Orrorin*.

Where *Orrorin* and *Ardipithecus* differ are in their teeth. *Orrorin* appears to have thick enamel, like a hominid or an orangutan, and *Ardipithecus* seems to have thin enamel, like other apes. This dental comparison might resolve the question "Who is the First Hominid?" in favor of *Orrorin*, except that *Orrorin*'s canine teeth imply the opposite conclusion. *Orrorin*'s single known canine is sizable and pointed and wears like an ape's canine. In contrast, the several known canines of *Ardipithecus* are all small-crowned and flat-wearing, like a hominid's canines.

Puzzlingly, *Ardipithecus* and *Orrorin* show different mosaics of hominid and ape features. Both may be bipeds, although *Ardipithecus* is a biped in the manner of *Australopithecus* and *Orrorin* is not. If one of these two newly announced species is the First Hominid, then the other must be banished to the ape lineage. The situation is deliciously complex and confusing.

It is also humbling. We thought we knew an ape from a person; we thought we could even identify a man in an ape suit or an ape in a tuxedo for what they were. Humans have long prided themselves on being very different from apes—but pride goeth before a fall. In this case, embarrassingly, we can't tell the ape from the hominid even though we have teeth, jaws, and arm and leg bones.

Paleoanthropologists must seriously reconsider the defining attributes of apes and hominids while we wait for new fossils. In the meantime, we should ponder our complicity, too, for we have been guilty of expecting evolution to be much simpler than it ever is.

Pat Shipman is an adjunct professor of anthropology at the Pennsylvania State University. Address: Department of Anthropology, 315 Carpenter Building, Pennsylvania State University, University Park, PA 16801. Internet:pls10@psu.edu

Food for THOUGHT

Dietary change was a driving force in human evolution

By William R. Leonard

W e walk on two legs, carry around enormous brains and have colonized every corner of the globe. Anthropologists and biologists have long sought to understand how our lineage came to differ so profoundly from the primate norm in these ways, and over the years all manner of hypotheses aimed at explaining each of these oddities have been put forth. But a growing body of evidence indicates that these miscellaneous quirks of humanity in fact have a common thread: they are largely the result of natural selection acting to maximize dietary quality and foraging efficiency. Changes in food availability over time, it seems, strongly influenced our hominid ancestors. Thus, in an evolutionary sense, we are very much what we ate.

Accordingly, what we eat is yet another way in which we differ from our primate kin. Contemporary human populations the world over have diets richer in calories and nutrients than those of our cousins, the great apes. So when and how did our ancestors' eating habits diverge from those of other primates? Further, to what extent have modern humans departed from the ancestral dietary pattern?

We humans are strange primates

Scientific interest in the evolution of human nutritional requirements has a long history. But relevant investigations started gaining momentum after 1985, when S. Boyd Eaton and Melvin J. Konner of Emory University published a seminal paper in the *New England Journal of Medicine* entitled "Paleolithic Nutrition." They argued that the prevalence in modern societies of many chronic diseases—obesity, hypertension, coronary heart disease and diabetes, among them—is the consequence of a mismatch between modern dietary patterns and the type of diet that our species evolved to eat as prehistoric hunter-gatherers. Since then, however, understanding of the evolution of human nutritional needs has advanced considerably—thanks

Overview/*Diet and Human Evolution*

- The characteristics that most distinguish humans from other primates are largely the results of natural selection acting to improve the quality of the human diet and the efficiency with which our ancestors obtained food. Some scientists have proposed that many of the health problems modern societies face are consequences of a discrepancy between what we eat and what our Paleolithic forebears ate.
- Yet studies of traditionally living populations show that modern humans are able to meet their nutritional needs using a wide variety of dietary strategies. We have evolved to be flexible eaters. The health concerns of the industrial world, where calorie-packed foods are readily available, stem not from deviations from a specific diet but from an imbalance between the energy we consume and the energy we expend.

in large part to new comparative analyses of traditionally living human populations and other primates—and a more nuanced picture has emerged. We now know that humans have evolved not to subsist on a single, Paleolithic diet but to be flexible eaters, an insight that has important implications for the current debate over what people today should eat in order to be healthy.

To appreciate the role of diet in human evolution, we must remember that the search for food, its consumption and, ultimately, how it is used for biological processes are all critical aspects of an organism's ecology. The energy dynamic between organisms and their environments—that is, energy expended in relation to energy acquired—has important adaptive consequences for survival and reproduction. These two components

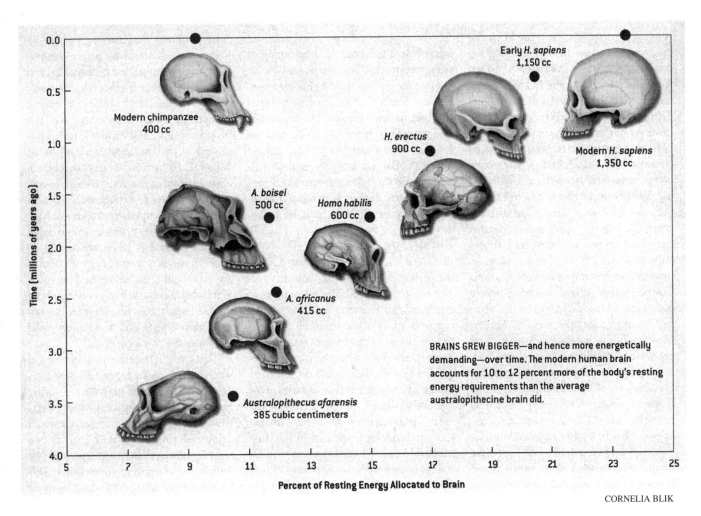

of Darwinian fitness are reflected in the way we divide up an animal's energy budget. Maintenance energy is what keeps an animal alive on a day-to-day basis. Productive energy, on the other hand, is associated with producing and raising offspring for the next generation. For mammals like ourselves, this must cover the increased costs that mothers incur during pregnancy and lactation.

The type of environment a creature inhabits will influence the distribution of energy between these components, with harsher conditions creating higher maintenance demands. Nevertheless, the goal of all organisms is the same: to devote sufficient funds to reproduction to ensure the long-term success of the species. Thus, by looking at the way animals go about obtaining and then allocating food energy, we can better discern how natural selection produces evolutionary change.

Becoming Bipeds

WITHOUT EXCEPTION, living nonhuman primates habitually move around on all fours, or quadrupedally, when they are on the ground. Scientists generally assume therefore that the last common ancestor of humans and chimpanzees (our closest living relative) was also a quadruped. Exactly when the last common ancestor lived is unknown, but clear indications of bipedalism—the trait that distinguished ancient humans from

other apes—are evident in the oldest known species of *Australopithecus,* which lived in Africa roughly four million years ago. Ideas about why bipedalism evolved abound in the paleoanthropological literature. C. Owen Lovejoy of Kent State University proposed in 1981 that two-legged locomotion freed the arms to carry children and foraged goods. More recently, Kevin D. Hunt of Indiana University has posited that bipedalism emerged as a feeding posture that enabled access to foods that had previously been out of reach. Peter Wheeler of Liverpool John Moores University submits that moving upright allowed early humans to better regulate their body temperature by exposing less surface area to the blazing African sun.

The list goes on. In reality, a number of factors probably selected for this type of locomotion. My own research, conducted in collaboration with my wife, Marcia L. Robertson, suggests that bipedalism evolved in our ancestors at least in part because it is less energetically expensive than quadrupedalism. Our analyses of the energy costs of movement in living animals of all sizes have shown that, in general, the strongest predictors of cost are the weight of the animal and the speed at which it travels. What is striking about human bipedal movement is that it is notably more economical than quadrupedal locomotion at walking rates.

Apes, in contrast, are not economical when moving on the ground. For instance, chimpanzees, which employ a peculiar

113

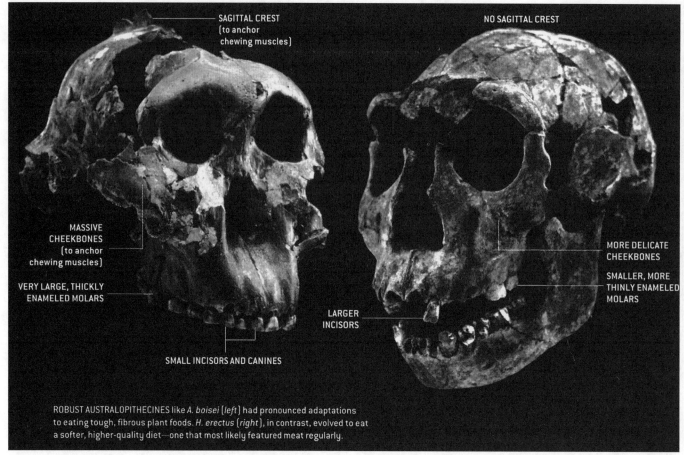

ROBUST AUSTRALOPITHECINES like *A. boisei* (*left*) had pronounced adaptations to eating tough, fibrous plant foods. *H. erectus* (*right*), in contrast, evolved to eat a softer, higher-quality diet—one that most likely featured meat regularly.

DAVID BRILL

form of quadrupedalism known as knuckle walking, spend some 35 percent more calories during locomotion than does a typical mammalian quadruped of the same size—a large dog, for example. Differences in the settings in which humans and apes evolved may help explain the variation in costs of movement. Chimps, gorillas and orangutans evolved in and continue to occupy dense forests where only a mile or so of trekking over the course of the day is all that is needed to find enough to eat. Much of early hominid evolution, on the other hand, took place in more open woodland and grassland, where sustenance is harder to come by. Indeed, modern human hunter-gatherers living in these environments, who provide us with the best available model of early human subsistence patterns, often travel six to eight miles daily in search of food.

These differences in day range have important locomotor implications. Because apes travel only short distances each day, the potential energetic benefits of moving more efficiently are very small. For far-ranging foragers, however, cost-effective walking saves many calories in maintenance energy needs—calories that can instead go toward reproduction. Selection for energetically efficient locomotion is therefore likely to be more intense among far-ranging animals because they have the most to gain.

For hominids living between five million and 1.8 million years ago, during the Pliocene epoch, climate change spurred this morphological revolution. As the African continent grew

drier, forests gave way to grasslands, leaving food resources patchily distributed. In this context, bipedalism can be viewed as one of the first strategies in human nutritional evolution, a pattern of movement that would have substantially reduced the number of calories spent in collecting increasingly dispersed food resources.

Big Brains and Hungry Hominids

NO SOONER HAD humans perfected their stride than the next pivotal event in human evolution—the dramatic enlargement of the brain—began. According to the fossil record, the australopithecines never became much brainier than living apes, showing only a modest increase in brain size, from around 400 cubic centimeters four million years ago to 500 cubic centimeters two million years later. *Homo* brain sizes, in contrast, ballooned from 600 cubic centimeters in *H. habilis* some two million years ago up to 900 cubic centimeters in early *H. erectus* just 300,000 years later. The *H. erectus* brain did not attain modern human proportions (1,350 cubic centimeters on average), but it exceeded that of living nonhuman primates.

From a nutritional perspective, what is extraordinary about our large brain is how much energy it consumes—roughly 16 times as much as muscle tissue per unit weight. Yet although humans have much bigger brains relative to body weight than do other primates (three times larger than expected), the total

INTO THE FIRE

EATING MORE ANIMAL FOODS is one way of boosting the caloric and nutrient density of the diet, a shift that appears to have been critical in the evolution of the human lineage. But might our ancient forebears have improved dietary quality another way? Richard Wrangham of Harvard University and his colleagues recently examined the importance of cooking in human evolution. They showed that cooking not only makes plant foods softer and easier to chew, it substantially increases their available energy content, particularly for starchy tubers such as potatoes and manioc. In their raw form, starches are not readily broken down by the enzymes in the human body. When heated, however, these complex carbohydrates become more digestible, thereby yielding more calories.

The researchers propose that *Homo erectus* was probably the first hominid to apply fire to food, starting perhaps 1.8 million years ago. They argue that early cooking of plant foods (especially tubers) enabled this species to evolve smaller teeth and bigger brains than those of their predecessors.

EARLY COOKING of plant foods, especially tubers, enabled brain expansion, argue Richard Wrangham of Harvard University and his colleages.

Additionally, the extra calories allowed *H. erectus* to start hunting—an energetically costly activity—more frequently.

From an energetics perspective, this is a logical enough line of reasoning. What makes the hypothesis difficult to swallow is the archaeological evidence Wrangham's team uses to make its case. The authors cite the East African sites of Koobi Fora and Chesowanja, which date to around 1.6 million and 1.4 million years ago, respectively, to indicate control of fire by *H. erectus*. These localities do indeed exhibit evidence of fires, but whether hominids were responsible for creating or harnessing the flames is a matter of some debate. The earliest unequivocal manifestations of fire use—stone hearths and burned animal bones from sites in Europe—are only some 200,000 years old.

Cooking was clearly an innovation that considerably improved the quality of the human diet. But it remains unclear when in our past this practice rose.

—*W.R.L.*

primates, and more still than the 3 to 5 percent allotted to the brain by other mammals.

By using estimates of hominid body size compiled by Henry M. McHenry of the University of California at Davis, Robertson and I have reconstructed the proportion of resting energy needs that would have been required to support the brains of our ancient ancestors. Our calculations suggest that a typical, 80- to 85-pound australopithecine with a brain size of 450 cubic centimeters would have devoted about 11 percent of its resting energy to the brain. For its part, *H. erectus*, which weighed in at 125 to 130 pounds and had a brain size of some 900 cubic centimeters, would have earmarked about 17 percent of its resting energy—that is, about 260 out of 1,500 kilocalories a day—for the organ.

NEANDERTAL HUNTERS

TO RECONSTRUCT what early humans ate, researchers have traditionally studied features on their fossilized teeth and skulls, archaeological remains of food-related activities, and the diets of living humans and apes. Increasingly, however, investigators have been tapping another source of data: the chemical composition of fossil bones. This approach has yielded some especially intriguing findings with regard to the Neandertals.

Michael Richards, now at the University of Bradford in England, and his colleagues recently examined isotopes of carbon (^{13}C) and nitrogen (^{15}N) in 29,000-year-old Neandertal bones from Vindija Cave in Croatia. The relative proportions of these isotopes in the protein part of human bone, known as collagen, directly reflect their proportions in the protein of the individual's diet. Thus, by comparing the isotopic "signatures" of the Neandertal bones to those of other animals living in the same environments, the authors were able to determine whether the Neandertals were deriving the bulk of their protein from plants or from animals.

The analyses show that the Vindija Neandertal had ^{15}N levels comparable to those seen in northern carnivores such as foxes and wolves, indicating that they obtained almost all their dietary protein from animal foods. Earlier work hinted that inefficient foraging might have been a factor in the subsequent demise of the Neandertals. But Richards and his collaborators argue that in order to consume as much animal food as they apparently did, the Neandertals had to have been skilled hunters. These findings are part of a growing body of literature that suggests Neandertal subsistence behavior was more complex than previously thought (see "Who Were the Neandertals?" by Kate Wong; SCIENTIFIC AMERICAN, April 2000).

—*W.R.L.*

resting energy requirements of the human body are no greater than those of any other mammal of the same size. We therefore use a much greater share of our daily energy budget to feed our voracious brains. In fact, at rest brain metabolism accounts for a whopping 20 to 25 percent of an adult human's energy needs—far more than the 8 to 10 percent observed in nonhuman

How did such an energetically costly brain evolve? One theory, developed by Dean Falk of Florida State University, holds that bipedalism enabled hominids to cool their cranial blood, thereby freeing the heat-sensitive brain of the temperature constraints that had kept its size in check. I suspect that, as

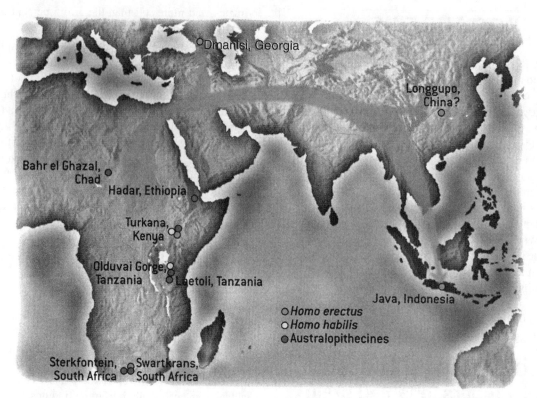

LAURIE GRACE (map)

AFRICAN EXODUS began as soon as *H. erectus* evolved around 1.8 million years ago, probably in part because it needed a larger home range than that of its smaller-bodied predecessors.

with bipedalism, a number of selective factors were probably at work. But brain expansion almost certainly could not have occurred until hominids adopted a diet sufficiently rich in calories and nutrients to meet the associated costs.

Comparative studies of living animals support that assertion. Across all primates, species with bigger brains dine on richer foods, and humans are the extreme example of this correlation, boasting the largest relative brain size and the choicest diet [see "Diet and Primate Evolution," by Katharine Milton; SCIENTIFIC AMERICAN, August 1993]. According to recent analyses by Loren Cordain of Colorado State University, contemporary hunter-gatherers derive, on average, 40 to 60 percent of their dietary energy from animal foods (meat, milk and other products). Modern chimps, in comparison, obtain only 5 to 7 percent of their calories from these comestibles. Animal foods are far denser in calories and nutrients than most plant foods. For example, 3.5 ounces of meat provides upward of 200 kilocalories. But the same amount of fruit provides only 50 to 100 kilocalories. And a comparable serving of foliage yields just 10 to 20 kilocalories. It stands to reason, then, that for early *Homo*, acquiring more gray matter meant seeking out more of the energy-dense fare.

Fossils, too, indicate that improvements to dietary quality accompanies evolutionary brain growth. All australopithecines had skeletal and dental features built for processing tough, low-quality plant foods. The later, robust australopithecines—a dead-end branch of the human family tree that lived alongside members of our own genus—had especially pronounced adaptations for grinding up fibrous plant foods, including massive, dish-shaped faces; heavily built mandibles; ridges, or sagittal

crests, atop the skull for the attachment of powerful chewing muscles; and huge, thickly enameled molar teeth. (This is not to say that australopithecines never ate meat. They almost certainly did on occasion, just as chimps do today.) In contrast, early members of the genus *Homo,* which descended from the gracile australopithecines, had much smaller faces, more delicate jaws, smaller molars and no sagittal crests—despite being far larger in terms of overall body size than their predecessors. Together these features suggest that early *Homo* was consuming less plant material and more animal foods.

As to what prompted *Homo*'s initial shift toward the higher-quality diet necessary for brain growth, environmental change appears to have once more set the stage for evolutionary change. The continued desiccation of the African landscape limited the amount and variety of edible plant foods available to hominids. Those on the line leading to the robust australopithecines coped with this problem morphologically, evolving anatomical specializations that enabled them to subsist on more widely available, difficult-to-chew foods. *Homo* took a different path. As it turns out, the spread of grasslands also led to an increase in the relative abundance of grazing mammals such as antelope and gazelle, creating opportunities for hominids capable of exploiting them. *H. erectus* did just that, developing the first hunting-and-gathering economy in which game animals became a significant part of the diet and resources were shared among members of the foraging groups. Signs of this behavior revolution are visible in the archaeological record, which shows an increase in animal bones at hominid sites during this period, along with evidence that the beasts were butchered using   stone tools.

116

VARIOUS DIETS can satisfy human nutritional requirements. Some populations subsist almost entirely on plant foods; others eat mostly animal foods. Although Americans consume less meat than do a number of the traditionally living people described here, they have on average higher cholesterol levels and higher levels of obesity (as indicated by body mass index) because they consume more energy than they expend and eat meat that is higher in fat.

Population	Energy Intake (kilocalories/day)	Energy from Animal Foods (%)	Energy from Plant Foods (%)	Total Blood Cholesterol (milligrams/deciliter)	Body Mass Index (weight/height squared)
HUNTER-GATHERERS					
!Kung (Botswana)	2,100	33	67	121	19
Inuit (North America)	2,350	96	4	141	24
PASTORALISTS					
Turkana (Kenya)	1,411	80	20	186	18
Evenki (Russia)	2,820	41	59	142	22
AGRICULTURALISTS					
Quechua (Highland Peru)	2,002	5	95	150	21
INDUSTRIAL SOCIETIES U.S.	2,250	23	77	204	26

Note: Energy intake figures reflect the adult average (males and females); blood cholesterol and body mass index (BMI) figures are given for males.
Healthy BMI = 18.5–24.9; overweight = 25.0–29.9; obese = 30 and higher.

These changes in diet and foraging behavior did not turn our ancestors into strict carnivores; however, the addition of modest amounts of animal foods to the menu, combined with the sharing of resources that is typical of hunter-gatherer groups, would have significantly increased the quality and stability of hominid diets. Improved dietary quality alone cannot explain *why* hominid brains grew, but it appears to have played a critical role in enabling that change. After the initial spurt in brain growth, diet and brain expansion probably interacted synergistically: bigger brains produced more complex social behavior, which led to further shifts in foraging tactics and improved diet, which in turn fostered additional brain evolution.

A Movable Feast

THE EVOLUTION of *H. erectus* in Africa 1.8 million years ago also marked a third turning point in human evolution: the initial movement of hominids out of Africa. Until recently, the locations and ages of known fossil sites suggested that early *Homo* stayed put for a few hundred thousand years before venturing out of the motherland and slowly fanning out into the rest of the Old World. Earlier work hinted that improvements in tool technology around 1.4 million years ago—namely, the advent of the Acheulean hand ax—allowed hominids to leave Africa. But new discoveries indicate that *H. erectus* hit the ground running, so to speak. Rutgers University geochronologist Carl Swisher III and his colleagues have shown that the earliest *H. erectus* sites outside of Africa, which are in Indonesia and the Republic of Georgia, date to between 1.8 million and 1.7 million years ago. It seems that the first appearance of *H. erectus* and its initial spread from Africa were almost simultaneous.

The impetus behind this newfound wanderlust again appears to be food. What an animal eats dictates to a large extent how much territory it needs to survive. Carnivorous animals generally require far bigger home ranges than do herbivores of comparable size because they have fewer total calories available to them per unit area.

Large-bodied and increasingly dependent on animal foods, *H. erectus* most likely needed much more turf than the smaller, more vegetarian australopithecines did. Using data on contemporary primates and human hunter-gatherers as a guide, Robertson, Susan C. Antón of Rutgers University and I have estimated that the larger body size of *H. erectus*, combined with a moderate increase in meat consumption, would have necessitated an eightfold to 10-fold increase in home range size compared with that of the late australopithecines—enough, in fact, to account for the abrupt expansion of the species out of Africa. Exactly how far beyond the continent that shift would have taken *H. erectus* remains unclear, but migrating animal herds may have helped lead it to these distant lands.

As humans moved into more northern latitudes, they encountered new dietary challenges. The Neandertals, who lived during the last ice ages of Europe, were among the first humans to inhabit arctic environments, and they almost certainly would have needed ample calories to endure under those circumstances. Hints at what their energy requirements might have been come from data on traditional human populations that live in northern settings today. The Siberian reindeer-herding populations known as the Evenki, which I have studied with Peter Katzmarzyk of Queen's University in Ontario and Victoria A. Galloway of the University of Toronto, and the Inuit (Eskimo) populations of the Canadian Arctic have resting metabolic rates that are about 15 percent higher than those of people of similar size living in temperate environments. The energetically expensive activities associated with living in a northern climate ratchet their caloric cost of living up further still. Indeed, whereas a 160-pound American male with a typical urban way of life requires about 2,600 kilocalories a day, a diminutive, 125-pound Evenki man needs more than 3,000 kilocalories a day to sustain himself. Using these modern northern populations as benchmarks, Mark Sorensen of Northwestern Univer-

A DIVERSITY OF DIETS

THE VARIETY OF SUCCESSFUL dietary strategies employed by traditionally living populations provides an important perspective on the ongoing debate about how high-protein, low-carbohydrate regimens such as the Atkins diet compare with those that underscore complex carbohydrates and fat restriction. The fact that both these schemes produce weight loss is not surprising, because both help people shed pounds through the same basic mechanism: limiting major sources of calories. When you create an energy deficit—that is, when you consume fewer calories than you expend—your body begins burning its fat stores and you lose weight.

The larger question about healthy weight-loss or weight-maintenance diets is whether they create eating patterns that are sustainable over time. On this point it appears that diets that severely limit large categories of foods (carbohydrates, for example) are much more difficult to sustain than are moderately restrictive diets. In the case of the Atkins-type regimen, there are also concerns about the potential long-term consequences of eating foods derived largely from feedlot animals, which tend to contain more fat in general and considerably more saturated fats than do their free-ranging counterparts.

In September the National Academy of Sciences's Institute of Medicine put forth new diet and exercise guidelines that mesh well with the ideas presented in this article. Not only did the institute set broader target ranges for the amounts of carbohydrates, fat and protein that belong in a healthy diet—in essence, acknowledging that there are various ways to meet our nutritional needs—the organization also doubled the recommended amount of moderately intense physical activity to an hour a day. By following these guidelines and balancing what we eat with exercise, we can live more like the Evenki of Siberia and other traditional societies—and more like our hominid ancestors.

—W.R.L.

sity and I have estimated that Neandertals most likely would have required as many as 4,000 kilocalories a day to survive. That they were able to meet these demands for as long as they did speaks to their skills as foragers.

Modern Quandaries

JUST AS PRESSURES to improve dietary quality influenced early human evolution, so, too, have these factors played a crucial role in the more recent increases in population size. Innovations such as cooking, agriculture and even aspects of modern food technology can all be considered tactics for boosting the quality of the human diet. Cooking, for one, augmented the energy available in wild plant foods. With the advents of agriculture, humans began to manipulate marginal plant species to increase their productivity, digestibility and nutritional content—essentially making plants more like animal foods. This kind of tinkering continues today, with genetic modification of crop species to make "better" fruits, vegetables and grains. Similarly, the development of liquid nutritional supplements and meal replacement bars is a continuation of the trend that our ancient ancestors started: gaining as much nutritional return from our food in as little volume and with as little physical effort as possible.

Overall, that strategy has evidently worked: humans are here today and in record numbers to boot. But perhaps the strongest testament to the importance of energy- and nutrient-rich foods in human evolution lies in the observation that so many health concerns facing societies around the globe stem from deviations from the energy dynamic that our ancestors established. For children in rural populations of the developing world, low-quality diets lead to poor physical growth and high rates of mortality during early life. In these cases, the foods fed to youngsters during and after weaning are often not sufficiently dense in energy and nutritional needs associated with this period of rapid growth and development. Although these children are typically similar in length and weight to their U.S. counterparts at birth, they are much shorter and lighter by the age of three, often resembling the smallest 2 to 3 percent of American children of the same age and sex.

In the industrial world, we are facing the opposite problem: rates of childhood and adult obesity are rising because the energy-rich foods we crave—notably those packed with fat and sugar—have become widely available and relatively inexpensive. According to recent estimates, more than half of adult Americans are overweight or obese. Obesity has also appeared in parts of the developing world where it was virtually unknown less than a generation ago. This seeming paradox has emerged as people who grew up malnourished move from rural areas to urban setting where food is more readily available. In some sense, obesity and other common diseases of the modern world are continuations of a tenor that started millions of years ago. We are victims of our own evolutionary success, having developed a calorie-packed diet while minimizing the amount of maintenance energy expended on physical activity.

The magnitude of this imbalance becomes clear when we look at traditionally living human populations. Studies of the Evenki reindeer herders that I have conducted in collaboration with Michael Crawford of the University of Kansas and Ludmila Osipova of the Russian Academy of Sciences in Novosibirsk indicate that the Evenki derive almost half their daily calories from meat, more than 2.5 times the amount consumed by the average American. Yet when we compare Evenki men with their U.S. peers, they are 20 percent leaner and have cholesterol levels that are 30 percent lower.

These differences partly reflect the compositions of the diets. Although the Evenki diet is high in meat, it is relatively low in fat (about 20 percent of their dietary energy comes from fat, compared with 35 percent in the average U.S. diet), because free-ranging animals such as reindeer have less body fat then cattle and other feedlot animals do. The composition of the fat is also different in free-ranging animals, tending to be lower in saturated fats and higher in the polyunsaturated fatty acids that protect against heart disease. More important, however, the Evenki way of life necessitates a much higher level of energy expenditure.

Thus, it is not just changes in diet that have created many of our pervasive health problems but the interaction of shifting diets and changing lifestyles. Too often modern health problems are portrayed as the result of eating "bad" foods that are departures from *the* natural human diet—an oversimplification embodied by the current debate over the relative merits of a high-protein, high-fat Atkins-type diet or a low-fat one that emphasizes complex carbohydrates. This is a fundamentally flawed approach to assessing human nutritional needs. Our species was not designed to subsist on a single, optimal diet. What is remarkable about human beings is the extraordinary variety of what we eat. We have been able to thrive in almost every ecosystem on the earth, consuming diets ranging from almost all animal foods among populations of the Arctic to primarily tubers and cereal grains among populations in the high Andes. Indeed, the hallmarks of human evolution have been the diversity of strategies that we have developed to create diets that meet our distinctive metabolic requirements and the ever increasing efficiency with which we extract energy and nutrients from the environment. The challenge our modern societies now face is balancing the calories we consume with the calories we burn.

MORE TO EXPLORE

Evolutionary Perspectives on Human Nutrition: The Influence of Brain and Body Size on Diet and Metabolism. William R. Leonard and Marcia L. Robertson in *American Journal of Human Biology,* Vol. 6, No. 1, pages 77–88; January 1994.

Rethinking the Energetics of Bipedality. William R. Leonard and Marcia L. Robertson in *Current Anthropology,* Vol. 38, No. 2, pages 304–309; April 1997.

Human Biology: An Evolutionary and Biocultural Approach. Edited by Sara Stinson, Barry Bogin, Rebecca Huss-Ashmore and Dennis O'Rourke. Wiley-Liss, 2000.

Ecology, Health and Lifestyle Change among the Evenki Herders of Siberia. William R. Leonard, Victoria A. Galloway, Evgueni Ivakine, Ludmila Osipova and Marina Kazakovtseva in *Human Biology of Pastoral Populations.* Edited by William R. Leonard and Michael H. Crawford. Cambridge University Press, 2002.

An Ecomorphological Model of the Initial Hominid Dispersal from Africa. Susan C. Antón, William R. Leonard and Marcia L. Robertson in *Journal of Human Evolution* (in press).

WILLIAM R. LEONARD is a professor of anthropology at Northwestern University. He was born in Jamestown, N.Y., and received his Ph.D. in biological anthropology at the University of Michigan at Ann Arbor in 1987. The author of more than 80 research articles on nutrition and energetics among contemporary and prehistoric populations, Leonard has studied indigenous agricultural groups in Ecuador, Bolivia and Peru and traditional herding populations in central and southern Siberia.

Scavenger Hunt

As paleoanthropologists close in on their quarry, it may turn out
to be a different beast from what they imaged

Pat Shipman

In both textbooks and films, ancestral humans (hominids) have been portrayed as hunters. Small-brained, big-browed, upright, and usually mildly furry, early hominid males gaze with keen eyes across the gold savanna, searching for prey. Skillfully wielding a few crude stone tools, they kill and dismember everything from small gazelles to elephants, while females care for young and gather roots, tubers, and berries. The food is shared by group members at temporary camps. This familiar image of Man the Hunter has been bolstered by the finding of stone tools in association with fossil animal bones. But the role of hunting in early hominid life cannot be determined in the absence of more direct evidence.

I discovered one means of testing the hunting hypothesis almost by accident. In 1978, I began documenting the microscopic damage produced on bones by different events. I hoped to develop a diagnostic key for identifying the postmortem history of specific fossil bones, useful for understanding how fossil assemblages were formed. Using a scanning electron microscope (SEM) because of its excellent resolution and superb depth of field, I inspected high-fidelity replicas of modern bones that had been subjected to known events or conditions. (I had to use replicas, rather than real bones, because specimens must fit into the SEM's small vacuum chamber.) I soon established that such common events as weathering, root etching, sedimentary abrasion, and carnivore

chewing produced microscopically distinctive features.

In 1980, my SEM study took an unexpected turn. Richard Potts (now of Yale University), Henry Bunn (now of the University of Wisconsin at Madison), and I almost simultaneously found what appeared to be stone-tool cut marks on fossils from Olduvai Gorge, Tanzania, and Koobi Fora, Kenya. We were working almost side by side at the National Museums of Kenya, in Nairobi, where the fossils are stored. The possibility of cut marks was exciting, since both sites preserve some of the oldest known archaeological materials. Potts and I returned to the United States, manufactured some stone tools, and started "butchering" bones and joints begged from our local butchers. Under the SEM, replicas of these cut marks looked very different from replicas of carnivore tooth scratches, regardless of the species of carnivore or the type of tool involved. By comparing the marks on the fossils with our hundreds of modern bones of known history, we were able to demonstrate convincingly that hominids using stone tools had processed carcasses of many different animals nearly two million years ago. For the first time, there was a firm link between stone tools and at least some of the early fossil animal bones.

This initial discovery persuaded some paleoanthropologists that the hominid hunter scenario was correct. Potts and I were not so sure. Our study had shown that many of the cut-marked fossils also

bore carnivore tooth marks and that some of the cut marks were in places we hadn't expected—on bones that bore little meat in life. More work was needed.

In addition to more data about the Olduvai cut marks and tooth marks, I needed specific information about the patterns of cut marks left by known hunters performing typical activities associated with hunting. If similar patterns occurred on the fossils, then the early hominids probably behaved similarly to more modern hunters; if the patterns were different, then the behavior was probably also different. Three activities related to hunting occur often enough in peoples around the world and leave consistent enough traces to be used for such a test.

First, human hunters systematically disarticulate their kills, unless the animals are small enough to be eaten on the spot. Disarticulation leaves cut marks in a predictable pattern on the skeleton. Such marks cluster near the major joints of the limbs: shoulder, elbow, carpal joint (wrist), hip, knee, and hock (ankle). Taking a carcass apart at the joints is much easier than breaking or cutting through bones. Disarticulation enables hunters to carry food back to a central place or camp, so that they can share it with others or cook it or even store it by placing portions in trees, away from the reach of carnivores. If early hominids were hunters who transported and shared their kills, disarticulation marks would occur near joints in frequencies comparable to those produced by modern human hunters.

Second, human hunters often butcher carcasses, in the sense of removing meat from the bones. Butchery marks are usually found on the shafts of bones from the upper part of the front or hind limb, since this is where the big muscle masses lie. Butchery may be carried out at the kill site—especially if the animal is very large and its bones very heavy—or it may take place at the base camp, during the process of sharing food with others. Compared with disarticulation, butchery leaves relatively few marks. It is hard for a hunter to locate an animal's joints without leaving cut marks on the bone. In contrast, it is easier to cut the meat away from the midshaft of the bone without making such marks. If early hominids shared their food, however, there ought to be a number of cut marks located on the midshaft of some fossil bones.

Finally, human hunters often remove skin or tendons from carcasses, to be used for clothing, bags, thongs, and so on. Hide or tendon must be separated from the bones in many areas where there is little flesh, such as the lower limb bones of pigs, giraffes, antelopes, and zebras. In such cases, it is difficult to cut the skin without leaving a cut mark on the bone. Therefore, one expects to find many more cut marks on such bones than on the flesh-covered bones of the upper part of the limbs.

Unfortunately, although accounts of butchery and disarticulation by modern human hunters are remarkably consistent, quantitative studies are rare. Further, virtually all modern hunter-gatherers use metal tools, which leave more cut marks than stone tools. For these reasons I hesitated to compare the fossil evidence with data on modern hunters. Fortunately, Diane Gifford of the University of California, Santa Cruz, and her colleagues had recently completed a quantitative study of marks and damage on thousands of antelope bones processed by Neolithic (Stone Age) hunters in Kenya some 2,300 years ago. The data from Prolonged Drift, as the site is called, were perfect for comparison with the Olduvai material.

Assisted by my technician, Jennie Rose, I carefully inspected more than 2,500 antelope bones from Bed I at Olduvai Gorge, which is dated to between 1.9 and 1.7 million years ago. We made high-fidelity replicas of every mark that we thought might be either a cut mark or a carnivore tooth mark. Back in the United States, we used the SEM to make positive identifications of the marks. (The replication and SEM inspection was time consuming, but necessary: only about half of the marks were correctly identified by eye or by light microscope.) I then compared the patterns of cut mark and tooth mark distributions on Olduvai fossils with those made by Stone Age hunters at Prolonged Drift.

By their location, I identified marks caused either by disarticulation or meat removal and then compared their frequencies with those from Prolonged Drift. More than 90 percent of the Neolithic marks in these two categories were from disarticulation, but to my surprise, only about 45 percent of the corresponding Olduvai cut marks were from disarticulation. This difference is too great to have occurred by chance; the Olduvai bones did not show the predicted pattern. In fact, the Olduvai cut marks attributable to meat removal and disarticulation showed essentially the same pattern of distribution as the carnivore tooth marks. Apparently, the early hominids were not regularly disarticulating carcasses. This finding casts serious doubt on the idea that early hominids carried their kills back to camp to share with others, since both transport and sharing are difficult unless carcasses are cut up.

When I looked for cut marks attributable to skinning or tendon removal, a more modern pattern emerged. On both the Neolithic and Olduvai bones, nearly 75 percent of all cut marks occurred on bones that bore little meat; these cut marks probably came from skinning. Carnivore tooth marks were much less common on such bones. Hominids were using carcasses as a source of skin and tendon. This made it seem more surprising that they disarticulated carcasses so rarely.

A third line of evidence provided the most tantalizing clue. Occasionally, sets of overlapping marks occur on the Olduvai fossils. Sometimes, these sets include both cut marks and carnivore tooth marks. Still more rarely, I could see under the SEM which mark had been made first, because its features were overlaid by those of the later mark, in much the same way as old tire tracks on a dirt road are obscured by fresh ones. Although only thirteen such sets of marks were found, in eight cases the hominids made the cut marks after the carnivores made their tooth marks. This finding suggested a new hypothesis. Instead of hunting for prey and leaving the remains behind for carnivores to scavenge, perhaps hominids were scavenging from the carnivores. This might explain the hominids' apparently unsystematic use of carcasses: they took what they could get, be it skin, tendon, or meat.

Man the Scavenger is not nearly as attractive an image as Man the Hunter, but it is worth examining. Actually, although hunting and scavenging are different ecological strategies, many mammals do both. The only pure scavengers alive in Africa today are vultures; not one of the modern African mammalian carnivores is a pure scavenger. Even spotted hyenas, which have massive, bone-crushing teeth well adapted for eating the bones left behind by others, only scavenge about 33 percent of their food. Other carnivores that scavenge when there are enough carcasses around include lions, leopards, striped hyenas, and jackals. Long-term behavioral studies suggest that these carnivores scavenge when they can and kill when they must. There are only two nearly pure predators, or hunters—the cheetah and the wild dog—that rarely, if ever, scavenge.

What are the costs and benefits of scavenging compared with those of predation? First of all, the scavenger avoids the task of making sure its meal is dead: a predator has already endured the energetically costly business of chasing or stalking animal after animal until one is killed. But while scavenging may be cheap, it's risky. Predators rarely give up their prey to scavengers without defending it. In such disputes, the larger animal, whether a scavenger or a predator, usually wins, although smaller animals in a pack may defeat a lone, larger animal. Both predators and scavengers suffer the dangers inherent in fighting for possession of a carcass. Smaller scavengers such as jackals or striped hyenas avoid disputes to some extent by specializing in darting in and removing a piece of a carcass without trying to take possession of the whole thing. These two strategies can be characterized as that of the bully or that of the sneak: bullies need to be large to be successful, sneaks need to be small and quick.

Because carcasses are almost always much rarer than live prey, the major cost peculiar to scavenging is that scavengers must survey much larger areas than predators to find food. They can travel slowly, since their "prey" is already dead, but endurance is important. Many predators specialize in speed at the expense of endurance, while scavengers do the opposite.

The more committed predators among the East African carnivores (wild dogs and cheetahs) can achieve great top speeds when running, although not for long. Perhaps as a consequence, these "pure" hunters enjoy a much higher success rate in hunting (about three-fourths of their chases end in kills) than any of the scavenger-hunters do (less than half of their chases are successful). Wild dogs and cheetahs are efficient hunters, but they are neither big enough nor efficient enough in their locomotion to make good scavengers. In fact, the cheetah's teeth are so specialized for meat slicing that they probably cannot withstand the stresses of bone crunching and carcass dismembering carried out by scavengers. Other carnivores are less successful at hunting, but have specializations of size, endurance, or (in the case of the hyenas) dentition that make successful scavenging possible. The small carnivores seem to have a somewhat higher hunting success rate than the large ones, which balances out their difficulties in asserting possession of carcasses.

In addition to endurance, scavengers need an efficient means of locating carcasses, which, unlike live animals, don't move or make noises. Vultures, for example, solve both problems by flying. The soaring, gliding flight of vultures expends much less energy than walking or cantering as performed by the part-time mammalian scavengers. Flight enables vultures to maintain a foraging radius

two to three times larger than that of spotted hyenas, while providing a better vantage point. This explains why vultures can scavenge all of their food in the same habitat in which it is impossible for any mammal to be a pure scavenger. (In fact, many mammals learn where carcasses are located from the presence of vultures.)

Since mammals can't succeed as full-time scavengers, they must have another source of food to provide the bulk of their diet. The large carnivores rely on hunting large animals to obtain food when scavenging doesn't work. Their size enables them to defend a carcass against others. Since the small carnivores—jackals and striped hyenas—often can't defend carcasses successfully, most of their diet is composed of fruit and insects. When they do hunt, they usually prey on very small animals, such as rats or hares, that can be consumed in their entirety before the larger competitors arrive.

The ancient habitat associated with the fossils of Olduvai and Koobi Fora would have supported many herbivores and carnivores. Among the latter were two species of large saber-toothed cats, whose teeth show extreme adaptations for meat slicing. These were predators with primary access to carcasses. Since their teeth were unsuitable for bone crushing, the saber-toothed cats must have left behind many bones covered with scraps of meat, skin, and tendon. Were early hominids among the scavengers that exploited such carcasses?

All three hominid species that were present in Bed I times (*Homo habilis, Australopithecus africanus, A. robustus*) were adapted for habitual, upright bipedalism. Many anatomists see evidence that these hominids were agile tree climbers as well. Although upright bipedalism is a notoriously peculiar mode of locomotion, the adaptive value of which has been argued for years (See Matt Cartmill's article, "Four Legs Good, Two Legs Bad," *Natural History*, November 1983), there are three general points of agreement.

First, bipedal running is neither fast nor efficient compared to quadrupedal gaits. However, at moderate speeds of 2.5 to 3.5 miles per hour, bipedal *walk-*

ing is more energetically efficient than quadrupedal walking. Thus, bipedal walking is an excellent means of covering large areas slowly, making it an unlikely adaptation for a hunter but an appropriate and useful adaptation for a scavenger. Second, bipedalism elevates the head, thus improving the hominid's ability to spot items on the ground—an advantage both to scavengers and to those trying to avoid becoming a carcass. Combining bipedalism with agile tree climbing improves the vantage point still further. Third, bipedalism frees the hands from locomotive duties, making it possible to carry items. What would early hominids have carried? Meat makes a nutritious, easy-to-carry package; the problem is that carrying meat attracts scavengers. Richard Potts suggests that carrying stone tools or unworked stones for toolmaking to caches would be a more efficient and less dangerous activity under many circumstances.

In short, bipedalism is compatible with a scavenging strategy. I am tempted to argue that bipedalism evolved because it provided a substantial advantage to scavenging hominids. But I doubt hominids could scavenge effectively without tools, and bipedalism predates the oldest known stone tools by more than a million years.

Is there evidence that, like modern mammalian scavengers, early hominids had an alternative food source, such as either hunting or eating fruits and insects? My husband, Alan Walker, has shown that the microscopic wear on an animal's teeth reflects its diet. Early hominid teeth wear more like that of chimpanzees and other modern fruit eaters than that of carnivores. Apparently, early hominids ate mostly fruit, as the smaller, modern scavengers do. This accords with the estimated body weight of early hominids, which was only about forty to eighty pounds—less than that of any of the modern carnivores that combine scavenging and hunting but comparable to the striped hyena, which eats fruits and insects as well as meat.

Would early hominids have been able to compete for carcasses with other carnivores? They were too small to use a bully strategy, but if they scavenged in groups, a combined bully-sneak strategy might have been possible. Perhaps they were able to drive off a primary predator long enough to grab some meat, skin, or marrow-filled bone before relinquishing the carcass. The effectiveness of this strategy would have been vastly improved by using tools to remove meat or parts of limbs, a task at which hominid teeth are poor. As agile climbers, early hominids may have retreated into the trees to eat their scavenged trophies, thus avoiding competition from large terrestrial carnivores.

In sum, the evidence on cut marks, tooth wear, and bipedalism, together with our knowledge of scavenger adaptation in general, is consistent with the hypothesis that two million years ago hominids were scavengers rather than accomplished hunters. Animal carcasses, which contributed relatively little to the hominid diet, were not systematically cut up and transported for sharing at base camps. Man the Hunter may not have appeared until 1.5 to 0.7 million years ago, when we do see a shift toward omnivory, with a greater proportion of meat in the diet. This more heroic ancestor may have been *Homo erectus*, equipped with Acheulean-style stone tools and, increasingly, fire. If we wish to look further back, we may have to become accustomed to a less flattering image of our heritage.

Pat Shipman is an assistant professor in the Department of Cell Biology and Anatomy at The Johns Hopkins University School of Medicine.

Reprinted with permission from *Natural History,* April 1984, pp. 20, 22–27. © 1984 by Natural History Magazine, Inc.

Chasing Dubois's Ghost

Pat Shipman

I first went to Java in October of 1998, chasing the ghost of Eugene Dubois. Dubois was the Dutch physician and anatomist who found the missing link there in 1891. He was a genius, a risk taker, one of the most stubborn men in the history of anthropology and the subject of my next book.

To Dubois, "missing link" meant the extinct form linking human beings with apes. Because few fossil hominids were known, scientists looked to comparative anatomy and embryology for evidence of human evolution. Dubois was almost alone in believing that the best proof would come from fossils. In 1887, he abruptly resigned his anatomy job at the University of Amsterdam and applied for a government grant to find the missing link. He received instead advice not to place so much stock in "that crazy book of Darwin's." His parents and colleagues condemned his plan as risky, dangerous and sure to be ruinous.

Dubois ignored their advice, preferring his own ironclad logic. One: Man evolved from apelike ancestors, so the place to find these ancestors was in the tropics of Africa and Asia inhabited by apes today. Two: One of the few known fossil apes, a putative chimpanzee ancestor, was discovered in Asia, in the Siwalik Hills of India. Three: The other mammals found with the Siwalik ape were also known from the Dutch East Indies (now Indonesia), a relatively easy place for Dubois to work. Four: One island, Sumatra, was full of limestone caves—where fossils were usually found in Europe—that had never been systematically explored.

The Dutch East Indies were a perfect place to find the missing link and a perfect place for failure. Dubois had support neither for his expedition nor for his family. Europeans in the Indies died of tropical diseases at horrific rates. The landscape was blanketed in dense tropical vegetation, cloaked in unbearably hot and humid weather and very steeply sloped in the volcanic regions where the caves were. Undaunted, Dubois enlisted for eight years as a military surgeon with the Royal Dutch East Indies Army, packed up his wife and infant daughter and sailed to Sumatra. He was not yet 30 years old.

Soon after disembarking from the steamer at Padang, Dubois began fossil hunting, finding thousands of mammalian fossils but no missing link. He also published his theory on the location of the missing link, observing pointedly that someone would beat the Dutch to it if research funds were not forthcoming. He was promptly relieved of medical duties and seconded to the Ministry of Education, Religion and Industry to search for fossils. In 1890, he shifted operations to Java and, brilliantly, also shifted his searching strategy. Instead of the cave sites that yielded so much in Europe, Dubois followed his unsupported intuition that open-air sites along the banks and point bars of the big, sluggish rivers might prove profitable.

In September of 1891, on a bend in the Bengawan Solo River near Trinil, Dubois's men excavated the tooth of a higher primate. The very next month, they found a beautiful skullcap, fossilized to a rich chocolate-brown color. The skullcap was a true treasure, boasting the prominent brow-ridges of an ape and the capacious braincase of a human being. In May of 1892 a dense, chocolate-colored left femur was excavated, unmistakably the thigh bone of a creature that walked bipedally. Five years, two weeks and three days after setting foot in the Indies, Eugene Dubois named his missing link *Pithecanthropus erectus* (it is now known as *Homo erectus*), using the generic name for the hypothetical ape-man suggested by Ernst Haeckel and adding *erectus* to emphasize its evident adaptation for upright walking.

Success and Skepticism

Further excavation yielded no more remains of *P.e.*, as he nicknamed it, but these three bones were a splendid confirmation of a hypothesis most thought foolish if not actually lunatic. That he nearly died several times over of fever, tiger and wild boar attacks, cave-ins and other adventures was unimportant.

Dubois decided to write a monograph, despite his limited scientific library, his scanty comparative collection of bones and a total lack of prototype for the sort of monograph he was trying to write. Before Dubois, no one had ever compared a fossil hominid to apes and to humans. Previous studies attempted to align the fossil with a human race. He created a new, transitional position for *Pithecanthropus*, halfway between apes and humans. Dubois completed his monograph in 1894, mailed it off to announce his find to the scientists of Europe and sailed home in 1895.

Instead of well-deserved accolades, Dubois was greeted with cruel skepticism. Academics who stayed comfortably in Europe while Dubois searched for fossils doubted his three specimens came from one individual and disagreed with his interpretations. From 1895 to 1900, Dubois defended his missing link with every weapon at his disposal. He barraged his critics with facts, geological diagrams, measurements and analyses. He thrust his fossils under their noses, making the missing link such a hot topic that more than 80 articles were written about *Pithecanthropus* before the end of the century. Then for more than 20 years, he turned his attention to other studies and refused to let anyone study *P.e.* Dubois always found it too inconvenient to interrupt his own work to show others the fossils, especially as this might open the door to still more controversy. He sequestered his fossils successfully for years, until international complaints reached the Royal Dutch Academy of Sciences, which suggested pointedly that one employed by the government as the curator of the Dubois Collection was obliged to make his fossil material accessible to fellow scientists. While he waited decades for vindication, Dubois single-handedly shaped the direction of research in paleoanthropology.

Java was the place that made Dubois who he was, and I knew I had to see it. Visiting Dubois's site, Trinil, was a revelation. My guide was apologetic because we arrived after the site museum had closed, but I didn't care. I walked happily through the huge wrought-iron gates and wandered into the small museum garden. "I did not come to see the museum. I came to see the place of Dubois," I explained. Then I spotted the monument Dubois erected in 1893 when he finished his work at Trinil. Seeing it in this foreign place was like encountering an old friend. I rushed over to place my hand on it. "You see, Anto?" I asked the guide. "This is it. This is why I came to Java."

On the monument is a bronze plaque.

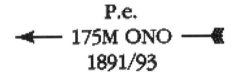

"P.e." is *Pithecanthropus erectus*; the numbers and arrow point to the find spot 175 meters east-northeast; the dates are the years of excavation.

"Anna Abortus"

The last, probably hopeless task on my agenda was to find the old European graveyard in Tulungagung so I could follow up on an enigmatic entry in Dubois's daily diary on August 30, 1893. "Anna abortus," he wrote in pencil, and then crossed the words out with thick, dark lines that nearly tore the page. Later, gently, he rewrote "Anna abortus." Anna was his wife, and they returned home to Holland with three children, Eugenie, Jean and Victor. This fourth child is mentioned neither in colonial ar-

chives nor in the remaining family letters. I wanted very much to find the grave.

Cemeteries in Java are not orderly, with neat rows of graves separated by grassy pathways. Graves are arranged helter-skelter, new ones squeezed in between the old at every sort of angle. Nearly all the graves in this cemetery appeared to be Javanese, among them many small children's graves.

Nevertheless, I finally saw what I was looking for, a tiny patch of ground surrounded by the old, crumbling double row of bricks. Such a small space, less than a foot square, to contain someone's heartache: a little headstone, no capstone, no inscription. There was no real proof that this was her grave, but I knew with a startling certainty that little Anna Jeanette Dubois was buried here. I had not considered her name—Anna after her mother, Jeanette after her grandfather—or sex before, but I knew them now, intuitively. Here, her mother had railed and wept at the cruelty of the tropics; here, her father had laid his fourth child to rest. Here, they left her behind, all alone, when they returned to Europe. It broke my heart.

Lost Time

My guide was startled by my sadness and later asked about the incident. He could not understand how I could feel "so sharp about someone dead 100 years." He explained that the Javanese mourn their dead mothers, fathers and grandparents, but not "someone you never see." Nothing I said about my emotional connection to this long-dead man whose words and work I had studied so closely seemed to resonate with him. I tried a metaphor, saying that I was walking in Dubois's footsteps, chasing his ghost, but this seemed equally incomprehensible. Then I remembered a passage in my phrasebook.

> Verbs in Indonesian are not conjugated. That is, unlike European languages, the form of the verb does not change according to the tense or the person. So, for example, **mereka pergi** can mean "they go", "they will go", "they were going", "they went", or "they have gone." … Usually the context in which you hear the verb will make it clear whether the speaker is referring to the past, present or future.

In Bahasa Indonesian, the past is implied, not demarcated. The linguistic difference reflects a perceived difference in the nature of time. Western time is a linear, unidirectional narrative; Javan time is not. This revelation confused me as profoundly as my search for the concrete remnants of history had confused many Indonesians on my journey.

If there is no past tense, is there no past? The past is the stuff of my work as a paleoanthropologist and historian of science. Thinking about a culture that functions without a past made my eyes cross. What did this mean, I wondered, for Dubois, searching for evidence of the deep past in a land where the past exists only by implication?

Then I recalled a moment of epiphany at the monument Dubois erected to mark the spot where he discovered the remains of *Pithecanthropus erectus*. I had looked up and seen a man up to his knees in river water, fishing, and standing on the old excavation.

I felt as if I had been slapped, so sudden was my insight. Dubois risked everything, found the missing link, erected a plinth to mark the spot for all time, and *he didn't put his own name on it*. During his lifetime, Dubois was called hard, stubborn and impossibly demanding by his colleagues; his wife left him; even a former student called him a "psychical monster." But now I saw the truth: Everything he did was about *P.e.*, not about himself. What was *not* there was more important than what was.

Much later, I learned that the closest equivalent for "history" in Bahasa Indonesian is "a long way away in time." It was the perfect phrase, a long way away in time: That was where I had been. Sometimes I was so close to Dubois that we shared expe-

riences. Yet those who guided me to him neither knew where I wanted to go nor recognized the place when we arrived.

I learned some simple and powerful lessons in Java. Things are not always as they seem. The past may be indistinguishable from the present. Context is everything: geological context, intellectual context, linguistic context, cultural context. In Java, it seems as if the physical laws of time and space are warped into a Möbius strip. One can never hope to see all that is there, and sometimes what is missing is most important of all.

Bibliography

Birks, T., F. Najoan Siregar and J. Buckley, eds. 1997. *Indonesian: A Rough Guide Phrasebook*. London: Lexus, pp. 9–10.

Shipman, P. In press. *The Man Who Found the Missing Link*. New York: Simon and Schuster.

Erectus Rising

Oh No. Not This. The Hominids Are Acting Up Again...

James Shreeve

Just when it seemed that the recent monumental fuss over the origins of modern human beings was beginning to quiet down, an ancient ancestor is once more running wild. Trampling on theories. Appearing in odd places, way ahead of schedule. Demanding new explanations. And shamelessly flaunting its contempt for conventional wisdom in the public press.

The uppity ancestor this time is *Homo erectus*—alias Java man, alias Peking man, alias a mouthful of formal names known only to the paleontological cognoscenti. Whatever you call it, *erectus* has traditionally been a quiet, average sort of hominid: low of brow, thick of bone, endowed with a brain larger than that of previous hominids but smaller than those that followed, a face less ape-like and projecting than that of its ancestors but decidedly more simian than its descendants'. In most scenarios of human evolution, *erectus*'s role was essentially to mark time—a million and a half years of it—between its obscure, presumed origins in East Africa just under 2 million years ago and its much more recent evolution into something deserving the name *sapiens*.

Erectus accomplished only two noteworthy deeds during its long tenure on Earth. First, some 1.5 million years ago, it developed what is known as the Acheulean stone tool culture, a technology exemplified by large, carefully crafted tear-shaped hand axes that were much more advanced than the bashed rocks that had passed for tools in the hands of earlier hominids. Then, half a million years later, and aided by those Acheulean tools, the species carved its way out of Africa and established a human presence in other parts of the Old World. But most of the time, *Homo erectus* merely existed, banging out the same stone tools millennium after millennium, over a time span that one archeologist has called "a period of unimaginable monotony."

Asian and African fossils were lumped into one far-flung taxon, a creature not quite like us but human enough to be welcomed into our genus: Homo erectus.

Or so read the old script. These days, *erectus* has begun to ad-lib a more vigorous, controversial identity for itself. Research within the past year has revealed that rather than being 1 million years old, several *erectus* fossils from Southeast Asia are in fact almost 2 million years old. That is as old as the oldest African members of the species, and it would mean that *erectus* emerged from its home continent much earlier than has been thought—in fact, almost immediately after it first appeared. There's also a jawbone, found in 1991 near the Georgian city of Tbilisi, that resembles *erectus* fossils from Africa and may be as old as 1.8 million years, though that age is still in doubt. These new dates—and the debates they've engendered—have shaken *Homo erectus* out of its interpretive stupor, bringing into sharp relief just how little agreement there is on the rise and demise of the last human species on Earth, save one.

"Everything now is in flux," says Carl Swisher of the Berkeley Geochronology Center, one of the prime movers behind the redating of *erectus* outside Africa. "It's all a mess."

The focal point for the flux is the locale where the species was first found: Java. The rich but frustration-soaked history of paleoanthropology on that tropical island began just over 100 years ago, when a young Dutch anatomy professor named Eugène Dubois conceived the idée fixe that the "missing link" between ape and man was to be found in the jungled remoteness of the Dutch East Indies. Dubois had never left Holland, much less traveled to the Dutch East Indies, and his pick for the spot on Earth where humankind first arose owed as much to a large part of the Indonesian archipelago's being a Dutch colony as it did to any scientific evidence. He nevertheless found this missing link—the top of an oddly thick skull with massive browridges—in 1891 on the banks of the Solo River, near a community called Trinil in central Java. About a year later a thighbone that Dubois thought might belong to the same individual was found nearby; it looked so much like a modern human thighbone that Dubois assumed this ancient primate had walked upright. He christened the creature *Pithecanthropus erectus*—"erect ape-man"—and returned home in triumph.

Finding the fossil proved to be the easy part. Though Dubois won popular acclaim, neither he nor his "Java man" received the full approbation of the anatomists of the day, who considered his ape-man either merely an ape or merely a man. In an apparent pique, Dubois cloistered away the fossils for a quarter-century, refusing others the chance to view his prized possessions. Later, other similarly primitive human remains began to turn up in China and East Africa. All shared a collection of anatomical traits, including a long, low braincase with prominent browridges and a flattened forehead; a sharp angle to the back of the skull when viewed in profile; and a deep, robustly built jaw showing no hint of a chin. Though initially given separate regional names, the fossils were eventually lumped together into one far-flung taxon, a creature not quite like us but human enough to be welcomed into our genus: *Homo erectus*.

Over the decades the most generous source of new *erectus* fossils has been the sites on or near the Solo River in Java. The harvest continues: two more skulls, including one of the most complete *erectus* skulls yet known, were found at a famous fossil site called Sangiran just in the past year. Though the Javan yield of ancient humans has been rich, something has always been missing—the crucial element of time. Unless the age of a fossil can be determined, it hangs in limbo, its importance and place in the larger scheme of human evolution forever undercut with doubt. Until researchers can devise better methods for dating bone directly—right now there are no techniques that can reliably date fossilized, calcified bone more than 50,000 years old—a specimen's age

has to be inferred from the geology that surrounds it. Unfortunately, most of the discoveries made on the densely populated and cultivated island of Java have been made not by trained excavators but by sharp-eyed local farmers who spot the bones as they wash out with the annual rains and later sell them. As a result, the original location of many a prized specimen, and thus all hopes of knowing its age, are a matter of memory and word of mouth.

Despite the problems, scientists continue to try to pin down dates for Java's fossils. Most have come up with an upper limit of around 1 million years. Along with the dates for the Peking man skulls found in China and the Acheulean tools from Europe, the Javan evidence has come to be seen as confirmation that *erectus* first left Africa at about that time.

By the early 1970s most paleontologists were firmly wedded to the idea that Africa was the only human-inhabited part of the world until one million years ago.

There are those, however, who have wondered about these dates for quite some time. Chief among them is Garniss Curtis, the founder of the Berkeley Geochronology Center. In 1971 Curtis, who was then at the University of California at Berkeley, attempted to determine the age of a child's skull from a site called Mojokerto, in eastern Java, by using the potassium-argon method to date volcanic minerals in the sediments from which the skull was purportedly removed. Potassium-argon dating had been in use since the 1950s, and Curtis had been enormously successful with it in dating ancient African hominids—including Louis Leakey's famous hominid finds at Olduvai Gorge in Tanzania. The method takes advantage of the fact that a radioactive isotope of potassium found in volcanic ash slowly and predictably decays over time into argon gas, which becomes trapped in the crystalline structure of the

mineral. The amount of argon contained in a given sample, measured against the amount of the potassium isotope, serves as a kind of clock that tells how much time has passed since a volcano exploded and its ash fell to earth and buried the bone in question.

Applying the technique to the volcanic pumice associated with the skull from Mojokerto, Curtis got an extraordinary age of 1.9 million years. The wildly anomalous date was all too easy to dismiss, however. Unlike the ash deposits of East Africa, the volcanic pumices in Java are poor in potassium. Also, not unexpectedly, a heavy veil of uncertainty obscured the collector's memories of precisely where he had found the fossil some 35 years earlier. Besides, most paleontologists were by this time firmly wedded to the idea that Africa was the only human-inhabited part of the world until 1 million years ago. Curtis's date was thus deemed wrong for the most stubbornly cherished of reasons: because it couldn't possibly be right.

In 1992 Curtis—under the auspices of the Institute for Human Origins in Berkeley—returned to Java with his colleague Carl Swisher. This time he was backed up by far more sensitive equipment and a powerful refinement in the dating technique. In conventional potassium-argon dating, several grams' worth of volcanic crystals gleaned from a site are needed to run a single experiment. While the bulk of these crystals are probably from the eruption that covered the fossil, there's always the possibility that other materials, from volcanoes millions of years older, have gotten mixed in and will thus make the fossil appear to be much older than it actually is. The potassium-argon method also requires that the researcher divide the sample of crystals in two. One half is dissolved in acid and passed through a flame; the wavelengths of light emitted tell how much potassium is in the sample. The other half is used to measure the amount of argon gas that's released when the crystals are heated. This two-step process further increases the chance of error, simply by giving the experiment twice as much opportunity to go wrong.

The refined technique, called argon-argon dating, neatly sidesteps most of these difficulties. The volcanic crystals are first placed in a reactor and bombarded with neutrons; when one of these neutrons penetrates the potassium nucleus, it displaces a proton, converting the potassium into an isotope of argon that doesn't occur in nature. Then the artificially created argon and the naturally occurring argon are measured in a single experiment. Because the equipment used to measure the isotopes can look for both types of argon at the same time, there's no need to divide the sample, and so the argon-argon method can produce clear results from tiny amounts of material.

In some cases—when the volcanic material is fairly rich in potassium—all the atoms of argon from a single volcanic crystal can be quick-released by the heat from a laser beam and then counted. By doing a number of such single-crystal experiments, the researchers can easily pick out and discard any data from older, contaminant crystals. But even when the researchers are forced to sample more than one potassium-poor crystal to get any reading at all—as was the case at Mojokerto—the argon-argon method can still produce a highly reliable age. In this case, the researchers carefully heat a few crystals at a time to higher and higher temperatures, using a precisely controlled laser. If all the crystals in a sample are the same age, then the amount of argon released at each temperature will be the same. But if contaminants are mixed in, or if severe weathering has altered the crystal's chemical composition, the argon measurements will be erratic, and the researchers will know to throw out the results.

Curtis and Swisher knew that in the argon-argon step-heating method they had the technical means to date the potassium-poor deposits at Mojokerto accurately. But they had no way to prove that those deposits were the ones in which the skull had been buried: all they had was the word of the local man who had found it. Then, during a visit to the museum in the regional capital, where the fossil was being housed, Swisher noticed something odd. The hardened sedi-

ments that filled the inside of the fossil's braincase looked black. But back at the site, the deposits of volcanic pumice that had supposedly sheltered the infant's skull were whitish in color. How could a skull come to be filled with black sediments if it had been buried in white ones? Was it possible that the site and the skull had nothing to do with each other after all? Swisher suspected something was wrong. He borrowed a penknife, picked up the precious skull, and nicked off a bit of the matrix inside.

"I almost got kicked out of the country at that point," he says. "These fossils in Java are like the crown jewels."

Luckily, his impulsiveness paid off. The knife's nick revealed white pumice under a thin skin of dark pigment: years earlier, someone had apparently painted the surface of the hardened sediments black. Since there were no other deposits within miles of the purported site that contained a white pumice visually or chemically resembling the matrix in the skull, its tie to the site was suddenly much stronger. Curtis and Swisher returned to Berkeley with pumice from that site and within a few weeks proclaimed the fossil to be 1.8 million years old, give or take some 40,000 years. At the same time, the geochronologists ran tests on pumice from the lower part of the Sangiran area, where *erectus* facial and cranial bone fragments had been found. The tests yielded an age of around 1.6 million years. Both numbers obviously shatter the 1-million-year barrier for *erectus* outside Africa, and they are a stunning vindication of Curtis's work at Mojokerto 20 years ago. "That was very rewarding," he says, "after having been told what a fool I was by my colleagues."

While no one takes Curtis or Swisher for a fool now, some of their colleagues won't be fully convinced by the new dates until the matrix inside the Mojokerto skull itself can be tested. Even then, the possibility will remain that the skull may have drifted down over the years into deposits containing older volcanic crystals that have nothing to do with its original burial site, or that it was carried by a river to another, older site. But Swisher contends that the chance of such an occurrence is remote: it would have to have happened at both Mojokerto and

Sangiran for the fossils' ages to be refuted. "I feel really good about the dates," he says. "But it has taken me a while to understand their implications."

The implications that can be spun out from the Javan dates depend on how one chooses to interpret the body of fossil evidence commonly embraced under the name *Homo erectus*. The earliest African fossils traditionally attributed to *erectus* are two nearly complete skulls from the site of Koobi Fora in Kenya, dated between 1.8 and 1.7 million years old. In the conventional view, these early specimens evolved from a more primitive, smaller-brained ancestor called *Homo habilis*, well represented by bones from Koobi Fora, Olduvai Gorge, and sites in South Africa.

If this conventional view is correct, then the new dates mean that *erectus* must have migrated out of Africa very soon after it evolved, quickly reaching deep into the farthest corner of Southeast Asia. This is certainly possible: at the time, Indonesia was connected to Asia by lower sea levels—thus providing an overland route from Africa—and Java is just 10,000 to 15,000 miles from Kenya, depending on the route. Even if *erectus* traveled just one mile a year, it would still take no more than 15,000 years to reach Java—a negligible amount of evolutionary time.

If *erectus* did indeed reach Asia almost a million years earlier than thought, then other, more controversial theories become much more plausible. Although many anthropologists believe that the African and Asian *erectus* fossils all represent a single species, other investigators have recently argued that the two groups are too different to be so casually lumped together. According to paleoanthropologist Ian Tattersall of the American Museum of Natural History in New York, the African skulls traditionally assigned to *erectus* often lack many of the specialized traits that were originally used to define the species in Asia, including the long, low cranial structure, thick skull bones, and robustly built faces. In his view, the African group de-

MEANWHILE, IN SIBERIA...

The presence of *Homo erectus* in Asia twice as long ago as previously thought has some people asking whether the human lineage might have originated in Asia instead of Africa. This long-dormant theory runs contrary to all current thinking about human evolution and lacks an important element: evidence. Although the new Javan dates do place the species in Asia at around the same time it evolved in Africa, all confirmed specimens of other, earlier hominids—the first members of the genus *Homo*, for instance, and the australopithecines, like Lucy—have been found exclusively in Africa. Given such an overwhelming argument, most investigators continue to believe that the hominid line began in Africa.

Most, but not all. Some have begun to cock an ear to the claims of Russian archeologist Yuri Mochanov. For over a decade Mochanov has been excavating a huge site on the Lena River in eastern Siberia—far from Africa, Java, or anywhere else on Earth an ancient hominid bone has ever turned up. Though he hasn't found any hominid fossils in Siberia, he stubbornly believes he's uncovered the next best thing: a trove of some 4,000 stone artifacts—crudely made flaked tools, but tools nonetheless—that he maintains are at least 2 million years old, and possibly 3 million. This, he says, would mean that the human lineage arose not in tropical Africa but in the cold northern latitudes of Asia.

"For evolutionary progress to occur, there had to be the appearance of new conditions: winter, snow, and, accompanying them, hunger," writes Mochanov.

"[The ancestral primates] had to learn to walk on the ground, to change their carriage, and to become accustomed to meat—that is, to become 'clever animals of prey.'" And to become clever animals of prey, they'd need tools.

Although he is a well-respected investigator, Mochanov has been unable to convince either Western anthropologists or his Russian colleagues of the age of his site. Until recently the chipped rocks he was holding up as human artifacts were simply dismissed as stones broken by natural processes, or else his estimate of the age of the site was thought to be wincingly wrong. After all, no other signs of human occupation of Siberia appear until some 35,000 years ago.

But after a lecture swing through the United States earlier this year—in which he brought more data and a few prime examples of the tools for people to examine and pass around—many archeologists concede that it is difficult to explain the particular pattern of breakage of the rocks by any known natural process. "Everything I have heard or seen about the context of these things suggests that they are most likely tools," says anthropologist Rick Potts of the Smithsonian Institution, which was host to Mochanov last January.

They're even willing to concede that the site might be considerably older than they'd thought, though not nearly as old as Mochanov estimates. (To date the site, Mochanov compared the tools with artifacts found early in Africa; he also employed an arcane dating technique little known outside Russia.) Preliminary results from an experimental dating technique performed on soil samples from the site by Michael Waters of Texas A&M and Steve Forman of Ohio State suggest that the layer of sediment bearing the artifacts is some 400,000 years old. That's a long way from 2 million, certainly, but it's still vastly older than anything else found in Siberia—and the site is 1,500 miles farther north than the famous Peking man site in China, previously considered the most northerly home of *erectus*.

"If this does turn out to be 400,000 years old, it's very exciting," says Waters. "If people were able to cope and survive in such a rigorous Arctic environment at such an early time, we would have to completely change our perception of the evolution of human adaptation."

"I have no problem with hominids being almost anywhere at that age—they were certainly traveling around," says Potts. "But the environment is the critical thing. If it was really cold up there"—temperatures in the region now often reach −50 degrees in deep winter—"we'd all have to scratch our heads over how these early hominids were making it in Siberia. There is no evidence that Neanderthals, who were better equipped for cold than anyone, were living in such climates. But who knows? Maybe a population got trapped up there, went extinct, and Mochanov managed to find it." He shrugs. "But that's just arm waving."

—*J. S*

serves to be placed in a separate species, which he calls *Homo ergaster*.

Most anthropologists believe that the only way to distinguish between species in the fossil record is to look at the similarities and differences between bones; the age of the fossil should not play a part. But age is often hard to ignore, and Tattersall believes that the new evidence for what he sees as two distinct populations living at the same time in widely separate parts of the Old World is highly suggestive. "The new dates help confirm that these were indeed two different species," he says. "In my view, *erectus* is a separate variant that evolved only in Asia."

Other investigators still contend that the differences between the African and Asian forms of *erectus* are too minimal to merit placing them in separate species.

But if Tattersall is right, his theory raises the question of who the original emigrant out of Africa really was. *Homo ergaster* may have been the one to make the trek, evolving into *erectus* once it was established in Asia. Or perhaps a population of some even more primitive, as-yet-unidentified common ancestor ventured forth, giving rise to *erectus* in Asia while a sister population evolved into *ergaster* on the home continent.

Furthermore, no matter who left Africa first, there's the question of what precipitated the migration, a question made even more confounding by the new dates. The old explanation, that the primal human expansion across the hem of the Old World was triggered by the sophisticated Acheulean tools, is no longer tenable with these dates, simply because the tools had not yet been invented when the earliest populations would have moved out. In hindsight, that notion seems a bit shopworn anyway. Acheulean tools first appear in Africa around 1.5 million years ago, and soon after at a site in the nearby Middle East. But they've never been found in the Far East, in spite of the abundant fossil evidence for *Homo erectus* in the region.

Until now, that absence has best been explained by the "bamboo line." According to paleoanthropologist Geoffrey Pope of William Paterson College in New Jersey, *erectus* populations venturing from Africa into the Far East found the land rich in bamboo, a raw material more easily worked into cutting and butchering tools than recalcitrant stone. Sensibly, they abandoned their less efficient stone industry for one based on the pliable plant, which leaves no trace of itself in the archeological record. This is still a viable theory, but the new dates from Java add an even simpler dimension to it: there are no Acheulean tools in the Far East because the first wave of *erectus* to leave Africa didn't have any to bring with them.

So what *did* fuel the quick-step migration out of Africa? Some researchers say the crucial development was not cultural but physical. Earlier hominids like *Homo habilis* were small-bodied creatures with more apelike limb proportions, notes pa-

leoanthropologist Bernard Wood of the University of Liverpool, while African *erectus* was built along more modern lines. Tall, relatively slender, with long legs better able to range over distance and a body better able to dissipate heat, the species was endowed with the physiology needed to free it from the tropical shaded woodlands of Africa that sheltered earlier hominids. In fact, the larger-bodied *erectus* would have required a bigger feeding range to sustain itself, so it makes perfect sense that the expansion out of Africa should begin soon after the species appeared. "Until now, one was always having to account for what kept *erectus* in Africa so long after it evolved," says Wood. "So rather than raising a problem, in some ways the new dates in Java solve one."

Of course, if those dates are right, the accepted time frame for human evolution outside the home continent is nearly doubled, and that has implications for the ongoing debate over the origins of modern human beings. There are two opposing theories. The "out of Africa" hypothesis says that *Homo sapiens* evolved from *erectus* in Africa, and then—sometime in the last 100,000 years—spread out and replaced the more archaic residents of Eurasia. The "multiregional continuity" hypothesis says that modern humans evolved from *erectus* stock in various parts of the Old World, more or less simultaneously and independently. According to this scenario, living peoples outside Africa should look for their most recent ancestors not in African fossils but in the anatomy of ancient fossils within their own region of origin.

As it happens, the multiregionalists have long claimed that the best evidence for their theory lies in Australia, which is generally thought to have become inhabited around 50,000 years ago, by humans crossing over from Indonesia. There are certain facial and cranial characteristics in modern Australian aborigines, the multiregionalists say, that can be traced all the way back to the earliest specimens of *erectus* at Sangiran—characteristics that differ from and precede those of any more recent, *Homo sapiens* arrival from Africa. But if the new Javan dates are right, then these unique characteristics,

and thus the aborigines' Asian *erectus* ancestors, must have been evolving separately from the rest of humankind for almost 2 million years. Many anthropologists, already skeptical of the multiregionalists' potential 1-million-year-long isolation for Asian *erectus*, find a 2-million-year-long isolation exceedingly difficult to swallow. "Can anyone seriously propose that the lineage of Australian aborigines could go back that far?" wonders paleoanthropologist Chris Stringer of the Natural History Museum in London, a leading advocate of the out-of-Africa theory.

The multiregionalists counter that they've never argued for *complete* isolation—that there's always been some flow of genes between populations, enough interbreeding to ensure that clearly beneficial *sapiens* characteristics would quickly be conferred on peoples throughout the Old World. "Just as genes flow now from Johannesburg to Beijing and from Melbourne to Paris, they've been flowing that way ever since humanity evolved," says Alan Thorne of the Australian National University in Canberra, an outspoken multiregionalist.

Stanford archeologist Richard Klein, another out-of-Africa supporter, believes the evidence actually *does* point to just such a long, deep isolation of Asian populations from African ones. The fossil record, he says, shows that while archaic forms of *Homo sapiens* were developing in Africa, *erectus* was remaining much the same in Asia. In fact, if some *erectus* fossils from a site called Ngandong in Java turn out to be as young as 100,000 years, as some researchers believe, then *erectus* was still alive on Java at the same time that fully modern human beings were living in Africa and the Middle East. Even more important, Klein says, is the cultural evidence. That Acheulean tools never reached East Asia, even after their invention in Africa, could mean the inventors never reached East Asia either. "You could argue that the new dates show that until very recently there was a long biological and cultural division between Asia on one hand, and Africa and Europe on the other," says Klein. In other words, there must have been two separate lineages of *erectus*, and since there aren't two separate lineages of modern humans, one of those must have gone extinct: presumably the Asian lineage, hastened into oblivion by the arrival of the more culturally adept, tool-laden *Homo sapiens*.

Naturally this argument is anathema to the multiregionalists. But this tenacious debate is unlikely to be resolved without basketfuls of new fossils, new ways of interpreting old ones—and new dates. In Berkeley, Curtis and Swisher are already busy applying the argon-argon method to the Ngandong fossils, which could represent some of the last surviving *Homo erectus* populations on Earth. They also hope to work their radiometric magic on a key *erectus* skull from Olduvai Gorge. In the meantime, at least one thing has become clear: *Homo erectus*, for so long the humdrum hominid, is just as fascinating, contentious, and elusive a character as any other in the human evolutionary story.

FURTHER READING

Eugène Dubois & the Ape-Man from Java. Bert Theunissen. Kluwer Academic, 1989. When a Dutch army surgeon, determined to prove Darwin right, traveled to Java in search of the missing link between apes and humans, he inadvertently opened a paleontological Pandora's box. This is Dubois's story, the story of the discovery of *Homo erectus*.

James Shreeve is the coauthor, with anthropologist Donald Johanson, of Lucy's Child: The Discovery of a Human Ancestor. *His book,* The Neandertal Enigma: Solving the Mystery of Modern Human Origins, *was published in 1995, and he is at work on a novel that a reliable source calls "a murder thriller about the species question."*

The Scavenging of "Peking Man"

New evidence shows that a venerable cave was neither hearth nor home.

By Noel T. Boaz and Russell L. Ciochon

China is filled with archaeological wonders, but few can rival the Peking Man Site at Zhoukoudian, which has been inscribed on UNESCO's World Heritage List. Located about thirty miles southwest of Beijing, the town of Zhoukoudian boasts several attractions, including ruins of Buddhist monasteries dating from the Ming Dynasty (1368–1644). But the town's main claim to fame is Longgushan, or Dragon Bone Hill, the site of the cave that yielded the first (and still the largest) cache of fossils of *Homo erectus pekinensis*, historically known as Peking man—a human relative who walked upright and whose thick skull bones and beetling brow housed a brain three-quarters the size of *H. sapiens*'s.

The remains of about forty-five individuals—more than half of them women and children—along with thousands of stone stools, debris from tool manufacturing, and thousands of animal bones, were contained within the hundred-foot-thick deposits that once completely filled the original cave. The task of excavation, initiated in 1921, was not completed until 1982. Some evidence unearthed at the site suggested that these creatures, who lived from about 600,000 to 300,000 years ago, had mastered the use of fire and practiced cannibalism. But despite years of excavation and analysis, little is certain about what occurred here long ago. In the past two years we have visited the cave site, reexamined the fossils, and

carried out new tests in an effort to sort out the facts.

To most of the early excavators, such as anatomist Davidson Black, paleontologist Pierre Teilhard de Chardin, and archaeologist Henri Breuil, the likely scenario was that these particular early humans lived in the cave where their bones and stone tools were found and that the animal bones were the remains of meals, proof of their hunting expertise. Excavation exposed ash in horizontal patches within the deposits or in vertical patches along the cave's walls; these looked very much like the residue of hearths built up over time.

A more sensational view, first advanced by Breuil in 1929, was that the cave contained evidence of cannibalism. If the animal bones at the site were leftovers from the cave dwellers' hunting forays, he argued, why not the human bones as well? And skulls were conspicuous among the remains, suggesting to him that these might be the trophies of headhunters. Perhaps, Breuil even proposed, the dull-witted *H. erectus* had been prey to a contemporary, advanced cousin, some ancestral form of *H. sapiens*. Most paleoanthropologists rejected this final twist, but the cannibalism hypothesis received considerable support.

In the late 1930s Franz Weidenreich, an eminent German paleoanthropologist working at Peking Union Medical College, described the *H. erectus* remains in

scientific detail. A trained anatomist and medical doctor, he concluded that some of the skulls showed signs of trauma, including scars and fresh injuries from attacks with both blunt and sharp instruments, such as clubs and stone tools. Most convincing to him and others was the systematic destruction of the skulls, apparently at the hands of humans who had decapitated the victims and then broken open the skull bases to retrieve the brains. Weidenreich also believed that the large longitudinal splits seen, for example, in some of the thighbones could only have been caused by humans and were probably made in an effort to extract the marrow.

Others held dissenting views. Chinese paleoanthropologist Pei Wenzhong, who codirected the early Zhoukoudian excavations, disagreed with Breuil and suggested in 1929 that the skulls had been chewed by hyenas. Some Western scientists also had doubts. In 1939 German paleontologist Helmuth Zapfe published his findings on the way hyenas at the Vienna zoo fed on cow bones. Echoing Pei's earlier observations, of which he was aware, Zapfe convincingly argued that many of the bones found at sites like Longgushan closely resembled modern bones broken up by hyenas. In fact, a new term, taphonomy, was coined shortly thereafter for the field Zapfe pioneered: the study of how, after death, animal and plant remains become modi-

Franz Weidenreich, who in the 1930s studied the fossils of Homo erectus *unearthed in China, is caricatured along with Ralph Von Koenigswald (wielding the shovel), who found fossils of* H. erectus *in Java. The fanciful setting is, according to the artist, "any place where the dead are disturbed."*

fied, moved, buried, and fossilized. Franz Weidenreich soon revised his prior interpretation of several *H. erectus* bones whose condition he had attributed to human cannibalistic activity, but he continued to argue that the long-bone splinters and broken skull bases must have resulted from human action.

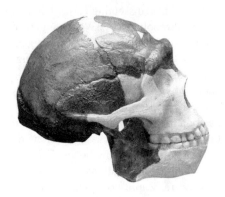

Above: A model of an H. erectus *skull, based on fossils of several individuals from the Peking Man Site at Zhoukoudian. Most of the missing bones, represented in white, mirror existing parts on the opposite side of the skull.*

Following disruptions in fieldwork during World War II (including the loss of all the *H. erectus* fossils collected at Longgushan up to that time, leaving only the casts that had been made of them), Chinese paleoanthropologists resumed investigation of the site. While rejecting the idea of cannibalism, they continued to look upon the cave as a shelter used by early humans equipped with stone tools and fire, as reflected in the title of paleoanthropologist Jia Lampo's book *The Cave Home of Peking Man*, published in 1975.

About this time, Western scientists began to appreciate and develop the field of taphonomy. A few scholars, notably U.S. archaeologist Lewis R. Binford, then reexamined the Longgushan evidence, but only from a distance, concluding that the burning of accumulated bat or bird guano may have accounted for the ash in the cave. With the founding in 1993 of the Zhoukoudian International Paleoanthropological Research Center at Beijing's Institute of Vertebrate Paleontology and Paleoanthropology, a new era of multidisciplinary and international re-

search at Longgushan began. At the institute, we have been able to collaborate with paleontologists Xu Qinqi and Liu Jinyi and with other scholars in a reassessment of the excavations.

It looked as if H. erectus *had smashed open the skulls to cannibalize the brains.*

One of taphonomy's maxims is that the most common animals at a fossil site and/or the animals whose remains there are the most complete are most likely the ones to have inhabited the area in life. Standing in the Beijing institute amid row after row of museum cases filled with mammal fossils from the cave, we were immediately struck by how few belonged to *H. erectus*—perhaps only 0.5 percent. This suggests that most of the time, this species did not live in the cave. Furthermore, none of the *H. erectus* skel-

AMNH

The early investigations at Zhoukoudian were coordinated by the Cenozoic Research Laboratory in Beijing. Staff members there included (left to right in foreground) Teilhard de Chardin, Franz Weidenreich, Yang Zhongjian, Pei Wenzhong, and Bian Meinian.

etons is complete. There is a dearth of limb bones, especially of forearms, hands, lower leg bones, and feet—indicating to us that these individuals died somewhere else and that their partial remains were subsequently brought to the cave. But how?

The answer was suggested by the remains of the most common and complete animal skeletons in the cave deposit: those of the giant hyena, *Pachycrocuta brevirostris*. Had *H. erectus*, instead of being the mighty hunters of anthropological lore, simply met the same ignominious fate as the deer and other prey species in the cave? This possibility, which had been raised much earlier by Pei and Zapfe, drew backing from subsequent studies by others. In 1970, for example, British paleontologist Anthony J. Sutcliffe reported finding a modern hyena den in Kenya that contained a number of human bones, including skulls, which the animals had apparently obtained from a nearby hospital cemetery. In the same year, South African zoologist C. K. Brain published the findings of his extensive feeding experiments with captive carnivores, akin to those of Zapfe three decades earlier. One of Brain's

conclusions was that carnivores tend to chew up and destroy the ends of the extremities, leaving, in the case of primates, very little of the hands and feet.

AMNH

During the 1930s, excavators dug down through the hundred-foot-thick deposits that contained the remains of "Peking man." The deposits, which also yielded animal bones, stone tools, and layers of ash, had completely filled an ancient cave.

To test the giant hyena hypothesis, we examined all the fossil casts and the few actual fossils of *H. erectus* from Longgushan. We looked for both carnivore bite marks and the shallow, V-shaped straight cuts that would be left by stone tools (although we realized that cut marks would probably not be detectable on the casts). We also analyzed each sample's fracture patterns. Breaks at right angles indicate damage long after death, when the bone is fossilized or fossilizing; fractures in fresh bone tend to be irregular, following natural structural lines. Breakage due to crushing by cave rocks is usually massive, and the fracture marks characteristically match rock fragments pushed into the bone.

We were surprised by our findings. Two-thirds of Longgushan's *H. erectus* fossils display what we are convinced are one or more of the following kinds of damage: puncture marks from a carnivore's large, pointed front teeth, most likely the canines of a hyena; long, scraping bite marks, typified by U-shaped grooves along the bone; and fracture patterns comparable to those created by modern hyenas when they chew bone. Moreover, we feel that the longitudinal

Franz Weidenreich at his laboratory at the American Museum of Natural History in the 1940s, with ape and human skulls

veals telltale surface etchings from stomach acid, indicating it was swallowed and then disgorged.

The pattern of damage on some of the skulls sheds light on how hyenas may have handled them. Bite marks on the brow ridge above the eyes indicate that this protrusion had been grasped and bitten by an animal in the course of chewing off the face. Most animals' facial bones are quite thin, and modern hyenas frequently attack or bite the face first; similarly, their ancient predecessors would likely have discovered this vulnerable region in *H. erectus*. Practically no such facial bones, whose structure is known to us from discoveries at other sites, have been found in the Longgushan cave.

The rest of the skull is a pretty tough nut to crack, however, even for *Pachycrocuta*, since it consists of bones half again as thick as those of a modern human, with massive mounds called tori above the eyes and ears and around the back of the skull. Puncture marks and elongated bite marks around the skulls reveal that the hyenas gnawed at and grappled with them, probably in an effort to crack open the cranium and consume the tasty, lipid-rich brain. We concluded that the hyenas probably succeeded best

A composite image of the skulls of Pachycrocuta and H. erectus, *shows how the giant hyena may have attacked the face. Beneath is a disgorged piece of an* H. erectus *thighbone.*

by chewing through the face, gaining a purchase on the bone surrounding the foramen magnum (the opening in the cranium where the spinal cord enters), and then gnawing away until the skull vault cracked apart or the opening was large enough to expose the brain. This is how we believe the skull bases were destroyed—not by the actions of cannibalistic *H. erectus*.

splitting of large bones—a feature that Weidenreich considered evidence of human activity—can also be attributed to a hyena, especially one the size of the extinct *Pachycrocuta*, the largest hyena known, whose preferred prey was giant elk and woolly rhinoceros. One of the *H. erectus* bones, part of a femur, even re-

An artist's depiction of the cave shows hyenas consuming the remains of an **H. erectus.**

Two-thirds of the fossils show bite marks or fractures inflicted by carnivores.

We know from geological studies of the cave that the animal bones found there could not have been washed in by rains or carried in by streams: the sediments in which the bones are found are either very fine-grained—indicating gradual deposition by wind or slow-moving water—or they contain angular, sharp-edged shards that would not have survived in a stream or flood. Some of the bones may have belonged to animals that died inside the cave during the course of living in it or frequenting it. Other bones were probably brought in and chewed on by hyenas and other carnivores.

Cut marks we observed on several mammal bones from the cave suggest that early humans did sometimes make use of Longgushan, even if they were not responsible for accumulating most of the bones. Stone tools left near the cave entrance also attest to their presence. Given its long history, the cave may have served a variety of occupants or at times have been configured as several separate, smaller shelters. Another possibility is that, in a form of time-sharing, early humans ventured partway into the cave during the day to scavenge on what the hyenas had not eaten and to find temporary shelter. They may not have realized that the animals, which roamed at twilight and at night, were sleeping in the dark recesses a couple of hundred feet away.

What about the ash in the cave, which has been taken as evidence that *H. erectus* used fire? Recently published work by geochemist Steve Weiner and his team at the Weizmann Institute of Science in Israel suggests that the fires were not from hearths. In detailed studies of the ash levels, they discovered no silica-rich layers, which would be left by the burning of wood. Wood (as well as grass and leaves) contains silica particles known as phytoliths—heat-resistant residues that are ubiquitous in archaeological hearth sites. The results indicate that fire was present in the cave but that its controlled use in hearths was not part of the story.

Still, a human hand may somehow be implicated in these fires. One possibility we are exploring in the next phase of our research is that Longgushan was a place where *Pachycrocuta* and *H. erectus* confronted each other as the early humans sought to snatch some of the meat brought back to the cave by the large hyenas. *Pachycrocuta* would have had the home court advantage, but *H. erectus*, perhaps using fire to hold the carnivore at bay, could have quickly sliced off slivers of meat. Although today we might turn up our noses at such carrion, it may have been a dependable and highly prized source of food during the Ice Age.

Reprinted with permission from *Natural History*, March 2001, pp. 46-51. © 2001 by Natural History Magazine, Inc.

UNIT 5
Late Hominid Evolution

Unit Selections

Key Points to Consider

- What evidence is there for hard times among the Neanderthals?

- Are Neanderthals part of our ancestry? Explain.

- If the Neanderthals were so smart, why did they disappear?

- When did language ability arise in our ancestry and why?

- When, where, and how did modern humans evolve?

 **Links: www.dushkin.com/online/**
These sites are annotated in the World Wide Web pages.

Human Prehistory
http://users.hol.gr/~dilos/prehis.htm

The most important aspect of human evolution is also the most difficult to decipher from the fossil evidence: our development as sentient, social beings, capable of communicating by means of language.

We detect hints of incipient humanity in the form of crudely chipped tools, the telltale signs of a home base, or the artistic achievements of ornaments and cave art. Yet none of these indicators of a distinctly hominid way of life can provide us with the nuances of the everyday lives of these creatures, their social relations, or their supernatural beliefs, if any. Most of what remains is the rubble of bones and stones from which we interpret what we can of their lifestyle, thought processes, and ability to communicate. Our ability to glean from the fossil record is not completely without hope, however. In fact, informed speculation is what makes possible such essays as "Hard Times Among the Neanderthals" by Erik Trinkaus, "Rethinking Neanderthals" by Joe Alper and "The Gift of Gab" by Matt Cartmill. Each is a fine example of careful, systematic, and thought-provoking work that is based upon an increased understanding of hominid fossil sites as well as the more general environmental circumstances in which our predecessors lived.

Beyond the technological and anatomical adaptations, questions have arisen as to how our hominid forebears organized themselves socially and whether modern-day human behavior is inherited as a legacy of our evolutionary past or is a learned product of contemporary circumstances. Attempts to address these questions have given rise to the technique referred to as the "ethnographic analogy." This is a method whereby anthropologists use "ethnographies" or field studies of modern-day hunters and gatherers whose lives we take to be the best approximations we have to what life might have been like for our ancestors. Granted, these contemporary foragers have been living under conditions of environmental and social change just as industrial peoples have. Nevertheless, it seems that, at least in some aspects of their lives, they have not changed as much as we have. So, if we are to make any enlightened assessments of prehistoric behavior patterns, we are better off looking at them than at ourselves.

As if to show that controversial interpretations of the evidence are not limited to the earlier hominid period, in this unit we also see how long-held beliefs about the rise of modern human behavior are being threatened by new fossil evidence (See "We Are All Africans" by Pat Shipman). For some scientists, the new evidence fits in quite comfortably with previously held positions; for others it seems that reputations, as well as theories, are at stake.

Hard Times Among the Neanderthals

Although life was difficult, these prehistoric people may not have been as exclusively brutish as usually supposed

Erik Trinkaus

Throughout the century that followed the discovery in 1856 of the first recognized human fossil remains in the Neander Valley (*Neanderthal* in German) near Düsseldorf, Germany, the field of human paleontology has been beset with controversies. This has been especially true of interpretations of the Neanderthals, those frequently maligned people who occupied Europe and the Near East from about 100,000 years ago until the appearance of anatomically modern humans about 35,000 years ago.

During the last two decades, however, a number of fossil discoveries, new analyses of previously known remains, and more sophisticated models for interpreting subtle anatomical differences have led to a reevaluation of the Neanderthals and their place in human evolution.

This recent work has shown that the often quoted reconstruction of the Neanderthals as semierect, lumbering caricatures of humanity is inaccurate. It was based on faulty anatomical interpretations that were reinforced by the intellectual biases of the turn of the century. Detailed comparisons of Neanderthal skeletal remains with those of modern humans have shown that there is nothing in Neanderthal anatomy that conclusively indicates locomotor, manipula-

tive, intellectual, or linguistic abilities inferior to those of modern humans. Neanderthals have therefore been added to the same species as ourselves—*Homo sapiens*—although they are usually placed in their own subspecies, *Homo sapiens neanderthalensis*.

Despite these revisions, it is apparent that there are significant anatomical differences between the Neanderthals and present-day humans. If we are to understand the Neanderthals, we must formulate hypotheses as to why they evolved from earlier humans about 100,000 years ago in Europe and the Near East, and why they were suddenly replaced about 35,000 years ago by peoples largely indistinguishable from ourselves. We must determine, therefore, the behavioral significance of the anatomical differences between the Neanderthals and other human groups, since it is patterns of successful behavior that dictate the direction of natural selection for a species.

In the past, behavioral reconstructions of the Neanderthals and other prehistoric humans have been based largely on archeological data. Research has now reached the stage at which behavioral interpretations from the archeological record can be significantly supplemented by analyses of the fossils themselves.

These analyses promise to tell us a considerable amount about the ways of the Neanderthals and may eventually help us to determine their evolutionary fate.

One of the most characteristic features of the Neanderthals is the exaggerated massiveness of their trunk and limb bones. All of the preserved bones suggest a strength seldom attained by modern humans. Furthermore, not only is this robustness present among the adult males, as one might expect, but it is also evident in the adult females, adolescents, and even children. The bones themselves reflect this hardiness in several ways.

First, the muscle and ligament attachment areas are consistently enlarged and strongly marked. This implies large, highly developed muscles and ligaments capable of generating and sustaining great mechanical stress. Secondly, since the skeleton must be capable of supporting these levels of stress, which are frequently several times as great as body weight, the enlarged attachments for muscles and ligaments are associated with arm and leg bone shafts that have been reinforced. The shafts of all of the arm and leg bones are modified tubular structures that have to absorb stress from bending and twisting without fracturing. When the habitual load on a bone in-

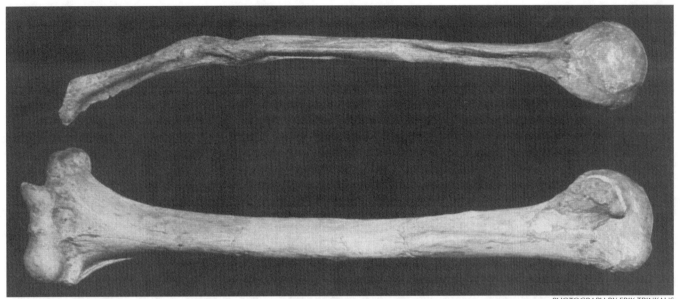

Diagonal lines on these two arm bones from Shanidar 1 are healed fractures. The bottom bone is normal. That on the top is atrophied and has a pathological tip, caused by either amputation or an improperly healed elbow fracture.

creases, the bone responds by laying down more bone in those areas under the greatest stress.

In addition, musculature and body momentum generate large forces across the joints. The cartilage, which covers joint surfaces, can be relatively easily overworked to the point where it degenerates, as is indicated by the prevalence of arthritis in joints subjected to significant wear and tear over the years. When the surface area of a joint is increased, the force per unit area of cartilage is reduced, decreasing the pressure on the cartilage.

Most of the robustness of Neanderthal arm bones is seen in muscle and ligament attachments. All of the muscles that go from the trunk or the shoulder blade to the upper end of the arm show massive development. This applies in particular to the muscles responsible for powerful downward movements of the arm and, to a lesser extent, to muscles that stabilize the shoulder during vigorous movements.

Virtually every major muscle or ligament attachment on the hand bones is clearly marked by a large roughened area or a crest, especially the muscles used in grasping objects. In fact, Neanderthal hand bones frequently have clear bony crests, where on modern human ones it is

barely possible to discern the attachment of the muscle on the dried bone.

In addition, the flattened areas on the ends of the fingers, which provide support for the nail and the pulp of the finger tip, are enormous among the Neanderthals. These areas on the thumb and the index and middle fingers are usually two to three times as large as those of similarly sized modern human hands. The overall impression is one of arms to rival those of the mightiest blacksmith.

Neanderthal legs are equally massive; their strength is best illustrated in the development of the shafts of the leg bones. Modern human thigh and shin bones possess characteristic shaft shapes adapted to the habitual levels and directions of the stresses acting upon them. The shaft shapes of the Neanderthals are similar to those in modern humans, but the cross-sectional areas of the shafts are much greater. This implies significantly higher levels of stress.

Further evidence of the massiveness of Neanderthal lower limbs is provided by the dimensions of their knee and ankle joints. All of these are larger than in modern humans, especially with respect to the overall lengths of the bones.

The development of their limb bones suggests that the Neanderthals frequently generated high levels of me-

chanical stress in their limbs. Since most mechanical stress in the body is produced by body momentum and muscular contraction, it appears that the Neanderthals led extremely active lives. It is hard to conceive of what could have required such exertion, especially since the maintenance of vigorous muscular activity would have required considerable expenditure of energy. That level of energy expenditure would undoubtedly have been maladaptive had it not been necessary for survival.

The available evidence from the archeological material associated with the Neanderthals is equivocal on this matter. Most of the archeological evidence at Middle Paleolithic sites concerns stone tool technology and hunting activities. After relatively little change in technology during the Middle Paleolithic (from about 100,000 years to 35,000 years before the present), the advent of the Upper Paleolithic appears to have brought significant technological advances. This transition about 35,000 years ago is approximately coincident with the replacement of the Neanderthals by the earliest anatomically modern humans. However, the evidence for a significant change in hunting patterns is not evident in the animal remains left behind. Yet even if a correlation between the robustness of

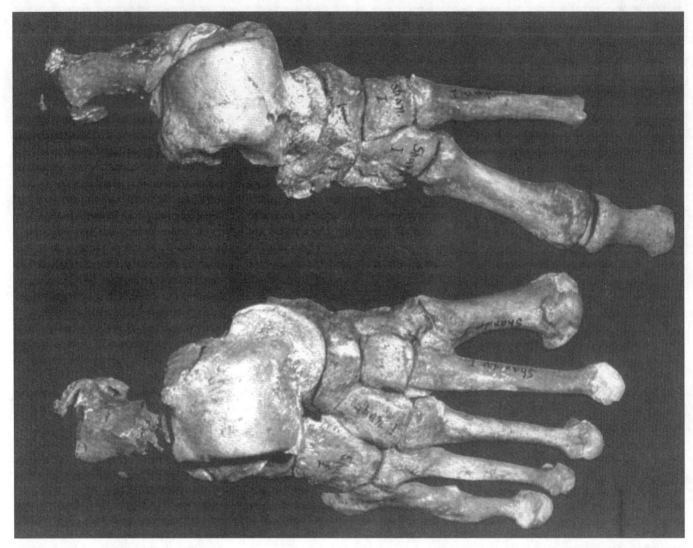

The ankle and big toe of Shanidar 1's bottom foot show evidence of arthritis, which suggests an injury to those parts. The top foot is normal though incomplete.

body build and the level of hunting efficiency could be demonstrated, it would only explain the ruggedness of the Neanderthal males. Since hunting is exclusively or at least predominantly a male activity among humans, and since Neanderthal females were in all respects as strongly built as the males, an alternative explanation is required for the females.

Some insight into why the Neanderthals consistently possessed such massiveness is provided by a series of partial skeletons of Neanderthals from the Shanidar Cave in northern Iraq. These fossils were excavated between 1953 and 1960 by anthropologist Ralph Solecki of Columbia University and have been studied principally by T. Dale Stewart, an anthropologist at the Smithsonian Institution, and myself. The most remarkable aspect of these skeletons is the number of healed injuries they contain. Four of the six reasonably complete adult skeletons show evidence of trauma during life.

The identification of traumatic injury in human fossil remains has plagued paleontologists for years. There has been a tendency to consider any form of damage to a fossil as conclusive evidence of prehistoric violence between humans if it resembles the breakage patterns caused by a direct blow with a heavy object. Hence a jaw with the teeth pushed in or a skull with a depressed fracture of the vault would be construed to indicate blows to the head.

The central problem with these interpretations is that they ignore the possibility of damage after death. Bone is relatively fragile, especially as compared with the rock and other sediment in which it is buried during fossilization. Therefore when several feet of sediment caused compression around fossil remains, the fossils will almost always break. In fact, among the innumerable cases of suggested violence between humans cited over the years, there are only a few exceptional examples that cannot be readily explained as the result of natural geologic forces acting after the death and burial of the individual.

The scar on the left ninth rib of Shanidar 3 is a partially healed wound inflicted by a sharp object. This wound is one of the few examples of trauma caused by violence.

One of these examples is the trauma of the left ninth rib of the skeleton of Shanidar 3, a partially healed wound inflicted by a sharp object. The implement cut obliquely across the top of the ninth rib and probably pierced the underlying lung. Shanidar 3 almost certainly suffered a collapsed left lung and died several days or weeks later, probably as a result of secondary complications. This is deduced from the presence of bony spurs and increased density of the bone around the cut.

The position of the wound on the rib, the angle of the incision, and the cleanness of the cut make it highly unlikely that the injury was accidentally inflicted. In fact, the incision is almost exactly what would have resulted if Shanidar 3 had been stabbed in the side by a right-handed adversary in face-to-face conflict. This would therefore provide conclusive evidence of violence between humans, the *only* evidence so far found of such violence among the Neanderthals.

In most cases, however, it is impossible to determine from fossilized remains the cause of an individual's death. The instances that can be positively identified as prehistoric traumatic injury are those in which the injury was inflicted prior to death and some healing took

place. Shortly after an injury to bone, whether a cut or a fracture, the damaged bone tissue is resorbed by the body and new bone tissue is laid down around the injured area. As long as irritation persists, new bone is deposited, creating a bulge or spurs of irregular bone extending into the soft tissue. If the irritation ceases, the bone will slowly re-form so as to approximate its previous, normal condition. However, except for superficial injuries or those sustained during early childhood, some trace of damage persists for the life of the individual.

In terms of trauma, the most impressive of the Shanidar Neanderthals is the first adult discovered, known as Shanidar 1. This individual suffered a number of injuries, some of which may be related. On the right forehead there are scars from minor surface injuries, probably superficial scalp cuts. The outside of the left eye socket sustained a major blow that partially collapsed that part of the bony cavity, giving it a flat rather than a rounded contour. This injury possibly caused loss of sight in the left eye and pathological alterations of the right side of the body.

Shanidar 1's left arm is largely preserved and fully normal. The right arm, however, consists of a highly atrophied but otherwise normal collarbone and

shoulder blade and a highly abnormal upper arm bone shaft. That shaft is atrophied to a fraction of the diameter of the left one but retains most of its original length. Furthermore, the lower end of the right arm bone has a healed fracture of the atrophied shaft and an irregular, pathological tip. The arm was apparently either intentionally amputated just above the elbow or fractured at the elbow and never healed.

This abnormal condition of the right arm does not appear to be a congenital malformation, since the length of the bone is close to the estimated length of the normal left upper arm bone. If, however, the injury to the left eye socket also affected the left side of the brain, directly or indirectly, by disrupting the blood supply to part of the brain, the result could have been partial paralysis of the right side. Motor and sensory control areas for the right side are located on the left side of the brain, slightly behind the left eye socket. This would explain the atrophy of the whole right arm since loss of nervous stimulation will rapidly lead to atrophy of the affected muscles and bone.

The abnormality of the right arm of Shanidar 1 is paralleled to a lesser extent in the right foot. The right ankle joint shows extensive arthritic degeneration,

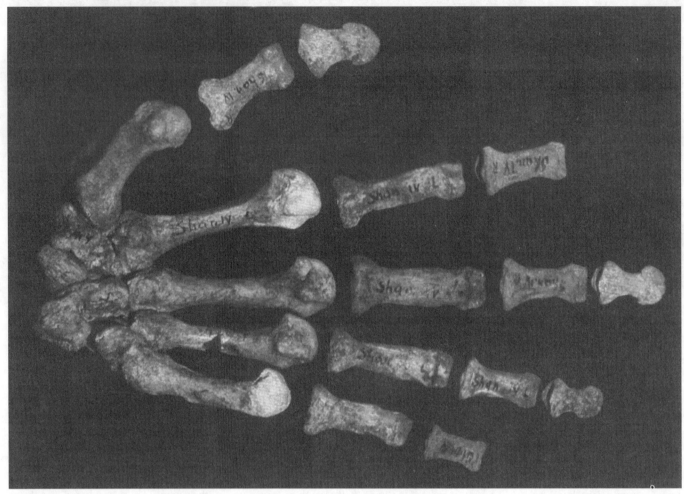

PHOTOGRAPH BY ERIK TRINKAUS

The right hand of Shanidar 4 demonstrates the enlarged finger tips and strong muscle markings characteristic of Neanderthal hands.

and one of the major joints of the inner arch of the right foot has been completely reworked by arthritis. The left foot, however, is totally free of pathology. Arthritis from normal stress usually affects both lower limbs equally; this degeneration therefore suggests that the arthritis in the right foot is a secondary result of an injury, perhaps a sprain, that would not otherwise be evident on skeletal remains. This conclusion is supported by a healed fracture of the right fifth instep bone, which makes up a major portion of the outer arch of the foot. These foot pathologies may be tied into the damage to the left side of the skull; partial paralysis of the right side would certainly weaken the leg and make it more susceptible to injury.

The trauma evident on the other Shanidar Neanderthals is relatively mi-

nor by comparison. Shanidar 3, the individual who died of the rib wound, suffered debilitating arthritis of the right ankle and neighboring foot joints, but lacks any evidence of pathology on the left foot; this suggests a superficial injury similar to the one sustained by Shanidar 1. Shanidar 4 had a healed broken rib. Shanidar 5 received a transverse blow across the left forehead that left a large scar on the bone but does not appear to have affected the brain.

None of these injuries necessarily provides evidence of deliberate violence among the Neanderthals; all of them could have been accidentally self-inflicted or accidentally caused by another individual. In either case, the impression gained of the Shanidar Neanderthals is of a group of invalids. The crucial variable, however, appears to be age. All four of

these individuals died at relatively advanced ages, probably between 40 and 60 years (estimating the age at death for Neanderthals beyond the age of 25 is extremely difficult); they therefore had considerable time to accumulate the scars of past injuries. Shanidar 2 and 6, the other reasonably complete Shanidar adults, lack evidence of trauma, but they both died young, probably before reaching 30.

Other Neanderthal remains, all from Europe, exhibit the same pattern. Every fairly complete skeleton of an elderly adult shows evidence of traumatic injuries. The original male skeleton from the Neander Valley had a fracture just below the elbow of the left arm, which probably limited movement of that arm for life. The "old man" from La Chapelle-aux-Saints, France, on whom most traditional

144

reconstructions of the Neanderthals have been based, suffered a broken rib. La Ferrassi 1, the old adult male from La Ferrassie, France, sustained a severe injury to the right hip, which may have impaired his mobility.

In addition, several younger specimens and ones of uncertain age show traces of trauma. La Quina 5, the young adult female from La Quina, France, was wounded on her right upper arm. A young adult from Sala, Czechoslovakia, was superficially wounded on the right forehead just above the brow. And an individual of unknown age and sex from the site of Krapina, Yugoslavia, suffered a broken forearm, in which the bones never reunited after the fracture.

The evidence suggests several things. First, life for the Neanderthals was rigor-ous. If they lived through childhood and early adulthood, they did so bearing the scars of a harsh and dangerous life. Furthermore, this incident of trauma correlates with the massiveness of the Neanderthals; a life style that so consistently involved injury would have required considerable strength and fortitude for survival.

There is, however, another, more optimistic side to this. The presence of so many injuries in a prehistoric human group, many of which were debilitating and sustained years before death, shows that individuals were taken care of long after their economic usefulness to the social group had ceased. It is perhaps no accident that among the Neanderthals, for the first time in human history, people lived to a comparatively old age. We also find among the Neanderthals the first intentional burials of the dead, some of which involved offerings. Despite the hardships of their life style, the Neanderthals apparently had a deep-seated respect and concern for each other.

Taken together, these different pieces of information paint a picture of life among the Neanderthals that, while harsh and dangerous, was not without personal security. Certainly the hardships the Neanderthals endured were beyond those commonly experienced in the prehistoric record of human caring and respect as well as of violence between individuals. Perhaps for these reasons, despite their physical appearance, the Neanderthals should be considered the first modern humans.

RETHINKING
NEANDERTHALS

Research suggests the so-called brutes fashioned tools,
buried their dead, maybe cared for the sick and even conversed.
But why, if they were so smart, did they disappear?

JOE ALPER

BRUNO MAUREILLE UNLOCKS THE GATE in a chain-link fence, and we walk into the fossil bed past a pile of limestone rubble, the detritus of an earlier dig. We're 280 miles southwest of Paris, in rolling farm country dotted with long-haired cattle and etched by meandering streams. Maureille, an anthropologist at the University of Bordeaux, oversees the excavation of this storied site called Los Pradelles, where for three decades researchers have been uncovering, fleck by fleck, the remains of humanity's most notorious relatives, the Neanderthals.

We clamber 15 feet down a steep embankment into a swimming pool-size pit. Two hollows in the surrounding limestone indicate where shelters once stood. I'm just marveling at the idea that Neanderthals lived here about 50,000 years ago when Maureille, inspecting a long ledge that a student has been painstakingly chipping away, interrupts my reverie and calls me over. He points to a whitish object resembling a snapped pencil that's embedded in the ledge. "Butchered reindeer bone," he says. "And here's a tool, probably used to cut meat from one of these bones." The tool, or lithic, is shaped like a hand-size D.

All around the pit, I now see, are other lithics and fossilized bones. The place, Maureille says, was probably a butchery where Neanderthals in small numbers processed the results of what appear to have been very successful hunts. That finding alone is significant, because for a long time paleoanthropologists have viewed Neanderthals as too dull and too clumsy to use efficient tools, never mind organize a hunt and divvy, up the game. Fact is, this site, along with others across Europe and in Asia, is helping overturn the familiar conception of Neanderthals as dumb brutes. Recent studies suggest they were imaginative enough to carve artful objects and perhaps clever enough to invent a language.

Neanderthals, traditionally designated *Homo sapiens neanderthalensis*, were not only "human" but also, it turns out, more "modern" than scientists previously allowed. "In the minds of the European anthropologists who first studied them, Neanderthals were the embodiment of primitive humans, subhumans if you will," says Fred H. Smith, a physical anthropologist at Loyola University in Chicago who has been studying Neanderthal DNA. "They were believed to be scavengers who made primitive tools and were incapable of language or symbolic thought." Now, he says, researchers believe that Neanderthals "were highly intelligent, able to adapt to a wide variety of ecological zones, and capable of developing highly functional tools to help them do so. They were quite accomplished."

Contrary to the view that Neanderthals were evolutionary failures—they died out about 28,000 years ago—they actually had quite a run. "If you take success to mean the ability to survive in hostile, changing environments, then Neanderthals were a great success," says archaeologist John Shea of the State University of New York at Stony Brook. "They lived 250,000 years or more in the harshest climates experienced by primates, not just humans." In contrast, we modern humans have only been around for 100,000 years or so and moved into colder, temperate regions only in the past 40,000 years.

Though the fossil evidence is not definitive, Neanderthals appear to have descended from an earlier human species, *Homo erectus*, between 500,000 to 300,000 years ago. Neanderthals shared many features with their ancestors—a prominent brow, weak chin, sloping skull and large nose—but were as big-brained as the anatomically modern humans that later colonized Europe, *Homo sapiens*. At the same time, Neanderthals were stocky, a build that would have conserved heat efficiently. From musculature marks on Neanderthal fossils and the heft of arm and leg bones, researchers conclude they were also incredibly strong. Yet their hands were remarkably like those of modern humans; a study published this past March in *Nature* shows that Neanderthals, contrary to previous thinking, could touch index finger and thumb, which would have given them considerable dexterity.

Neanderthal fossils suggest that they must have endured a lot of pain. "When you look at adult Neanderthal fossils, particularly the bones of the arms and skull, you see [evidence of] fractures," says Erik Trinkaus, an anthropologist at Washington University in St. Louis. "I've yet to see an adult Neanderthal skeleton that doesn't have at least one fracture, and in adults in their 30s, it's common to see multiple healed fractures." (That they suffered so many broken bones suggests they hunted large animals up close, probably stabbing prey with heavy spears—a risky tactic.) In addition, fossil evidence indicates that Neanderthals suffered from a wide range of ailments, including pneumonia and malnourishment. Still, they persevered, in some cases living to the ripe old age of 45 or so.

Perhaps surprisingly, Neanderthals must also have been caring: to survive disabling injury or illness requires the help of fellow clan members, paleoanthropologists say. A telling example came from an Iraqi cave known as Shanidar, 250 miles north of Baghdad, near the border with Turkey and Iran. There, archaeologist Ralph Solecki discovered nine nearly complete Neanderthal skeletons in the late 1950s. One belonged to a 40- to 45-year-old male with several major fractures. A blow to the left side of his head had crushed an eye socket and almost certainly blinded him. The bones of his right shoulder and upper arm appeared shriveled, most likely the result of a trauma that led to the amputation of his right forearm. His right foot and lower right leg had also been broken while he was alive. Abnormal wear in his right knee, ankle and foot shows that he suffered from injury-induced arthritis that would have made walking painful, if not impossible. Researchers don't know how he was injured but believe that he could not have survived long without a hand from his fellow man.

"This was really the first demonstration that Neanderthals behaved in what we think of as a fundamentally human way," says Trinkaus, who in the 1970s helped reconstruct and catalog the Shanidar fossil collection in Baghdad. (One of the skeletons is held by the Smithsonian Institution's National Museum of Natural History.) "The result was that those of us studying Neanderthals started thinking about these people in terms of their behavior and not just their anatomy."

NEANDERTHALS INHABITED a vast area roughly from present-day England east to Uzbekistan and south nearly to the Red Sea. Their time spanned periods in which glaciers advanced and retreated again and again, But the Neanderthals adjusted. When the glaciers moved in and edible plants became scarcer, they relied more heavily on large, hoofed animals for food, hunting the reindeer and wild horses that grazed the steppes and tundra.

THERE ARE HINTS OF CANNIBALISM: DEER AND NEANDERTHAL BONES AT THE SAME SITE BEAR IDENTICAL SCRAPE MARKS.

Paleoanthropologists have no idea how many Neanderthals existed (crude estimates are in the many thousands), but archaeologists have found more fossils from Neanderthals than from any extinct human species. The first Neanderthal fossil was uncovered in Belgium in 1830, though nobody accurately identified it for more than a century. In 1848, the Forbes Quarry in Gibraltar yielded one of the most complete Neanderthal skulls ever found, but it, too, went unidentified, for 15 years. The name Neanderthal arose after quarrymen in Germany's Neander Valley found a cranium and several long bones in 1856; they gave the specimens to a local naturalist, Johann Karl Fuhlrott, who soon recognized them as the legacy of a previously unknown type of human. Over the years, France, the Iberian Peninsula, southern Italy and the Levant have yielded abundances of Neanderthal remains, and those finds are being supplemented by newly opened excavations in Ukraine and Georgia. "It seems that everywhere we look, we're finding Neanderthal remains," says Loyola's Smith. "It's an exciting time to be studying Neanderthals."

Clues to some Neanderthal ways of life come from chemical analyses of fossilized bones, which confirm that Neanderthals were meat eaters. Microscopic studies hint at cannibalism; fossilized deer and Neanderthal bones found at the same site bear identical scrape marks, as though the same tool removed the muscle from both animals.

The arrangement of fossilized Neanderthal skeletons in the ground demonstrates to many archaeologists that Neanderthals buried their dead. "They might not have done so with elaborate ritual, since there has never been solid evidence that they included symbolic objects in graves, but it is clear that they did not just dump their dead with the rest of the trash to be picked over by hyenas and other scavengers," says archaeologist Francesco d'Errico of the University of Bordeaux.

Paleoanthropologists generally agree that Neanderthals lived in groups of 10 to 15, counting children. That assessment is based on a few lines of evidence, including the limited remains at burial sites and the modest size of rock shelters. Also, Neanderthals were top predators, and some top predators, such as lions and wolves, live in small groups.

Steven Kuhn, an archaeologist at the University of Arizona, says experts "can infer quite a bit about who Neanderthal was by studying tools in conjunction with the other artifacts they left behind." For instance, recovered stone tools are typically fashioned from nearby sources of flint or quartz, indicating to some researchers that a Neanderthal group did not necessarily range far.

The typical Neanderthal tool kit contained a variety of implements, including large spear points and knives that would have been halted, or set in wooden handles. Other tools were suitable for cutting meat, cracking open bones (to get at fat-rich marrow) or scraping hides (useful for clothing, blankets or shelter). Yet other stone tools were used for woodworking; among the very few wooden artifacts associated with Neanderthal sites are objects that resemble spears, plates and pegs.

I get a feel for Neanderthal handiwork in Maureille's office, where plastic milk crates are stacked three high in front of his desk. They're stuffed with plastic bags full of olive and tan flints from Les Pradelles. With his encouragement, I take a palm-size, D-shaped flint out of a bag. Its surface is scarred as though by chipping, and the flat side has a thin edge. I readily imagine I could scrape a hide with it or whittle a stick. The piece, Maureille says, is about 60,000 years old. "As you can see from the number of lithics we've found," he adds, referring to the crates piling up in his office, "Neanderthals were prolific and accomplished toolmakers."

AMONG THE NEW APPROACHES to Neanderthal study is what might be called paleo-mimicry, in which researchers themselves fashion tools to test their ideas. "What we do is make our own tools out of flint, use them as a Neanderthal might have, and then look at the fine detail of the cutting edges with a high-powered microscope," explains Michael Bisson, chairman of anthropology at McGill University in Montreal. "A tool used to work wood will have one kind of wear pattern that differs from that seen when a tool is used to cut meat from a bone, and we can see those different patterns on the implements recovered from Neanderthal sites." Similarly, tools used to scrape hide show few microscopic scars, their edges having been smoothed by repeated rubbing against skin, just as stropping a straight razor will hone its edge. As Kuhn, who has also tried to duplicate Neanderthal handicraft, says: "There is no evidence of really fine, precise work, but they were skilled in what they did."

Based on the consistent form and quality of the tools found at sites across Europe and western Asia, it appears likely that Neanderthal was able to pass along his toolmaking techniques to others. "Each Neanderthal or Neanderthal group did not have to reinvent the wheel when it came to their technologies," says Bisson.

The kinds of tools that Neanderthals began making about 200,000 years ago are known as Mousterian, after the site in France where thousands of artifacts were first found. Neanderthals struck off pieces from a rock "core" to make an implement, but the "flaking" process was not random; they evidently examined a core much as a diamond cutter analyzes a rough gemstone today, trying to strike just the spot that would yield "flakes," for knives or spear points, requiring little sharpening or shaping.

Around 40,000 years ago, Neanderthals innovated again. In what passes for the blink of an eye in paleoanthropology, some Neanderthals were suddenly making long, thin stone blades and halting more tools. Excavations in southwest France and northern Spain have uncovered Neanderthal tools betraying a more refined technique involving, Kuhn speculates, the use of soft hammers made of antler or bone.

What happened? According to the conventional wisdom, there was a culture clash. In the early 20th century, when researchers first discovered those "improved" lithics—called Châtelperronian and Uluzzian, depending on where they were found—they saw the relics as evidence that modern humans, Homo sapiens or Cro-Magnon, had arrived in Neanderthal ter-

ritory. That's because the tools resembled those unequivocally associated with anatomically modern humans, who began colonizing western Europe 38,000 years ago. And early efforts to assign a date to those Neanderthal lithics yielded time frames consistent with the arrival of modern humans.

But more recent discoveries and studies, including tests that showed the lithics to be older than previously believed, have prompted d'Errico and others to argue that Neanderthals advanced on their own. "They could respond to some change in their environment that required them to improve their technology," he says. "They could behave like modern humans."

Meanwhile, these "late" Neanderthals also discovered ornamentation, says d'Errico and his archaeologist colleague João Zilhão of the University of Lisbon. Their evidence includes items made of bone, ivory and animal teeth marked with grooves and perforations. The researchers and others have also found dozens of pieces of sharpened manganese dioxide—black crayons, essentially—that Neanderthals probably used to color animal skins or even their own. In his office at the University of Bordeaux, d'Errico hands me a chunk of manganese dioxide. It feels silky, like soapstone. "Toward the end of their time on earth," he says, "Neanderthals were using technology as advanced as that of contemporary anatomically modern humans and were using symbolism in much the same way."

AS NEANDERTHALS RETREATED, MODERN HUMANS WERE RIGHT ON THEIR HEELS. THE TWO MAY HAVE MATED—OR TRIED TO.

Generally, anthropologists and archaeologists today proffer two scenarios for how Neanderthals became increasingly resourceful in the days be fore they vanished. On the one hand, it may be that Neanderthals picked up a few new technologies from invading humans in an effort to copy their cousins. On the other, Neanderthals learned to innovate in parallel with anatomically modern human beings, our ancestors,

MOST RESEARCHERS AGREE that Neanderthals were skilled hunters and craftsmen who made tools, used fire, buried their dead (at least on occasion), cared for their sick and injured and even had a few symbolic notions. Likewise, most researchers believe that Neanderthals probably had some facility, for language, at least as we usually think of it. It's not far-fetched to think that language skills developed when Neanderthal groups mingled and exchanged mates; such interactions may have been necessary for survival, some researchers speculate, because Neanderthal groups were too small to sustain the species. "You need to have a breeding population of at least 250 adults, so some kind of exchange had to take place," says archaeologist Ofer Bar-Yosef of Harvard University. "We see this type of behavior in all hunter-gatherer cultures, which is essentially what Neanderthals had."

But if Neanderthals were so smart, why did they go extinct? "That's a question we'll never really have an answer to," says Clive Finlayson, who runs the Gibraltar Museum, "though it doesn't stop any of us from putting forth some pretty elaborate scenarios." Many researchers are loath even to speculate on the cause of Neanderthals' demise, but Finlayson suggests that a combination of climate change and the cumulative effect of repeated population busts eventually did them in. "I think it's the culmination of 100,000 years of climate hitting Neanderthals hard, their population diving during the cold years, rebounding some during warm years, then diving further when it got cold again," Finlayson says.

As Neanderthals retreated into present-day southern Spain and parts of Croatia toward the end of their time, modern human beings were right on their heels. Some researchers, like Smith, believe that Neanderthals and Cro-Magnon humans probably mated, if only in limited numbers. The question of whether Neanderthals and modern humans bred might be resolved within a decade by scientists studying DNA samples from Neanderthal and Cro-Magnon fossils.

But others argue that any encounter was likely to be hostile. "Brotherly love is not the way I'd describe any interaction between different groups of humans," Shea says. In fact, he speculates that modern humans were superior warriors and wiped out the Neanderthals. "Modern humans are very competitive and really good at using projectile weapons to kill from a distance," he says, adding they also probably worked together better in large groups, providing a battlefield edge.

In the end, Neanderthals, though handy, big-brained, brawny and persistent, went the way of every human species but one. "There have been a great many experiments at being human preceding us and none of them made it, so we should not think poorly of Neanderthal just because they went extinct," says Rick Potts, head of the Smithsonian's Human Origins Program. "Given that Neanderthal possessed the very traits that we think guarantee our success should make us pause about our place here on earth."

JOE ALPER, *a freelance writer in Louisville, Colorado, is a frequent contributor to* Science *magazine. This is his first article for* SMITHSONIAN. *Paris-based* ERIC SANDER *photographed "Master Class" in our October 2002 issue.* STAN FELLOWS' *illustrations appeared in "Hamilton Takes Command," in the January issue.*

The Gift *of* Gab

Grooves and holes in fossil skulls may reveal when our ancestors began to speak. The big question, though, is what drove them to it?

By Matt Cartmill

People can talk. Other animals can't. They can all communicate in one way or another—to lure mates, at the very least—but their whinnies and wiggles don't do the jobs that language does. The birds and beasts can use their signals to attract, threaten, or alert each other, but they can't ask questions, strike bargains, tell stories, or lay out a plan of action.

Those skills make *Homo sapiens* a uniquely successful, powerful, and dangerous mammal. Other creatures' signals carry only a few limited kinds of information about what's happening at the moment, but language lets us tell each other in limitless detail about what used to be or will be or might be. Language lets us get vast numbers of big, smart fellow primates all working together on a single task—building the Great Wall of China or fighting World War II or flying to the moon. It lets us construct and communicate the gorgeous fantasies of literature and the profound fables of myth. It lets us cheat death by pouring out our knowledge, dreams, and memories into younger people's minds. And it does powerful things for us inside our own minds because we do a lot of our thinking by talking silently to ourselves. Without language, we would be only a sort of upright chimpanzee with funny feet and clever hands. With it, we are the self-possessed masters of the planet.

How did such a marvelous adaptation get started? And if it's so marvelous, why hasn't any other species come up with anything similar? These may be the most important questions we face in studying human evolution. They are also the least understood. But in the past few years, linguists and anthropologists have been making some breakthroughs, and we are now beginning to have a glimmering of some answers.

COULD NEANDERTHALS talk? They seem to have had nimble tongues, but some scientists think the geometry of their throats prevented them from making many clear vowel sounds.

We can reasonably assume that by at least 30,000 years ago people were talking—at any rate, they were producing carvings, rock paintings, and jewelry, as well as ceremonial graves containing various goods. These tokens of art and religion are high-level forms of symbolic behavior, and they imply that the everyday symbol-handling machinery of human language must have been in place then as well.

Language surely goes back further than that, but archeologists don't agree on just how far. Some think that earlier, more basic human behaviors—hunting in groups, tending fires, making tools—also demanded language. Others think

these activities are possible without speech. Chimpanzees, after all, hunt communally, and with human guidance they can learn to tend fires and chip flint.

Paleontologists have pored over the fossil bones of our ancient relatives in search of evidence for speech abilities. Because the most crucial organ for language is the brain, they have looked for signs in the impressions left by the brain on the inner surfaces of fossil skulls, particularly impressions made by parts of the brain called speech areas because damage to them can impair a person's ability to talk or understand language. Unfortunately, it turns out that you can't tell whether a fossil hominid was able to talk simply by looking at brain impressions on the inside of its skull. For one thing, the fit between the brain and the bony braincase is loose in people and other large mammals, and so the impressions we derive from fossil skulls are disappointingly fuzzy. Moreover, we now know that language functions are not tightly localized but spread across many parts of the brain.

Faced with these obstacles, researchers have turned from the brain to other organs used in speech, such as the throat and tongue. Some have measured the fossil skulls and jaws of early hominids, tried to reconstruct the shape of their vocal tracts, and then applied the laws of acoustics to them to see whether they might have been capable of producing human speech.

All mammals produce their vocal noises by contracting muscles that compress the rib cage. The air in the lungs is driven out through the windpipe to the larynx, where it flows between the vocal cords. More like flaps than cords, these structures vibrate in the breeze, producing a buzzing sound that becomes the voice. The human difference lies in what happens to the air after it gets past the vocal cords.

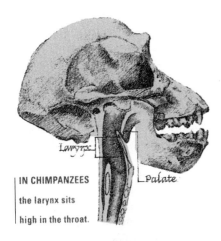

IN CHIMPANZEES the larynx sits high in the throat.

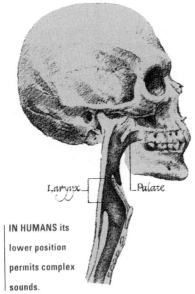

IN HUMANS its lower position permits complex sounds.

ILLUSTRATIONS BY DUGALD STERMER

In people, the larynx lies well below the back of the tongue, and most of the air goes out through the mouth when we talk. We make only a few sounds by exhaling through the nose—for instance, nasal consonants like *m* or *n*, or the so-called nasal vowels in words like the French *bon* and *vin*. But in most mammals, including apes, the larynx sticks farther up behind the tongue, into the back of the nose, and most of the exhaled air passes out through the nostrils. Nonhuman mammals make mostly nasal sounds as a result.

At some point in human evolution the larynx must have descended from its previous heights, and this change had some serious drawbacks. It put the opening of the windpipe squarely in the path of descending food, making it dangerously easy for us to choke to death if a chunk of meat goes down the wrong way—something that rarely happens to a dog or a cat. Why has evolution exposed us to this danger?

Some scientists think that the benefits outweighed the risks, because lowering the larynx improved the quality of our vowels and made speech easier to understand. The differences between vowels are produced mainly by changing the size and shape of the airway between the tongue and the roof of the mouth. When the front of the tongue almost touches the palate, you get the *ee* sound in *beet*; when the tongue is humped up high in the back (and the lips are rounded), you get the *oo* sound in *boot*, and so on. We are actually born with a somewhat apelike throat, including a flat tongue and a larynx lying high up in the neck, and this arrangement makes a child's vowels sound less clearly separated from each other than an adult's.

Philip Lieberman of Brown University thinks that an ape-like throat persisted for some time in our hominid ancestors. His studies of fossil jaws and skulls persuade him that a more modern throat didn't evolve until some 500,000 years ago, and that some evolutionary lines in the genus *Homo* never did acquire modern vocal organs. Lieberman concludes that the Neanderthals, who lived in Europe until perhaps 25,000 years ago, belonged to a dead-end lineage that never developed our range of vowels, and that their speech—if they had any at all—would have been harder to understand than ours. Apparently, being easily understood wasn't terribly important to them—not important enough, at any rate, to outweigh the risk of inhaling a chunk of steak into a lowered larynx. This suggests that vocal communication wasn't as central to their lives as it is to ours.

Many paleoanthropologists, especially those who like to see Neanderthals as a separate species, accept this story. Others have their doubts. But the study of other parts of the skeleton in fossil hominids supports some of Lieberman's conclusions. During the 1980s a nearly complete skeleton of a young *Homo* male was recovered from 1.5-million-year-old deposits in northern Kenya. Examining the vertebrae attached to the boy's rib cage, the English anatomist Ann MacLarnon discovered that his spinal cord was proportionately thinner in this region than it is in people today. Since that part of the cord controls most of the muscles that drive air in and out of the lungs, MacLarnon concluded that the youth may not have had the kind of precise neural control over breathing movements that is needed for speech.

This year my colleague Richard Kay, his student Michelle Balow, and I were able to offer some insights from yet another part of the hominid body. The tongue's movements are controlled almost solely by a nerve called the hypoglossal. In its course from the brain to the tongue, this nerve passes through a hole in the skull, and Kay, Balow, and I found that this bony canal is relatively big in modern humans—about twice as big in cross section as that of a like-size chimpanzee. Our larger canal presumably reflects a bigger hypoglossal nerve, giving us the precise control over tongue movements that we need for speech.

We also measured this hole in the skulls of a number of fossil hominids. Australopithecines have small canals like those of apes, suggesting that they couldn't talk. But later *Homo* skulls, beginning with a 400,000-year-old skull from Zambia, all have big, humanlike hypoglossal canals. These are also the skulls that were the first to house brains as big as our own. On these counts our work supports Lieberman's ideas. We disagree only on the matter of Neanderthals. While he claims their throats couldn't have produced human speech, we find that their skulls also had human-size canals for the hypoglossal nerve, suggesting that they could indeed talk.

THE VERDICT IS STILL out on the language abilities of Neanderthals. I tend to think they must have had fully human language. After all, they had brains larger than those of most humans.

In short, several lines of evidence suggest that neither the australopithecines nor the early, small-brained species of *Homo* could talk. Only around half a million years ago did the first big-brained *Homo* evolve language. The verdict is still out on the language abilities of Neanderthals. I tend to think that they must have had fully human language. After all, they had brains larger than those of most modern humans, made elegant stone tools, and knew how to use fire. But if Lieberman and his friends are right about those vowels, Neanderthals may have sounded something like the Swedish chef on *The Muppet Show*.

We are beginning to get some idea of when human language originated, but the fossils can't tell us how it got started, or what the intermediate stages between animal calls and human language might have been like. When trying to understand the origin of a trait that doesn't fossilize, it's sometimes useful to look for similar but simpler versions of it in other creatures living today. With luck, you can find a series of forms that suggest how simple primitive makeshifts could have evolved into more complex and elegant versions. This is how Darwin attacked the problem of the evolution of the eye. Earlier biologists had pointed to the human eye as an example of a marvelously perfect organ that must have been specially created all at once in its final form by God. But Darwin pointed out that animal eyes exist in all stages of complexity, from simple skin cells that can detect only the difference between light and darkness, to pits lined with such cells, and so on all the way to the eyes of people and other vertebrates. This series,

he argued, shows how the human eye could have evolved from simpler precursors by gradual stages.

Can we look to other animals to find simpler precursors of language? It seems unlikely. Scientists have sought experimental evidence of language in dolphins and chimpanzees, thus far without success. But even if we had no experimental studies, common sense would tell us that the other animals can't have languages like ours. If they had, we would be in big trouble because they would organize against us. They don't. Outside of Gary Larson's *Far Side* cartoons and George Orwell's *Animal Farm*, farmers don't have to watch their backs when they visit the cowshed. There are no conspiracies among cows, or even among dolphins and chimpanzees. Unlike human slaves or prisoners, they never plot rebellions against their oppressors.

Even if language as a whole has no parallels in animal communication, might some of its peculiar properties be foreshadowed among the beasts around us? If so, that might tell us something about how and in what order these properties were acquired. One such property is reference. Most of the units of human languages refer to things—to individuals (like *Fido*), or to types of objects (*dog*), actions (*sit*), or properties (*furry*). Animal signals don't have this kind of referential meaning. Instead, they have what is called instrumental meaning: this is, they act as stimuli that trigger desired responses from others. A frog's mating croak doesn't *refer* to sex. Its purpose is to get some, not to talk about it. People, too, have signals of this purely animal sort—for example, weeping, laughing, and screaming—but these stand outside language. They have powerful meanings for us but not the kind of meaning that words have.

Some animal signals have a focused meaning that looks a bit like reference. For example, vervet monkeys give different warning calls for different predators. When they hear the "leopard" call, vervets climb trees and anxiously look down; when they hear the "eagle" call, they hide in low bushes or look up. But although the vervets' leopard call is in some sense about leopards, it isn't a word for leopard. Like a frog's croak or

human weeping, its meaning is strictly instrumental; it's a stimulus that elicits an automatic response. All a vervet can "say" with it is "*Eeek!* A leopard!"—not "I really hate leopard!" or "No leopards here, thank goodness" or "A leopard ate Alice yesterday."

AUSTRALOPITHECUS africanus and other early hominids couldn't speak.

In these English sentences, such referential words as *leopard* work their magic through an accompanying framework of nonreferential, grammatical words, which set up an empty web of meaning that the referential symbols fill in. When Lewis Carroll tells us in "Jabberwocky" that "the slithy toves did gyre and gimble in the wabe," we have no idea what he is talking about, but we do know certain things—for instance, that all this happened in the past and that there was more than one tove but only one wabe. We know these things because of the grammatical structure of the sentence, a structure that linguists call syntax. Again, there's nothing much like it in any animal signals.

But if there aren't any intermediate stages between animal calls and human speech, then how could language evolve? What was there for it to evolve from? Until recently, linguists have shrugged off these questions—or else concluded that language didn't evolve at all, but just sprang into existence by accident, through some glorious random mutation. This theory drives Darwinians crazy, but the linguists have been content with it because it fits neatly into some key ideas in modern linguistics.

Forty years ago most linguists thought that people learn to talk through the same sort of behavior reinforcement used in training an animal to do tricks: when children use a word correctly or produce a grammatical sentence, they are rewarded. This picture was swept away in the late 1950s by the revolutionary ideas of Noam Chomsky. Chomsky argued that the structures of syntax lie in unconscious linguistic patterns—

so-called deep structures—that are very different from the surface strings of words that come out of our mouths. Two sentences that look different on the surface (for instance, "A leopard ate Alice" and "Alice was eaten by a leopard") can mean the same thing because they derive from a single deep structure. Conversely, two sentences with different deep structures and different meanings can look exactly the same on the surface (for example, "Fleeing leopards can be dangerous"). Any models of language learning based strictly on the observable behaviors of language, Chomsky insisted, can't account for these deep-lying patterns of meaning.

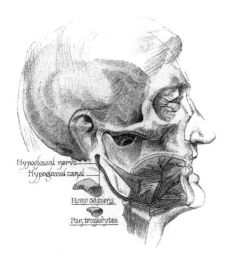

THE TONGUE-CONTROLLING

hypoglossal nerve is larger in

humans than in chimps.

Chomsky concluded that the deepest structures of language are innate, not learned. We are all born with the same fundamental grammar hard-wired into our brains, and we are preprogrammed to pick up the additional rules of the local language, just as baby ducks are hard-wired to follow the first big animal they see when they hatch. Chomsky could see no evidence of other animals' possessing this innate syntax machinery. He concluded that we can't learn anything about the origins of language by studying other animals and they can't learn language from us. If language learning were just a matter of proper training, Chomsky rea-

soned, we ought to be able to teach English to lab rats, or at least to apes.

As we have seen, apes aren't built to talk. But they can be trained to use sign language or to point to word-symbols on a keyboard. Starting in the 1960s, several experimenters trained chimpanzees and other great apes to use such signs to ask for things and answer questions to get rewards. Linguists, however, were unimpressed. They said that the apes' signs had a purely instrumental meaning: the animals were just doing tricks to get a treat. And there was no trace of syntax in the random-looking jumble of signs the apes produced; an ape that signed "You give me cookie please" one minute might sign "Me cookie please you cookie eat give" the next.

Duane Rumbaugh and Sue Savage-Rumbaugh set to work with chimpanzees at the Yerkes Regional Primate Research Center in Atlanta to try to answer the linguists' criticisms. After many years of mixed results, Sue made a surprising break-through with a young bonobo (or pygmy chimp) named Kanzi. Kanzi had watched his mother, Matata, try to learn signs with little success. When Sue gave up on her and started with Kanzi, she was astonished to discover that he already knew the meaning of 12 of the keyboard symbols. Apparently, he had learned them without any training or rewards. In the years that followed, he learned new symbols quickly and used them referentially, both to answer questions and to "talk" about things that he intended to do or had already done. Still more amazingly, he had a considerable understanding of spoken English—including its syntax. He grasped such grammatical niceties as case structures ("Can you throw a potato to the turtle?") and if-then implication ("You can have some cereal if you give Austin your monster mash to play with"). Upon hearing such sentences, Kanzi behaved appropriately 72 percent of the time—more than a 30-month-old human child given the same tests.

Kanzi is a primatologist's dream and a linguist's nightmare. His language-learning abilities seem inexplicable. He didn't need any rewards to learn language, as the old behaviorists would have predicted; but he also defies the

Chomskyan model, which can't explain why a speechless ape would have an innate tendency to learn English. It looks as though some animals can develop linguistic abilities for reasons unrelated to language itself.

BRAIN ENLARGEMENT in hominids may have been the result of evolutionary pressures that favored intelligence. As a side effect, human evolution crossed a threshold at which language became possible.

Neuroscientist William Calvin of the University of Washington and linguist Derek Bickerton of the University of Hawaii have a suggestion as to what those reasons might be. In their forthcoming book, *Lingua ex Machina*, they argue that the ability to create symbols—signs that refer to things—is potentially present in any animal that can learn to interpret natural signs, such as a trail of footprints. Syntax, meanwhile, emerges from the abstract thought required for a social life. In apes and some other mammals with complex and subtle social relationships, individuals make alliances and act altruistically towards others, with the implicit understanding that their favors will be returned. To succeed in such societies, animals need to choose trustworthy allies and to detect and punish cheaters who take but never give anything in return. This demands fitting a shifting constellation of individuals into an abstract mental model of social roles (debtors, creditors, allies, and so on) connected by social expectations ("If you scratch my back, I'll scratch yours"). Calvin and Bickerton believe that such abstract models of social obligation furnished the basic pattern for the deep structures of syntax.

These foreshadowings of symbols and syntax, they propose, laid the groundwork for language in a lot of social animals but didn't create language itself. That had to wait until our ancestors evolved brains big enough to handle the large-scale operations needed to generate and process complex strings of signs. Calvin and Bickerton suggest that brain enlargement in our ancestry was the result of evolutionary pressures that favored intelligence and motor coordination for making tools and throwing weapons. As a side effect of these selection pressures, which had nothing to do with communication, human evolution crossed a threshold at which language became possible. Big-brained, nonhuman animals like Kanzi remain just on the verge of language.

FOSSILS HINT that language dawned 500,000 years ago.

This story reconciles natural selection with the linguists' insistence that you can't evolve language out of an animal communication system. It is also consistent with what we know about language from the fossil record. The earliest hominids with modern-size brains also seem to be the first ones with modern-size hypoglossal canals. Lieberman thinks that these are also the first hominids with modern vocal tracts. It may be no coincidence that all three of these changes seem to show up together around half a million years ago. If Calvin and Bickerton are right, the enlargement of the brain may have abruptly brought language into being at this time, which would have placed new selection pressures on the evolving throat and tongue.

This account may be wrong in some of its details, but the story in its broad outlines solves so many puzzles and ties up so many loose ends that something like it must surely be correct. It also promises to resolve our conflicting views of the boundary between people and animals. To some people, it seems obvious that human beings are utterly different from any beasts. To others, it's just as obvious that many other animals are essentially like us, only with fewer smarts and more fur. Each party finds the other's view of humanity alien and threatening. The story of language origins sketched above suggests that both parties are right: the human difference is real and profound, but it is rooted in aspects of psychology and biology that we share with our close animal relatives. If the growing consensus on the origins of language can join these disparate truths together, it will be a big step forward in the study of human evolution.

MATT CARTMILL is a professor at Duke, where he teaches anatomy and anthropology and studies animal locomotion. Cartmill is also the author of numerous articles and books on the evolution of people and other animals, including an award-winning book on hunting, A View to a Death in the Morning. *He is the president of the American Association of Physical Anthropologists.*

We Are All Africans

Pat Shipman

Nice hypothesis, you may say, but *is it true?* The heart of the scientific method lies in that skeptic's simple question. A merely plausible explanation of what we observe will not suffice, nor will a hypothesis bolstered only by some expert's endorsement. Modern science is wonderfully egalitarian, and it demands proof that all can see: measurements, objects or evidence of some kind. Scientific hypotheses must be both well-defined and firmly supported, preferably by several different types of data.

If a hypothesis meets these requirements, does this mean it is true? No, according to the philosopher Karl Popper, who believed that hypotheses could never be proven true—only false. Frederick Nietzsche claimed that the great charm of hypotheses was that they were refutable. While Nietzsche may be correct in the abstract, my experience suggests that scientists do not gleefully bury hypotheses in which they have invested many years of research.

In the study of human evolution, dueling hypotheses are commonplace because of long-standing, frequently erupting feuds about the interpretation of the fossil record. The field is so argumentative, in part, because the theories reflect directly on the nature and origin of humans. There is immense room for giving and taking offense when the subject is oneself. Too, the primary data of paleoanthropology—fossilized remains of our ancestors and near-relatives—are rare and difficult to obtain. Hence, it is not a simple matter to collect more evidence to clarify or support hypotheses. Fossil hunting requires tremendous knowledge and effort, good organizational skills, substantial grants, and a huge dollop of luck. New theories are, sadly, easier to come by than new primary evidence.

Thus it is a joyous occasion when my paleoanthropologist colleagues appear to resolve one of the most bitterly debated questions in the discipline: the issue of when, where and how modern humans evolved. For simplicity, I use "modern humans" or "recent humans" to denote the species to which I (and all the readers of this magazine) belong, but the formal term is either "anatomically modern *Homo sapiens*" or "*Homo sapiens sapiens.*" Humans who lived in the past and did not have modern anatomy are often referred to as archaic or primitive.

Opposable Theories

For decades, paleoanthropologists have argued over two competing theories about the origin of our kind. The older notion, which owes its crude beginnings to Charles Darwin, is the *Out of Africa hypothesis.* This theory maintains that modern humans evolved in Africa and then spread around the world. Boiled down to its essence, the hypothesis states that modern humans are both relatively recent (100,000 to 200,000 years old) and African in origin. A major prediction of this hypothesis is that the earliest remains of modern humans will be found in Africa, dated to an appropriate time period.

The rival *Multiregional hypothesis* argues that modern humans evolved in many locations around the world from a precursor species, *Homo erectus*, approximately one to two million years ago. According to this school of thought, these regional populations evolved along parallel paths and reached modernity at roughly the same time. Because the populations were largely isolated from one another, they developed distinctive regional features, which people recognize today as "racial" differences. The Multiregional hypothesis predicts that the fossilized remains of the earliest modern humans will be found all over the Old World and that these scattered fossils will all date from about the same time. Furthermore, the theory requires these early populations to show anatomical and genetic continuity with the current inhabitants of the same region. For example, Multiregionalists believe that Neandertals, an archaic human form, are most closely related to modern indigenous Europeans.

Unfortunately for adherents of the Multiregional hypothesis, recent results are weighing heavily against them. Three very different strains of evidence have converged to offer convincing support for the rival theory.

Evidence for "Eve"

In April of this year, Sarah Tishkoff of the University of Maryland and a team of coworkers reported genetic analyses of more than 600 living Tanzanians from 14 different tribes and four linguistic groups. They analyzed mitochondrial DNA (mtDNA)—the tool of choice for tracing ancestry because it is inherited only through the mother as part of the ovum. The number of mutations that have accumulated in mtDNA is a rough measure of the time that has passed since that lineage first appeared. The owner of the first modern human mtDNA (by definition, a woman) is often referred to as "Eve," although many women of that time are likely to have shared similar mtDNA.

Tishkoff and her colleagues chose to investigate East African peoples for specific reasons. The number of linguistic and cultural differences is unusually high in the region, as is the variation in physical appearance—East Africans are tall or short, darker-skinned or lighter-skinned, round-faced or narrow-faced, and so on. This observation suggested that the genetic composition of the population is highly diverse, and as expected, the team found substantial variation in the mtDNA. In fact, members of five of the lineages showed an exceptionally high number of mutations compared with other populations, indicating that these East African lineages are of great antiquity. Identified by tribal affiliation, these are: the Sandawe, who speak a "click" language related to that of the Bushmen of the Kalahari desert; the Burunge and Gorowaa, who migrated to Tanzania from Ethiopia within the last five thousand years; and the Maasai and the Datog, who probably originated in the Sudan. The efforts of the University of Maryland group reflect a substantially larger database and more certain geographic origins for its subjects than earlier mtDNA studies. Further, the work by Tishkoff's team reveals that these five East African populations have even older origins than the !Kung San of southern Africa, who previously had the oldest known mtDNA.

"These samples showed really deep, old lineages with lots of genetic diversity," Tishkoff says. "They are the oldest lineages identified to date. And that fact makes it highly likely that 'Eve' was an East or Northeast African. My guess is that the region of Ethiopia or the Sudan is where modern humans originated."

By assuming that mtDNA mutates at a constant rate, Tishkoff's team estimated that the oldest lineages in their study originated 170,000 years ago, although she cautions that the method only gives an approximate date. Nonetheless, this finding is neatly congruent with new fossil evidence.

Idaltu Means "Elder"

This past June, an international team headed by Tim White and F. Clark Howell of the University of California at Berkeley, and Berhane Asfaw of the Rift Valley Research Service in Addis Ababa announced the discovery of three fossilized human skulls in the Herto Bouri area of Ethiopia. Volcanic layers immediately above and below the layer were dated to 154,000 and 160,000 years using radioisotopes, meaning that the owners of the skulls lived sometime between those dates.

The most remarkable of the three specimens is an adult male cranium: With the exception of a few missing teeth and some damage on the left side of the skull, the fossil is complete. There is also part of another male skull and an immature cranium from a six- or seven-year-old child.

Once these specimens were cleaned and pieced together, the team was able to make some telling observations. Like modern humans, the owners of these skulls had small faces tucked under capacious braincases, making the facial profile vertical. The cranial volume of the most complete specimen, designated BOU-VP-16/1, is 1,450 cubic centimeters—large even for modern humans. The braincase of the other adult skull may have been even bigger. Although the African Herto skulls are longer and more robust than those of recent humans, the

team considers the Herto specimens to be the earliest modern *Homo sapiens* yet found—direct ancestors of people living today. In an unknowing echo of Tishkoff's genetic findings, Tim White concludes, "We are all, in this sense, Africans."

Because the discoverers of the Herto skulls were unable to find convincing links between these fossils and archaic humans from any single geographic region, they put the three specimens into a new subspecies, *Homo sapiens idaltu*. The subspecies name *idaltu* comes from the Afar language of Ethiopia. It means "elder."

Even paleoanthropologists who were not associated with the finds overwhelmingly agree that the Herto skulls are the earliest securely dated modern humans yet found, meshing with the Out of Africa hypothesis. The Herto fossils also fit neatly into an African succession: Older skulls from the region include *Homo erectus* fossils from Daka, dated to about 1 million years ago, and the archaic Bodo skull, estimated to be about 500,000 years old. Meanwhile, fossils from Omo Kibish, also in Ethiopia, are more recent than the Herto skulls, according to a reanalysis of those remains. For a long time, the Omo Kibish specimens were regarded as ambiguous: They were fragmentary, making their anatomy less clear, and the site was originally dated using older, less reliable methods. However, a recent relocation of the site turned up new pieces that glued onto specimens found in 1967, and the site was re-dated to about 125,000 years using modern techniques. Further evidence comes from the Qafzeh site in Israel—on a plausible route from Africa—where there is a 92,000-year-old modern human skull.

These findings establish the earliest modern humans in Africa, but they do not exclude the simultaneous evolution of modern man in other parts of the world, as suggested by the Multiregional hypothesis. The most pertinent test of Multiregionalism focuses on Neandertals, which are a uniquely European form of primitive humans. According to Multiregionalists, Neandertals (which lived between about 200,000 and 27,000 years ago) are a transitional form that connects European *Homo erectus* to modern *Homo sapiens sapiens*. Could the Herto skulls simply be the regional, African equivalent of Neandertals?

"No," says co-leader Berhane Asfaw definitively. "The Herto skulls show that people in Africa had already developed the anatomy of modern humans while European Neandertals were still quite different." Indeed, the Herto skulls, though robust, lack many of the diagnostic anatomical features of Neandertal skulls. Asfaw states, "We can conclusively say that Neandertals had nothing to do with modern humans based on these skulls and on the genetic evidence."

Neandertals as European Ancestors?

The genetic evidence to which he refers has accumulated over the last six years, but the most dramatic advance came in 1999, when a team led by Svante Pääbo of the Max Planck Institute for Evolutionary Anthropology in Leipzig, Germany, became the first to extract mtDNA from the original Neandertal specimen. His group's success was a spectacular tour de force of meticulous technique and solid research design. The ancient mtDNA was compared with mtDNA from more than 2,000 people living in various regions around the world and differed from each of the modern regional groups by an average of 27 mutations (out of a possible 379 that were examined). Contrary to the predictions of the Multiregional hypothesis, the mtDNA of Neandertals was not closer to that of the modern Europeans. The work was a strong blow to the theory that humans evolved in several places simultaneously.

Multiregionalists Milford Wolpoff of the University of Michigan and Alan Thorne, then of Australian National University in Canberra, challenged the conclusions. They urged an investigation of mtDNA from additional Neandertals, in case the single individual used by Pääbo's team was particularly unusual. They also suggested that Neandertal mtDNA might be closer to samples from the fossilized remains of early modern humans in Europe than from living Europeans.

Since these criticisms were levied, several teams have carried out additional studies of mtDNA from Neandertals and fossilized modern humans. All have shown that Neandertal samples differ significantly from modern mtDNA, which is indistinguishable from fossilized modern human mtDNA. Giorgio Bertorelle of the University of Ferrara in Italy led one of these teams, which published important results last May. Bertorelle's team compared mtDNA from two early modern humans (Cro-Magnons) from Italy, dated to 23,000 and 24,720 years old, with four mtDNA sequences of Neandertals from 42,000 to 29,000 years ago. The chronological proximity of the Neandertal and modern fossils was key because it increased the likelihood that Neandertal mtDNA would strongly resemble the early modern human mtDNA—if the former evolved into the latter, as the Multiregional hypothesis states.

Bertorelle and colleagues found that the Cro-Magnon mtDNA was unlike the Neandertal samples, differing from them at 22 and 28 sites out of 360. Instead, the Cro-Magnon mtDNA sequences fell squarely within the range of variation of living humans. One of the Italian Cro-Magnons had a sequence shared by 359 (14 percent) of 2,566 modern samples in Europe and the Near East, and the other differs by only one mutation.

"The early modern humans had sequences that living individuals still have," concluded Bertorelle, "they [have] … nothing to do with Neandertal sequences." He and Asfaw might chime in unison that Neandertals cannot represent a regional European transition from *Homo erectus* to modern *Homo sapiens*

The identity between Cro-Magnon and modern human mtDNA sequences in this study and others is striking, and it has caused some researchers to worry about the possibility of mtDNA contamination from researchers or others who have handled the fossils. Although contamination is a major problem in such studies, Bertorelle asserts spiritedly that his data are clean, stating that his group performed nine different tests to check for contamination and followed the most stringent procedures and methodology. He also points out the irony of questioning the validity of the mtDNA of a prehistoric human only because it is identical to that of modern humans.

Compelling Congruity

The Out of Africa hypothesis has become compelling because these different studies have all yielded congruent answers. Tishkoff's work points to East Africa in general, and Ethiopia/Sudan in particular, as the region where the oldest modern human lineages are found—and probably evolved. Studies of ancient mtDNA by groups led by Pääbo, Bertorelle and others emphasize the genetic discrepancies between Neandertals and modern humans and demonstrate that some early anatomically modern fossils were also genetically modern—undermining the Multiregional hypothesis.

Despite the power of these genetic studies, only the fossils can tell us what our ancestors actually looked like, what they actually did and where they actually lived. It is singularly satisfying that the White-Howell-Asfaw team has discovered fossilized human remains from the right place (Ethiopia) and time (about 160,000 years ago) that also have the right (modern human) anatomy. The authors of the Out of Africa hypothesis are celebrating.

I don't expect that the subscribers of the Multiregional hypothesis will be waving a white flag of surrender, although they have lost the great majority of their supporters. At least one of the theory's most ardent proponents, Wolpoff, is still steadfast in defense of the hypothesis he has so long espoused. While it remains possible that new findings will shift the balance in favor of the Multiregional viewpoint, the consilience of such evidence creates a powerful testament. It would take many new fossils and many new genetic studies to resculpt this intellectual landscape.

Pat Shipman is an adjunct professor of anthropology at the Pennsylvania State University. Address: Department of Anthropology, 315 Carpenter Building, Pennsylvania State University, University Park, PA 16801. pls10@psu.edu

Bibliography

Caramelli, D., C. Lalueza-Fox, C. Vernesi, M. Lari, A. Casoli, F. Mallegni, B. Chiarelli, I. Dupanloup, J. Bertranpetit, G. Barbujani and G. Bertorelle. 2003. Evidence for a genetic discontinuity between Neandertals and 24,000-year-old anatomically modern Europeans. *Proceedings of the National Academy of Science of the United States of America* 100:6593-6597.

Barbujani, G., and G. Bertorelle. 2003. Were Cro-Magnons too like us for DNA to tell? Nature 424:127.

Krings, M., A. Stone, R. W. Schmitz, H. Krainitzki, M. Stoneking and S. Pääbo. 1997. Neandertal DNA sequences and the origin of modern humans. Cell 90:19-30.

Tishkoff, S. A., K. Gonder, J. Hirbo, H. Mortensen, K. Powell, A. Knight and J. Mountain. 2003. The genetic diversity of linguistically diverse Tanzanian populations: A multilocus analysis. *American Journal of Physical Anthropology Supplement* 36:208-209.

White, T. D., B. Asfaw, D. DaGusta, H. Gilbert, G. D. Richards, G. Suwa and F. C. Howell. 2003. Pleistocene *Homo sapiens* from Middle Awash, Ethiopia. *Nature* 423:742-747.

UNIT 6

Human Diversity

Unit Selections

Key Points to Consider

- Discuss whether the human species can be subdivided into racial categories. Support your position.

- How and why did the concept of race develop?

- Would you have allowed archaeologists to study the remains of Kennewick Man, or would you have immediately repatriated the bones to Native Americans? Why?

- Why does skin color vary among humans?

- Why are humans nearly hairless?

- To what extent is height a barometer of the health of a society, and why?

 **Links: www.dushkin.com/online/**
These sites are annotated in the World Wide Web pages.

Hominid Evolution Survey
http://www.geocities.com/SoHo/Atrium/1381/index.html

Human Genome Project Information
http://www.ornl.gov/TechResources/Human_Genome/home.html

OMIM Home Page-Online Mendelian Inheritance in Man
http://www3.ncbi.nlm.nih.gov/omim/

The Human Diversity Resource Page
http://community-1.webtv.net/SoundBehavior/DIVERSITYFORSOUND/

A more recent attempt to salvage the idea of human races has been to perceive them not so much as reproductively isolated entities but as so many clusters of gene frequencies, separable only by the fact that the proportions of traits (such as skin color, hair form, etc.) differ in each artificially constructed group. George W. Gill (in "Does Race Exist? A Proponent's Perspective") appreciates the practical value of this approach in the area of forensic physical anthropology. In a similar manner, our ability to reconstruct human prehistory is dependent upon an understanding of human variation, as can be seen in "The Lost Man" by Douglas Preston.

When it comes to *explaining* human variation, however, C. Loring Brace (in "Does Race Exist? An Antagonist's Perspective") claims that it would be more productive to study human traits in terms of their particular adaptiveness (as in "Skin Deep" by Nina G. Jablonski and George Chaplin, "The Tall and the Short of It" by Barry Bogin and "The Bare Truth").

Lest anyone think that anthropologists are "in denial" regarding the existence of human races and that the viewpoints expressed in these articles are merely expressions of contemporary political correctness, it should be pointed out that serious, scholarly attempts to classify people in terms of precise, biological units have been going on now for 200 years and, so far, nothing of value has come of them.

Complicating the matter, as Jonathan Marks elucidates in "Black, White, Other," is that there actually are two concepts of race: the strictly biological one, which was originally set forth by Linnaeus in the 1700s, and the one of popular culture, which has been around since time immemorial. These "two constantly intersecting ways of thinking about the divisions between us," says Marks, have resulted not only in fuzzy thinking about racial biology, but they have also infected the way we think about people and, therefore, the way we treat each other in the social sense.

What we should recognize, claim most anthropologists, is that, despite the superficial physical and biological differences between us, when it comes to intelligence, all human beings are basically the same. The degrees of variation within our species may be accounted for by the subtle and changing selective forces experienced as one moves from one geographical area to another. However, no matter what the environmental pressures have been, the same intellectual demands have been made upon us all. This is not to say, of course, that we do not vary from each other as individuals. Rather, what is being said is that when we look at these artificially created groups of people called "races," we find the same range of intellectual skills within each group. Indeed, even when we look at traits other than intelligence, we find much greater variation within each group than we find between groups.

It is time, therefore, to put the idea of human races to rest, at least as far as science is concerned. If such notions remain in the realm of social discourse, then so be it. That is where the problems associated with notions of race have to be solved anyway. At least, says Marks, in speaking for the anthropological community: "You may group humans into a small number of races if you want to, but you are denied biology as a support for it."

The field of biological anthropology has come a long way since the days when one of its primary concerns was the classification of human beings according to racial type. Although human diversity is still a matter of major interest in terms of how and why we differ from one another, most anthropologists have concluded that human beings cannot be sorted into sharply distinct entities. Without denying the fact of human variation throughout the world, the prevailing view today is that the differences between us exist along geographical gradients, as differences in degree, rather than in terms of the separate and discrete reproductive entities perceived in the past.

One of the old ways of looking at human "races" was that each such group was a subspecies of humans that, if left reproductively isolated long enough, would eventually evolve into separate species. While this concept of subspecies, or racial varieties within a species, would seem to apply to some living creatures (such as the dog and wolf or the horse and zebra) and might even be relevant to hominid diversification in the past, the current consensus is that it is not happening today, at least not within the human species.

A REPORTER AT LARGE

The Lost Man

Is it possible that the first Americans weren't who we think they were?
And why is the government withholding Kennewick Man, who might turn out
to be the most significant archeological find of the decade?

DOUGLAS PRESTON

On Sunday, July 28, 1996, in the middle of the afternoon, two college students who were watching a hydroplane race on the Columbia River in Kennewick, Washington, decided to take a shortcut along the river's edge. While wading through the shallows, one of them stubbed his toe on a human skull partly buried in the sand. The students picked it up and, thinking it might be that of a murder victim, hid it in some bushes and called the police.

Floyd Johnson, the Benton County coroner, was called in, and the police gave him the skull in a plastic bucket. Late in the afternoon, Johnson called James Chatters, a forensic anthropologist and the owner of a local consulting firm called Applied Paleoscience. "Hey, buddy, I got a skull for you to look at," Johnson said. Chatters had often helped the police identify skeletons and distinguish between those of murder victims and those found in Indian burial sites. He is a small, determined, physically powerful man of forty-eight who used to be a gymnast and a wrestler. His work occasionally involves him in grisly or spectacular murders, where the victims are difficult to identify, such as burnings and dismemberments.

"When I looked down at the skull," Chatters told me, "right off the bat I saw it had a very large number of Caucasoid features"—in particular, a long, narrow braincase, a narrow face, and a slightly projecting upper jaw. But when Chatters took it out of the bucket and laid it on his worktable he began to see some unusual traits. The crowns of the teeth were worn flat, a common characteristic of prehistoric Indian skulls, and the color of the bone indicated that it was fairly old. The skull sutures had fused, indicating that the individual was past middle age. And, for a prehistoric Indian of what was then an advanced age, he or she was in exceptional health; the skull had, for example, all its teeth and no cavities.

As dusk fell, Chatters and Johnson went out to the site to see if they could find the rest of the skeleton. There, working in the dying light, they found more bones, lying around on sand and mud in about two feet of water. The remains were remarkably complete: only the sternum, a few rib fragments, and some tiny hand, wrist, and foot bones were missing. The bones had evidently fallen out of a bank during recent flooding of the Columbia River.

The following day, Chatters and Johnson spread the bones out in Chatters's laboratory. In forensic anthropology, the first order of business is to determine sex, age, and race. Determin-

ing race was particularly important, because if the skeleton turned out to be Native American it fell under a federal law called the Native American Graves Protection and Repatriation Act, or NAGPRA. Passed in 1990, NAGPRA requires the government—in this case, the Army Corps of Engineers, which controls the stretch of the Columbia River where the bones were found—to ascertain if human remains found on federal lands are Native American and, if they are, to "repatriate" them to the appropriate Indian tribe.

Chatters determined that the skeleton was male, Caucasoid, from an individual between forty and fifty-five years old, and about five feet nine inches tall—much taller than most prehistoric Native Americans in the Northwest. In physical anthropology, the term "Caucasoid" does not necessarily mean "white" or "European"; it is a descriptive term applied to certain biological features of a diverse category that includes, for example, some south-Asian groups as well as Europeans. (In contrast, the term "Caucasian" is a culturally defined racial category.) "I thought maybe we had an early pioneer or fur trapper," he said. As he was cleaning the pelvis, he noticed a gray object embedded in the bone, which had partly healed and fused around it. He took the bone to be X-rayed, but the object did not show up, meaning that it was not made of metal. So he requested a CAT scan. To his surprise, the scan revealed the object to be part of a willow-leaf-shaped spear point, which had been thrust into the bone and broken off. It strongly resembled a Cascade projectile point—an Archaic Indian style in wide use from around nine thousand to forty-five hundred years ago.

The Army Corps of Engineers asked Chatters to get a second opinion. He put the skeleton into his car and drove it a hundred miles to Ellensburg, Washington, where an anthropologist named Catherine J. MacMillan ran a forensic consulting business called the Bone-Apart Agency. "He didn't say anything," MacMillan told me. "I examined the bones, and I said 'Male, Caucasian.' He said 'Are you sure?' and I said 'Yeah.' And then he handed me the pelvis and showed me the ancient point embedded in it, and he said, 'What do you think now?' And I said, 'That's extremely interesting, but it still looks Caucasian to me.'" "In her report to the Benton County coroner's office she wrote that in her opinion the skeleton was "Caucasian male."

Toward the end of the week, Chatters told Floyd Johnson and the Army Corps of Engineers that he thought they needed to get a radiocarbon date on Kennewick Man. The two parties agreed, so Chatters sent the left fifth metacarpal bone—a tiny bone in the hand—to the University of California at Riverside.

On Friday, August 23rd, Jim Chatters received a telephone call from the radiocarbon lab. The bone was between ninety-three hundred and ninety-six hundred years old. He was astounded. "It was just a phone call," he said. "I thought, Maybe there's been a mistake. I had to see the report with my own eyes." The report came on Monday, in the form of a fax. "I got very nervous then," Chatters said. He knew that, because of their age, the bones on his worktable had to be one of the most important archeological finds of the decade. "It was just a tremendous responsibility." The following Tuesday, the coroner's office issued a press release on the find, and it was reported in the Seattle *Times*, and other local papers.

Chatters called in a third physical anthropologist, Grover S. Krantz, a professor at Washington State University. Krantz looked at the bones on Friday, August 30th. His report noted some characteristics common to both Europeans and Plains Indians but concluded that "this skeleton cannot be racially or culturally associated with any existing American Indian group." He also wrote, "The Native Repatriation Act has no more applicability to this skeleton than it would if an early Chinese expedition had left one of its members there."

Fifteen minutes after Krantz finished looking at the bones, Chatters received a call from Johnson. Apologetically, the coroner said, "I'm going to have to come over and get the bones." The Army Corps of Engineers had demanded that all study of the bones cease, and had required him to put the skeleton in the county sheriff's evidence locker. On the basis of the carbon date, the Corps had evidently decided that the skeleton was Native American and that it fell under NAGPRA.

"When I heard this, I panicked," Chatters said. "I was the only one who'd recorded any information on it. There were all these things I should have done. I didn't even have photographs of the post-cranial skeleton. I thought, Am I going to be the last scientist to see these bones?"

On September 9th, the Umatilla Indians, leading a coalition of five tribes and bands of the Columbia River basin, formally claimed the skeleton under NAGPRA, and the Corps quickly made a preliminary decision to "repatriate" it. The Umatilla Indian Reservation lies just over the border, in northeastern Oregon, and the other tribes live in Washington and Idaho; all consider the Kennewick area part of their traditional territories. The Umatillas announced that they were going to bury the skeleton in a secret site, where it would never again be available to science.

Three weeks later, the *New York Times* picked up the story, and from there it went to *Time* and on around the world. Television crews from as far away as France and Korea descended on Kennewick. The Corps received more than a dozen other claims for the skeleton, including one from a group known as the Asatru Folk Assembly, the California-based followers of an Old Norse religion, who wanted the bones for their own religious purposes.

On September 2nd, the Corps had directed that the bones be placed in a secure vault at the Pacific Northwest National Laboratory, in Richland, Washington. Nobody outside of the Corps has seen them since. They are now at the center of a legal controversy that will likely determine the course of American archeology.

WHAT was a Caucasoid man doing in the New World more than ninety-three centuries ago? In the reams of press reports last fall, that question never seemed to be dealt with. I called up Douglas Owsley, who is the Division Head for Physical Anthropology at the National Museum of Natural History, Smithsonian Institution, in Washington, D.C., and an expert on Paleo-American remains. I asked him how many well-preserved skeletons that old had been found in North America.

He replied, "Including Kennewick, about seven."

Then I asked if any others had Caucasoid features, and there was a silence that gave me the sense that I was venturing onto controversial ground.

He guardedly replied, "Yes."

"How many?"

"Well," he said, "in varying degrees, all of them."

Kennewick Man's bones are part of a growing quantity of evidence that the earliest inhabitants of the New World may have been a Caucasoid people. Other, tentative evidence suggests that these people may have originally come from Europe. The new evidence is fragmentary, contradictory, and controversial. Critical research remains to be done, and many studies are still unpublished. At the least, the new evidence calls into question the standard Beringian Walk theory, which holds that the first human beings to reach the New World were Asians of Mongoloid stock, who crossed from Siberia to Alaska over a land bridge. The new evidence involves three basic questions. Who were the original Americans? Where did they come from? And what happened to them?

"You're dealing with such a black hole," Owsley told me. "It's hard to draw any firm conclusions from such a small sample of skeletons, and there is more than one group represented. That's why Kennewick is so important."

KENNEWICK MAN made his appearance at the dawn of a new age in physical anthropology. Scientists are now able to extract traces of organic material from a person's bone and perform a succession of powerful biochemical assays which can reveal an astonishing amount of information about the person. In March, for example, scientists at Oxford University announced that they had compared DNA extracted from the molar cavity of a nine-thousand-year-old skeleton known as Cheddar Man to DNA collected from fifteen pupils and five adults from old families in the village of Cheddar, in Somersetshire. They had established a blood tie between Cheddar Man and a schoolteacher who lived just half a mile from the cave where the bones were found.

In the few weeks that Kennewick Man was in the hands of scientists, they discovered a great deal about him. Isotopic-carbon studies of the bones indicate that he had a diet high in marine food—that he may have been a fisherman who ate a lot of salmon. He seems to have been a tall, good-looking man, slender and well proportioned. (Studies have shown that "handsomeness" is largely the result of symmetrical features and good health, both of which Kennewick Man had.) Archeological finds of similar age in the area suggest that he was part of a small band of people who moved about, hunting, fishing, and gathering wild plants. He may have lived in a simple sewn tent or mat hut that could be disassembled and carried. Some nearby sites contain large numbers of fine bone needles, indicating that a lot of delicate sewing was going on: Kennewick Man may have worn tailored clothing. For a person at that time to live so long in relatively good health indicates that he was

clever or lucky, or both, or had family and close friends around him.

He appears to have perished from recurring infections caused by the stone point in his hip. Because of the way his bones were found, and the layer of soil from which they presumably emerged, it may be that he was not deliberately buried but died near the river and was swept away and covered up in a flood. He may have perished alone on a fishing trip, far from his family.

Chatters made a cast of the skull before the skeleton was taken from his office. In the months since, he has been examining it to figure out how Kennewick Man may have looked. He plans to work with physical anthropologists and a forensic sculptor to make a facial reconstruction. "On the physical characteristics alone, he could fit on the streets of Stockholm without causing any kind of notice," Chatters told me. "Or on the streets of Jerusalem or New Delhi, for that matter. I've been looking around for someone who matches this Kennewick gentleman, looking for weeks and weeks at people on the street, thinking, This one's got a little bit here, that one a little bit there. And then, one evening, I turned on the TV, and there was Patrick Stewart"—Captain Picard, of "Star Trek"—"and I said, 'My God, there he is! Kennewick Man!'"

IN September, following the requirements of NAGPRA, the Corps advertised in a local paper its intention of repatriating the skeleton secreted in the laboratory vault. The law mandated a thirty-day waiting period after the advertisements before the Corps could give a skeleton to a tribe.

Physical anthropologists and archeologists around the country were horrified by the seizure of the skeleton. They protested that it was not possible to demonstrate a relationship between nine-thousand-year-old remains and any modern tribe of the area. "Those tribes are relatively new," says Dennis Stanford, the chairman of the Department of Anthropology at the Smithsonian's National Museum of Natural History. "They pushed out other tribes that were there." Both Owsley and Richard L.

Jantz, a biological anthropologist at the University of Tennessee, wrote letters to the Army Corps of Engineers in late September saying that the loss to science would be incalculable if Kennewick Man were to be reburied before being studied. They received no response. Robson Bonnichsen, the director of the Center for the Study of the First Americans, at Oregon State University, also wrote to the Corps and received no reply. Three representatives and a United States senator from the state of Washington got in touch with the Corps, pleading that it allow the skeleton to be studied before reburial, or, at least, refrain from repatriating the skeleton until Congress could take up the issue. The Corps rebuffed them.

The Umatillas themselves issued a statement, which was written by Armand Minthorn, a tribal religious leader. Minthorn, a small, well-spoken young man with long braids, is a member of a new generation of Native American activists, who see religious fundamentalism—in this case, the Washat religion—as a road back to Native American traditions and values:

> Our elders have taught us that once a body goes into the ground, it is meant to stay there until the end of time.... If this individual is truly over 9,000 years old, that only substantiates our belief that he is Native American. From our oral histories, we know that our people have been part of this land since the beginning of time. We do not believe that our people migrated here from another continent, as the scientists do.... Scientists believe that because the individual's head measurement does not match ours, he is not Native American. Our elders have told us that Indian people did not always look the way we look today. Some scientists say that if this individual is not studied further, we, as Indians, will be destroying evidence of our history. We already know our history. It is passed on to us through our elders and through our religious practices.

Despite the mounting protests, the Corps refused to reconsider its decision to ban scientific study of the Kennewick skeleton. As the thirty-day waiting period came to a close, anthropologists around the country panicked. Just a week before it ended, on October 23rd, a group of eight anthropologists filed suit against the Corps. The plaintiffs included Douglas Owsley, Robson Bonnichsen, and also Dennis Stanford. Stanford, one of the country's top Paleo-Indian experts, is a formidable opponent. While attending graduate school in New Mexico, he roped in local rodeos, and helped support his family by leasing an alfalfa farm. There's still a kind of laconic, frontier toughness about him. "Kennewick Man has the potential to change the way we view the entire peopling of the Americas," he said to me. "We had to act. Otherwise, I might as well retire."

The eight are pursuing the suit as individuals. Their academic institutions are reluctant to get involved in a lawsuit as controversial as this, particularly at a time when most of them are negotiating with tribes over their own collections.

In the suit, the scientists have argued that Kennewick Man may not meet the NAGPRA definition of "Native American" as being "of, or relating to, a tribe, people, or culture that is indigenous to the United States." The judge trying the case has asked both sides to be prepared to define the word "indigenous" as it is used in NAGPRA. This will be an interesting exercise, since no human beings are indigenous to the New World: we are all immigrants.

The scientists have also argued that the Corps had had no evidence to support its claim that the skeleton had a connection to the Umatillas. Alan Schneider, the scientists' attorney, says, "Our analysis of NAGPRA is that first you have to make a determination if the human remains are Native American. And then you get to the question of cultural affiliation. The Army Corps assumed that anyone who died in the continental United States prior to a certain date is automatically Native American."

The NAGPRA law appears to support the scientists' point of view. It says that when there are no known lineal descendants "cultural affiliation" should be determined using "geographical, kinship, biological, archeological, anthropologi-

cal, linguistic, folkloric, oral traditional, historical," or other "relevant information or expert opinion" before human remains are repatriated. In other words, human remains must often be studied before anyone can say whom they are related to.

The Corps, represented by the Justice Department, has refused to comment on most aspects of the case. "It's really as if the government didn't want to know the truth about Kennewick Man," Alan Schneider told me in late April. "It seems clear that the government will *never* allow this skeleton to be studied, for any reason, unless it is forced to by the courts."

Preliminary oral arguments in the case were heard on June 2nd in the United States District Court for the District of Oregon. The scientists asked for immediate access to study the bones, and the Corps asked for summary judgment. Judge John Jelderks denied both motions, and said that he would have a list of questions for the Corps that it is to answer within a reasonable time. With the likelihood of appeals, the case could last a couple of years longer, and could ultimately go to the Supreme Court.

Schneider was not surprised that the Corps had sided with the Indians. "It constantly has a variety of issues it has to negotiate with Native American tribes," he told me, and he specified, among others, land issues, water rights, dams, salmon fishing, hydroelectric projects, and toxic-waste dumps. The Corps apparently decided, Schneider speculated, that in this case its political interests would be better served by supporting the tribes than by supporting a disgruntled group of anthropologists with no institutional backing, no money, and no political power. There are large constituencies for the Indians' point of view: fundamentalist Christians and liberal supporters of Indian rights. Fundamentalists of all varieties tend to object to scientific research into the origins of humankind, because the results usually contradict their various creation myths. A novel coalition of conservative Christians and liberal activists was important in getting NAGPRA through Congress.

KENNEWICK MAN, early as he is, was not one of the first Americans. But he could be their descendant. There is evidence that those mysterious first Americans were a Caucasoid people. They may have come from Europe and may be connected to the Clovis people of America. Kennewick may provide evidence of a connection between the Old World and the New.

The Clovis mammoth hunters were the earliest widespread culture that we know of in the Americas. They appeared abruptly, seemingly out of nowhere, all over North and South America about eleven thousand five hundred years ago—two thousand years before Kennewick. (They were called Clovis after a town in New Mexico near an early site— a campground beside an ancient spring which is littered with projectile points, tools, and the remains of fires.) We have only a few fragments of human bone from the Clovis people and their immediate descendants, the Folsom, and these remains are so damaged that nothing can be learned from them at present.

The oldest bones that scientists have been able to study are the less than a dozen human remains that are contemporaneous with Kennewick. They date from between eight thousand and nearly eleven thousand years ago—the transition period between the Paleo-Indian and the Archaic Indian traditions. Most of the skeletons have been uncovered accidentally in recent years, primarily because of the building boom in the West. (Bones do not survive well in the East: the soil is too wet and acidic.) Some other ancient skeletons, though, have been discovered gathering dust in museum drawers. Among these oldest remains are the Spirit Cave mummy and Wizard's Beach Willie, both from Nevada; the Hourglass Cave and Gordon's Creek skeletons, from Colorado; the Buhl Burial, from Idaho; and remains from Texas, California, and Minnesota.

Douglas Owsley and Richard Jantz made a special study of several of these ancient remains. The best-preserved specimen they looked at was a partial mummy from Spirit Cave, Nevada, which is more than nine thousand years old. Owsley and Jantz compared the

Spirit Cave skull with thirty-four population samples from around the world, including ten Native American groups. In an as yet unpublished letter to the Nevada State Museum, they concluded that the Spirit Cave skull was "very different" from any historic-period Native American groups. They wrote, "In terms of its closest classification, it does have a 'European' or 'Archaic Caucasoid' look, because morphometrically it is most similar to the Ainu from Japan and a Medieval period Norse population." Additional early skeletons that they and others have looked at also show Caucasoid-like traits that, in varying degrees, resemble Kennewick Man's. Among these early skeletons, there are no close resemblances to modern Native Americans.

But, even though the skeletons do look Caucasoid, other evidence indicates that the concept of "race" may not be applicable to human beings of ten or fifteen thousand years ago. Recent studies have discovered that all Eurasians may have looked Caucasoid-like in varying degrees. In addition, some researchers believe that the Caucasoid type first emerged in Western Asia or the Middle East, rather than in Europe. The racial differences we see today may be a late (and trivial) development in human evolution. If this is the case, then Kennewick may indeed be a direct ancestor of today's Native Americans—an idea that some preliminary DNA and dental studies seem to support.

BIOLOGY, however, isn't the whole story. There is some archeological evidence that the Clovis people of America—Kennewick Man's predecessors—came from Europe, which could account for his Caucasoid features. When the Clovis people appeared in the New World, they possessed an advanced stone and bone technology, and employed it in hunting big game. (It is no small feat to kill a mammoth or a mastodon with a hand-held spear or an atlatl.) If the Clovis people—or their precursors—had migrated to North America from Asia, one would expect to find early forms of their distinctive tools, of

the right age, in Alaska or eastern Siberia. We don't. But we do find such artifacts in Europe and parts of Russia.

Bruce Bradley is the country's leading expert on Paleo-Indian flaked-stone technology. In 1970, as a recent college graduate, Bradley spent time in Europe studying paleolithic artifacts, including those of the Solutrean people, who lived in southwestern France and Spain between twenty thousand and sixteen thousand years ago. During his stay in Europe, Bradley learned how to flake out a decent Solutrean point. Then he came back to America and started studying stone tools made by the Clovis people. He noticed not only striking visual similarities between the Old World Solutrean and the New World Clovis artifacts, as many researchers had before, but also a strikingly similar use of flaking technology.

"The artifacts don't just look identical," Bradley told me. "They are *made* the same way." Both the European Solutrean and the American Clovis stone tools are fashioned using the same complex flaking techniques. He went on, "As far as I know, overshot flaking is unique to Solutrean and Clovis, and the only diving flaking that is more than eleven thousand years old is that of Solutrean and Clovis."

To argue his case, he drove from Cortez, Colorado, where he lives, to see me, in Santa Fe, bringing with him a trunkful of Solutrean artifacts, casts of Clovis bone and stone tools, and detailed illustrations of artifacts, along with a two-pound chunk of gray Texas flint and some flaking tools.

Silently, he laid a piece of felt on my desk and put on it a cast of a Clovis knife from Blackwater Draw, New Mexico. On top of that, he put a broken Solutrean knife from Laugerie-Haute, in France. They matched perfectly—in size, shape, thickness, and pattern of flaking. As we went through the collection, the similarities could be seen again and again. "It isn't just the flaking as you see it on the finished piece that is the same," Bradley explained. "Both cultures had a very specific way of preparing the edge before striking it to get a very specific type of flake. I call these deep technologies. These are not mere resemblances—they

are deep, complex, abstract concepts applied to the stone."

I remarked that according to other archeologists I had talked to the resemblances were coincidental, the result of two cultures—one Old World, the other New World—confronting the same problems and solving them in the same way. "Maybe," Bradley said. "But a lot of older archeologists were not trained with technology in mind. They see convergence of form or look, but they don't see the technology that goes into it. I'm not saying this is the final answer. But there is so much similarity that we cannot say, 'This is just coincidence,' and ignore it."

To show me what he meant, he brought out the piece of gray flint, and we went into the back yard. "This isn't just knocking away at a stone," he said, hefting the piece of flint and examining it from various angles with narrowed eyes. "After the initial flaking of a spear point, there comes a stage where you have almost limitless choices on how to continue." He squatted down and began to work on the flint with hammer stones and antler billets, his hands deftly turning and shaping the material—knapping, chipping, scraping, pressing, flaking. The pile of razor-sharp flakes grew bigger, and the chunk of flint began to take on a definite shape. Over the next ninety minutes, Bradley reduced the nodule to a five-inch-long Clovis spear point.

It was a revelation to see that making a Clovis point was primarily an intellectual process. Sometimes ten minutes would pass while Bradley examined the stone and mapped out the next flaking sequence. "After thirty years of intense practice, I'm still at the level of a mediocre Clovis craftsman," he said, wiping his bloodied hands and reviving himself with a cup of cocoa. "This is as difficult and complex as a game of chess."

Those are not the only similarities between the Old World Solutrean and the New World Clovis cultures. As we went through Bradley's casts of Clovis artifacts, he compared them with pictures of similar Solutrean artifacts. The Clovis people, for example, produced enigmatic bone rods that were bevelled on both ends and crosshatched; so did the Solutrean. The Clovis people fashioned distinctive spear points out of mammoth ivory; so did the Solutrean. Clovis and Solutrean shaft wrenches (tools thought to have been used for straightening spears) look almost identical. At the same time, there are significant differences between the Clovis and the Solutrean tool kits; the Clovis people fluted their spear points, for instance, while the Solutrean did not.

"To get to the kind of complexity you find in Clovis tools, I see a long technological development," Bradley said. "It isn't one person in one place inventing something. But there is no evolution in Clovis technology. It just appears, full blown, all over the New World, around eleven thousand five hundred years ago. Where's the evolution? *Where did that advanced Clovis technology come from?*"

When I mentioned the idea of a possible Old World Solutrean origin for the New World Clovis to Lawrence Straus, a Solutrean expert at the University of New Mexico, he said, "There are two gigantic problems with it—thousands of years of separation and thousands of miles of ocean." Pointing out that the Solutrean technology itself appeared relatively abruptly in the South of France, he added, "I think this is a fairly clear case of mankind's ability to reinvent things."

But Bradley and other archeologists have pointed out that these objections may not be quite so insurmountable. Recently, in southern Virginia, archeologists discovered a layer of non-Clovis artifacts beneath a Clovis site. The layer dates from fifteen thousand years ago—much closer to the late Solutrean period, sixteen thousand five hundred years ago. Only a few rough tools have been found, but if more emerge they might provide evidence for the independent development of Clovis—or provide a link to the Solutrean. The as yet unnamed culture may be precisely the precursor to Clovis which archeologists have been looking for since the nineteen-thirties. The gap between Solutrean and Clovis may be narrowing.

The other problem is how the Solutrean people—if they are indeed the ancestors of the Clovis—might have reached America in the first place. Although most of them lived along river-

banks and on the seacoast of France and Spain, there is no evidence that they had boats. No Paleo-Indian boats have been found on the American side, either, but there is circumstantial evidence that the Paleo-Indians used boats. The ancestors of the Australian aborigines got to Australia in boats from the Indonesian archipelago at least fifty thousand years ago.

But the Solutrean people may not have needed boats at all: sixteen thousand years ago, the North Atlantic was frozen from Norway to Newfoundland. Seasonal pack ice probably extended as far south as Britain and Nova Scotia. William Fitzhugh, the director of the Arctic Studies Center, at the Smithsonian, points out that if human beings had started in France, crossed the English Channel, then hopped along the archipelago from Scotland to the Faeroes to Iceland to Greenland to Newfoundland, and, finally, Nova Scotia, the biggest distance between landfalls would have been about five hundred miles, which Fitzhugh says could have been done on foot over ice. It would still have been a stupendous journey, but perhaps not much more difficult than the Beringian Walk, across thousands of miles of tundra, muskeg, snow, and ice.

"For a long time, most archeologists have been afraid to challenge the Beringian Walk paradigm," Bradley said. "I don't want to try to convince anybody. But I do want to shake the bushes. You could put all the archeological evidence for the Asian-Clovis connection in an envelope and mail it for thirty-two cents. The evidence for a European-Clovis connection you'd have to send in a U.P.S. box, at least."

Robson Bonnichsen, the director of the Center for the Study of the First Americans, at Oregon State University, is another archeologist whose research is challenging the established theories. "There is a presumption, written into almost every textbook on prehistory, that Paleo-Americans such as Clovis are the direct ancestors of today's Native Americans," he told me. "But now we have a very limited number of skeletons from that early time, and it's not clear that that's true. We're getting some hints from people working with genetic data that these earliest populations might

have some shared genetic characteristics with latter-day European populations. A lot more research is needed to sort all this out. Now, for the first time, we have the technology to do this research, especially in molecular biology. Which is why we *must* study Kennewick."

This summer, Bonnichsen hopes to go to France and recover human hair from Solutrean and other Upper Paleolithic sites. He will compare DNA from that hair with DNA taken from naturally shed Paleo-American hair recovered from the United States to see if there is a genetic link. Human hair can survive thousands of years in the ground, and, using new techniques, Bonnichsen and his research team have been finding hair in the places where people worked and camped.

BONNICHSEN and most other archeologists tend to favor the view that if the ancestors of Clovis once lived in Europe they came to America via Asia—the Beringian Walk theory with somewhat different people doing the walking. C. Vance Haynes, Jr., the country's top Paleo-Indian geochronologist, who is a professor of anthropology at the University of Arizona, and is a plaintiff in the lawsuit, said to me, "When I look at Clovis and ask myself where in the world the culture was derived from, I would say Europe." In an article on the origins of Clovis, Haynes noted that there were extraordinary resemblances between New World Clovis and groups that lived in Czechoslovakia and Ukraine twenty thousand years ago. He noted at least nine "common traits" shared by Clovis and certain Eastern European cultures: large blades, end scrapers, burins, shaft wrenches, cylindrical bone points, knapped bone, unifacial flake tools, red ochre, and circumferentially chopped mammoth tusks. He also pointed out that an eighteen-thousand-year-old burial site of two children near Lake Baikal, in Central Asia, exhibits remarkable similarities to what appears to be a Clovis burial site of two cremated children in Montana. The similarities extend beyond tools and points buried with the remains: red ochre, a kind of iron oxide, was placed in both graves. This suggests a migratory group carrying its technology from Europe across Asia. "If you want to speculate, I see a band moving eastward from Europe through Siberia, and meeting people there, and having cultural differences," Haynes said to me. "Any time there's conflict, it drives people, and maybe it just drove them right across the Bering land bridge. And exploration could have been as powerful a driving force thirteen thousand years ago as it was in 1492."

ONCE the Clovis people or their predecessors reached the New World, what happened to them? This is the second—and equally controversial—half of the theory: that the Clovis people or their immediate successors, the Folsom people, may have been supplanted by the ancestors of today's Native Americans. In this scenario, Kennewick Man may have been part of a remnant Caucasoid population related to Clovis and Folsom. Dennis Stanford, of the Smithsonian, said to me, "For a long time, I've held the theory that the Clovis and the Folsom were overwhelmed by a migration of Asians over the Bering land bridge. It may not just have been a genetic swamping or a pushing aside. The north Asians may have been carrying diseases that the Folsom and the Clovis had no resistance to"—just as European diseases wiped out a large percentage of the Native American population after the arrival of Columbus. Stanford explained that at several sites the Paleo-Indian tradition of Clovis and Folsom was abruptly replaced by Archaic Indian traditions, which had advanced but very different lithic technologies. The abruptness of the transition and the sharp change in technology, Stanford feels, suggest a rapid replacement of Folsom by the Archaic cultural complex, rather than an evolution from one into the other. The Archaic spear point embedded in Kennewick Man's hip could even be evidence of an ancient conflict: the Archaic Indian tradition was just beginning to appear in the Pacific Northwest at the time of Kennewick Man's death.

OWSLEY and other physical anthropologists who have studied the skulls of

the earliest Americans say that the living population they most closely match is the mysterious Ainu, the aboriginal inhabitants of the Japanese islands. Called the Hairy People by the Japanese, the Ainu are considered by some researchers to be a Causasoid group who, before mixing with the Japanese, in the late nineteenth and twentieth centuries, had European faces, wavy hair, thick beards, and a European-type distribution of body hair. Early travellers reported that some also had blue eyes. Linguists have not been able to connect the Ainu language with any other on earth. The American Museum of Natural History, in New York, has a collection of nineteenth-century photographs of pure-blood Ainu, which I have examined: they stare from the glass plates like fierce, black-bearded Norwegians.

Historically, the Ainu have been the "Indians" of Japan. After the ancestors of the Japanese migrated from the mainland a couple of thousand years ago, they fought the Ainu and pushed them into the northernmost islands of the Japanese archipelago. The Japanese later discriminated against the Ainu, forcing their children to attend Japanese schools, and suppressing their religion and their language. Today, most Ainu have lost their language and many of their distinct physical characteristics, although there has recently been a movement among them to recapture their traditions, their religion, their language, and their songs. Like the American Indians, the Ainu suffer high rates of alcoholism. The final irony is that the Ainu, like the American Indians for Americans, have become a popular Japanese tourist attraction. Many Ainu now make a living doing traditional dances and selling handicrafts to Japanese tourists. The Japanese are as fascinated by the Ainu as we are by the Indians. The stories are mirror images of each other, with only the races changed.

If the Ainu are a remnant population of those people who crossed into America thirteen or more millennia ago, then they are right where one might expect to find them, in the extreme eastern part of Asia. Stanford says, "That racial type goes all the way to Europe, and I suspect that originally they were the same racial group at both ends. At that point in time,

this racial diversification hadn't developed. They could have come into the New World from two directions at once, east and west."

THERE is a suspicion among anthropologists that some of the people behind the effort to rebury Kennewick and other ancient skeletons are afraid that the bones could show that the earliest Americans were Caucasoid. I asked Armand Minthorn about this. "We're not afraid of the truth," he said calmly. "We already know our truth. We're not telling the scientists what *their* truth is".

The Umatillas were infuriated by the research that Chatters did on the skeleton before it was seized by the Corps. "Scientists have dug up and studied Native Americans for decades," Minthorn wrote. "We view this practice as desecration of the body and a violation of our most deeply-held religious beliefs." Chatters told me that he had received "vitriolic" and "abusive" telephone calls from tribe members, accusing him of illegalities and racism. (The latter was an odd charge, since Chatters's wife is of Native American descent.) A client of his, he said, received an unsigned letter from one of the tribes, telling the client not to work with Chatters anymore. "They're going to ruin my livelihood," the forensic consultant said.

In a larger sense, the anger of the Umatillas and other Native American tribes is understandable, and even justified. If you look into the acquisition records of most large, old natural-history museums, you will see a history of unethical, and even grisly, collecting practices. Fresh graves were dug up and looted, sometimes in the dead of night. "It is most unpleasant to steal bones from a grave," the eminent anthropologist Franz Boas wrote in his diary just around the turn of the century, "but what is the use, someone has to do it." Indian skulls were bought and sold among collectors like arrowheads and pots. Skeletons were exhibited with no regard for tribal sensitivities. During the Indian wars, warriors who had been killed on the battlefield were sometimes decapitated by Army doctors so that scientists back in the East could study their heads. The

ANTHROPOLOGY

Anthropologists 1, Army Corps 0

American anthropologists won a round in an important legal battle last week, when a U.S. District Court in Portland, Oregon, ordered the Army Corps of Engineers to reopen the case of 9300-year-old human skeleton found on federal land in Washington state. The corps, which has jurisdiction over the skeleton—one of the oldest in the Americas—had planned to turn it over to American Indian tribes for reburial last October under the 1990 Native American Graves Protection and Repatriation Act (NAGPRA). But scientists sued to prevent the handover until they had studied the bones.

Now, although the court stopped short of allowing study of the skeleton, it opened the door for future research by recognizing that the scientists have a legitimate claim that must be considered. "It's a landmark ruling," exulted Alan Schneider, the Portland attorney for the scientists. "This is the first case where a court has held that a third party like a scientist has standing to challenge a government agency's overenforcement of NAGPRA."

The male skeleton, known as "Kennewick Man" for the town where it was discovered in the bank of the Columbia River last summer, is a rare representative of the earliest people to inhabit the Americas. It also had a projectile point embedded in its pelvis and facial features that may be Caucasoid-like, offering clues about early Americans (*Science,* 11 October 1996, p. 172).

As soon as the skeleton was discovered, Smithsonian Institution skeletal biologist Douglas Owsley sought permission to study it, and a team at the University of California, Davis, extracted ancient DNA from a bit of its finger bone for analysis. Owsley and others say that without scientific study it's impossible to know whether the skeleton has a biological or cultural tie to any living people—knowledge needed to determine which tribe, if any, should receive it.

But Owsley says he was told by the corps "flat-out that there would be no scientific study." The corps ordered a halt to the DNA work as soon as it learned of it in October, and announced that it would hand over the skeleton to the Confederated Tribes of the Umatilla Indian Reservation under the auspices of NAGPRA, which requires remains or cultural objects to be given to a culturally affiliated tribe. It later rescinded that order but has kept the skeleton locked away and unavailable for study. Court documents suggest that corps officials were concerned about alienating the Indians. In an 18 September 1996 e-mail message, a corps official wrote: "All risk to us seems to be associated with not repatriating the remains."

In the new decision, U.S. District Court Magistrate John Jelderks invalidated all the corps' orders in the case and criticized the "flawed" procedures used by the agency, which he said "acted before it had all the evidence or fully appreciated the scope of the problem." Jelderks also asked the corps to report back to him with its decision on the case and to answer several questions, including whether repatriation under NAGPRA required a biological or cultural link between bones and living tribes, and how such a link would be determined.

Corps attorney Daria Zane declined to comment for the record. As for the scientists, although they still can't study the skeleton, they're pleased. "Hopefully, the Army Corps will come to its senses," says Owsley. "They are using government lawyers and taxpayers' dollars to argue against academic freedom."

—**Ann Gibbons**

From *Science,* Vol. 277, July 11, 1997, p. 173. © 1997 by The American Association for the Advancement of Science. Reprinted by permission

American Museum of Natural History "collected" six live Inuits in Greenland and brought them to New York to study; four of them died of respiratory diseases, whereupon the museum macerated their corpses and installed the bones in its collection. When I worked at the museum, in the nineteen-eighties, entire hallways were lined with glass cases containing Indian bones and mummified body parts—a small fraction of the museum's collection, which includes an estimated twenty thousand or more human remains, of all races. Before NAGPRA, the Smithsonian had some thirty-five thousand sets of human remains in storage; around eighteen thousand of them were Native American.

Now angry Native Americans, armed with NAGPRA and various state reburial laws, are emptying such museums of bones and grave goods. Although most anthropologists agree that burials identified with particular tribes should be returned, many have been horrified to discover that some tribes are trying to get everything—even skeletons and priceless funerary objects that are thousands of years old.

An amendment that was introduced in Congress last January would tighten NAGPRA further. The amended law could have the effect of hindering much archeology in the United States involving human remains, and add to the cost of construction projects that inadvertently uncover human bones. (Or perhaps the law would merely guarantee that such remains would be quietly destroyed.)

Native Americans have already claimed and reburied two of the earliest skeletons, the Buhl Burial and the Hourglass Cave skeleton, both of which apparently had some Caucasoid characteristics. The loss of the Buhl Burial was particularly significant to anthropologists, because it was more than ten thousand years old—a thousand years older than Kennewick Man—and had been found buried with its grave goods. The skeleton, of a woman between eighteen and twenty years old, received, in the opinion of some anthropologists, inadequate study before it was turned over to the Shoshone-Bannock tribe. The Northern Paiute have asked that the Spirit Cave mummy be reburied. If these early skeletons are all put back in the ground, anthropologists say, much of the history of the peopling of the Americas will be lost.

WHEN Darwin proposed his theory of natural selection, it was seized upon and distorted by economists, social engineers, and politicians, particularly in England: they used it to justify all sorts of vicious social and economic policies. The scientific argument about the original peopling of the Americas threatens to be distorted in a similar way. Some tabloids and radio talk shows have referred to Kennewick as a "white man" and have suggested that his discovery changes everything with respect to the rights of Native Americans in this country. James Chatters said to me, "There are some less racially enlightened folks in the neighborhood who are saying, 'Hey, our ancestors were here first, so we don't owe the Indians anything.'"

This is clearly racist nonsense: these new theories cannot erase or negate the existing history of genocide, broken treaties, and repression. But it does raise an interesting question: If the original inhabitants of the New World were Europeans who were pushed out by Indians, would it change the Indians' position in the great moral landscape?

"No," Stanford said in reply to this question. "Whose ancestors are the people who were pushed out? And who did the pushing? The answer is that we're all the descendants of those folks. If you go back far enough, eventually we all have a common ancestor—*we're all the same.* When the story is finally written, the peopling of the Americas will turn out to be far more complicated than anyone imagined. There have been a lot of people who came here, at many different times. Some stayed and some left, some made it and some didn't, some got pushed out and some did the pushing. It's the history of humankind: the tough guy gets the ground."

Chatters put it another way. "We didn't go digging for this man. He fell out—he was actually a volunteer. I think it would be wrong to stick him back in the ground without waiting to hear the story he has to tell. We need to look at things as human beings, not as one race or another. The message this man brings to us is one of unification: there may be some commonality in our past that will bring us together."

Skin Deep

Throughout the world, human skin color has evolved to be dark enough to
prevent sunlight from destroying the nutrient folate but light enough
to foster the production of vitamin D

By Nina G. Jablonski and George Chaplin

Among primates, only humans have

a mostly naked skin that comes in different colors. Geographers and anthropologists have long recognized that the distribution of skin colors among indigenous populations is not random: darker peoples tend to be found nearer the equator, lighter ones closer to the poles. For years, the prevailing theory has been that darker skins evolved to protect against skin cancer. But a series of discoveries has led us to construct a new framework for understanding the evolutionary basis of variations in human skin color. Recent epidemiological and physiological evidence suggests to us that the worldwide pattern of human skin color is the product of natural selection acting to regulate the effects of the sun's ultraviolet (UV) radiation on key nutrients crucial to reproductive success.

From Hirsute to Hairless

THE EVOLUTION OF SKIN PIGMENTATION is linked with that of hairlessness, and to comprehend both these stories, we need to page back in human history. Human beings have been evolving as an independent lineage of apes since at least seven million years ago, when our immediate ancestors diverged from those of our closest relatives, chimpanzees. Because chimpanzees have changed less over time than humans have, they can provide an idea of what human anatomy and physiology must have been like. Chimpanzees' skin is light in color and is covered by hair over most of their bodies. Young animals have pink faces, hands, and feet and become freckled or dark in these areas only as they are exposed to sun with age. The earliest humans almost certainly had a light skin covered with hair. Presumably hair loss occurred first, then skin color changed. But that leads to the question, When did we lose our hair?

The skeletons of ancient humans—such as the well-known skeleton of Lucy, which dates to about 3.2 million years ago—give us a good idea of the build and the way of life of our ancestors. The daily activities of Lucy and other hominids that lived before about three million years ago appear to have been similar to those of primates living on the open savannas of Africa today. They probably spent much of their day foraging for food over three to four miles before retiring to the safety of trees to sleep.

By 1.6 million years ago, however, we see evidence that this pattern had begun to change dramatically. The famous skeleton of Turkana Boy—which belonged to the species *Homo ergaster*—is that of a long-legged, striding biped that probably walked long distances. These more active early humans faced the problem of staying cool and protecting their brains from overheating. Peter Wheeler of John Moores University in Liverpool, England, has shown that this was accomplished through an increase in the number of sweat glands on the surface of the body and a reduction in the covering of body hair. Once rid of most of their hair, early members of the genus *Homo* then encountered the challenge of protecting their skin from the damaging effects of sunlight, especially UV rays.

Built-in Sunscreen

IN CHIMPANZEES, the skin on the hairless parts of the body contains cells called melanocytes that are capable of synthesizing the dark-brown pigment melanin in response to exposure to UV radiation. When humans became mostly hairless, the ability of the skin to produce melanin assumed new importance. Melanin is nature's sunscreen: it is a large organic molecule that Overview/ Skin Color Evolution serves the dual purpose of physically and chemically filtering the harmful effects of UV radiation; it absorbs UV rays, causing them to lose energy, and it neutralizes harmful chemicals called free radicals that form in the skin after damage by UV radiation.

Overview/Skin Color Evolution

- After losing their hair as an adaptation for keeping cool, early hominids gained pigmented skins. Scientists initially thought that such pigmentation arose to protect against skin-cancer-causing ultraviolet [UV] radiation.
- Skin cancers tend to arise after reproductive age, however. An alternative theory suggests that dark skin might have evolved primarily to protect against the breakdown of folate, a nutrient essential for fertility and for fetal development.
- Skin that is too dark blocks the sunlight necessary for catalyzing the production of vitamin D, which is crucial for maternal and fetal bones. Accordingly, humans have evolved to be light enough to make sufficient vitamin B yet dark enough to protect their stores of folate.
- As a result of recent human migrations, many people now live in areas that receive more [or less] UV radiation than is appropriate for their skin color.

Anthropologists and biologists have generally reasoned that high concentrations of melanin arose in the skin of peoples in tropical areas because it protected them against skin cancer. James E. Cleaver of the University of California at San Francisco, for instance, has shown that people with the disease xeroderma pigmentosum, in which melanocytes are destroyed by exposure to the sun, suffer from significantly higher than normal rates of squamous and basal cell carcinomas, which are usually easily treated. Malignant melanomas are more frequently fatal, but they are rare (representing 4 percent of skin cancer diagnoses) and tend to strike only light-skinned people. But all skin cancers typically arise later in life, in most cases after the first reproductive years, so they could not have exerted enough evolutionary pressure for skin protection alone to account for darker skin colors. Accordingly, we began to ask what role melanin might play in human evolution.

The Folate Connection

IN 1991 ONE OF US (Jablonski) ran across what turned out to be a critical paper published in 1978 by Richard F. Branda and John W. Eaton, now at the University of Vermont and the University of Louisville, respectively. These investigators showed that light-skinned people who had been exposed to simulated strong sunlight had abnormally low levels of the essential B vitamin folate in their blood. The scientists also observed that subjecting human blood serum to the same conditions resulted in a 50-percent loss of folate content within one hour.

The significance of these findings to reproduction—and hence evolution—became clear when we learned of

research being conducted on a major class of birth defects by our colleagues at the University of Western Australia. There Fiona J. Stanley and Carol Bower had established by the late 1980s that folate deficiency in pregnant women is related to an increased risk of neural tube defects such as spina bifida, in which the arches of the spinal vertebrae fail to close around the spinal cord. Many research groups throughout the world have since confirmed this correlation, and efforts to supplement foods with folate and to educate women about the importance of the nutrient have become widespread.

We discovered soon afterward that folate is important not only in preventing neural tube defects but also in a host of other processes. Because folate is essential for the synthesis of DNA in dividing cells, anything that involves rapid cell proliferation, such as spermatogenesis (the production of sperm cells), requires folate. Male rats and mice with chemically induced folate deficiency have impaired spermatogenesis and are infertile. Although no comparable studies of humans have been conducted, Wai Yee Wong and his colleagues at the University Medical Center of Nijmegen in the Netherlands have recently reported that folic acid treatment can boost the sperm counts of men with fertility problems.

Such observations led us to hypothesize that dark skin evolved to protect the body's folate stores from destruction. Our idea was supported by a report published in 1996 by Argentine pediatrician Pablo Lapunzina, who found that three young and otherwise healthy women whom he had attended gave birth to infants with neural tube defects after using sun beds to tan themselves in the early weeks of pregnancy. Our evidence about the breakdown of folate by UV radiation thus supplements what is already known about the harmful (skin-cancer-causing) effects of UV radiation on DNA.

Human Skin on the Move

THE EARLIEST MEMBERS of *Homo sapiens*, or modern humans, evolved in Africa between 120,000 and 100,000 years ago and had darkly pigmented skin adapted to the conditions of UV radiation and heat that existed near the equator. As modern humans began to venture out of the tropics, however, they encountered environments in which they received significantly less UV radiation during the year. Under these conditions their high concentrations of natural sunscreen probably proved detrimental. Dark skin contains so much melanin that very little UV radiation, and specifically very little of the shorter-wavelength UVB radiation, can penetrate the skin. Although most of the effects of UVB are harmful, the rays perform one indispensable function: initiating the formation of vitamin D in the skin. Dark-skinned people living in the tropics generally receive sufficient UV radiation during the year for UVB to penetrate the skin and allow them to make vitamin D. Outside the tropics this is not the case.

The solution, across evolutionary time, has been for migrants to northern latitudes to lose skin pigmentation.

The connection between the evolution of lightly pigmented skin and vitamin D synthesis was elaborated by W. Farnsworth Loomis of Brandeis University in 1967. He established the importance of vitamin D to reproductive success because of its role in enabling calcium absorption by the intestines, which in turn makes possible the normal development of the skeleton and the maintenance of a healthy immune system. Research led by Michael Holick of the Boston University School of Medicine has, over the past 20 years, further cemented the significance of vitamin D in development and immunity. His team also showed that not all sunlight contains enough UVB to stimulate vitamin D production. In Boston, for instance, which is located at about 42 degrees north latitude, human skin cells begin to produce vitamin D only after mid-March. In the wintertime there isn't enough UVB to do the job. We realized that this was another piece of evidence essential to the skin color story.

During the course of our research in the early 1990s, we searched in vain to find sources of data on actual UV radiation levels at the earth's surface. We were rewarded in 1996, when we contacted Elizabeth Weatherhead of the Cooperative Institute for Research in Environmental Sciences at the University of Colorado at Boulder. She shared with us a database of measurements of UV radiation at the earth's surface taken by NASA's Total Ozone Mapping Spectrophotometer satellite between 1978 and 1993. We were then able to model the distribution of UV radiation on the earth and relate the satellite data to the amount of UVB necessary to produce vitamin D.

We found that the earth's surface could be divided into three vitamin D zones: one comprising the tropics, one the subtropics and temperate regions, and the last the circumpolar regions north and south of about 45 degrees latitude. In the first, the dosage of UVB throughout the year is high enough that humans have ample opportunity to synthesize vitamin D all year. In the second, at least one month during the year has insufficient UVB radiation, and in the third area not enough UVB arrives on average during the entire year to prompt vitamin D synthesis. This distribution could explain why indigenous peoples in the tropics generally have dark skin, whereas people in the subtropics and temperate regions are lighter-skinned but have the ability to tan, and those who live in regions near the poles tend to be very light skinned and burn easily.

One of the most interesting aspects of this investigation was the examination of groups that did not precisely fit the predicted skin-color pattern. An example is the Inuit people of Alaska and northern Canada. The Inuit exhibit skin color that is somewhat darker than would be predicted given the UV levels at their latitude. This is probably caused by two factors. The first is that they are relatively recent inhabitants of these climes, having migrated to North America only roughly 5,000 years ago.

The second is that the traditional diet of the Inuit is extremely high in foods containing vitamin D, especially fish and marine mammals. This vitamin D-rich diet offsets the problem that they would otherwise have with vitamin D synthesis in their skin at northern latitudes and permits them to remain more darkly pigmented.

Our analysis of the potential to synthesize vitamin D allowed us to understand another trait related to human skin color: women in all populations are generally lighter-skinned than men. (Our data show that women tend to be between 3 and 4 percent lighter than men.) Scientists have often speculated on the reasons, and most have argued that the phenomenon stems from sexual selection—the preference of men for women of lighter color. We contend that although this is probably part of the story, it is not the original reason for the sexual difference. Females have significantly greater needs for calcium throughout their reproductive lives, especially during pregnancy and lactation, and must be able to make the most of the calcium contained in food. We propose, therefore, that women tend to be lighter-skinned than men to allow slightly more UVB rays to penetrate their skin and thereby increase their ability to produce vitamin D. In areas of the world that receive a large amount of UV radiation, women are indeed at the knife's edge of natural selection, needing to maximize the photoprotective function of their skin on the one hand and the ability to synthesize vitamin D on the other.

Where Culture and Biology Meet

AS MODERN HUMANS MOVED throughout the Old World about 100,000 years ago, their skin adapted to the environmental conditions that prevailed in different regions. The skin color of the indigenous people of Africa has had the longest time to adapt because anatomically modern humans first evolved there. The skin-color changes that modern humans underwent as they moved from one continent to another—first Asia, then Austro-Melanesia, then Europe and, finally, the Americas—can be reconstructed to some extent. It is important to remember, however, that those humans had clothing and shelter to help protect them from the elements. In some places, they also had the ability to harvest foods that were extraordinarily rich in vitamin D, as in the case of the Inuit. These two factors had profound effects on the tempo and degree of skin-color evolution in human populations.

Africa is an environmentally heterogeneous continent. A number of the earliest movements of contemporary humans outside equatorial Africa were into southern Africa. The descendants of some of these early colonizers, the Khoisan (previously known as Hottentots), are still found in southern Africa and have significantly lighter skin than indigenous equatorial Africans do—a clear adaptation to the lower levels of UV radiation that prevail at the southern extremity of the continent.

Interestingly, however, human skin color in southern Africa is not uniform. Populations of Bantu-language speakers who live in southern Africa today are far darker than the Khoisan. We know from the history of this region that Bantu speakers migrated into this region recently—probably within the past 1,000 years—from parts of West Africa near the equator. The skin-color difference between the Khoisan and Bantu speakers such as the Zulu indicates that the length of time that a group has inhabited a particular region is important in understanding why they have the color they do.

Cultural behaviors have probably also strongly influenced the evolution of skin color in recent human history. This effect can be seen in the indigenous peoples who live on the eastern and western banks of the Red Sea. The tribes on the western side, which speak so-called Nilo-Hamitic languages, are thought to have inhabited this region for as long as 6,000 years. These individuals are distinguished by very darkly pigmented skin and long, thin bodies with long limbs, which are excellent biological adaptations for dissipating heat and intense UV radiation. In contrast, modern agricultural and pastoral groups on the eastern bank of the Red Sea, on the Arabian Peninsula, have lived there for only about 2,000 years. These earliest Arab people, of European origin, have adapted to very similar environmental conditions by almost exclusively cultural means—wearing heavy protective clothing and devising portable shade in the form of tents. (Without such clothing, one would have expected their skin to have begun to darken.) Generally speaking, the more recently a group has migrated into an area, the more extensive its cultural, as opposed to biological, adaptations to the area will be.

Perils of Recent Migrations

DESPITE GREAT IMPROVEMENTS in overall human health in the past century, some diseases have appeared or reemerged in populations that had previously been little affected by them. One of these is skin cancer, especially basal and squamous cell carcinomas, among light-skinned peoples. Another is rickets, brought about by severe vitamin D deficiency, in dark-skinned peoples. Why are we seeing these conditions?

As people move from an area with one pattern of UV radiation to another region, biological and cultural adaptations have not been able to keep pace. The light-skinned people of northern European origin who bask in the sun of Florida or northern Australia increasingly pay the price in the form of premature aging of the skin and skin cancers, not to mention the unknown cost in human life of folate depletion. Conversely, a number of dark-skinned

MORE TO EXPLORE

The Evolution of Human Skin Coloration. Nina G. Jablonski and George Chaplin in *Journal of Human Evolution*, Vol. 39, No. 1, pages 57-106; July 1, 2000. An abstract of the article is available online at **www.idealibrary.com/links/doi/10.1006/jhev.2000.0403**

Why Skin Comes in Colors. Blake Edgar in *California Wild*, Vol. 53, No. 1, pages 6-7; Winter 2000. The article is also available at **www.calacademy.org/calwild/winter2000/html/horizons.html**

The Biology of Skin Color: Black and White. Gina Kirchweger in *Discover*, Vol. 22, No. 2, pages 32-33; February 2001. The article is also available at **www.discover.com/feb_01/featbiology.html**

people of southern Asian and African origin now living in the northern U.K., northern Europe or the northeastern U.S. suffer from a lack of UV radiation and vitamin D, an insidious problem that manifests itself in high rates of rickets and other diseases related to vitamin D deficiency.

The ability of skin color to adapt over long periods to the various environments to which humans have moved reflects the importance of skin color to our survival. But its unstable nature also makes it one of the least useful characteristics in determining the evolutionary relations between human groups. Early Western scientists used skin color improperly to delineate human races, but the beauty of science is that it can and does correct itself. Our current knowledge of the evolution of human skin indicates that variations in skin color, like most of our physical attributes, can be explained by adaptation to the environment through natural selection. We look ahead to the day when the vestiges of old scientific mistakes will be erased and replaced by a better understanding of human origins and diversity. Our variation in skin color should be celebrated as one of the most visible manifestations of our evolution as a species.

NINA G. JABLONSKI and *GEORGE CHAPLIN* work at the California Academy of Sciences in San Francisco, where Jablonski is Irvine Chair and curator of anthropology and Chaplin is a research associate in the department of anthropology. Jablonski's research centers on the evolutionary adaptations of monkeys, apes and humans. She is particularly interested in how primates have responded to changes over time in the global environment. Chaplin is a private geographic information systems consultant who specializes in describing and analyzing geographic trends in biodiversity. In 2001 he was awarded the Student of the Year prize by the Association of Geographic Information in London for his master's thesis on the environmental correlates of skin color.

Black, White, Other

Racial categories are cultural constructs masquerading as biology

Jonathan Marks

While reading the Sunday edition of the *New York Times* one morning last February, my attention was drawn by an editorial inconsistency. The article I was reading was written by attorney Lani Guinier. (Guinier, you may remember, had been President Clinton's nominee to head the civil rights division at the Department of Justice in 1993. Her name was hastily withdrawn amid a blast of criticism over her views on political representation of minorities.) What had distracted me from the main point of the story was a photo caption that described Guinier as being "half-black." In the text of the article, Guinier had described herself simply as "black."

How can a person be black and half black at the same time? In algebraic terms, this would seem to describe a situation where $x = 1/2\, x$, to which the only solution is $x = 0$.

The inconsistency in the *Times* was trivial, but revealing. It encapsulated a longstanding problem in our use of racial categories—namely, a confusion between biological and cultural heredity. When Guinier is described as "half-black," that is a statement of biological ancestry, for one of her two parents is black. And when Guinier describes herself as black, she is using a cultural category, according to which one can either be black or white, but not both.

Race—as the term is commonly used—is inherited, although not in a strictly biological fashion. It is passed down according to a system of folk heredity, an all-or-nothing system that is different from the quantifiable heredity of biology. But the incompatibility of the two notions of race is sometimes starkly evident—as when the state decides that racial differences are so important that interracial marriages must be regulated or outlawed entirely. Miscegenation laws in this country (which stayed on the books in many states through the 1960s) obliged the legal system to define who belonged in what category. The resulting formula stated that anyone with one-eighth or more black ancestry was a "negro." (A similar formula, defining Jews, was promulgated by the Germans in the Nuremberg Laws of the 1930s.)

Applying such formulas led to the biological absurdity that having one black great-grandparent was sufficient to define a person as black, but having seven white great grandparents was insufficient to define a person as white. Here, race and biology are demonstrably at odds. And the problem is not semantic but conceptual, for race is presented as a category of nature.

Human beings come in a wide variety of sizes, shapes, colors, and forms—or, because we are visually oriented primates, it certainly seems that way. We also come in larger packages called populations; and we are said to belong to even larger and more confusing units, which have long been known as races. The history of the study of human variation is to a large extent the pursuit of those human races—the attempt to identify the small number of fundamentally distinct kinds of people on earth.

This scientific goal stretches back two centuries, to Linnaeus, the father of biological systematics, who radically established *Homo sapiens* as one species within a group of animals he called Primates. Linnaeus's system of naming groups within groups logically implied further breakdown. He consequently sought to establish a number of subspecies within *Homo sapiens*. He identified five: four geographical species (from Europe, Asia, Africa, and America) and one grab-bag subspecies called *monstrosus*. This category was dropped by subsequent researchers (as was Linnaeus's use of criteria such as personality and dress to define his subspecies).

While Linnaeus was not the first to divide humans on the basis of the continents on which they lived, he had given the division a scientific stamp. But in attempting to determine the proper number of subspecies, the heirs of Linnaeus always seemed to find different answers, depending upon the criteria they applied. By the mid-twentieth century, scores of anthropologists—led by Harvard's Earnest Hooton—had expended enormous energy on the problem. But these scholars could not convince one another about the precise nature of the fundamental divisions of our species.

Part of the problem—as with the *Times*'s identification of Lani Guinier—was that we humans have two constantly intersecting ways of thinking about the divisions among us. On the one hand, we like to think of "race"—as Linnaeus did—as an objective, biological category. In this sense, being a member of a race is supposed to be the equivalent of being a member of a species or of a phylum—except that race, on the analogy of subspecies, is an even narrower (and presumably more exclusive and precise) biological category.

The other kind of category into which we humans allocate ourselves—when we say "Serb" or "Hutu" or "Jew" or "Chicano" or "Republican" or "Red Sox fan"—is cultural. The label refers to little or nothing in the natural attributes of its members. These members may not live in the same region and may not even know many others like themselves. What they share is neither strictly nature nor strictly community. The groupings are constructions of human social history.

Membership in these *un*biological groupings may mean the difference between life and death, for they are the categories that allow us to be identified (and accepted or vilified) socially. While membership in (or allegiance to) these categories may be assigned or adopted from birth, the differentia that mark members from nonmembers are symbolic and abstract; they serve to distinguish people who cannot be readily distinguished by nature. So important are these symbolic distinctions that some of the strongest animosities are often expressed between very similar-looking peoples. Obvious examples are Bosnian Serbs and Muslims, Irish and English, Huron and Iroquois.

Obvious natural variation is rarely so important as cultural difference. One simply does not hear of a slaughter of the short people at the hands of the tall, the glabrous at the hands of the hairy, the red-haired at the hands of the brown-haired. When we do encounter genocidal violence between different looking peoples, the two groups are invariably socially or culturally distinct as well. Indeed, the tragic frequency of hatred and genocidal violence between biologically indistinguishable peoples implies that biological differences such as skin color are not motivations but, rather, excuses. They allow nature to be invoked to reinforce group identities and antagonisms that would exist without these physical distinctions. But are there any truly "racial" biological distinctions to be found in our species?

Obviously, if you compare two people from different parts of the world (or whose ancestors came from different parts of the world), they will differ physically, but one cannot therefore define three or four or five basically different kinds of people, as a biological notion of race would imply. The anatomical properties that distinguish people—such as pigmentation, eye form, body build—are not clumped in discrete groups, but distributed along geographical gradients, as are nearly all the genetically determined variants detectable in the human gene pool.

These gradients are produced by three forces. Natural selection adapts populations to local circumstances (like climate) and thereby differentiates them from other populations. Genetic drift (random fluctuations in a gene pool) also differentiates populations from one another, but in non-adaptive ways. And gene flow (via intermarriage and other child-producing unions) acts to homogenize neighboring populations.

In practice, the operations of these forces are difficult to discern. A few features, such as body build and the graduated distribution of the sickle cell anemia gene in populations from western Africa, southern Asia, and the Mediterranean can be plausibly related to the effects of selection. Others, such as the graduated distribution of a small deletion in the mitochondrial DNA of some East Asian, Oceanic, and Native American peoples, or the degree of flatness of the face, seem unlikely to be the result of selection and are probably the results of random biohistorical factors. The cause of the distribution of most features, from nose breadth to blood group, is simply unclear.

The overall result of these forces is evident, however. As Johann Friedrich Blumenbach noted in 1775, "you see that all do so run into one another, and that one variety of mankind does so sensibly pass into the other, that you cannot mark out the limits between them." (Posturing as an heir to Linnaeus, he nonetheless attempted to do so.) But from humanity's gradations in appearance, no defined groupings resembling races readily emerge. The racial categories with which we have become so familiar are the result of our imposing arbitrary cultural boundaries in order to partition gradual biological variation.

Unlike graduated biological distinctions, culturally constructed categories are ultrasharp. One can be French or German, but not both; Tutsi or Hutu, but not both; Jew or Catholic, but not both; Bosnian Muslim or Serb, but not both; black or white, but not both. Traditionally, people of "mixed race" have been obliged to choose one and thereby identify themselves unambiguously to census takers and administrative bookkeepers—a practice that is now being widely called into question.

A scientific definition of race would require considerable homogeneity within each group, and reasonably discrete differences between groups, but three kinds of data militate against this view: First, the groups traditionally described as races are not at all homogeneous. Africans and Europeans, for instance, are each a collection of biologically diverse populations. Anthropologists of the 1920s widely recognized *three* European races: Nordic, Alpine, and Mediterranean. This implied that races could exist within races. American anthropologist Carleton Coon identified *ten* European races in 1939. With such protean use, the term race came to have little value in describing actual biological entities within *Homo sapiens*. The scholars were not only grappling with a broad north-south gradient in human appearance across Europe, they were trying to bring the data into line with their belief in profound and fundamental constitutional differences between groups of people.

But there simply isn't one European race to contrast with an African race, nor three, nor ten: the question (as scientists long posed it) fails to recognize the actual patterning of diversity in the human species. Fieldwork revealed, and genetics later quantified, the existence of far more biological diversity within any group than between groups. Fatter and thinner people exist everywhere, as do people with type O and type A blood. What generally varies from one population to the next is the *proportion* of people in these groups expressing the trait or gene. Hair color varies strikingly among Europeans and native Australians, but little among other peoples. To focus on discovering differences between presumptive races, when the vast majority of detectable variants do not help differentiate them, was thus to define a very narrow—if not largely illusory—problem in human biology. (The fact that Africans are biologically more diverse than Europeans, but have rarely been split into so many races, attests to the cultural basis of these categorizations.)

Second, differences between human groups are only evident when contrasting geographical extremes. Noting these extremes, biologists of an earlier era sought to identify representatives of "pure," primordial races presumably located in Norway, Senegal, and Thailand. At no time, however, was our species composed of a few populations within which everyone looked pretty much the same. Ever since some of our ancestors left Africa to spread out through the Old World, we humans have always lived in the "in-between" places. And human populations have also always been in genetic contact with one another. Indeed, for tens of thousands of years, humans have had trade networks; and where goods flow, so do genes. Consequently, we have no basis for considering *extreme* human forms the most pure, or most representative, of some ancient primordial populations. Instead, they represent populations adapted to the most disparate environments.

And third, between each presumptive "major" race are unclassifiable populations and people. Some populations of India, for example, are darkly pigmented (or "black"), have Europeanlike ("Caucasoid") facial features, but inhabit the continent of Asia (which should make them "Asian"). Americans might tend to ignore these "exceptions" to the racial categories, since immigrants to the United States from West Africa, Southeast Asia, and northwest Europe far outnumber those from India. The very existence of unclassifiable peoples undermines the idea that there are just three human biological groups in the Old World. Yet acknowledging the biological distinctiveness of such groups leads to a rapid proliferation of categories. What about Australians? Polynesians? The Ainu of Japan?

Categorizing people is important to any society. It is, at some basic psychological level, probably necessary to have group identity about who and what you are, in contrast to who and what you are not. The concept of race, however, specifically involves the recruitment of biology to validate those categories of self-identity.

Mice don't have to worry about that the way humans do. Consequently, classifying them into subspecies entails less of a responsibility for a scientist than classifying humans into sub-species does. And by the 1960s, most anthropologists realized they could not defend any classification of *Homo sapiens* into biological subspecies or races that could be considered reasonably objective. They therefore stopped doing it, and stopped identifying the endeavor as a central goal of the field. It was a biologically intractable problem—the old square-peg-in-a-round-hole enterprise; and people's lives, or welfares, could well depend on the ostensibly scientific pronouncement. Reflecting on the social history of the twentieth century, that was a burden anthropologists would no longer bear.

This conceptual divorce in anthropology—of cultural from biological phenomena was one of the most fundamental scientific revolutions of our time. And since it affected assumptions so rooted in our everyday experience, and resulted in conclusions so counterintuitive—like the idea that the earth goes around the sun, and not vice-versa—it has been widely underappreciated.

Kurt Vonnegut, in *Slaughterhouse Five*, describes what he remembered being taught about human variation: "At that time, they were teaching that there was absolutely no difference between anybody. They may be teaching that still." Of course there are biological differences between people, and between populations. The question is: How are those differences patterned? And the answer seems to be: Not racially. Populations are the only readily identifiable units of humans, and even they are fairly fluid, biologically similar to populations nearby, and biologically different from populations far away.

In other words, the message of contemporary anthropology is: You may group humans into a small number of races if you want to, but you are denied biology as a support for it.

New York-born Jonathan Marks earned an undergraduate degree in natural science at Johns Hopkins. After getting his Ph.D. in anthropology, Marks did a post-doc in genetics at the University of California at Davis and is now an associate professor of anthropology at Yale University. He is the coauthor, with Edward Staski, of the introductory textbook Evolutionary Anthropology *(San Diego: Harcourt, Brace Jovanovich, 1992). His new book,* Human Biodiversity: Genes, Race, and History *is published (1995) by Aldine de Gruyter.*

DOES RACE EXIST?

A proponent's perspective

by George W. Gill

Slightly over half of all biological/physical anthropologists today believe in the traditional view that human races are biologically valid and real. Furthermore, they tend to see nothing wrong in defining and naming the different populations of *Homo sapiens*. The other half of the biological anthropology community believes either that the traditional racial categories for humankind are arbitrary and meaningless, or that at a minimum there are better ways to look at human variation than through the "racial lens."

Are there differences in the research concentrations of these two groups of experts? Yes, most decidedly there are. As pointed out in a recent 2000 edition of a popular physical anthropology textbook, forensic anthropologists (those who do skeletal identification for law-enforcement agencies) are overwhelmingly in support of the idea of the basic biological reality of human races, and yet those who work with blood-group data, for instance, tend to reject the biological reality of racial categories.

I happen to be one of those very few forensic physical anthropologists who actually does research on the particular traits used today in forensic racial identification (i.e., "assessing ancestry," as it is generally termed today). Partly this is because for more than a decade now U.S. national and regional forensic anthropology organizations have deemed it necessary to quantitatively test both traditional and new methods for accuracy in legal cases. I volunteered for this task of testing methods and developing new methods in the late 1980s. What have I found? Where do I now stand in the "great race debate?" Can I see truth on one side or the other—or on both sides—in this argument?

Findings

First, I have found that forensic anthropologists attain a high degree of accuracy in determining geographic racial affinities (white, black, American Indian, etc.) by utilizing both new and traditional methods of bone analysis. Many well-conducted studies were reported in the late 1980s and 1990s that test methods objectively for percentage of correct placement. Numerous individual methods involving midfacial measurements, femur traits, and so on are over 80 percent accurate alone, and in combination produce very high levels of accuracy. No forensic anthropologist would make a racial assessment based upon just *one* of these methods, but in combination they can make very reliable assessments, just as in

determining sex or age. In other words, multiple criteria are the key to success in all of these determinations.

I have a respected colleague, the skeletal biologist C. Loring Brace, who is as skilled as any of the leading forensic anthropologists at assessing ancestry from bones, yet he does not subscribe to the concept of race. Neither does Norman Sauer, a board-certified forensic anthropologist. My students ask, "How can this be? They can identify skeletons as to racial origins but do not believe in race!" My answer is that we can often *function* within systems that we do not believe in.

As a middle-aged male, for example, I am not so sure that I believe any longer in the chronological "age" categories that many of my colleagues in skeletal biology use. Certainly parts of the skeletons of some 45-year-old people look older than corresponding portions of the skeletons of some 55-year-olds. If, however, law enforcement calls upon me to provide "age" on a skeleton, I can provide an answer that will be proven sufficiently accurate should the decedent eventually be identified. I may not believe in society's "age" categories, but I can be very effective at "aging" skeletons. The next question, of course, is how "real" is age biologically? My answer is that if one can use biological criteria to assess age with reasonable accuracy, then age has some basis in biological reality even if the particular "social construct" that defines its limits might be imperfect. I find this true not only for age and stature estimations but for sex and race identification.

The "reality of race" therefore depends more on the definition of reality than on the definition of race. If we choose to accept the system of racial taxonomy that physical anthropologists have traditionally established—major races: black, white, etc.—then one can classify human skeletons within it just as well as one can living humans. The bony traits of the nose, mouth, femur, and cranium are just as revealing to a good osteologist as skin color, hair form, nose form, and lips to the perceptive observer of living humanity. I have been able to prove to myself over the years, in actual legal cases, that I am *more* accurate at assessing race from skeletal remains than from looking at living people standing before me. So those of us in forensic anthropology know that the skeleton reflects race, whether "real" or not, just as well if not better than superficial soft tissue does. The idea that race is "only skin deep" is simply not true, as any experienced forensic anthropologist will affirm.

Position on race

Where I stand today in the "great race debate" after a decade and a half of pertinent skeletal research is clearly more on the side of the reality of race than on the "race denial" side. Yet I do see why many other physical anthropologists are able to ignore or deny the race concept. Blood-factor analysis, for instance, shows many traits that cut across racial boundaries in a purely *clinal* fashion with very few if any "breaks" along racial boundaries. (A cline is a gradient of change, such as from people with a high frequency of blue eyes, as in Scandinavia, to people with a high frequency of brown eyes, as in Africa.)

Morphological characteristics, however, like skin color, hair form, bone traits, eyes, and lips tend to follow geographic boundaries coinciding often with climatic zones. This is not surprising since the selective forces of climate are probably the primary forces of nature that have shaped human races with regard not only to skin color and hair form but also the underlying bony structures of the nose, cheekbones, etc. (For example, more prominent noses humidify air better.) As far as we know, blood-factor frequencies are *not* shaped by these same climatic factors.

So, serologists who work largely with blood factors will tend to see human variation as clinal and races as not a valid construct, while skeletal biologists, particularly forensic anthropologists, will see races as biologically real. The common person on the street who sees only a person's skin color, hair form, and face shape will also tend to see races as biologically real. They are not incorrect. Their perspective is just different from that of the serologist.

So, yes, I see truth on both sides of the race argument.

Those who believe that the concept of race is valid do not discredit the notion of clines, however. Yet those with the clinal perspective who believe that races are not real do try to discredit the evidence of skeletal biology. Why this bias from the "race denial" faction? This bias seems to stem largely from socio-political motivation and not science at all. For the time being at least, the people in "race denial" are in "reality denial" as well. Their motivation (a positive one) is that they have come to believe that the race concept is socially dangerous. In other words, they have convinced themselves that race promotes racism. Therefore, they have pushed the politically correct agenda that human races are not biologically real, no matter what the evidence.

Consequently, at the beginning of the 21st century, even as a majority of biological anthropologists favor the reality of the race perspective, not one introductory textbook of physical anthropology even presents that perspective as a possibility. In a case as flagrant as this, we are not dealing with science but rather with blatant, politically motivated censorship. But, you may ask, are the politically correct actually correct? Is there a relationship between thinking about race and racism?

Race and racism

Does discussing human variation in a framework of racial biology promote or reduce racism? This is an important question, but one that does not have a simple answer. Most social scientists over the past decade have convinced themselves that it runs the risk of promoting racism in certain quarters. Anthropologists of the 1950s, 1960s, and early 1970s, on the other hand, believed that they were combating racism by openly discussing race and by teaching courses on human races and racism. Which approach has worked best? What do the intellectuals among racial minorities believe? How do students react and respond?

Three years ago, I served on a NOVA-sponsored panel in New York, in which panelists debated the topic "Is There Such a Thing as Race?" Six of us sat on the panel, three proponents of the race concept and three antagonists. All had authored books or papers on race. Loring Brace and I were the two anthropologists "facing off" in the debate. The ethnic composition of the panel was three white and three black scholars. As our conversations developed, I was struck by how similar many of my concerns regarding racism were to those of my two black teammates. Although recognizing that embracing the race concept can have risks attached, we were (and are) more fearful of the form of racism likely to emerge if race is denied and dialogue about it lessened. We fear that the social taboo about the subject of race has served to suppress open discussion about a very important subject in need of dispassionate debate. One of my teammates, an affirmative-action lawyer, is afraid that a denial that races exist also serves to encourage a denial that racism exists. He asks, "How can we combat racism if no one is willing to talk about race?"

Who will benefit?

In my experience, minority students almost invariably have been the strongest supporters of a "racial perspective" on human variation in the classroom. The first-ever black student in my human variation class several years ago came to me at the end of the course and said, "Dr. Gill, I really want to thank you for changing my life with this course." He went on to explain that, "My whole life I have wondered about why I am black, and if that is good or bad. Now I know the reasons why I am the way I am and that these traits are useful and good."

A human-variation course with another perspective would probably have accomplished the same for this student if he had ever noticed it. The truth is, innocuous contemporary human-variation classes with their politically correct titles and course descriptions do not attract the attention of minorities or those other students who could most benefit. Furthermore, the politically correct "race denial" perspective in society as a whole suppresses dialogue, allowing ignorance to replace knowledge and suspicion to replace familiarity. This encourages ethnocentrism and racism more than it discourages it.

Dr. George W. Gill is a professor of anthropology at the University of Wyoming. He also serves as the forensic anthropologist for Wyoming law-enforcement agencies and the Wyoming State Crime Laboratory.

DOES RACE EXIST?

An antagonist's perspective

by C. Loring Brace

I am going to start this essay with what may seem to many as an outrageous assertion: There is no such thing as a biological entity that warrants the term "race."

The immediate reaction of most literate people is that this is obviously nonsense. The physician will retort, "What do you mean 'there is no such thing as race'? I see it in my practice everyday!" Jane Doe and John Roe will be equally incredulous. Note carefully, however, that my opening declaration did not claim that "there is no such thing as race." What I said is that there is no "biological entity that warrants the term 'race'." "You're splitting hairs," the reader may retort. "Stop playing verbal games and tell us what you really mean!"

And so I shall, but there is another charge that has been thrown my way, which I need to dispel before explaining the basis for my statement. Given the tenor of our times at the dawn of the new millennium, some have suggested that my position is based mainly on the perception of the social inequities that have accompanied the classification of people into "races." My stance, then, has been interpreted as a manifestation of what is being called "political correctness." My answer is that it is really the defenders of the concept of "race" who are unwittingly shaped by the political reality of American history. [Read a *proponent's perspective,* that of anthropologist George Gill.]

But all of this needs explaining. First, it is perfectly true that the long-term residents of the various parts of the world have patterns of features that we can easily identify as characteristic of the areas from which they come. It should be added that they have to have resided in those places for a couple of hundred thousand years before their regional patterns became established. Well, you may ask, why can't we call those regional patterns "races"? In fact, we can and do, but it does not make them coherent biological entities. "Races" defined in such a way are products of our perceptions. "Seeing is believing" will be the retort, and, after all, aren't we seeing reality in those regional differences?

I should point out that this is the same argument that was made against Copernicus and Galileo almost half a millennium ago. To this day, few have actually made the observations and done the calculations that led those Renaissance scholars to challenge the universal perception that the sun sets in the evening to rise again at the dawn. It was just a matter of common sense to believe that the sun revolves around the Earth, just as it was common sense to "know" that the Earth was flat. Our beliefs concerning "race" are based on the same sort of common sense, and they are just as basically wrong.

The nature of human variation

I would suggest that there are very few who, of their own experience, have actually perceived at first hand the nature of human variation. What we know of the characteristics of the various regions of the world we have largely gained vicariously and in misleadingly spotty fashion. Pictures and the television camera tell us that the people of Oslo in Norway, Cairo in Egypt, and Nairobi in Kenya look very different. And when we actually meet natives of those separate places, which can indeed happen, we can see representations of those differences at first hand. But if one were to walk up beside the Nile from Cairo, across the Tropic of Cancer to Khartoum in the Sudan and on to Nairobi, there would be no visible boundary between one people and another. The same thing would be true if one were to walk north from Cairo, through the Caucasus, and on up into Russia, eventually swinging west across the northern end of the Baltic Sea to Scandinavia. The people at any adjacent stops along the way look like one another more than they look like anyone else since, after all, they are related to one another. As a rule, the boy marries the girl next door throughout the whole world, but next door goes on without stop from one region to another.

We realize that in the extremes of our transit—Moscow to Nairobi, perhaps—there is a major but gradual change in skin color from what we euphemistically call white to black, and that this is related to the latitudinal difference in the intensity of the ultraviolet component of sunlight. What we do not see, however, is the myriad other traits that are distributed in a fashion quite unrelated to the intensity of ultraviolet radiation. Where skin color is concerned, all the northern populations of the Old World are lighter than the long-term inhabitants near the equator. Although Europeans and Chinese are obviously different, in skin color they are closer to each other than either is to equatorial Africans. But if we test the distribution of the widely known ABO blood-group system, then Europeans and Africans are closer to each other than either is to Chinese.

Then if we take that scourge sickle-cell anemia, so often thought of as an African disease, we discover that, while it does reach high frequencies in some parts of sub-Saharan Africa, it did not originate there. Its distribution includes southern Italy, the eastern Mediterranean, parts of the Middle East, and over into India. In fact, it represents a kind of adaptation that aids survival in the face of a particular kind of malaria, and wherever that malaria is a prominent threat, sickle-cell anemia tends to occur in higher frequencies. It would appear that the gene that controls that trait was introduced to sub-Saharan Africa by traders from those parts of the Middle East where it had arisen in conjunction with the conditions created by the early development of agriculture.

Every time we plot the distribution of a trait possessing a survival value that is greater under some circumstances than under others, it will have a different pattern of geographical variation, and no two such patterns will coincide. Nose form, tooth size, relative arm and leg length, and a whole series of other traits are distributed each in accordance with its particular controlling selective force. The gradient of the distribution of each is called a "cline" and those clines are completely independent of one another. This is what lies behind the aphorism, "There are no races, there are only clines." Yes, we can recognize people from a given area. What we are seeing, however, is a pattern of features derived from common ancestry in the area in question, and these are largely without different survival value. To the extent that the people in a given region look more like one another than they look like people from other regions, this can be regarded as "family resemblance writ large." And as we have seen, each region grades without break into the one next door.

There is nothing wrong with using geographic labels to designate people. Major continental terms are just fine, and sub-regional refinements such as Western European, Eastern African, Southeast Asian, and so forth carry no unintentional baggage. In contrast, terms such as "Negroid," "Caucasoid,"

and "Mongoloid" create more problems than they solve. Those very terms reflect a mix of narrow regional, specific ethnic, and descriptive physical components with an assumption that such separate dimensions have some kind of common tie. Biologically, such terms are worse than useless. Their continued use, then, is in social situations where people think they have some meaning.

America and the race concept

The role played by America is particularly important in generating and perpetuating the concept of "race." The human inhabitants of the Western Hemisphere largely derive from three very separate regions of the world—Northeast Asia, Northwest Europe, and Western Africa—and none of them has been in the New World long enough to have been shaped by their experiences in the manner of those long-term residents in the various separate regions of the Old World.

It was the American experience of those three separate population components facing one another on a daily basis under conditions of manifest and enforced inequality that created the concept in the first place and endowed it with the assumption that those perceived "races" had very different sets of capabilities. Those thoughts are very influential and have become enshrined in laws and regulations. This is why I can conclude that, while the word "race" has no coherent biological meaning, its continued grip on the public mind is in fact a manifestation of the power of the historical continuity of the American social structure, which is assumed by all to be essentially "correct."

Finally, because of America's enormous influence on the international scene, ideas generated by the idiosyncrasies of American history have gained currency in ways that transcend American intent or control. One of those ideas is the concept of "race," which we have exported to the rest of the world without any realization that this is what we were doing. The adoption of the biologically indefensible American concept of "race" by an admiring world has to be the ultimate manifestation of political correctness.

Dr. C. Loring Brace is professor anthropology and curator of biological anthropology at the Museum of Anthropology, University of Michigan, Ann Arbor.

The bare truth

Why are humans nearly hairless? And why do some wish to become more so?

At THE back of a hairdresser's shop, just off Piccadilly in London, an Irish beautician called Genevieve is explaining what a "Brazilian" is as she practises her art on your correspondent. A Brazilian strip, some are surprised to learn, is nothing to do with Latin American football. Between each excruciating rip, she explains that she is going to remove nearly all my pubic hair, except for a narrow vertical strip of hairs the width of a couple of fingers. This is known colloquially as the "landing strip".

In only a few years, this form of waxing has gone from the esoteric to the everyday and is starting to rival the ordinary bikini wax in popularity. At the same time the bikini wax is becoming a normal procedure for women of all ages: the youngest person Genevieve has waxed is a 12-year-old girl. Women are styling their pubic hair into hearts, stars and arrows. It is one of the more notable developments in hairdressing since the permanent wave.

The agony involved raises the question of why women increasingly feel the need to remove a natural covering of hair. One theory is that they are trying to acquire a prepubescent look in order to please men. The waxers, though, will let you into another little secret which suggests that, even if this is true, it is not the whole story. Some men too, both straight and gay, are waxing their most intimate parts. Ouch.

At a biological level this behaviour seems even odder. Most other mammals seem quite content with a luxuriant growth of fur. The idea of a chimpanzee pulling out the hair on its genital regions is ridiculous. Perhaps waxing is little more than a pseudo-sexual fad: another example of the kind of erotic titivation, such as body piercing and tattooing, that was once popular mainly among sailors, hippies and prostitutes. There is another possibility, though. It could be an extension of a longer-running animal story: humanity's evolution towards near nakedness.

Humans are clearly obsessed with having too much hair. Last year men and women spent $8 billion removing it with razor blades, reports Gillette, which makes the things. Of this, $2 billion was spent by America's 100m men on beard removal. More than 90% of American men over 15 shave about five times a week. But as beards are, biologically, a sexual signal indicating masculinity, why shave them off?

Men have been shaving since antiquity, although the habit really got going only when Gillette replaced the cut-throat razor with the safety razor in 1903. Gus Van Beek, a curator of archaeology at the Smithsonian Institution in Washington, DC, says that Egyptian tomb paintings of men show them without beards, or at least without real beards. When beards are depicted, they are false ones. This is known, says Mr Van Beek, because detached falsies have been found.

Beards may have been considered a disadvantage in hand-to-hand combat, since they can be grabbed. Yet much of the body, or so it is thought, was shaven by the ancient Egyptians. Mr Van Beek says that their razors would have been made first of copper, then of bronze and, much later, of brass. But the ancient Egyptians would not have gone in for the Sphinx, which is another style of pubic wax, named after the completely hairless Egyptian cat.

Great for scouring pots

It is not clear when women began shaving their legs. One idea, almost certainly wrong, is that the fashion began in the 1920s when western women's skirts became shorter. Typically, today's women start shaving at a slightly younger age than men do but they shave an area nine times as large. Although the average male beard has the same number of hairs as a woman's legs and underarms combined (7,000 to 15,000 hairs), the beard is denser and grows much faster. The average American man spends about 33 days of his life removing facial hair. Dry beard hair, says an alarming Gillette fact sheet on shaving, is "extremely abrasive and about as tough as copper wire of the same thickness."

Though beards and hairy legs may be unwanted, head hair is greatly desired. Many men go to great lengths in their efforts to keep the hair on their heads. Male-pattern baldness, or androgenetic alopecia, is the commonest form of hair loss. By the age of 50, over half of all men are experiencing some thinning or loss of hair at the top or front of their scalp. It is caused by genetics and hormones, specifically the male hormone dihydrotestosterone.

If fat is a feminist issue, then baldness is a male one, according to statistics compiled by members of the American Academy of Cosmetic Surgery. The main reason a man will have cosmetic surgery (apart, that is, from botox injections) is for the transplantation or restoration of his hair. Roughly the same number of American men are having their hair revived as women are having their breasts augmented. In online chat groups, bald men from all over the world discuss their misery and inability to attract a mate (or "gf"). "I'd rather be fat than bald," bemoans one.

Human beings' hairy preoccupations are curious because, compared with their closest animal relations, humans have very little hair to begin with. Hair is unique to mammals, and is one of the most obvious and defining characteristics of the group. It may have first evolved when sensory hairs—rather like a cat's whiskers—were multiplied over the body and became a useful insulator. Many scientists believe the evolution of hair is related to the evolution of warm-bloodedness: the ability to maintain a constant internal temperature. This may have given mammals an advantage in their early, nocturnal, environment, when they lived in the shadow of dinosaurs. Mammals have probably had hair for about 200m years, but since hair does not generally fossilise, scientists are not quite sure.

Of the 5,000-plus species of mammal, the only other (mostly) hairless creatures are elephants, rhinoceroses, hippopotamuses, walruses, whales and naked mole rats. It is easy to see why these few animals are not so hairy. Elephants and rhinoceroses are some of the largest of mammals, live in hot places and have trouble staying cool. The others live, at least part of the time, in water—where hair is not very useful—or underground, where temperature does not fluctuate as much as on the surface. Pigs are different. Their relative hairlessness has been bred into them fairly recently, in rather the same way as the unfortunate Mexican hairless dog.

A scientist might argue that humans are not, technically, "hairless". Many have the same density of hair follicles as an ape of the same body size would have. But human hair is generally fine and short, and so humans look naked compared with their closest animal relations. How bare they are, though, does vary racially—which may explain why one Thai lady has requested that her European boyfriend should have his entire body waxed. But completely hairless human skin is found in only a few areas such as the soles of the feet, the areolae round the nipples, the umbilicus, and the palms and undersurface of the fingers and toes.

Despite the title of Desmond Morris's 1967 book, "The Naked Ape", scientists do not know when in evolutionary history the "great denudation" took place. Or, for that matter, why. One of the more imaginative theories is that humans were once aquatic apes. This, it is argued, would explain why humans have hair on their heads: since the aquatic ape's head would have to be held out of the water, it would have needed protection from the glare of the sun.

The aquatic-ape theory is also used to explain why humans are relatively nimble in water, certainly compared with chimpanzees; and why the hair on the human back points in a direction that would reduce resistance from the water while swimming. But, as is often pointed out, the idea lacks hard evidence.

Cool, man

For many decades, the most popular explanation of hairlessness was that humans lost their hair to keep cool. Too much hair made humans—very active apes—hot, like elephants. Elephants evolved huge floppy ears to radiate heat back into their surroundings. But when hominids moved out of the forests and into the savannah, the same task could be carried out by the entire body, thanks to hominids' upright posture (which exposed less skin to the sun) and their lack of hair.

Unfortunately, as Mr Morris points out, there are problems with this idea, too. One is that no other animals of human size, indeed, no other savannah mammals at all, have shed their fur. Where are the naked lions? Another is that, though bare skin increases the chances of heat loss, it also increases the chances of heat gain, and the risk of damage from the sun. And nakedness makes humans vulnerably cold at night, even in Africa.

Mark Pagel, at the University of Reading, and Sir Walter Bodmer, at the John Radcliffe Hospital in Oxford, have a new idea. They believe that parasites are the key to human hairlessness. Humans, they say, lost their hair in order to reduce the burden of parasites such as fleas and ticks, some of which would have transmitted disease. Early humans probably lived close together in hunter-gatherer groups, in which the rate of parasite transmission was high. Hairless skin was easier to keep clean. Cultural adaptations, such as the use of fire, shelter and clothing, allowed humans to become furless.

Humans . . . lost their hair in order to reduce the burden of parasites such as fleas and ticks, some of which would have transmitted disease

What convinces them, they say, is the recent evidence of the great toll that ticks, lice and fleas have on the survival of furry and feathered creatures. Many animals die from parasites, and fleas carry the plague. Other scientists have recently discovered that when foreign species arrive on new shores they typically come with half as many parasites as they had at home. This gives them a huge competitive advantage over the local species, and explains why some become pests.

In 1874 Charles Darwin noted that, in the tropics, hairlessness would help humans to free themselves from ticks and other parasites. He showed some support for the idea in a passage reporting, "It is said to be a practice with the

Australians, when the vermin get troublesome, to singe themselves."

Some even argue that early cave paintings prove that cavemen were removing hairs from their face for similar reasons. At first, it is said, they plucked hair out using a pair of seashells as tweezers, and later they scraped away at it with razors made of flint or horn. Since horn becomes blunt quickly, it may almost be said that stone-age man invented the disposable razor. Others may have singed their facial hair with burning twigs. Why? Perhaps because it became sweaty and dirty, made eating awkward and played host to nits.

My husband is a hairy man ...

The parasite theory may also help explain why women are less hairy than men. Mates of either sex would have chosen each other because of their lack of hair, argue Mr Pagel and Sir Walter, since this would suggest that the chosen one was likelier to be free of disease. But as men are more likely than women to select mates on their appearance, it may be that the evolutionary pressure driving hairlessness was greater in women than in men.

Hairiness is also related to the level of a predominantly male hormone. Hence, being less hairy may be a sexual signal of femininity. The companies that advertise female shaving, waxing and depilatory products often play on the fear that hair is dirty. The message is clear: if you don't want to look like a dirty man in a hygiene-obsessed world, get rid of your body hair. And as the fashion for revealing clothing and microscopic underwear spreads, so too does the desire to show only smooth, naked skin—a desire often reinforced by society. Consider the outcry when Julia Roberts waved to a crowd and revealed, to the horror of many, a hairy armpit.

More and more of the body is on display, and not always pleasurably. For many women, for instance, men's hairy backs and chests are an acquired taste. Smoother certainly usually means easier on the eye. Mr Pagel says he is struck by how many advertisements for women's clothes and scent show them with their backs exposed. This may, conventionally, be thought of as a normal, sexually suggestive, display. But Mr Pagel adds, "We do not normally regard backs as secondary sexual characteristics and so it occurred to me that what these advertisements may be subconsciously displaying is the 'health' and 'fitness' of the model by revealing a large area of unblemished skin."

Some evolutionary biologists, though, are bristling at the parasite theory. Robin Dunbar, of the University of Liverpool, is sceptical. Parasites, he says, would have become a problem only when shelters were first established. But hairlessness, he says, evolved before shelters did. Some research suggests it evolved when walking upright became popular among hominids more than 2m years ago.

Mr Dunbar supports the cooling theory, and argues that when humans invaded the open plains, hair loss doubled the distance they could travel on a pint of water. Moreover, the presence or absence of hair clearly affects insulation because hair length changes on animals in different environments: elephants in cold places became the woolly mammoth. And it is now thought that humans started wearing clothes rather recently—work on the genetics and evolutionary origins of clothes lice suggests they first appeared some time between 30,000 and 114,000 years ago—certainly far too late to explain why humans lost most of their hair.

... but I am sexy

Whatever the explanation for the loss of hair, another explanation is needed for why men and women kept dense hair in three places: their heads, armpits and pubes. In particular, those who believe in the parasite theory must explain why humans merely shed some of their hair and not all of it, since the head, armpits and pubic areas are the very regions where human parasitic infections tend to occur.

The answer is sex, of course. David Stoddart, an olfactory biologist with Australia's Antarctic programme, points out that armpit and pubic hair grows just where the major scent glands are to be found. Hair is a means of wafting this scent about. Thus a tuft of hair allows humans, like other animals, to advertise to mates that something of interest is happening on the skin below.

Humans' crowning glory, the hair on their heads, is easier to explain. Again, it is a human characteristic that was shaped by sexual selection. A luxuriant head of hair is, and has always been, desirable in a mate. At least since the days of the Assyrians—between the 17th and seventh centuries BC—hair has been dressed, and has been an important signal for attracting and choosing partners. In Europe in the late 1760s, women's hair rose from the head and took on extraordinary proportions. Fashionable women might dress their hair powdered, draped over wire or basketwork foundations, and crowned with feathers, flowers, baskets of fruit, or even a miniature ship in full sail.

That still leaves beards. The theory here is that sexual selection has kept facial hair in men, presumably because this advertises their male hormones. But why, then, do so many men, in so many cultures, shave them off? Perhaps the fear of parasites is driving some men to be clean-shaven. Maybe the goatee is a compromise between being clean and manly. Or, perhaps, shaving is popular because facial shape in humans is a sexually dimorphic characteristic. Men tend to have squarer jaws than women, and they shave to highlight this. If so, this would explain the trend for emphasising the edge of the jawline with a fringe of hair. But moustaches are a mystery, to evolutionary biologists and to practically everyone else.

Commentary

The Tall and the Short of It

By Barry Bogin

BAFFLED BY YOUR FUTURE PROSPECTS? As a biological anthropologist, I have just one word of advice for you: plasticity. *Plasticity* refers to the ability of many organisms, including humans, to alter themselves—their behavior or even their biology—in response to changes in the environment. We tend to think that our bodies get locked into their final form by our genes, but in fact we alter our bodies as the conditions surrounding us shift, particularly as we grow during childhood. Plasticity is as much a product of evolution's fine-tuning as any particular gene, and it makes just as much evolutionary good sense. Rather than being able to adapt to a single environment, we can, thanks to plasticity, change our bodies to cope with a wide range of environments. Combined with the genes we inherit from our parents, plasticity accounts for what we are and what we can become.

Anthropologists began to think about human plasticity around the turn of the century, but the concept was first clearly defined in 1969 by Gabriel Lasker, a biological anthropologist at Wayne State University in Detroit. At that time scientists tended to consider only those adaptations that were built into the genetic makeup of a person and passed on automatically to the next generation. A classic example of this is the ability of adults in some human societies to drink milk. As children, we all produce an enzyme called lactase, which we need to break

down the sugar lactose in our mother's milk. In many of us, however, the lactase gene slows down dramatically as we approach adolescence—probably as the result of another gene that regulates its activity. When that regulating gene turns down the production of lactase, we can no longer digest milk.

Lactose intolerance—which causes intestinal gas and diarrhea—affects between 70 and 90 percent of African Americans, Native Americans, Asians, and people who come from around the Mediterranean. But others, such as people of central and western European descent and the Fulani of West Africa, typically have no problem drinking milk as adults. That's because they are descended from societies with long histories of raising goats and cattle. Among these people there was a clear benefit to being able to drink milk, so natural selection gradually changed the regulation of their lactase gene, keeping it functioning throughout life.

That kind of adaptation takes many centuries to become established, but Lasker pointed out that there are two other kinds of adaptation in humans that need far less time to kick in. If people have to face a cold winter with little or no heat, for example, their metabolic rates rise over the course of a few weeks and they produce more body heat. When summer returns, the rates sink again.

Lasker's other mode of adaptation concerned the irreversible, lifelong mod-

ification of people as they develop—that is, their plasticity. Because we humans take so many years to grow to adulthood, and because we live in so many different environments, from forests to cities and from deserts to the Arctic, we are among the world's most variable species in our physical form and behavior. Indeed, we are one of the most plastic of all species.

In an age when DNA is king, it's worth considering why Americans are no longer the world's tallest people, and some Guatemalans no longer pygmies.

One of the most obvious manifestations of human malleability is our great range of height, and it is a subject I've made a special study of for the last 25 years. Consider these statistics: in 1850 Americans were the tallest people in the world, with American men averaging 5'6". Almost 150 years later, American men now average 5'8", but we have fallen in the standings and are now only the third tallest people in the world. In first place are the Dutch. Back in 1850 they averaged only 5'4"—the shortest men in Europe—but today they are a towering 5'10". (In these two groups, and just about everywhere else, women average about five inches less than men at all times.)

So what happened? Did all the short Dutch sail over to the United States? Did the Dutch back in Europe get an infusion of "tall genes"? Neither. In both America and the Netherlands life got better, but more so for the Dutch, and height increased as a result. We know this is true thanks in part to studies on how height is determined. It's the product of plasticity in our childhood and in our mothers' childhood as well. If a girl is undernourished and suffers poor health, the growth of her body, including her reproductive system, is usually reduced. With a shortage of raw materials, she can't build more cells to construct a bigger body; at the same time, she has to invest what materials she can get into repairing already existing cells and tissues from the damage caused by disease. Her shorter stature as an adult is the result of a compromise her body makes while growing up.

Such a woman can pass on her short stature to her child, but genes have nothing to do with it for either of them. If she becomes pregnant, her small reproductive system probably won't be able to supply a normal level of nutrients and oxygen to her fetus. This harsh environment reprograms the fetus to grow more slowly than it would if the woman was healthier, so she is more likely to give birth to a smaller baby. Low-birth-weight babies (weighing less than 5.5 pounds) tend to continue their prenatal program of slow growth through childhood. By the time they are teenagers, they are usually significantly shorter than people of normal birth weight. Some particularly striking evidence of this reprogramming comes from studies on monozygotic twins, which develop from a single fertilized egg cell and are therefore identical genetically. But in certain cases, monozygotic twins end up being nourished by unequal portions of the placenta. The twin with the smaller fraction of the placenta is often born with low birth weight, while the other one is normal. Follow-up studies show that this difference between the twins can last throughout their lives.

As such research suggests, we can use the average height of any group of peo-

ple as a barometer of the health of their society. After the turn of the century both the United States and the Netherlands began to protect the health of their citizens by purifying drinking water, installing sewer systems, regulating the safety of food, and, most important, providing better health care and diets to children. The children responded to their changed environment by growing taller. But the differences in Dutch and American societies determined their differing heights today. The Dutch decided to provide public health benefits to all the public, including the poor. In the United States, meanwhile, improved health is enjoyed most by those who can afford it. The poor often lack adequate housing, sanitation, and health care. The difference in our two societies can be seen at birth: in 1990 only 4 percent of Dutch babies were born at low birth weight, compared with 7 percent in the United States. For white Americans the rate was 5.7 percent, and for black Americans the rate was a whopping 13.3 percent. The disparity between rich and poor in the United States carries through to adulthood: poor Americans are shorter than the better-off by about one inch. Thus, despite great affluence in the United States, our average height has fallen to third place.

People are often surprised when I tell them the Dutch are the tallest people in the world. Aren't they shrimps compared with the famously tall Tutsi (or "Watusi," as you probably first encountered them) of Central Africa? Actually, the supposed great height of the Tutsi is one of the most durable myths from the age of European exploration. Careful investigation reveals that today's Tutsi men average 5'7" and that they have maintained that average for more than 100 years. That means that back in the 1800s, when puny European men first met the Tutsi, the Europeans suffered strained necks from looking up all the time. The two-to-three-inch difference in average height back then could easily have turned into fantastic stories of African giants by European adventures and writers.

The Tutsi could be as tall or taller than the Dutch if equally good health care and diets were available in Rwanda and Bu-

rundi, where the Tutsi live. But poverty rules the lives of most African people, punctuated by warfare, which makes the conditions for growth during childhood even worse. And indeed, it turns out that the Tutsi and other Africans who migrate to Western Europe or North America at young ages end up taller than Africans remaining in Africa.

At the other end of the height spectrum, Pygmies tell a similar story. The shortest people in the world today are the Mbuti, the Efe, and other Pygmy peoples of Central Africa. Their average stature is almost 4'9" for adult men and 4'6" for women. Part of the reason Pygmies are short is indeed genetic: some evidently lack the genes for producing the growth-promoting hormones that course through other people's bodies, while others are genetically incapable of using these hormones to trigger the cascade of reactions that lead to growth. But another important reason for their small size is environmental. Pygmies living as hunter-gatherers in the forests of Central African countries appear to be undernourished, which further limits their growth. Pygmies who live on farms and ranches outside the forest are better fed than their hunter-gatherer relatives and are taller as well. Both genes and nutrition thus account for the size of Pygmies.

Peoples in other parts of the world have also been labeled pygmies, such as some groups in Southeast Asia and the Maya of Guatemala. Well-meaning explorers and scientists have often claimed that they are genetically short, but here we encounter another myth of height. A group of extremely short people in New Guinea, for example, turned out to eat a diet deficient in iodine and other essential nutrients. When they were supplied with cheap mineral and vitamin supplements, their supposedly genetic short stature vanished in their children, who grew to a more normal height.

ANOTHER WAY FOR THESE SO-CALLED pygmies to stop being pygmies is to immigrate to the United States. In my own research, I study the growth of two groups of Mayan children. One group lives in their homeland of Guatemala, and the other is a group of refugees living in the United States. The Maya in Guatemala live in the village of San Pedro, which has no safe source of drinking water. Most of the water is contaminated with fertilizers and pesticides used on nearby agricultural fields. Until recently, when a deep well was dug, the townspeople depended on an unreliable supply of water from rain-swollen streams. Most homes still lack running water and have only pit toilets. The parents of the Mayan children work mostly at clothing factories and are paid only a few dollars a day.

I began working with the schoolchildren in this village in 1979, and my research shows that most of them eat only 80 percent of the food they need. Other research shows that almost 30 percent of the girls and 20 percent of the boys are deficient in iodine, that most of the children suffer from intestinal parasites, and that many have persistent ear and eye infections. As a consequence, their health is poor and their height reflects it: they average about three inches shorter than better-fed Guatemalan children.

The Mayan refugees I work with in the United States live in Los Angeles and in the rural agricultural community of Indiantown in central Florida. Although the adults work mostly in minimum-wage jobs, the children in these communities are generally better off than their counterparts in Guatemala. Most Maya arrived in the 1980s as refugees escaping a civil war as well as a political system that threatened them and their children. In the United States they found security and started new lives, and before long their children began growing faster and bigger. My data show that the average increase in height among the first generation of these immigrants was 2.2 inches, which means that these so-called pygmies have undergone one of the largest single-generation increases in height ever recorded. When people such as my own grandparents migrated from the poverty of rural life in Eastern Europe to the cities of the United States just after World War I, the increase in height of the next generation was only about one inch.

One reason for the rapid increase in stature is that in the United States the

Maya have access to treated drinking water and to a reliable supply of food. Especially critical are school breakfast and lunch programs for children from low-income families, as well as public assistance programs such as the federal Woman, Infants, and Children (WIC) program and food stamps. That these programs improve health and growth is no secret. What is surprising is how fast they work. Mayan mothers in the United States tell me that even their babies are bigger and healthier than the babies they raised in Guatemala, and hospital statistics bear them out. These women must be enjoying a level of health so improved from that of their lives in Guatemala that their babies are growing faster in the womb. Of course, plasticity means that such changes are dependent on external conditions, and unfortunately the rising height—and health—of the Maya is in danger from political forces that are attempting to cut funding for food stamps and the WIC program. If that funding is cut, the negative impact on the lives of poor Americans, including the Mayan refugees, will be as dramatic as were the former positive effects.

Height is only the most obvious example of plasticity's power; there are others to be found everywhere you look. The Andes-dwelling Quechua people of Peru are well-adapted to their high-altitude homes. Their large, barrel-shaped chests house big lungs that inspire huge amounts of air with each breath, and they manage to survive on the lower pressure of oxygen they breathe with an unusually high level of red blood cells. Yet these secrets of mountain living are not hereditary. Instead the bodies of young Quechua adapt as they grow in their particular environment, just as those of European children do when they live at high altitudes.

One way for the so-called pygmies of Guatemala to stop being pygmies is to immigrate to the United States.

Plasticity may also have a hand in determining our risks for developing a number of diseases. For example, scientists have long been searching for a cause for Parkinson's disease. Because Parkinson's tends to run in families, it is natural to think there is a genetic cause. But while a genetic mutation linked to some types of Parkinson's disease was reported in mid-1997, the gene accounts for only a fraction of people with the disease. Many more people with Parkinson's do not have the gene, and not all people with the mutated gene develop the disease.

Ralph Garruto, a medical researcher and biological anthropologist at the National Institutes of Health, is investigating the role of the environment and human plasticity not only in Parkinson's but in Lou Gehrig's disease as well. Garruto and his team traveled to the islands of Guam and New Guinea, where rates of both diseases are 50 to 100 times higher than in the United States. Among the native Chamorro people of Guam these diseases kill one person out of every five over the age of 25. The scientists found that both diseases are linked to a shortage of calcium in the diet. This shortage sets off a cascade of events that result in the digestive system's absorbing too much of the aluminum present in the diet. The aluminum wreaks havoc on various parts of the body, including the brain, where it destroys neurons and eventually causes paralysis and death.

The most amazing discovery made by Garruto's team is that up to 70 percent of the people they studied in Guam had some brain damage, but only 20 percent progressed all the way to Parkinson's or Lou Gehrig's disease. Genes and plasticity seem to be working hand in hand to produce these lower-than-expected rates of disease. There is a certain amount of genetic variation in the ability that all people have in coping with calcium shortages—some can function better than others. But thanks to plasticity, it's also possible for people's bodies to gradually develop ways to protect themselves against aluminum poisoning. Some people develop biochemical barriers to the aluminum they eat, while others develop ways to prevent the aluminum from reaching the brain.

An appreciation of plasticity may temper some of our fears about these diseases and even offer some hope. For if Parkinson's and Lou Gehrig's diseases can be prevented among the Chamorro by plasticity, then maybe medical researchers can figure out a way to produce the same sort of plastic changes in you and me. Maybe Lou Gehrig's disease and Parkinson's disease—as well as many other, including some cancers—aren't our genetic doom but a product of our development, just like variations in human height. And maybe their danger will in time prove as illusory as the notion that the Tutsi are giants, or the Maya pygmies—or Americans still the tallest of the tall.

BARRY BOGIN is a professor of anthropology at the University of Michigan in Dearborn and the author of Patterns of Human Growth.

UNIT 7
Living With the Past

Unit Selections

Key Points to Consider

- What are the ways to prevent epidemics in the human species?

- What social policy issues are involved in the nature versus nurture debate?

- Does the concept of natural selection have relevance to the treatment of disease? Defend your answer.

- What is the nature of the bush-meat crisis in Africa and what can be done about it?

 **Links: www.dushkin.com/online/**
These sites are annotated in the World Wide Web pages.

Ancestral Passions
http://www.canoe.ca/JamBooksReviewsA/ancestral_morell.html
Forensic Science Reference Page
http://www.lab.fws.gov
Zeno's Forensic Page
http://forensic.to/forensic.html

Anthropology continues to evolve as a discipline, not only in the tools and techniques of the trade, but also in the application of whatever knowledge we stand to gain about ourselves. Sometimes an awareness of our biological and behavioral past may help us to better understand the present. For instance, in showing how our evolutionary past may make a difference in bodily health, Lori Oliwenstein (in "Dr. Darwin") talks about how the symptoms of disease must first be interpreted as to whether they represent part of the aggressive strategy of microbes or the defensive mechanisms of the patient before treatment can be applied.

As we reflect upon where we have been and how we came to be as we are in the evolutionary sense, the inevitable question arises as to what will happen next. This is the most difficult issue of all, since our biological future depends so much on long-range ecological trends that no one seems to be able to predict. There is no better example of this problem than the recent explosion of new diseases, as described in "The Viral Superhighway" by George Armelagos. Some wonder if we will even survive long enough as a species to experience any significant biological changes. Perhaps our capacity for knowledge is outstripping the wisdom to use it wisely, and the consequent destruction of our earthly environments and wildlife (as addressed in "Great Apes as Food") is placing us in ever greater danger of creating the circumstances of our own extinction.

Counterbalancing this pessimism is the view that because it has been our conscious decision making (and not the genetically predetermined behavior that characterizes some species) that has gotten us into this mess, then it will be the conscious will of our generation and future generations that will get us out of it. But, can we wait much longer for humanity to collectively come to its senses? Or is it already too late?

TABOOS

Great Apes as Food

dale peterson

Gorilla meat, so Joseph Melloh, a former commercial meat hunter from Cameroon, once told me, is "sweet, very sweet." Some people have a strong preference for it. "If you love somebody," Joseph explained, "you love somebody. If you don't, no matter how it's viewed, you know, how beautiful the woman is: no way. Same for those who eat gorilla meat as their precious meat. Just because they love it."

Chimpanzee, on the other hand, tastes "definitely different from gorilla. For one thing, chimpanzee meat stinks a little bit."[1]

That the three African apes—chimpanzees, bonobos, and gorillas—have traditionally been a food source for many people living in Central Africa's Congo Basin (a largely forested region claimed by the nations of Cameroon, Central African Republic, Congo, Democratic Republic of Congo, Equatorial Guinea, and Gabon) should surprise no one. Around the globe, people living in or on the edges of the world's great forests have always taken the protein offered by wild animals: true in Asia, Europe, and the Americas, as well as in Africa. But the African tropical forests are particularly rich in variety and have provided Central Africans a very diverse wealth of game species—collectively known as bushmeat. Gabonese, one informant tells me, eat every kind of *bushmeat* except owls, frogs, small lizards, and giant land snails.[2] Southern Congolese, a member of one southern ethnic group once declared, will eat almost every animal, gorillas included—but for various reasons still eschew the meat of chimpanzees.3

It is important to remember, however, that traditional eating habits in Central Africa depend not upon one's membership in the modern nation states, which are, after all, a recent invention, but rather upon one's allegiance to a tribe or ethnic group; and the tribal or ethnic food preferences and taboos in this part of the world remain subtle and complex as a result of subtle and complex historical traditions.[4]

Some religious prohibitions (notably, the Muslim prohibition against eating primate meat) and a number of village or tribal traditions have kept apes off the menu in a scattered patchwork across the continent. The local traditions are often rationalized according to familiar myths, and in the case of apes these ancient tales ordinarily evoke the theme of kinship. The Oroko of southwestern Cameroon consider that, since people are occasionally turned into chimps, any hunter discovering and sparing a wild chimp will find the grateful ape has deliberately chased other animals his way; conversely, killing the chimp can cast misfortune onto the hunter's family. (Nevertheless, a dead chimp is still edible food for the Oroko.)[5] The Kouyou of northern Congo traditionally forbade the hunting of at least four species—gorillas, chimpanzees, leopards, and bongo antelopes—and in the case of the two apes, that prohibition was based upon their closeness to humans. Likewise, the Mongandu people of north central Democratic Republic of Congo (former Zaire) have always, since anyone can remember, eaten everything in their forests except for leopards, tree hyraxes, and bonobos. While their neighbors to the south of the Luo River, the Mongo people, will happily hunt and eat bonobos, the Mongandu say that bonobos are simply too much like people to eat. They look human, and when actual humans are not watching, these animals will even stand upright on their hind legs.[6] (Chimpanzees and gorillas also sometimes walk upright, but bonobos, in fact, are the ape most distinguished by this surprising tendency. They will even walk considerable distances on two legs, often when their hands are full, so the Mongandu prohibition is based upon good observation and a sensible interpretation.)[7]

And yet the human resemblance that places apes on the prohibited list for some traditions actually lands them on the preferred list in others. Apes look like humans but possess a superhuman strength.[8] This combination may help explain why apes are, in some places, culturally valued as a food for ambitious men who would like to acquire the strength, and perhaps also the supposed virility, of an ape. For this reason, possibly, ape meat is strictly a man's meat for the Zime of Cameroon, so one tribe member told me.[9] Baka villagers in the southeast of that nation once told me the same thing.[10] For the Ewondo of Cameroon, according to one informant, women can eat gorilla meat at any time except during pregnancy, out of concern about the effects such potent fare might have on the unborn child.[11] This important "masculine" meat also turns out to be a special treat sometimes offered to visiting dignitaries and other powerful men. The recently elected governor of Cameroon's Eastern Province was regularly served up gorilla as he toured his new constituency. Likewise, the Bishop of Bertoua, according to one report, is offered gorilla hands and feet (considered the best parts) when he goes visiting.[12]

Many Central Africans still prefer the taste of bushmeat, in all its prolific variety, but millions of recent urbanites also value bushmeat as a reminder of their cultural identity and roots in traditional villages.

These food preferences, based partly upon symbolic value, blend into the preferential logic expressed by symbolic medicine. Symbolic (or "fetish") medicine is a thriving business in the big cities of Central Africa;[13] my own experience suggests that a person can rather easily locate ape parts in the city fetish markets. In Brazzaville, Congo's capital, I once looked over gorilla heads and hands. The hands, so the fetish dealer explained, are used especially by athletes who would like to be stronger. They boil pieces of the flesh until the water is all gone. Then they grind the remnants at the bottom of the pot down to a powder and press the powder into a cut in the skin, thus magically absorbing great strength from the great ape.[14] Likewise, according to Mbongo George, an active commercial meat hunter in southeastern Cameroon, rubbing pulverized gorilla flesh into your back will cure a backache, and chimp bones tied to the hips of a pregnant young girl will ease the process of labor when her own hips are narrow.[15]

ASIDE FROM BONES AND HAIR, virtually every part of an ape is edible, with some rare exceptions. In parts of Cameroon, at least, a male gorilla's testicles and scrotum will be rejected for reasons, so I am told, of taste.[16] But the ape's in-testines and soft organs make the central ingredients of a soup or stew. A gorilla's head is so big it might be cooked in its own pot. Likewise, gorilla hands and feet, especially desirable parts, may be cooked separately.

Ape meat, both smoked and fresh, is singed over a fire to remove any hair, then washed thoroughly, and cooked by boiling—a couple of hours for gorilla. Out in a hunters' camp the final meal may be quite simple: boiled meat with salt, oils, a few wild spices, perhaps a vegetable or two. In villages and towns and cities, though, a wide variety of oils and spices, starches and vegetables is available, and the cooking of ape or any other kind of bushmeat is likely to produce a rich and tasty soup or stew.[17]

YES THERE ARE ALTERNATIVES to bushmeat in Central Africa. The city markets offer domestic meats, both imported and home grown—and, indeed, at least some of the bushmeats sold in the city markets are more expensive than some domestic meats. I am persuaded this is true for chimpanzee and elephant meat compared to beef and pork, at least, because I once asked an ordinary citizen in Cameroon's capital city of Yaoundé to buy—bargaining as he would in ordinary circumstances—equivalent-by-weight amounts of chimpanzee, elephant, beef, and pork. In that way, I acquired a strange collection of flesh in my hotel room (severed hand of chimp, slice of elephant trunk, cube of cow, etc.), which I weighed and otherwise compared, and concluded that city people were paying approximately twice as much for chimpanzee and elephant as for beef and pork. Why would anyone pay more for chimp and elephant? Taste is clearly an important consideration in people's food preferences, though not the only one. Many Central Africans still prefer the taste of bushmeat, in all its prolific variety, but millions of recent urbanites also value bushmeat as a reminder of their cultural identity and roots in traditional villages.

In the rural areas where people are in many cases still living in a style close to traditional village life, the market cost hierarchy is reversed, with domestic meats more and bushmeat less expensive. For many rural Africans, then, bushmeat is also attractive simply because it's cheaper.

The standard dynamics of supply and demand mean that this pattern of consumption is about to hit a wall. While Africa is by far the most impoverished continent on the planet, it is also (and not coincidentally) the fastest growing. A natural rate of increase of 3.1 percent per year for Middle Africa indicates that human numbers are doubling every twenty-three years in this part of the world.[18] If food consumption habits continue, in short, demand for bushmeat as a source of dietary protein will double in little more than two decades.[19]

While the demand increases so rapidly, the supply is simply collapsing as a result of at least three factors. First, traditional hunting technologies are being replaced by ever more efficient modern ones, including wire snares, shotguns, and military hardware, and, as a direct consequence, animals across the Basin are being very efficiently *mined*, rather than *harvested*, out of the forests. Wire snares are particularly devastating because they kill indiscriminately; and, since snare lines are only periodically checked, they allow for considerable waste from rot.[20] Wire snares tend to maim rather than kill bigger animals like the apes, but modern shotguns loaded with large-ball *chevrotine* cartridges enable many of today's hunters to target such larger and more dangerous species with impunity.[21] Apes, who would have been unapproachably dangerous quarry for many (though certainly not all) hunters even a few years ago, are now attractive targets offering a very good deal in hunting economics: ratio of meat to cartridge.

Second, a one-billion-dollar-per-year commercial logging industry, run primarily by European and Asian firms to supply ten million cubic meters per year of construction, marine, and finish hardwoods primarily for the pleasure and benefit of European and Asian consumers, has during the last two decades cast a vast network of roads and tracks and trails into profoundly ancient and previously remote forests across the Congo Basin.[22] Loggers degrade these forests, haul in large numbers of workers and families, and often hire hunters to supply the bushmeat to feed the workers and their dependents. Most seriously, though, the loggers' roads and tracks and trails allow hunters in and meat out for the first time in history (and the ecological history of these great forests takes us back to the era of the dinosaurs). Vast areas of forest that even a decade ago were protected by their remoteness are today no longer protected at all.

Biologists theoretically examining the sustainability of hunting consider... the ability of a species to replenish itself.

Third, as a result of the new hunting technologies and the new opportunity offered by all those roads and tracks and trails cut by the European and Asian loggers, a small army of African entrepreneurs has found new economic opportunity in the bushmeat trade, which has quite suddenly become efficient and utterly commercialized. Bushmeat is now big business. Bushmeat is now no longer merely feeding the people in small rural villages and other subsistence communities but instead reaching very deeply into the forests and then stretching very broadly out to the towns and big cities throughout Central Africa. In Gabon alone, the trade currently amounts to a fifty-million-dollar-per-year exchange.[23] Altogether, this commerce today draws out of Central Africa's Congo Basin forests an estimated and astonishing five million metric tons of animal meat per year.[24] That amount is absolutely unsustainable. The depletion of the supply of wild animals and their meat, in short, is not even remotely balanced by the replenishment offered via natural reproduction in a stable ecosystem.[25]

A GENERALLY ACCEPTED estimate holds that around 1 percent of the total bushmeat trade involves the meat of the great apes—chimpanzees, bonobos, and gorillas. A blind and drunk optimist might imagine that 1 percent even of five million metric tons is a somewhat tolerable amount. It is not, of course. And even in the best of circumstances, where apes happen to inhabit legally protected forests (that is, national parks and reserves), a recent survey based on responses from professional field workers tells us that chimpanzees are hunted in 50 percent of their protected areas, bonobos in 88 percent, and gorillas in 56 percent.[26]

The impact of the current explosion in market hunting across the Congo Basin is threatening the existence of several wild animal species—but it disproportionately devastates the great apes. Biologists theoretically examining the sustainability of hunting consider, among other things, the ability of a species to replenish itself. A species with a quick rate of replenishment can likely, other factors being equal, withstand a high rate of depletion from hunting. Thinking about the impact hunting has on the survival of any particular species, in other words, requires us to examine that species' reproduction rates, and the great apes are unfortunately very slow reproducers. Perhaps because they are intelligent animals requiring extended periods of immature dependency while the young learn from their elders, apes wean late, reach independence and puberty late, and produce surprisingly few offspring. Altogether, the apes show about one quarter the reproduction rate of most other mammals.[27]

... apes are susceptible to a large variety of diseases that will also infect humans, including bacterial meningitis, chicken pox, diphtheria, Epstein-Barr virus, hepatitis A and B, influenza, measles, mumps, pneumonia, rubella, small pox, whooping cough, and so on.

Given such a slow reproduction rate, biologists calculate that chimpanzees and bonobos can theoretically withstand a loss of only about 2 percent of their numbers per year and still maintain a steady population. Gorillas may be able to tolerate losses of 4 percent per year. Monkeys have about the same low tolerance for loss, ranging from 1 to 4 percent, depending on the species. Ungulates, depending on the species, should be able to withstand yearly losses ranging most typically around 25 percent; and rodents can do just fine with losses from 13 percent to 80 percent per year, again depending on the species. In an ideal world, hunters would be equipped with pocket calculators to keep track of how sustainable their hunting is. In the real world, commercial hunters usually shoot whatever happens to wander in front of their guns. As a result, active hunting in a forest tends to deplete the fauna in a predictable progression. Apes and monkeys go first. Ungulates next. Rodents last. Indeed, it ought to be possible to measure the faunal disintegration of a forest by comparing the ratio of monkeys to rats sold in local markets.[28]

The best, most recent estimates tell us that approximately 150,000 to 250,000 wild chimpanzees survive in the wild, at the most some 50,000 bonobos remain, and roughly 120,000 wild gorillas are still there.[29] Based on the "informed consensus of experts," though, the commercial hunting of apes for meat is "out of control and unsustainable," and it continues "to spread and accelerate."[30] With the current levels and patterns of demand for apes as food, how long can they last?

One measure of how fast commercial hunting can reduce an ape population has been provided by the recent history of eastern Democratic Republic of Congo's Kahuzi-Biega National Park, supposedly protected as a UNESCO World Heritage Site but not protected well enough to keep out the professional hunters. In only three years during the last decade, hunters in Kahuzi-Biega earned a living by transforming into meat ("if our worst fears prove founded," so one investigator writes cautiously) some 80 to 90 percent of the 17,000 individuals who until then comprised the subspecies *Gorilla gorilla grauerai*.[31]

In sum, conserving biodiversity—saving the apes from extinction—amounts to one argument against using apes as a human food. A second argument has to do with public health. Perhaps all meats amount to a fair bridge for animal-to-human infection. Domestic meats, for example, offer *E. coli 0157*, salmonella, and the hypothetical "prion" that causes Mad Cow Disease among cattle and the deadly Creutzfeldt-Jakob syndrome among humans who eat cattle. But most domestic meats are regularly inspected and controlled to protect the carnivorous public, while bushmeat is not. Ape meat is particularly suspect if only because it is illegal, often sold covertly, and therefore particularly difficult to monitor or control.

The final argument against apes as food is …the moral argument. The great apes… are special animals because they are so close to human.

Chimpanzees and gorillas, in any event, appear to be about as vulnerable to the extremely infectious and frequently lethal Ebola virus as people are, and recent events in Central and West Africa have demonstrated that apes can also, like humans, readily transmit that virus not only to each other but also to any humans nearby—hunters handling meat, for instance.[32] Virologists have also recently identified an SIV virus endemic to chimpanzees as the culprit, the historical source of HIV 1 (subtypes M, N, and O) in humans, which accounts for the infection of

around 99 percent of today's globally distributed AIDS victims.[33] The remaining 1 percent have been infected with HIV 2, a closely related virus that we now know comes from an SIV endemic to the West African monkey popularly known as Sooty Mangabey. A reasonable presumption is that the three historical moments of viral transmission from chimpanzees to humans (producing today's three viable HIV 1 subtypes)—three separate episodes when a chimpanzee SIV successfully leapt into a human host—occurred not during the eating of ape meat, since cooking kills viruses, but during the butchering phase.[34] In any case, since that event has already happened, a person might imagine that the danger has passed: deed already done. In fact, apes are susceptible to a large variety of diseases that will also infect humans, including bacterial meningitis, chicken pox, diphtheria, Epstein-Barr virus, hepatitis A and B, influenza, measles, mumps, pneumonia, rubella, smallpox, whooping cough, and so on.[35] Far more serious, however, is the possible scenario of a person already infected with HIV 1 or HIV 2 coming into intimate contact (through butchering, for instance) with one of a number of related viruses—the SIVs endemic among several monkey species—thereby producing a successful cross, a recombinant virus that could become HIV 3. The government of Cameroon recently sponsored an extended study on primate viruses where researchers tested the blood of 788 monkeys kept as pets or sold as meat and discovered that around one fifth of those samples were infected with numerous varieties of SIV, including five previously unknown types. So the potential for new epidemics based on recombinants should be taken very seriously.[36]

The final argument against apes as food is perhaps the one many people think of first but often have trouble describing fully or convincingly, and that is the moral argument. The great apes—the three species commonly known as chimpanzees, bonobos, gorillas in Africa, and orangutans in Southeast Asia—are special animals because they are so close to human.

This idea is one long held in several, though not all, African traditions, as I have already suggested, and now, increasingly, in the European tradition. One of the earliest European reports on the existence of the great apes in Africa, English sailor Andrew Battell's tale (told to a collector of explorers' narratives probably in 1607) of two types of humanoid "monsters" in Africa may have provided the seminal inspiration for Shakespeare's evocatively humanoid "howling monster" Caliban, in *The Tempest* (1611).[37] A few live apes created some more generalized interest, as they began arriving in Europe by the middle of the seventeenth century; and in 1698, British physician Edward Tyson dissected the recently deceased body of the first live chimpanzee ever to appear in England and announced before the Royal Society the existence of *Homo Sylvestrius*, an animal with a profound anatomical similarity to humans.[38] That sort of rather casual enthusiasm was, during the nineteenth century, replaced by less casual studies in comparative anatomy. Charles Darwin himself was inspired to speculate that the African great apes would most likely turn out to be our own closest living relatives, though he lacked the data to prove it.[39]

Around the turn of the century, George Nuttall, an American expert on ticks lecturing in bacteriology at Cambridge University, pressed the comparative science beyond observable anatomy by examining the molecular structure of blood from different species, via antibody reactivity, and demonstrated the surprising fact that the blood of apes resembles human blood far more than it resembles monkey blood.[40] By midcentury, behavioral studies in the field began adding to the picture—perhaps most dramatically through Jane Goodall's first observations in 1960 that the chimpanzees of Gombe Stream Reserve in East Africawere making and using simple tools to capture termites.[41] Subsequent behavioral research shows that wild chimpanzees fashion and exploit an impressive variety of tools according to locally different cultural traditions and that they live in provocatively humanlike social systems, complete with a Machiavellian style of male power-politics and lethal, male-driven territorial wars between adjacent chimp communities.[42] Around the same time, laboratory projects in the United States and Japan were starting to demonstrate the astonishing reality that apes—all four species—are capable of learning and using sign language for communication purposes.[43] A few of those early studies still continue at full strength, as I write, and they have successfully responded to the earliest cries of disbelief from astonished skeptics.[44]

By the end of the twentieth century, techniques and technologies for genetic analysis had become sophisticated enough that it was possible not only to demonstrate to the satisfaction of every scientifically informed observer the undeniable reality of this closeness between humans and the great apes, but also to quantify it. The numbers go like this: Humans and orangutans share 96.4 percent of their genetic code. Humans and gorillas are genetically 97.7 percent identical. And, finally, humans share with both chimpanzees and bonobos an amazing 98.7 percent of their DNA. Genetically, you and I are 98.7 percent identical to both those ape species.[45]

A somewhat careless reader required to examine two books in which 98.7 percent of the words, sentences, and paragraphs are identical and placed in the identical order might complain at the serious injustice of having been forced to read the same book twice. A moderately careful reader, perhaps noticing that the two books have different titles—*Homo sapiens* for one and *Pan troglodytes* for the other—might express outrage at the unimaginative effrontery of this plagiarism.

No wonder, then, that the apes we see in zoos and on stage, in laboratories or in the wild, provoke that strange shock of recognition, serve as that often unexamined source of fascination and sometimes revulsion, of jokes and insults, of hidden concerns and even considered eth-

ical assessments. The four non-human apes, our closest relatives, mirror our faces and bodies, our hands and fingers, our fingernails and fingerprints. They seem to share our perceptual world. They appear to express something very much like the human repertoire of emotions. They look into a mirror and act as if they recognize themselves as individuals,[46] laugh in amusing circumstances,[47] are manifestly capable of learning symbolic language, share with us several recognizable expressions and gestures….[48] Chimpanzees, the hunters sometimes say, will beg for their lives when cornered, with that desperately hunched posture, pleading expression, and pathetically outstretched hand—oh, quite in the style of real beggars you see in the city.

Notes

1. Joseph Melloh, interviewed in Lomié, Cameroon, by the author, August 2000. Taste is surely one reason why people prefer some foods over others. Since I have never myself eaten ape meat, I cannot form a reasonable opinion about the taste. Interestingly enough, though, a mystery meat experiment (not including ape meat) conducted with thirty European and thirty Nigerian tasters reached the conclusion that both groups harbored a distinct preference for the taste of wild animal meat, while both also ranked domestic beef near the bottom. The Europeans gave their highest scores to the taste of cane rat, while Nigerians preferred bushbuck and giant snail most of all. G.H.G. Martin, "Carcass Composition and Palatability in Some Wild Animals," *World Animal Review* 53 (1985): 40–44.
2. David Edderai, interviewed in Libreville, Gabon, by the author, August 2000.
3. Dale Peterson and Jane Goodall, *Visions of Caliban: On Chimpanzees and People* (Boston: Houghton Mifflin, 1993), 66.
4. Cameroon, for instance, is a single modern nation, but the 15.5 million people living within Cameroon's borders worship according to three major religious systems (Christian, Muslim, and indigenous African), speak twenty-four major African languages and two European languages (English and French), and retain their own cultural identity as members of more than two hundred different tribes. Thus, describing "Cameroonean food traditions" is likely to be incorrect in the particular even while it may be correct in the general.
5. Benis Egoh, letter to author, February 2002.
6. Takayoshi Kano, letter to author, 1996; see also Takayoshi Kano, *The Last Ape: Pygmy Chimpanzee Behavior and Ecology* (Stanford, CA: Stanford University Press, 1992).
7. Personal observation; also Kano, *The Last Ape*, 125.
8. One early experiment in the United States demonstrated that even caged, bored, and out-of-condition chimpanzees can be, pound for pound, three-and-a-half to four-and-a-half times stronger than uncaged, eager, and fully in shape college football players. John Bauman, "Observations on the Strength of the Chimpanzee and Its Implications," *Journal of Mammalogy* 1 (1926): 1–9.
9. Mbongo George, interviewed in Djodibe (hunting camp), Cameroon, by the author, August 2000.
10. Several villagers interviewed in Casablanca, Cameroon by the author, August, 2000.

11. Pierre Efe interviewed in Yaoundé, Cameroon, by the author, August 2000.

12. Karl Ammann, letter to author, September 2000.

13. Personal observation; see also Moses A. Adeola, "Importance of Wild Animals and Their Parts in the Culture, Religious Festivals and Traditional Medicine of Nigeria," *Environmental Conservation* 19 (1992): 125–134.

14. Peterson and Goodall, *Visions of Caliban*, 66.

15. Mbongo George, interviewed in Djodibe (hunting camp), Cameroon, by the author, August 2000.

16. Ammann, letter to author, March 2002.

17. Mbongo George, interviewed in Djodibe (hunting camp), Cameroon, by the author, August 2000; François Kameni, interviewed in Yaoundé, Cameroon, by the author, August 2000; Marcellin Agnagna, letter to author, March 2001; Benis Egoh, letter to author, February 2002; Christina Ellis, letter to author, March 2002; Joseph Nnomo Abah, *L'Art Culinaire Dans le Sud Forestier du Cameroun* (Silver Spring, MD: The Jane Goodall Institute, 2001).

18. *The World Population Data Sheet* (Washington, D.C.: Population Reference Bureau, 1998).

19. Standard consumption rates include a Congo Basin average of forty-seven kilograms per person per year of meat, reasonably comparable to the thirty kilograms per person per year in the "northern industrial countries." David S. Wilkie, "Bushmeat Trade in the Congo Basin," in *Great Apes and Humans: The Ethics of Coexistence*, edited by Benjamin B. Beck, et al. (Washington, D.C.: Smithsonian Institution Press, 2001), 89.

20. Andrew J. Noss, "Cable Snare," *Conservation Biology* 12 (1998): 390–398.

21. Raymond B. Hames compares the efficiency of traditional and modern weapons and reaches the conclusion that shotguns are 231 percent more efficient (meat per hunting time) than bow and arrow. One problem is that time saved using a shotgun may be lost in economic activities required to buy shotgun cartridges. See Raymond B. Hames, "A Comparison of the Efficiencies of the Shotgun and the Bow in Neotropical Forest Hunting," *Human Ecology* 7 (1979): 219–252.

22. *Sold Down the River: The Need to Control Transnational Forestry Corporations, a European Case Study* (Cambridge: Forests Monitor, 2001).

23. Elisabeth A. Steel, *A Study of the Value and Volume of Bushmeat Commerce in Gabon* (Libreville, Gabon: WWF and Gabon Ministère des Eaux et Forêts et d'Environnement, 1994).

24. According to a recent study by John Fa, reported in Fred Pearce, "Death in the Jungle," *New Scientist*, 9 March, 2002, 14; a survey of earlier studies on bushmeat consumption rates can be found in David S. Wilkie and Julia F. Carpenter, "The Impact of Bushmeat Hunting on Forest Fauna and Local Economies in the Congo Basin: A Review of the Literature" (unpublished draft manuscript, 2001).

25. See, for instance, David S. Wilkie and Julia F. Carpenter, "Bushmeat Hunting in the Congo Basin: An Assessment of Impacts and Options for Mitigation," *Biodiversity and Conservation* 8 (1999): 927–955; or "U.N. Warns of 'Bushmeat' Crisis," Reuters News Service, 12 March 2001.

26. Andrew J. Marshall, James Holland Jones, and Richard W. Wrangham, *The Plight of the Apes: A Global Survey of Great Ape Populations* (Cambridge, MA: Briefing for United States Representatives Miller and Saxon, 2002), 10.

27. Ibid.

28. Sustainable offtakes for apes, Ibid.; for general concept and all other species, John G. Robinson, "Appendix: Calculating Maximum Sustainable Harvests and Percentage Offtakes," in *Hunting for Sustainability in Tropical Forests*, edited by John G. Robinson and Elizabeth L. Bennett (New York: Columbia University Press, 2000), 499–519.

29. Tom Butynski, "Africa's Great Apes," in *Great Apes: The Ethics of Coexistence*, 3–56.

30. Ibid.

31. Ian Redmond, *Coltan Boom, Gorilla Bust: The Impact of Coltan Mining on Gorillas and Other Wildlife in Eastern D. R. Congo* (private report sponsored by the Dian Fossey Gorilla Fund and the Born Free Foundation, 2001), 3.

32. Joel G. Breman, et al., "A Search for Ebola Virus in Animals in the Democratic Republic of the Congo and Cameroon: Ecologic, Virologic, and Serologic Surveys, 1979–1980," *Journal of Infectious Diseases* 179 (Suppl 1, 1999): s139–147; Pierre Formenty, et al., "Ebola Virus Outbreak Among Wild Chimpanzees Living in a Rain Forest of Côte d'Ivoire," *Journal of Infectious Diseases* 179 (Suppl 1, 1999): s120–126; Pierre Formenty, et al., "Human Infection Due to Ebola Virus, Subtype Côte d'Ivoire: Clinical and Biologic Presentation," *Journal of Infectious Diseases* 179 (Suppl 1, 1999): s48–53; Alain-Jean Georges, "Ebola Hemorrhagic Fever Outbreaks in Gabon, 1994–1997: Epidemiologic and Health Control Issues," *Journal of Infectious Diseases* 179 (Suppl 1, 1999): s65–75; C.J. Peters, and J.W. LeDuc, "An Introduction to Ebola: The Virus and the Disease," Journal of Infectious Diseases 179 (Suppl 1, 1999): ix–xvi.

33. Beatrice Hahn, et al., "AIDS as a Zoonosis: Scientific and Public Health Implications," Science 287 (2000): 607–614; Feng Gao, et al., "Origin of HIV-1 in the Chimpanzee *Pan troglodytes troglodytes*," *Nature* 397 (1999): 436–441.

34. Hahn, et al., "AIDS as a Zoonosis."

35. Tom Butynski, "Africa's Endangered Great Apes," *Africa Environment and Wildlife* 8 (2000), 30.

36. Martine Peeters, et al., "Risk to Human Health From a Plethora of Simian Immunodeficiency Viruses in Primate Bushmeat," *Emerging Infectious Diseases* 8 (2002).

37. See Samuel Purchas, *Hakluytus Posthumus, or Purchase His Pilgrimes, Contayning a History of the World in Sea Voyages and Lande Travels by Englishmen and Others* (Glasgow: James MacLehose and Sons, 1625, rpt. 1905). The full argument supporting the theory of Battell's influence on the creation of Shakespeare's Caliban is elaborated in Peterson and Goodall.

38. Geoffrey Bourne, *Primate Odyssey* (New York: G. P. Putnam's Sons, 1974), 281, 282.

39. Nineteenth-century anatomical comparisons include those reported in Thomas H. Huxley, *Man's Place in Nature* (New York: D. Appleton, 1863; 1894).

40. George H. F. Nuttall, *Blood Immunity and Blood Relationship: A Demonstration of Certain Blood-relationships Amongst Animals by Means of the Precipitin Test for Blood* (Cambridge: Cambridge University Press, 1904); see also Richard Wrangham and Dale Peterson, *Demonic Males: Apes and the Origins of Human Violence* (Boston: Houghton Mißßin, 1996), 35–37.

41. See, for example, Jane Goodall, *The Chimpanzees of Gombe: Patterns of Behavior* (Cambridge, MA: The Belknap Press of Harvard University, 1986), 248–251.

42. Ibid., 530–534.

43. See, for example, Roger Fouts, *Next of Kin: What Chimpanzees Have Taught Me About Who We Are* (New York: William Morrow, 1997); R. Allen Gardner and Beatrix T. Gardner, eds., *Teaching Sign Language to Chimpanzees* (Albany, NY: SUNY Press, 1989); H. Lyn White Miles, "Language and the Orang-utan: The Old 'Person of the Forest,'" in *The Great Ape Project: Equality Beyond Humanity*, eds. Paola Cavalieri and Peter Singer (New York: St. Martin's Press, 1993); Francine Patterson and Eugene Linden, *The*

Education of Koko (New York: Holt, Rinehart and Winston, 1981); and Sue Savage-Rumbaugh and Roger Lewin, *Kanzi: The Ape at the Brink of the Human Mind* (New York: John Wiley and Sons, 1994).

44. The most vocal skeptic: Herbert S. Terrace. See his "In the Beginning was the 'Name,'" *American Psychologist* (September 1985): 1011–1028; and *Nim* (New York: Columbia University Press, 1979; 1987). To find the best and most thorough response to the criticism, see Savage-Rumbaugh and Lewin; also Fouts.

45. Charles C. Sibley and Jon E. Ahlquist, "The Phylogeny of the Hominoid Primates, As Indicated by DNA-DNA Hybridization," *Journal of Molecular Evolution* 20 (1984): 2–15; also Feng-Chin Chen and Wen-Hsiung Li, "Genomic Divergences Between Human and Other Hominoids and the Effective Population Size of the Common Ancestor of Humans and Chimpanzees," *American Journal of Human Genetics* 68 (2001): 444–456.

46. George G. Gallup, Jr., "Chimpanzees: Self-Recognition," *Science* 167 (1970): 86, 87; George G. Gallup, Jr., "Self-Recognition in Primates," *American Psychologist* 32 (1977): 329–338.

47. Peterson and Goodall, *Visions of Caliban*, 180, 181.

48. Adriaan Kortlandt, "Handgebrauch bei Freilebenden Schimpansen," in *Handgebrauch und Verständigung bei Affen und Frümenschen*, ed. B. Rensch (Bern: Huber, 1968): 59–102.

Dale Peterson has written, co-authored, and edited several books, including *Storyville, USA; Chimpanzee Travels; The deluge and the Ark; Visions of Caliban* (with Jane Goodall); and *Demonic Males* (with Richard Wrangham). His latest work, *Eating Apes*, just released from the University of California Press, is the first book to expose the threat to great apes posed by Central Africa's bushmeat crisis.

The Viral Superhighway

Environmental disruptions and international travel have brought on a new era in human illness, one marked by diabolical new diseases

By George J. Armelagos

So the Lord sent a pestilence upon Israel from the morning until the appointed time; and there died of the people from Dan to Beer-sheba seventy thousand men.
—2 Sam. 24:15

SWARMS OF CROP-DESTROYING LO-custs, rivers fouled with blood, lion-headed horses breathing fire and sulfur: the Bible presents a lurid assortment of plagues, described as acts of retribution by a vengeful God. Indeed, real-life epidemics—such as the influenza outbreak of 1918, which killed 21 million people in a matter of months—can be so sudden and deadly that it is easy, even for non-believers, to view them as angry messages from the beyond.

How reassuring it was, then, when the march of technology began to give people some control over the scourges of the past. In the 1950s the Salk vaccine, and later, the Sabin vaccine, dramatically reduced the incidence of polio. And by 1980 a determined effort by health workers worldwide eradicated smallpox, a disease that had afflicted humankind since earliest times with blindness, disfigurement and death, killing nearly 300 million people in the twentieth century alone.

But those optimistic years in the second half of our century now seem, with hindsight, to have been an era of inflated expectations, even arrogance. In 1967 the surgeon general of the United States, William H. Stewart, announced that vic-tory over infectious diseases was imminent—a victory that would close the book on modern plagues. Sadly, we now know differently. Not only have deadly and previously unimagined new illnesses such as AIDS and Legionnaires' disease emerged in recent years, but historical diseases that just a few decades ago seemed to have been tamed are returning in virulent, drug-resistant varieties. Tuberculosis, the ancient lung disease that haunted nineteenth-century Europe, af-flicting, among others, Chopin, Dostoyevski and Keats, is aggressively mutating into strains that defy the standard medicines; as a result, modern TB victims must undergo a daily drug regimen so elaborate that health-department workers often have to personally monitor patients to make sure they comply [see "A Plague Returns," by Mark Earnest and John A. Sbarbaro, September/October 1993]. Meanwhile, bacteria and viruses in foods from chicken to strawberries to alfalfa sprouts are sickening as many as 80 million Americans each year.

And those are only symptoms of a much more general threat. Deaths from infectious diseases in the United States rose 58 percent between 1980 and 1992. Twenty-nine new diseases have been reported in the past twenty-five years, a few of them so bloodcurdling and bizarre that descriptions of them bring to mind tacky horror movies. Ebola virus, for instance, can in just a few days reduce a healthy person to a bag of teeming flesh spilling blood and organ parts from every orifice. Creutzfeldt-Jakob disease, which killed the choreographer George Balanchine in 1983, eats away at its victims' brains until they resemble wet sponges. Never slow to fan mass hysteria, Hollywood has capitalized on the phenomenon with films such as *Outbreak*, in which a monkey carrying a deadly new virus from central Africa infects unwitting Californians and starts an epidemic that threatens to annihilate the human race.

The reality about infectious disease is less sensational but alarming nonetheless. Gruesome new pathogens such as Ebola are unlikely to cause a widespread epidemic because they sicken and kill so quickly that victims can be easily identified and isolated; on the other hand, the seemingly innocuous practice of over-prescribing antibiotics for bad colds could ultimately lead to untold deaths, as familiar germs evolve to become untreatable. We are living in the twilight of the antibiotic era: within our lifetimes, scraped knees and cut fingers may return to the realm of fatal conditions.

Through international travel, global commerce and the accelerating destruction of ecosystems worldwide, people are inadvertently exposing themselves to a Pandora's box of emerging microbial threats. And the recent rumblings of biological terrorism from Iraq highlight the appalling potential of disease organisms for being manipulated to vile ends. But although it may appear that the apocalypse has arrived, the truth is that people today are not facing a unique predicament. Emerging diseases have long loomed like a shadow over the human race.

PEOPLE AND PATHOGENS HAVE A LONG history together. Infections have been detected in the bones of human ancestors more than a million years old, and evidence from the mummy of the Egyptian pharaoh Ramses V suggests that he may have died from smallpox more than 3,000 years ago. Widespread outbreaks of disease are also well documented. Between 1347 and 1351 roughly a third of the population of medieval Europe was wiped out by bubonic plague, which is carried by fleas that live on rodents. In 1793, 10 percent of the population of Philadelphia succumbed to yellow fever, which is spread by mosquitoes. And in 1875 the son of a Fiji chief came down with measles after a ceremonial trip to Australia. Within four months more than 20,000 Fijians were dead from the imported disease, which spreads through the air when its victims cough or sneeze.

According to conventional wisdom in biology, people and invading microorganisms evolve together: people gradually become more resistant, and the microorganisms become less virulent. The result is either mutualism, in which the relation benefits both species, or commensalism, in which one species benefits without harming the other. Chicken pox and measles, once fatal afflictions, now exist in more benign forms. Logic would suggest, after all, that the best interests of an organism are not served if it kills its host; doing so would be like picking a fight with the person who signs your paycheck.

But recently it has become clear to epidemiologists that the reverse of that cooperative paradigm of illness can also be true: microorganisms and their hosts sometimes exhaust their energies devising increasingly powerful weaponry and defenses. For example, several variants of human immunodeficiency virus (HIV) may compete for dominance within a person's body, placing the immune system under ever-greater siege. As long as a virus has an effective mechanism for jumping from one person to another, it can afford to kill its victims

[see "The Deadliest Virus," by Cynthia Mills, January/February 1997].

If the competition were merely a question of size, humans would surely win: the average person is 10^{17} times the size of the average bacterium. But human beings, after all, constitute only one species, which must compete with 5,000 kinds of viruses and more than 300,000 species of bacteria. Moreover, in the twenty years it takes humans to produce a new generation, bacteria can reproduce a half-million times. That disparity enables pathogens to evolve ever more virulent adaptations that quickly outstrip human responses to them. The scenario is governed by what the English zoologist Richard Dawkins of the University of Oxford and a colleague have called the "Red Queen Principle." In Lewis Carroll's *Through the Looking Glass* the Red Queen tells Alice she will need to run faster and faster just to stay in the same place. Staving off illness can be equally elusive.

THE CENTERS FOR DISEASE CONTROL and Prevention (CDC) in Atlanta, Georgia, has compiled a list of the most recent emerging pathogens. They include:

- *Campylobacter*, a bacterium widely found in chickens because of the commercial practice of raising them in cramped, unhealthy conditions. It causes between two million and eight million cases of food poisoning a year in the United States and between 200 and 800 deaths.

- *Escherichia coli* 0157:H7, a dangerously mutated version of an often harmless bacterium. Hamburger meat from Jack in the Box fast-food restaurants that was contaminated with this bug led to the deaths of at least four people in 1993.

- Hantaviruses, a genus of fast-acting, lethal viruses, often carried by rodents, that kill by causing the capillaries to leak blood. A new hantavirus known as *sin nombre* (Spanish for "nameless") surfaced in 1993 in the southwestern United States, causing the sudden and mysterious deaths of thirty-two people.

- HIV, the deadly virus that causes AIDS (acquired immunodeficiency syndrome). Although it was first observed in people as recently as 1981, it has spread like wildfire and is now a global scourge, affecting more than 30 million people worldwide.

- The strange new infectious agent that causes bovine spongiform encephalopathy, or mad cow disease, which recently threw the British meat industry and consumers into a panic. This bizarre agent, known as a prion, or "proteinaceous infectious particle," is also responsible for Creutzfeldt-Jakob disease, the brain-eater I mentioned earlier. A Nobel Prize was awarded last year to the biochemist Stanley B. Prusiner of the University of California, San Francisco, for his discovery of the prion.

- *Legionella pneumophila*, the bacterium that causes Legionnaires' disease. The microorganism thrives in wet environments; when it lodges in air-conditioning systems or the mist machines in supermarket produce sections, it can be expelled into the air, reaching people's lungs. In 1976 thirty-four participants at an American Legion convention in Philadelphia died—the incident that led to the discovery and naming of the disease.

- *Borrelia burgdorferi*, the bacterium that causes Lyme disease. It is carried by ticks that live on deer and white-footed mice. Left untreated, it can cause crippling, chronic problems in the nerves, joints and internal organs.

HOW IRONIC, GIVEN SUCH A ROGUES' gallery of nasty characters, that just a quarter-century ago the Egyptian demographer Abdel R. Omran could observe that in many modern industrial nations the major killers were no longer infectious diseases. Death, he noted, now came not from outside but rather from within the body, the result of gradual deterioration. Omran traced the change to the middle of the nineteenth century, when the industrial revolution took hold in the United States and parts of Europe. Thanks to better nutrition, improved public-health measures and medical advances such as mass immunization and the introduction of antibiotics, microorganisms were brought under control. As people began living longer, their aging bodies succumbed to "diseases of civilization": cancer, clogged arteries, diabetes, obesity and osteoporosis. Omran was the first to formally recognize that shift in the disease environment. He called it an "epidemiological transition."

Like other anthropologists of my generation, I learned of Omran's theory early in my career, and it soon became a basic tenet—a comforting one, too, implying as it did an end to the supremacy of microorganisms. Then, three years ago, I began working with the anthropologist Kathleen C. Barnes of Johns Hopkins University in Baltimore, Maryland, to formulate an expansion of Omran's ideas. It occurred to us that his epidemiological transition had not been a unique event. Throughout history human populations have undergone shifts in their relations with disease—shifts, we noted, that are always linked to major changes in the way people interact with the environment. Barnes and I, along with James Lin, a master's student at Johns Hopkins University School of Hygiene and Public Health, have since developed a new theory: that there have been not one but three major epidemiological transitions; that each one has been sparked by human activities; and that we are living through the third one right now.

The first epidemiological transition took place some 10,000 years ago, when people abandoned their nomadic existence and began farming. That profoundly new way of life disrupted ecosystems and created denser living conditions that led, as I will soon detail, to new diseases. The second epidemiological transition was the salutary one Omran singled out in 1971, when the war against infectious diseases seemed to have been won. And in the past two decades the emergence of illnesses such as hepatitis C, cat scratch disease (caused by the bacterium *Bartonella henselae*), Ebola and others on CDC's list has created a third epidemiological transition, a disheartening set of changes that in many

ways have reversed the effects of the second transition and coincide with the shift to globalism. Burgeoning population growth and urbanization, widespread environmental degradation, including global warming and tropical deforestation, and radically improved methods of transportation have given rise to new ways of contracting and spreading disease.

We are, quite literally, making ourselves sick.

WHEN EARLY HUMAN ANCESTORS moved from African forests onto the savanna millions of years ago, a few diseases came along for the ride. Those "heirloom" species—thus designated by the Australian parasitologist J. F. A. Sprent because they had afflicted earlier primates—included head and body lice; parasitic worms such as pinworms, tapeworms and liver flukes; and possibly herpes virus and malaria.

Global Warming could allow the mosquitoes that carry dengue fever to survive as far north as New York City.

For 99.8 percent of the five million years of human existence, hunting and gathering was the primary mode of subsistence. Our ancestors lived in small groups and relied on wild animals and plants for their survival. In their foraging rounds, early humans would occasionally have contracted new kinds of illnesses through insect bites or by butchering and eating disease-ridden animals. Such events would not have led to widespread epidemics, however, because groups of people were so sparse and widely dispersed.

About 10,000 years ago, at the end of the last ice age, many groups began to abandon their nomadic lifestyles for a more efficient and secure way of life. The agricultural revolution first appeared in the Middle East; later, farming centers developed independently in China and Central America. Permanent

villages grew up, and people turned their attention to crafts such as toolmaking and pottery. Thus when people took to cultivating wheat and barley, they planted the seeds of civilization as well.

With the new ways, however, came certain costs. As wild habitats were transformed into urban settings, the farmers who brought in the harvest with their flint-bladed sickles were assailed by grim new ailments. Among the most common was scrub typhus, which is carried by mites that live in tall grasses, and causes a potentially lethal fever. Clearing vegetation to create arable fields brought farmers frequently into mite-infested terrain.

Irrigation brought further hazards. Standing thigh-deep in watery canals, farm workers were prey to the worms that cause schistosomiasis. After living within aquatic snails during their larval stage, those worms emerge in a free-swimming form that can penetrate human skin, lodge in the intestine or urinary tract, and cause bloody urine and other serious maladies. Schistosomiasis was well known in ancient Egypt, where outlying fields were irrigated with water from the Nile River; descriptions of its symptoms and remedies are preserved in contemporary medical papyruses.

The domestication of sheep, goats and other animals cleared another pathway for microorganisms. With pigs in their yards and chickens roaming the streets, people in agricultural societies were constantly vulnerable to pathogens that could cross interspecies barriers. Many such organisms had long since reached commensalism with their animal hosts, but they were highly dangerous to humans. Milk from infected cattle could transmit tuberculosis, a slow killer that eats away at the lungs and causes its victims to cough blood and pus. Wool and skins were loaded with anthrax, which can be fatal when inhaled and, in modern times, has been developed by several nations as a potential agent of biological warfare. Blood from infected cattle, injected into people by biting insects such as the tsetse fly, spread sleeping sickness, an often-fatal disease marked by tremors and protracted lethargy.

A SECOND MAJOR EFFECT OF AGRI-culture was to spur population growth and, perhaps more important, density. Cities with populations as high as 50,000 had developed in the Near East by 3000 B.C. Scavenger species such as rats, mice and sparrows, which congregate wherever large groups of people live, exposed city dwellers to bubonic plague, typhus and rabies. And now that people were crowded together, a new pathogen could quickly start an epidemic. Larger populations also enabled diseases such as measles, mumps, chicken pox and smallpox to persist in an endemic form—always present, afflicting part of the population while sparing those with acquired immunity.

Thus the birth of agriculture launched humanity on a trajectory that has again and again brought people into contact with new pathogens. Tilling soil and raising livestock led to more energy-intensive ways of extracting resources from the earth—to lumbering, coal mining, oil drilling. New resources led to increasingly complex social organization, and to new and more frequent contacts between various societies. Loggers today who venture into the rain forest disturb previously untouched creatures and give them, for the first time, the chance to attack humans. But there is nothing new about this drama; only the players have changed. Some 2,000 years ago the introduction of iron tools to sub-Saharan Africa led to a slash-and-burn style of agriculture that brought people into contact with *Anopheles gambiae*, a mosquito that transmits malaria.

Improved transportation methods also help diseases extend their reach: microorganisms cannot travel far on their own, but they are expert hitchhikers. When the Spanish invaded Mexico in the early 1500s, for instance, they brought with them diseases that quickly raged through Tenochtitlán, the stately, temple-filled capital of the Aztec Empire. Smallpox, measles and influenza wiped out millions of Central America's original inhabitants, becoming the invisible weapon in the European conquest.

I N THE PAST THREE DECADES PEOPLE AND their inventions have drilled, polluted,

engineered, paved, planted and deforested at soaring rates, changing the biosphere faster than ever before. The combined effects can, without hyperbole, be called a global revolution. After all, many of them have worldwide repercussions: the widespread chemical contamination of waterways, the thinning of the ozone layer, the loss of species diversity. And such global human actions have put people at risk for infectious diseases in newly complex and devastating ways. Global warming, for instance, could expose millions of people for the first time to malaria, sleeping sickness and other insect-borne illnesses; in the United States, a slight overall temperature increase would allow the mosquitoes that carry dengue fever to survive as far north as New York City.

Major changes to the landscape that have become possible in the past quarter-century have also triggered new diseases. After the construction of the Aswan Dam in 1970, for instance, Rift Valley fever infected 200,000 people in Egypt, killing 600. The disease had been known to affect livestock, but it was not a major problem in people until the vast quantities of dammed water became a breeding ground for mosquitoes. The insects bit both cattle and humans, helping the virus jump the interspecies barrier.

In the eastern United States, suburbanization, another relatively recent phenomenon, is a dominant factor in the emergence of Lyme disease—10,000 cases of which are reported annually. Thanks to modern earth-moving equipment, a soaring economy and population pressures, many Americans have built homes in formerly remote, wooded areas. Nourished by lawns and gardens and unchecked by wolves, which were exterminated by settlers long ago, the deer population has exploded, exposing people to the ticks that carry Lyme disease.

Meanwhile, widespread pollution has made the oceans a breeding ground for microorganisms. Epidemiologists have suggested that toxic algal blooms—fed by the sewage, fertilizers and other contaminants that wash into the oceans—harbor countless viruses and bacteria. Thrown together into what amounts to a dirty genetic soup, those pathogens can undergo gene-swapping and mutations,

engendering newly antibiotic-resistant strains. Nautical traffic can carry ocean pathogens far and wide: a devastating outbreak of cholera hit Latin America in 1991 after a ship from Asia unloaded its contaminated ballast water into the harbor of Callao, Peru. Cholera causes diarrhea so severe its victims can die in a few days from dehydration; in that outbreak more than 300,000 people became ill, and more than 3,000 died.

The modern world is becoming—to paraphrase the words of the microbiologist Stephen S. Morse of Columbia University—a viral superhighway. Everyone is at risk.

Our newly global society is characterized by huge increases in population, international travel and international trade—factors that enable diseases to spread much more readily than ever before from person to person and from continent to continent. By 2020 the world population will have surpassed seven billion, and half those people will be living in urban centers. Beleaguered third-world nations are already hard-pressed to provide sewers, plumbing and other infrastructure; in the future, clean water and adequate sanitation could become increasingly rare. Meanwhile, political upheavals regularly cause millions of people to flee their homelands and gather in refugee camps, which become petri dishes for germs.

More than 500 million people cross international borders each year on commercial flights. Not only does that traffic volume dramatically increase the chance a sick person will infect the inhabitants of a distant area when she reaches her destination; it also exposes the sick person's fellow passengers to the disease, because of poor air circulation on planes. Many of those passengers can, in turn, pass the disease on to others when they disembark.

T HE GLOBAL ECONOMY THAT HAS arisen in the past two decades has established a myriad of connections between far-flung places. Not too long ago bananas and oranges were rare treats in northern climes. Now you can walk into your neighborhood market and find food that has been flown and trucked in from all over the world: oranges from Israel, apples from New Zealand, avocados from California. Consumers in affluent nations expect to be able to buy whatever they want whenever they want it. What people do not generally realize, however, is that this global network of food production and delivery provides countless pathways for pathogens. Raspberries from Guatemala, carrots from Peru and coconut milk from Thailand have been responsible for recent outbreaks of food poisoning in the United States. And the problem cuts both ways: contaminated radish seeds and frozen beef from the United States have ended up in Japan and South Korea.

Finally, the widespread and often indiscriminate use of antibiotics has played a key role in spurring disease. Forty million pounds of antibiotics are manufactured annually in the United States, an eightyfold increase since 1954. Dangerous microorganisms have evolved accordingly, often developing antibiotic-resistant strains. Physicians are now faced with penicillin-resistant gonorrhea, multiple-drug-resistant tuberculosis and E. coli variants such as 0157:H7. And frighteningly, some enterococcus bacteria have become resistant to all known antibiotics. Enterococcus infections are rare, but staphylococcus infections are not, and many strains of staph bacteria now respond to just one antibiotic, vancomycin. How long will it be before run-of-the-mill staph infections—in a boil, for instance, or in a surgical incision—become untreatable?

Although civilization can expose people to new pathogens, cultural progress also has an obvious countervailing effect: it can provide tools—medicines, sensible city planning, educational campaigns about sexually transmitted diseases—to fight the encroachments of disease. Moreover, since biology seems to side with microorganisms anyway, people have little choice but to depend on protective cultural practices to keep pace: vaccinations, for instance, to confer immunity, combined with practices such as handwashing by physicians between patient visits, to limit contact between people and pathogens.

All too often, though, obvious protective measures such as using only clean hypodermic needles or treating urban drinking water with chlorine are neglected, whether out of ignorance or a wrongheaded emphasis on the short-term financial costs. The worldwide disparity in wealth is also to blame: not surprisingly, the advances made during the second epidemiological transition were limited largely to the affluent of the industrial world.

Such lapses are now beginning to teach the bitter lesson that the delicate balance between humans and invasive microorganisms can tip the other way again. Overconfidence—the legacy of the second epidemiological transition—has made us especially vulnerable to emerging and reemerging diseases. Evolutionary principles can provide this useful corrective: in spite of all our medical and technological hubris, there is no quick fix. If human beings are to overcome the current crisis, it will be through sensible changes in behavior, such as increased condom use and improved sanitation, combined with a commitment to stop disturbing the ecological balance of the planet.

The Bible, in short, was not far from wrong: We do bring plagues upon ourselves—not by sinning, but by refusing to heed our own alarms, our own best judgment. The price of peace—or at least peaceful coexistence—with the microorganisms on this planet is eternal vigilance.

George J. Armelagos is a professor of anthropology at Emory University in Atlanta, Georgia. He has coedited two books on the evolution of human disease: PALEOPATHOLOGY AT THE ORIGINS OF AGRICULTURE, *which deals with prehistoric populations, and* DISEASE IN POPULATIONS IN TRANSITION, *which focuses on contemporary societies.*

This article is reprinted by permission of *The Sciences* and is from the January/February 1998 issue, pp. 24–29. Individual subscriptions are $28 per year. Write to: The Sciences, 2 East 63rd Street, New York, NY 10021.

Dr. Darwin

*With a nod to evolution's god, physicians are looking at illness
through the lens of natural selection to find out why we get sick
and what we can do about it.*

Lori Oliwenstein

PAUL EWALD KNEW FROM THE BEGINNING that the Ebola virus outbreak in Zaire would fizzle out. On May 26, after eight days in which only six new cases were reported, that fizzle became official. The World Health Organization announced it would no longer need to update the Ebola figures daily (though sporadic cases continued to be reported until June 20).

The virus had held Zaire's Bandundu Province in its deadly grip for weeks, infecting some 300 people and killing 80 percent of them. Most of those infected hailed from the town of Kikwit. It was all just as Ewald predicted. "When the Ebola outbreak occurred," he recalls, "I said, as I have before, these things are going to pop up, they're going to smolder, you'll have a bad outbreak of maybe 100 or 200 people in a hospital, maybe you'll have the outbreak slip into another isolated community, but then it will peter out on its own."

> *"If you look at it from an evolutionary point of view, you can sort out the 95 percent of disease organisms that aren't a major threat from the 5 percent that are."*

Ewald is no soothsayer. He's an evolutionary biologist at Amherst College in Massachusetts and perhaps the world's leading expert on how infectious diseases—and the organisms that cause them—evolve. He's also a force behind what some are touting as the next great medical revolution: the application of Darwin's theory of natural selection to the understanding of human diseases.

A Darwinian view can shed some light on how Ebola moves from human to human once it has entered the population. (Between human outbreaks, the virus resides in some as yet unknown living reservoir.) A pathogen can survive in a population, explains Ewald, only if it can easily transmit its progeny from one host to another. One way to do this is to take a long time to disable a host, giving him plenty of time to come into contact with other potential victims. Ebola, however, kills quickly, usually in less than a week. Another way is to survive for a long time outside the human body, so that the pathogen can wait for new hosts to find it. But the Ebola strains encountered thus far are destroyed almost at once by sunlight, and even if no rays reach them, they tend to lose their infectiousness outside the human body within a day. "If you look at it from an evolutionary point of view, you can sort out the 95 percent of disease organisms that aren't a major threat from the 5 percent that are," says Ewald. "Ebola really isn't one of those 5 percent."

The earliest suggestion of a Darwinian approach to medicine came in 1980, when George Williams, an evolutionary biologist at the State University of New York at Stony Brook, read an article in which Ewald discussed using Darwinian theory to illuminate the origins of certain symptoms of infectious disease—things like fever, low iron counts, diarrhea. Ewald's approach struck a chord in Williams. Twenty-three years earlier he had written a paper proposing an evolutionary framework for senescence, or aging. "Way back in the 1950s I didn't worry about the practical aspects of senescence, the medical aspects," Williams notes. "I was pretty young then." Now, however, he sat up and took notice.

While Williams was discovering Ewald's work, Randolph Nesse was discovering Williams's. Nesse, a psychiatrist and a founder of the University of Michigan Evolution and Human Behavior Program, was exploring his own interest in the aging process, and he and Williams soon got together. "He had wanted to find a physician to work with on medical problems," says Nesse, "and I had long wanted to find an evolutionary biologist, so it was a very natural match for us." Their collaboration led to a 1991 article that most researchers say signaled the real birth of the field.

Nesse and Williams define Darwinian medicine as the hunt for evolutionary explanations of vulnerabilities to disease. It can, as Ewald noted, be a way to interpret the body's defenses, to try to figure out, say, the reasons we feel pain or get runny noses when we have a cold, and to determine what we should—or shouldn't—be doing about those defenses. For instance, Darwinian researchers like physiologist Matthew Kluger of the Lovelace Institute in Albuquerque now say that a moderate rise in body temperature is more than just a symptom of disease; it's an evolutionary adaptation the body uses to fight infection by making itself inhospitable to invading microbes. It would seem, then, that if you lower the fever, you may prolong the infection. Yet no one is ready to say whether we should toss out our aspirin bottles. "I would love to see a dozen proper studies of whether it's wise to bring fever down when someone has influenza," says Nesse. "It's never been done, and it's just astounding that it's never been done."

Diarrhea is another common symptom of disease, one that's sometimes the result of a pathogen's manipulating your body for its own good purposes, but it may also be a defense mechanism mounted by your body. Cholera bacteria, for example, once they invade the human body, induce diarrhea by producing toxins that make the intestine's cells leaky. The resultant diarrhea then both flushes competing beneficial bacteria from the gut and gives the cholera bacteria a ride into the world, so that they can find another hapless victim. In the case of cholera, then, it seems clear that stopping the diarrhea can only do good.

But the diarrhea that results from an invasion of shigella bacteria—which cause various forms of dysentery—seems to be more an intestinal defense than a bacterial offense. The infection causes the muscles surrounding the gut to contract more frequently, apparently in an attempt to flush out the bacteria as quickly as possible. Studies done more than a decade ago showed that using drugs like Lomotil to decrease the gut's contractions and cut down the diarrheal output actually prolong infection. On the other hand, the ingredients in over-the-counter preparations like Pepto Bismol, which don't affect how frequently the gut contracts, can be used to stem the diarrheal flow without prolonging infection.

Seattle biologist Margie Profet points to menstruation as another "symptom"

that may be more properly viewed as an evolutionary defense. As Profet points out, there must be a good reason for the body to engage in such costly activities as shedding the uterine lining and letting blood flow away. That reason, she claims, is to rid the uterus of any organisms that might arrive with sperm in the seminal fluid. If an egg is fertilized, infection may be worth risking. But if there is no fertilized egg, says Profet, the body defends itself by ejecting the uterine cells, which might have been infected. Similarly, Profet has theorized that morning sickness during pregnancy causes the mother to avoid foods that might contain chemicals harmful to a developing fetus. If she's right, blocking that nausea with drugs could result in higher miscarriage rates or more birth defects.

Darwinian medicine isn't simply about which symptoms to treat and which to ignore. It's a way to understand microbes—which, because they evolve so much more quickly than we do, will probably always beat us unless we figure out how to harness their evolutionary power for our own benefit. It's also a way to realize how disease-causing genes that persist in the population are often selected for, not against, in the long run.

Sickle-cell anemia is a classic case of how evolution tallies costs and benefits. Some years ago, researchers discovered that people with one copy of the sickle-cell gene are better able to resist the protozoans that cause malaria than are people with no copies of the gene. People with two copies of the gene may die, but in malaria-plagued regions such as tropical Africa, their numbers will be more than made up for by the offspring left by the disease-resistant kin.

Cystic fibrosis may also persist through such genetic logic. Animal studies indicate that individuals with just one copy of the cystic fibrosis gene may be more resistant to the effects of the cholera bacterium. As is the case with malaria and sickle-cell, cholera is much more prevalent than cystic fibrosis; since there are many more people with a single, resistance-conferring copy of the

gene than with a disease-causing double dose, the gene is stably passed from generation to generation.

> *"I used to hunt saber-toothed tigers all the time, thousands of years ago. I got lots of exercise and all that sort of stuff. Now I sit in front of a computer and don't get exercise, so I've changed my body chemistry."*

"With our power to do gene manipulations, there will be temptations to find genes that do things like cause aging, and get rid of them," says Nesse. "If we're sure about everything a gene does, that's fine. But an evolutionary approach cautions us not to go too fast, and to expect that every gene might well have some benefit as well as costs, and maybe some quite unrelated benefit."

Darwinian medicine can also help us understand the problems encountered in the New Age by a body designed for the Stone Age. As evolutionary psychologist Charles Crawford of Simon Fraser University in Burnaby, British Columbia, put it: "I used to hunt saber-toothed tigers all the time, thousands of years ago. I got lots of exercise and all that sort of stuff. Now I sit in front of a computer, and all I do is play with a mouse, and I don't get exercise. So I've changed my body biochemistry in all sorts of unknown ways, and it could affect me in all sorts of ways, and we have no idea what they are."

Radiologist Boyd Eaton of Emory University and his colleagues believe such biochemical changes are behind today's breast cancer epidemic. While it's impossible to study a Stone Ager's biochemistry, there are still groups of hunter-gatherers around—such as the San of Africa—who make admirable stand-ins. A foraging life-style, notes Eaton, also means a life-style in which menstruation begins later, the first child is born earlier, there are more children altogether, they are breast-fed for years rather than months, and menopause comes somewhat earlier. Overall, he says, American women today probably experience 3.5 times more menstrual cycles than our ancestors did 10,000 years ago. During each cycle a woman's body is flooded with the hormone estrogen, and breast cancer, as research has found, is very much estrogen related. The more frequently the breasts are exposed to the hormone, the greater the chance that a tumor will take seed.

Depending on which data you choose, women today are somewhere between 10 and 100 times more likely to be stricken with breast cancer than our ancestors were. Eaton's proposed solutions are pretty radical, but he hopes people will at least entertain them; they include delaying puberty with hormones and using hormones to create pseudopregnancies, which offer a woman the biochemical advantages of pregnancy at an early age without requiring her to bear a child.

In general, Darwinian medicine tells us that the organs and systems that make up our bodies result not from the pursuit of perfection but from millions of years of evolutionary compromises designed to get the greatest reproductive benefit at the lowest cost. We walk upright with a spine that evolved while we scampered on four limbs; balancing on two legs leaves our hands free, but we'll probably always suffer some back pain as well.

"What's really different is that up to now people have used evolutionary theory to try to explain why things work, why they're normal," explains Nesse. "The twist—and I don't know if it's simple or profound—is to say we're trying to understand the abnormal, the vulnerability to disease. We're trying to understand why natural selection has not made the body better, why natural selection has left the body with vulnerabilities. For every single disease, there is an answer to that question. And for very few of them is the answer very clear yet."

One reason those answers aren't yet clear is that few physicians or medical researchers have done much serious surveying from Darwin's viewpoint. In many cases, that's because evolutionary theories are hard to test. There's no way to watch human evolution in progress—

at best it works on a time scale involving hundreds of thousands of years. "Darwinian medicine is mostly a guessing game about how we think evolution worked in the past on humans, what it designed for us," say evolutionary biologist James Bull of the University of Texas at Austin. "It's almost impossible to test ideas that we evolved to respond to this or that kind of environment. You can make educated guesses, but no one's going to go out and do an experiment to show that yes, in fact humans will evolve this way under these environmental conditions."

Yet some say that these experiments can, should, and will be done. Howard Howland, a sensory physiologist at Cornell, is setting up just such an evolutionary experiment, hoping to interfere with the myopia, or nearsightedness, that afflicts a full quarter of all Americans. Myopia is thought to be the result of a delicate feedback loop that tries to keep images focused on the eye's retina. There's not much room for error: if the length of your eyeball is off by just a tenth of a millimeter, your vision will be blurry. Research has shown that when the eye perceives an image as fuzzy, it compensates by altering its length.

This loop obviously has a genetic component, notes Howland, but what drives it is the environment. During the Stone Age, when we were chasing buffalo in the field, the images we saw were usually sharp and clear. But with modern civilization came a lot of close work. When your eye focuses on something nearby, the lens has to bend, and since bending that lens is hard work, you do as little bending as you can get away with. That's why, whether you're conscious of it or not, near objects tend to be a bit blurry. "Blurry image?" says the eye. "Time to grow." And the more it grows, the fuzzier those buffalo get. Myopia seems to be a disease of industrial society.

To prevent that disease, Howland suggests going back to the Stone Age—or at least convincing people's eyes that that's where they are. If you give folks with normal vision glasses that make their eyes think they're looking at an object in the distance when they're really looking at one nearby, he says, you'll

avoid the whole feedback loop in the first place. "The military academies induct young men and women with twenty-twenty vision who then go through four years of college and are trained to fly an airplane or do some difficult visual task. But because they do so much reading, they come out the other end nearsighted, no longer eligible to do what they were hired to do," Howland notes. "I think these folks would very much like not to become nearsighted in the course of their studies." He hopes to be putting glasses on them within a year.

THE NUMBING PACE OF EVOlution is a much smaller problem for researchers interested in how the bugs that plague us do their dirty work. Bacteria are present in such large numbers (one person can carry around more pathogens than there are people on the planet) and evolve so quickly (a single bacterium can reproduce a million times in one human lifetime) that experiments we couldn't imagine in humans can be carried out in microbes in mere weeks. We might even, says Ewald, be able to use evolutionary theory to tame the human immunodeficiency virus.

"HIV is mutating so quickly that surely we're going to have plenty of sources of mutants that are mild as well as severe," he notes. "So now the question is, which of the variants will win?" As in the case of Ebola, he says, it will all come down to how well the virus manages to get from one person to another.

"If there's a great potential for sexual transmission to new partners, then the viruses that reproduce quickly will spread," Ewald says. "And since they're reproducing in a cell type that's critical for the well-being of the host—the helper T cell—then that cell type will be decimated, and the host is likely to suffer from it." On the other hand, if you lower the rate of transmission—through abstinence, monogamy, condom use—then the more severe strains might well die out before they have a chance to be passed very far. "The real question," says Ewald, "is, exactly how mild can you make this virus as a result of reducing the rate at which it could be transmitted to new partners, and how long will it take for this change to occur?" There are already strains of HIV in Senegal with such low virulence, he points out, that most people infected will die of old age. "We don't have all the answers. But I think we're going to be living with this virus for a long time, and if we have to live with it, let's live with a really mild virus instead of a severe virus."

Though condoms and monogamy are not a particularly radical treatment, that they might be used not only to stave off the virus but to tame it is a radical notion—and one that some researchers find suspect. "If it becomes too virulent, it will end up cutting off its own transmission by killing its host too quickly," notes James Bull. "But the speculation is that people transmit HIV primarily within one to five months of infection, when they spike a high level of virus in the blood. So with HIV, the main period of transmission occurs a few months into the infection, and yet the virulence—the death from it—occurs years later. The major stage of transmission is decoupled from the virulence." So unless the protective measures are carried out by everyone, all the time, we won't stop most instances of transmission; after all, most people don't even know they're infected when they pass the virus on.

But Ewald thinks these protective measures are worth a shot. After all, he says, pathogen taming has occurred in the past. The forms of dysentery we encounter in the United States are quite mild because our purified water supplies have cut off the main route of transmission for virulent strains of the bacteria.

Not only did hygienic changes reduce the number of cases, they selected for the milder shigella organisms, those that leave their victim well enough to get out and about. Diphtheria is another case in point. When the diphtheria vaccine was invented, it targeted only the most severe form of diphtheria toxin, though for economic rather than evolutionary reasons. Over the years, however, that choice has weeded out the most virulent strains of diphtheria, selecting for the ones that cause few or no symptoms. Today those weaker strains act like another level of vaccine to protect us against new, virulent strains.

"We did with diphtheria what we did with wolves. We took an organism that caused harm, and unknowingly, we domesticated it into an organism that protects us."

"You're doing to these organisms what we did to wolves," says Ewald. "Wolves were dangerous to us, we domesticated them into dogs, and then they helped us, they warned us against the wolves that were out there ready to take our babies. And by doing that, we've essentially turned what was a harmful organism into a helpful organism. That's the same thing we did with diphtheria; we took an organism that was causing harm, and without knowing it, we do-

mesticated it into an organism that is protecting us against harmful ones."

Putting together a new scientific discipline—and getting it recognized—is in itself an evolutionary process. Though Williams and Neese say there are hundreds of researchers working (whether they know it or not) within this newly built framework, they realize the field is still in its infancy. It may take some time before *Darwinian medicine* is a household term. Nesse tells how the editor of a prominent medical journal, when asked about the field, replied, "Darwinian medicine? I haven't heard of it, so it can't be very important."

But Darwinian medicine's critics don't deny the field's legitimacy; they point mostly to its lack of hard-and-fast answers, its lack of clear clinical guidelines. "I think this idea will eventually establish itself as a basic science for medicine, " answers Nesse. "What did people say, for instance, to the biochemists back in 1900 as they were playing out the Krebs cycle? People would say, 'So what does biochemistry really have to do with medicine? What can you cure now that you couldn't before you knew about the Krebs cycle?' And the biochemists could only say, 'Well, gee, we're not sure, but we know what we're doing is answering important scientific questions, and eventually this will be useful.' And I think exactly the same applies here."

Lori Oliwenstein, a former DISCOVER senior editor, is now a freelance journalist based in Los Angeles.

Test Your Knowledge Form

We encourage you to photocopy and use this page as a tool to assess how the articles in *Annual Editions* expand on the information in your textbook. By reflecting on the articles you will gain enhanced text information. You can also access this useful form on a product's book support Web site at *http://www.dushkin.com/online/*.

NAME:

DATE:

TITLE AND NUMBER OF ARTICLE:

BRIEFLY STATE THE MAIN IDEA OF THIS ARTICLE:

LIST THREE IMPORTANT FACTS THAT THE AUTHOR USES TO SUPPORT THE MAIN IDEA:

WHAT INFORMATION OR IDEAS DISCUSSED IN THIS ARTICLE ARE ALSO DISCUSSED IN YOUR TEXTBOOK OR OTHER READINGS THAT YOU HAVE DONE? LIST THE TEXTBOOK CHAPTERS AND PAGE NUMBERS:

LIST ANY EXAMPLES OF BIAS OR FAULTY REASONING THAT YOU FOUND IN THE ARTICLE:

LIST ANY NEW TERMS/CONCEPTS THAT WERE DISCUSSED IN THE ARTICLE, AND WRITE A SHORT DEFINITION:

We Want Your Advice

ANNUAL EDITIONS revisions depend on two major opinion sources: one is our Advisory Board, listed in the front of this volume, which works with us in scanning the thousands of articles published in the public press each year; the other is you—the person actually using the book. Please help us and the users of the next edition by completing the prepaid article rating form on this page and returning it to us. Thank you for your help!

ANNUAL EDITIONS: Physical Anthropology 05/06

ARTICLE RATING FORM

Here is an opportunity for you to have direct input into the next revision of this volume.
We would like you to rate each of the articles listed below, using the following scale:

1. **Excellent: should definitely be retained**
2. **Above average: should probably be retained**
3. **Below average: should probably be deleted**
4. **Poor: should definitely be deleted**

Your ratings will play a vital part in the next revision.
Please mail this prepaid form to us as soon as possible.
Thanks for your help!

RATING	ARTICLE	RATING	ARTICLE
	1. The Growth of Evolutionary Science		39. Great Apes as Food
	2. Darwin's Influence on Modern Thought		40. The Viral Superhighway
	3. 15 Answers to Creationist Nonsense		41. Dr. Darwin
	4. Profile of an Anthropologist: No Bone Unturned		
	5. Go Ahead, Kiss Your Cousin		
	6. Curse and Blessing of the Ghetto		
	7. The Saltshaker's Curse		
	8. Of Mice, Men and Genes		
	9. What You Can Learn From Drunk Monkeys		
	10. What Are Friends For?		
	11. Fossey in the Mist		
	12. The Mind of the Chimpanzee		
	13. Got Culture?		
	14. Dim Forest, Bright Chimps		
	15. Rethinking Primate Aggression		
	16. Disturbing Behaviors of the Orangutan		
	17. Are We in Anthropodenial?		
	18. Mothers and Others		
	19. A Woman's Curse?		
	20. What's Love Got to Do With It?		
	21. Apes of Wrath		
	22. Hunting the First Hominid		
	23. Food for Thought: Dietary Change Was a Driving Force in Human Evolution		
	24. Scavenger Hunt		
	25. Chasing Dubois's Ghost		
	26. *Erectus* Rising		
	27. The Scavenging of "Peking Man"		
	28. Hard Times Among the Neanderthals		
	29. Rethinking Neanderthals		
	30. The Gift of Gab		
	31. We are All Africans		
	32. The Lost Man		
	33. Skin Deep		
	34. Black, White, Other		
	35. Does Race Exist? A Proponent's Perspective		
	36. Does Race Exist? An Antagonist's Perspective		
	37. The Bare Truth		
	38. The Tall and the Short of It		

(Continued on next page)

BUSINESS REPLY MAIL
FIRST CLASS MAIL PERMIT NO. 551 DUBUQUE IA

POSTAGE WILL BE PAID BY ADDRESEE

McGraw-Hill/Dushkin
2460 KERPER BLVD
DUBUQUE, IA 52001-9902

NO POSTAGE
NECESSARY
IF MAILED
IN THE
UNITED STATES

ABOUT YOU

Name   Date

Are you a teacher? ☐ A student? ☐
Your school's name

Department

Address   City   State   Zip

School telephone #

YOUR COMMENTS ARE IMPORTANT TO US!

Please fill in the following information:
For which course did you use this book?

Did you use a text with this ANNUAL EDITION? ☐ yes ☐ no
What was the title of the text?

What are your general reactions to the *Annual Editions* concept?

Have you read any pertinent articles recently that you think should be included in the next edition? Explain.

Are there any articles that you feel should be replaced in the next edition? Why?

Are there any World Wide Web sites that you feel should be included in the next edition? Please annotate.

May we contact you for editorial input? ☐ yes ☐ no
May we quote your comments? ☐ yes ☐ no